TURKEY

Studies in Critical Social Sciences Book Series

Haymarket Books is proud to be working with Brill Academic Publishers (www.brill.nl) to republish the *Studies in Critical Social Sciences* book series in paperback editions. This peer-reviewed book series offers insights into our current reality by exploring the content and consequences of power relationships under capitalism, and by considering the spaces of opposition and resistance to these changes that have been defining our new age. Our full catalog of *SCSS* volumes can be viewed at https://www.haymarketbooks.org/series_collections/4-studies-in-critical-social-sciences.

Series Editor
David Fasenfest (Wayne State University)

Editorial Board
Eduardo Bonilla-Silva (Duke University)
Chris Chase-Dunn (University of California–Riverside)
William Carroll (University of Victoria)
Raewyn Connell (University of Sydney)
Kimberlé W. Crenshaw (University of California–LA and Columbia University)
Heidi Gottfried (Wayne State University)
Karin Gottschall (University of Bremen)
Alfredo Saad Filho (King's College London)
Chizuko Ueno (University of Tokyo)
Sylvia Walby (Lancaster University)
Raju Das (York University)

Turkey

The Pendulum between Military Rule and Civilian Authoritarianism

Fatıh Çağatay Cengız

Haymarket Books
Chicago, IL

First published in 2020 by Brill Academic Publishers, The Netherlands
© 2020 Koninklijke Brill NV, Leiden, The Netherlands

Published in paperback in 2021 by
Haymarket Books
P.O. Box 180165
Chicago, IL 60618
773-583-7884
www.haymarketbooks.org

ISBN: 978-1-64259-612-0

Distributed to the trade in the US through Consortium Book Sales and Distribution (www.cbsd.com) and internationally through Ingram Publisher Services International (www.ingramcontent.com).

This book was published with the generous support of Lannan Foundation and Wallace Action Fund.

Special discounts are available for bulk purchases by organizations and institutions. Please call 773-583-7884 or email info@haymarketbooks.org for more information.

Cover design by Jamie Kerry and Ragina Johnson.

Printed in the United States.

10 9 8 7 6 5 4 3 2 1

Library of Congress Cataloging-in-Publication data is available.

Contents

Acknowledgements IX
List of Figures, Box and Tables X

Introduction: Conceptualisation of Kemalism, Bonapartism, and Procedural Democracy 1

1 The Kemalist State 24
    1 The Historical Legacy 24
    2 The 1923 İzmir Economic Congress and National Developmentalism 27
    3 The Statist and Ultra-nationalist Phase in the Kemalist Capitalist State 31
    4 Industrial Upgrading (1960–1980) 33
    5 Failed Democratic Transition under the Democrat Party (1950–1960) 36
    6 The 1960 Coup and 1971 Memorandum in the Context of the Cold War 41
    7 Institutionalisation of "Kemalism without Mustafa Kemal" 48
    8 Bourgeoisification of the Military 56

2 The Construction of a New Society after the 1980 Military Coup 60
    1 The Completion of the National Developmentalist Project 60
    2 The Absorption of Kemalism into Neoliberalism 64
    3 Islamisation of Society after the 1980s 69
    4 Turgut Özal in Power (1983–1989 and 1989–1993): Post-Kemalist Rule 73
    5 Political Liberalisation in the 1990s under Post-Bonapartist Rule 79
    6 Second-generation Devout Turkish Bourgeoisie 84
        6.1 MÜSİAD (*The Independent Industrialists' and Businessmen's Association*) 87
        6.2 ASKON (*The Anatolian Tigers Business Association*) 93
        6.3 TUSKON (*Turkish Confederation of Businessmen and Industrialists*) 94

3 War of Manoeuvre by Islamic Fundamentalism against the Kemalist State   97
  1 The Political Trajectory of Islamic Parties Led by Necmettin Erbakan in Turkey   100
     1.1 *The National Order Party (1970–1971)*   100
     1.2 *The National Salvation Party (1972–1981)*   103
     1.3 *The Welfare Party (1983–1998)*   106
  2 The Just Economic System: a Petty-bourgeois Utopia in the Era of Neoliberalism   112
  3 The National View (*Milli Görüş*) as Common Ideational Ground for Islamic Parties   116
  4 The Islamic Alternative to the Kemalist State   118
  5 The Military Intervention of 28 February 1997   124
  6 The Rupture in Islamic Politics   127

4 War of Position by the AKP against the Kemalist State   130
  1 The Restructuring of the State after the End of the Cold War   130
  2 The Rise of the AKP in the Post-crisis Period and Continuation of Neoliberal Economic Policies   134
     2.1 *The 2001 Economic Crisis*   135
     2.2 *The Economy under AKP Rule*   137
  3 Procedural Democratisation under the Influence of the EU   149
  4 The AKP Tactics towards the Military: the Modern Capitalist Prince and a "War of Position"   157

5 Authoritarian Turn, Sub-imperialist Foreign Policy, and the Failed Coup of 15 July 2016   165
  1 The Expansion of the Gülen Movement   165
  2 The Ergenekon and Sledgehammer (*Balyoz*) Trials   167
  3 Authoritarian Wave in Domestic Policy   172
  4 Sub-imperialism and Neo-Ottomanism in Foreign Policy: Strategic Depth or Strategic Failure?   177
     4.1 *Sub-imperialism in Question*   178
     4.2 *The Military Dimension of Turkey's Sub-imperialist Role*   180
     4.3 *Continuity in Turkish Foreign Policy in the 1990s*   184
     4.4 *The Economic Foundation of Neo-Ottomanism: Turkish Exports and Capital in the Region*   186
     4.5 *Turkish Companies as Agents of Regional Economic Power*   191
     4.6 *Political Tools for Turkish Sub-imperialism*   196
  5 Neo-Ottomanism in Practice   199
  6 The State Crisis Ahead of Turkey's Failed Coup   203

6 **Concluding Observations** 215
  1. Basic Structural Economic Limitations of Turkey's Sub-imperialist Expansion: the Sustainability and Capacity Problem of the Turkish Economy 219
  2. Is Erdoğan an Islamic Bonaparte? 221
  3. Any Hope: Waiting for Godot? 223

References 225
Index 266

Acknowledgements

This book is the condensed and updated version of my four-year PhD endeavour at the School of Oriental and African Studies (SOAS, University of London) that was finalised in December 2015. My dissertation was the product of an enormous amount of intellectual guidance from Professor Gilbert Achcar, to whom my academic development is greatly indebted. I am also grateful to Professor Achcar for sharing his experience, accepting me as his graduate teaching assistant continuing his academic support by reading the updated version of this book even after I finalised my PhD, and encouraging me to publish it. I feel lucky to have him as my lifelong supervisor, both during and after my PhD. I am also thankful to four anonymous scholars who read the earlier version of the book and made constructive comments and criticisms.

The book aims to shed light on the dynamics of the demise of the Kemalist state in Turkey after the late 1990s. It problematises the way in which neoliberal globalisation after the 1980s created conditions that made changes in civil-military relations possible. On that matter, the mutation of Islamic politics in Turkey was an instrumental factor in achieving the break between military and parliamentary power. The rise of the Justice and Development Party (*Adalet ve Kalkınma Partisi*, AKP) in 2002 embodies the mutation in Islamic politics in Turkey, to the extent that the AKP has been able to unify the interests of big finance capital and peripheral capital. By representing these different fractions of the bourgeoisie, the AKP has managed to overcome the political omnipotence of the Turkish military, concurrently leading to the institutional necrosis of the Kemalist/Bonapartist state. A breakaway from its predecessor's Islamic genealogy enabled the party to carry out a democratic transition until 2010/2011. However, a reversal of the previous wave of democratisation in domestic policy and contradictions in Turkey's sub-imperialist foreign policy laid the ground for a state crisis, which peaked with the coup attempt of 15 July 2016. The book also analyses the anatomy of the failed coup and concludes with observations on recent development.

Figures, Box and Tables

Figures

1. Exports and imports (% of GDP), 1960–1980   61
2. The development of real wages and salaries (TL/day), 1963–1988   70
3. Number of mobile telephone and internet subscribers in Turkey, 1994–2014   80
4. *Milli Görüş* parties and the party that won the municipal elections, 1963–2019   107
5. *Milli Görüş* parties and the party that won the general elections, 1950–2018   107
6. The characteristics of economic systems according to *Milli Görüş*   114
7. Interest repayments/total expenditure, 1990–2017   136
8. Annual inflation in consumer prices (%), 1990–2018   139
9. Turkey's gross external debt (million $), 1989–2019   140
10. Turkey's gross external debt to GDP (%), 1989–2019   140
11. Budget balance to GDP (%), 2002–2019   141
12. Privatisation revenue by years (million $)   141
13. Gross fixed capital formation to GDP, total and private sector, (%), 1968–2018   141
14. GDP per capita annual growth rate (%), 1961–2018   143
15. GDP per capita average annual growth rate in comparison (%)   144
16. Poverty rates according to the international threshold of 4.3 dollars per day, 2002–2015   148
17. Total number of convicts and detainees in penal institutions, 1970–2018   174
18. Turkish exports by years (million $), 1960–2019   187
19. Export of manufactured goods (% of Exports), 1960–2018   187
20. Turkish exports by two country groups (billion $), 2004–2019   188
21. Inward FDI flows and FDI stocks in Turkey (million $), 1980–2010   189
22. Outward FDI flows and FDI stocks of Turkey (million $), 1980–2010   190
23. Turkish exports and imports (billion $), 1980–2019   219
24. High-technology exports in some selected emerging countries and Turkey (% of manufactured exports)   221

Box

1. Constitutional amendments in 1995   82

Tables

1. Martial law and state of emergency in Turkey and their durations 16
2. Structure of manufacturing, share in production value (%), 1963–1980 35
3. Internal structure of state manufacturing, share in production value (%), 1963–1980 35
4. Concentration in manufacturing (1985) 36
5. National defence expenditure, 1950–1960 41
6. Political parties banned by the Constitutional Court since 1983 55
7. Relative share of public and private sectors in total fixed capital investments, 1973–1988 76
8. Distribution of fixed capital investment (as of total) 77
9. Sectoral distribution of MÜSİAD members (2014) 90
10. Sectoral distribution of TÜSİAD members (2013) 91
11. Annual GDP growth in some selected emerging countries and Turkey (%), 2002–2013 145
12. Chronology of Turkey-EU relations 152
13. 29 largest Turkish multinationals ($ million), (2012) 192

INTRODUCTION

Conceptualisation of Kemalism, Bonapartism, and Procedural Democracy

In his groundbreaking book *Social Origins of Dictatorship and Democracy*, Barrington Moore formulated the motto "No bourgeois, no democracy", arguing that the growth of democracy is associated with the heroic role played by town dwellers (1966: 418). It is clear that Moore's formula was *uncritically* applied to Turkey by mainstream scholars who argue that the persistence of a weak bourgeoisie *vis-à-vis* a strong state tradition is key to the underdevelopment of Turkey's democracy.

In his book *The State Tradition in Turkey*, Metin Heper (1985) notes that business life in Turkey was inherently submissive to the strong state, which led to an understanding of the Turkish state as *Leviathan* in the Hobbesian sense. Herper argues that interest group associations in Turkey were unable to articulate their demands in a straightforward manner (1991: 16), contending that interest groups in Turkey could not engage in even partisan activities and, instead, chose to stay out of politics while the state remained unresponsive to civil society (Heper, 1991: 17–18). From this perspective, the interests of state elites, which are autonomous from social relations, are translated into a hegemonic set of interests adopted by political parties and civil society. It is claimed that "[t]his monist conception of public interest, developed by the State elites, was later adopted by the political elites ... the State-centred polity was replaced by a party-centred polity but not by a civil society-centred one" (Heper, 1985: 20).

Heper touches on the causes of Turkish interest groups' inability to articulate their demands, quoting the chairman of TÜSİAD (the Turkish Industrialists and Businessmen's Association):

> In this country, our philosophy has always been that of taking the paternal State ('devlet baba') as paramount, refraining from challenging it, and of pursuing an economic policy not in spite of, but along with the paternal State... Hesitancy on part of members of the private sector to run for public office stems from the philosophy of not challenging the paternal State, from the belief that the State is still influential, and that alienating the State would not bode well for them (Heper, 1985: 103; 1991: 16).

It is argued that this strong, paternal state was built upon the Ottoman legacy that, unlike Western examples, failed to integrate peripheral forces and urban middle layers—such as "the feudal nobility, the cities, the burghers, and later industrial labour"—into the centre (Mardin, 1973: 170). In addition, the state bureaucracy had a firm grip on the economy and society, and the Ottoman polity therefore lacked multiple confrontations and compromises (Heper, 1976; Mardin, 1973: 170). Similarly, the Marxist writer Fikret Başkaya (2010) argues that the legacy of the strong Ottoman state still continues in Republican Turkey, where the state apparatus subordinates civil society and weilds the real power, such that the army becomes the "principal state party" (*asıl devlet partisi*). According to liberals, the strong state not only subordinates civil society but also creates an inefficient and unproductive economic system by consolidating bureaucratic power (Altan, 1993: 41).

Therefore, literature focused on "strong state tradition" largely concludes that "the recalcitrance of the Turkish public bureaucracy to bourgeois politics" (Heper, 1976) is businessmen's primary concern with regards to the prospects for productive and efficient commercial life (Buğra, 1994). According to Ayşe Buğra (1994: 261), "the most striking characteristic of the Turkish experience is the reluctance of the political authority to accept associations as the legitimate medium of interest representation". Turkish businessmen are portrayed as timid, humble, and ashamed of gaining wealth *vis-à-vis* the autonomous and strong state bureaucracy (Buğra, 1994: 261; Heper, 1985). The result of the state's inability to commit to a coherent, long–term industrial strategy and reduce business uncertainty has precipitated forms of rentier and speculative activity amongst Turkish business. This is despite the fact that the Turkish state has a substantial degree of autonomy to discipline big businesses into conforming with national objectives (Buğra, 1994: 22–23).

By referring to the strong state tradition in Turkey, where the government tends to regard its political power as absolute, Buğra claims that the government in power fully controls the state bureaucracy and legal system (1994: 23). Furthermore, as these mechanisms are subservient to the government, the state bureaucracy and legal system cannot settle potential or actual disputes between the government and social groups (Buğra, 1994: 156–157). Hence, according to Buğra (1994: 163), these systems cannot function as stable mechanisms of mediation in state-business relations. Consequently, "...haphazard policy changes often become reflected in legal modifications and changes in bureaucratic rules which, in turn, enhance the instability of the economic environment" (1994: 97).

Due to the existence of absolute state power in the Republican period, this approach portrays the Turkish bourgeoisie as predatory and self-maximising

(Buğra, 1994; Heper, 1985). The bureaucratic oligarchy created an environment in which "the bureaucracy [in Turkey] remained a class whose location in the social system allowed it to attempt the transformation of that system while maintaining its location" (Keyder, 1987a: 48). As a consequence of Turkey's strong state *vis-à-vis* weak bourgeoisie, Buğra perceives the Turkish businessmen's self-perception as lacking "confidence about the legitimacy of activities carried out in pursuit of pecuniary gain" (Buğra, 1994: 5). The animosity between the autonomous state and the interests of the Turkish bourgeoisie has precipitated an industrial environment in which Turkish businessmen see the state as "the major source of their difficulties" (Buğra, 1994: 5).

Having said this, this "strong state tradition" literature on state-society relations properly regards the Turkish army as the principal power holder, the possessor of a privileged status in the state, and founder, guardian, and moderniser of the Kemalist state; however, this literature's methodological position wrongly prioritises the main social conflict between political and state elites (Demirel, 2004; Hale, 1994; Harris, 1965; Heper 1976, 1985, 1991; Heper and Evin, 1988; Karabelias, 2009; Lerner and Robinson, 1960; Momayezi, 1988; Narli, 2000; Nye, 1977; Sakallioğlu, 1997; Tachau and Heper, 1983). Thus, this analysis' main downfall is that it neglects to see state power as an agent of capitalist development in Turkey. Instead, this literature largely assumes that the Turkish state has been the main source of instability and insecurity for capitalist development (Buğra, 1991; Heper, 1985). The methodological selection ignores a relational analysis between the state's militarist-nationalist institutionalisation and capitalist institutionalisation (Akça, 2010a: 354–364). Rather, the state and capital relations are taken as *external* to each other and autonomous from class contradictions in society. The demarcation of the state apparatus from social power relations is absolutised, disregarding hybrid formations, policy links, and the disunity of state managers (Jessop, 2008: 64). As a consequence, this literature argues that the Turkish state has *incapacitated* the development of the internal endogenous dynamics of capitalism (Buğra, 1994: 23). However, it becomes impossible to characterise the state solely as an obstacle to capital accumulation when one takes into account the implementation of state-led industrialisation in the 1930s and state entrepreneurship through the Five-Year Development Plans of the 1930s and 1960s (Boratav, 2006).

Second, the state-tradition perspective has a tendency to position the basic cleavage in society between the bureaucracy as an autonomous class, which remains above class politics, and the bourgeoisie (Keyder, 1987a; Heper, 1976). However, the civil/military bureaucracy cannot constitute a social class *per se*. The bureaucracy is strictly tied to the dominant ruling class in society. In terms of a class analysis, the civil/military bureaucracy can be conceptualised as a social category defined "by its relation to the state apparatuses" (Poulantzas, 1975: 23). This means that "...social categories have a class membership, their agents generally belonging to several different social classes" (Poulantzas, 1975: 24). This conceptualisation is important to this book because once the civil/military bureaucracy is positioned as a *class* against the interests of the bourgeoisie, the Turkish state automatically becomes the prime *impediment* to capitalist development. Unsurprisingly, in the 1980s such a conceptualisation of the capitalist state, in the context of the centre-periphery dichotomy, translated into a neoliberal political discourse that posited minimal state intervention in the economy (Güngen and Erten, 2005: 8).

Third, by downplaying the state's class content—and instead emphasising the state's autonomy and the analytical superiority of a state-centred perspective over Marxism—the state tradition perspective sees the state as class-neutral and neglects the logic of social reproduction (Cammack, 1990). Consequently, this perspective posits "a possibility of the state going beyond the social dominance of the capitalist class and therefore, to be a *class neutral* state" (Chang, 2008: 22).

Finally, the "strong state" analysis translates class relations into relations between rational individuals or different interest groups, in turn mystifying the unequal social relations in society. As Dae-oup Chang suggests in criticising the mainstream understanding of the developmental state in South Korea,

> this image of the independence of the state resulted, therefore, from a very narrow and a-historical understanding of the relations of the state with capitalist society as the relations between different societal forces, or more exactly societal organisations as set of individual-societal actors, rather than from a serious attempt to understand the nature of the capitalist state in relation to particularly capitalist social relations (Chang, 2008: 24).

As a consequence, the "strong state" analysis purposefully ignores the unequal power relations between capital and labour.

In addition to the "strong state tradition" approach, the existing literature largely employs the "centre-periphery" dichotomy in explaining the general trends of Turkish politics. Academic works mainly concentrate on the confrontation between the authoritarian secularism of the Republican elite at the centre, and the broad masses adherence to Islamic principles and values on the periphery (Gellner, 1981; Göle, 1997; Heper, 1981; Mardin, 1995; Öniş, 1997: 744; Toprak, 2006). For the most part, the manifestation of this dichotomy in Turkish politics is deemed central to the Islamic resurgence in Turkey and the autonomous role of the military in politics. This analysis argues that the genealogy of the Turkish state can be explained through the ideational conflicts between the authoritarian civilian/military state elite and the broad masses. Metin Heper (1981), for instance, analyses the state-religion relationship in the early phase of Republican Turkey through referencing the effects of the Cultural Revolution on the broad masses in the 1920s and 1930s. Heper argues that the visibility of the Islamic resurgence in Turkey has much to do with the psychological and cultural consequences of the Kemalist regime's secularisation process. The substitution of Kemalist nationalism for Islam failed to offer a system of beliefs and practices for the masses, which in turn led to a confrontation between "radical secularists and Islamists" (Heper, 1981). A similar line of reasoning is evident in Emelie Olson (1985), Yeşim Arat (1998), Aynur İlyasoğlu (1996), and Hasan Ünal Nalbantoğlu's analysis (1993), in the sense that modernisation or Westernisation from above is seen to have prompted a religious reaction to the secular elite and its dominant ideology.

According to Nilüfer Göle, the implementation of "didactic secularism" (1997: 49) with a modern pedagogical ideology was intended to "demystify religion" (Gellner, 1981: 68) in Turkey and build a society in line with Western values. In the modernisation and secularisation process initiated by the Kemalist regime, the Ottoman past was seen as backward, culturally submissive and a heritage to avoid. The radical cultural reforms—such as the substitution of the Latin script for the Arabic script in 1928, the removal of Persian and Arabic influences from Turkish in order to purify the language, and the institutional establishment of the Turkish Linguistic Society (*Türk Dil Kurumu*) in 1932 to create a pure language—were all intended to effect a deep-rooted rupture with the Ottoman legacy and its associated political elites (Göle, 1997: 49–50). In this perspective, Islamic revivalism in Turkey is seen as antithetical to the modernisation process of Turkey's secular elites (Göle, 1997). It is postulated that "[t]he Islamists are the counter-elites of Republicans but the elites of their followers" (Göle, 1997: 57–58). In this context, Mehmet Altan coined the phrase "Second Republic" in pointing to the need to reverse the general features of the Kemalist state, which he named the "First Republic". According to Altan (1993: 37), the First Republic is a military state in which the National Security Council stands above parliament and embodies national sovereignty. Altan (1993:42) advocates for a transition from the political state—the First Republic or the Kemalist state—to the liberal state, the Second Republic.

Thus, with respect to Islamic politics in Turkey, the centre-periphery dichotomy offers a wealth of information about the ideological clashes in society. However, such a framework, which is based on the confrontation between the secular elites and conservative masses, constructs each identity as fixed rather than flexible. In other words, the centre-periphery dichotomy attributes a *secular character* to state elites, namely the military and civil bureaucracy, and a *conservative character* to the masses. This approach glosses over the fact that Turkey's military elites utilised Islam as a tool for achieving social order even before the 1980 coup, in the political convulsions of the 1970s. As religion has been a bulwark against nationalist and socialist tendencies in Turkey, the military—as a core nucleus of the state apparatus—did not refrain from blending religion with a new form of nationalism in order to create a new form of state ideology (Şen, 2010: 61–66). Secondly, the centre-periphery dichotomy does not explain why Islamic politics rose particularly after the 1990s, as religion has always been important to the Turkish masses. In other words, this dichotomy neglects the historical-political aspect of the resurgence of religion. In addition, this analysis is blind to the changing social base of Islamic revivalism in Turkey. In the context of neoliberal globalisation, the social base of Turkey's Islamic movement includes: the newly emerging professional middle classes, who are socially conservative and challenge Kemalist modernisation; peripheral capitalists; and the working class who migrated to the cities and encountered precarious working conditions (Gülalp, 2001). Thirdly, although the centre-periphery analysis aptly addresses the ideological consequences of the Kemalist state's modernisation/Westernisation process, this analysis remains silent on this process's economic aspect, namely its attempt to create a bourgeois society.

Therefore, divergent understandings of state-society relations in Turkey leads to contradictory evaluations of the nature of the Justice and Development Party (*Adalet ve Kalkınma Partisi*, AKP) and the conceptualisation of (formal and procedural) democracy. On the one hand, the wholesale adoption of the centre-periphery dichotomy in explaining the general cleavages of Turkish politics leads to an esentialised notion of the AKP as a democratic party. While this approach accurately defines the AKP-engineered process in Turkey until 2010/2011 as a "bourgeois democratic transition", it nevertheless adopts a linear view of history, implying that the bourgeois democratic transition is irreversible and will necessarily evolve into full-fledged democracy in Turkey. This linear view of history inevitably led some liberals and liberal-leftists to unconditionally support the AKP against the state elites. For instance, Ahmel İnsel (2003: 306) argued that the AKP victory in the 2002 elections "will finally make the normalization of Turkey's century-old Westernization adventure possible". Socialist Ömer Laçiner went further, depicting the AKP victory in the 2007 general election as "a postmodern bourgeois democratic revolution", the "consolidation of the republic and of the bourgeois democracy" and the end of the political crises instigated in the 1980s (2007: 43–49). Sociologist Ferhat Kentel whose article was also published in an Islamic fundamentalist journal called *Haksöz*, on the other hand, defined the AKP victory after the 2010 constitutional referendum as a "chain democracy" and "conservative revolution" (2010).

On the other side of the spectrum, there has been a growing tendency in Turkish academia and left, since the AKP's abrupt turn to authoritarianism after 2011, to either essentialise the party's power—by arguing that it has, *from the beginning*, been authoritarian in nature, right-wing populist in politics, and regressive in social imagination—or label it a "wolf in sheep's clothing". In addition, this line of thinking confuses "bourgeois democratic transition" with "substantial democracy". As this vein has an idealised form of democracy, one that goes hand in hand with economic and social justice, they belittle "bourgeois democratic transition" and/or totally reject everything associated with the term and its applicability to the Turkish context. They also fervently criticise those who use the concept to define the process that Turkey underwent until 2010/2011 and scapegoate these same people for Turkey's subsequent authoritarian turn. Merdan Yanardağ, for instance, argued that democratisation is the "new tool of global capitalism for domination"; a similar term—human rights—was instrumentalised for imperialist interventions in Yugoslavia, Afghanistan, Iraq, Libya and Syria (2015: 126). In his book *Liberal İhanet* [The Liberal Treachery], Yanardağ therefore took aim at those who saw the AKP-engineered process until 2011 as a "bourgeois democratic transition". Yanardağ (2015) suggested that liberal Turkish intellectuals who supported the AKP betrayed the nation and were instrumental in the transition to Turkey's current Islamic fascist regime. According to Yanardağ (2015: 13–17), liberals formed a "reactionary historical bloc" with conservatives and postmodern intellectuals, hegemonising the reactionary critique of the Republic. Aras Aladağ (2013), on the other hand, argued that the adherence of left liberals to the AKP's conservative hegemonic project traces back to the 1980s, when state-civil society antinomy became their methodological approach. According to Aladağ (2013: 23), the methodological approach adopted by left liberals understands democratisation as a struggle *together* with the bourgeoisie against tutelary forces, not as a struggle *against* the bourgeoisie and social, economic order.

Moreover, some Stalinist leftists in Turkey suggest that the struggle against the tutelary regime attempted to replace the First Republic (or the Kemalist state) with the Second Republic, a regime that asks for an articulation with international capital, the spread of religious reactionism—instead of secularism—and the abolishment of the welfare state (Nalçacı, 2012: 29). Such arguments also revolve around the rejection of the term "military tutelage"[1] in Turkey, which ruled for decades. Even more, some people in the Kemalist left despised the transition to democracy in 1946, arguing that this first attempt at transitioning to democracy was the reason for the defeat of Kemalism:

> Kemalism was defeated against the reactionary forces, imperialism, religious forces, and ethnic nationalists which have been mobilised against the nation state [since 1980s]. [However], there is a background [of this mobilisation]. Since 1919, the struggle between the progressive and reactionary forces has never finished. Sometimes, the progressive forces won [the struggle], sometimes the other forces prevailed. According to me, the biggest checkmate came about with the acceptance of democracy in 1946 [in Turkey]. 1946 was [the year of] the first elections [in Turkey]. Everything [had become] for democracy. What I mean by democracy is not the ideal state order. It is an American project. ... The Democrat Party, the first party of Turkey, is not a leftist party. It is a party which is open to the collaboration with the US. ... According to me, 1946–1947 is the point of failure. While abandoning the independence, the collaboration style does not assure that the independence can be sustained any longer (Birgül Ayman Güler, 2013, personal communication).

Putting aside this exaggerated view that Kemalism was defeated due to Turkey's transition to democracy in 1946, it is more accurate to acknowledge that Kemalism was defeated due to Turkey's transition to democracy in 1946, it is better to account that Kemalism has been so far the official "religion" of the Turkish state. It facilitated the establishment of modern bourgeois society in Turkey through a "revolution from above" under the control of the military. By doing this, Kemalism—the unifying ideology of the Republic—created an

---

1 The concept of "military tutelage" was first introduced for the Turkish context as being "a temporary guardian of the single party" in the English edition of a book titled *Political Parties: their organization and activity in the modern state* by French sociologist Maurice Duverger in 1954, arguing the positive aspects of the single party regime in preparing country for democracy (The original book was published in 1951 and titled *Les Partis Politiques*). Following Duverger, Walter F. Weiker developed the concept and presented it with a positive attribute in his book *Political Tutelage and Democracy in Turkey: The Free Party and its Aftermaths* in 1973. It was argued that particular stages of development and modernisation in Turkey between 1930 and 1946 *under the political tutelage of the single party rule* facilitated the transition to a multi-party system in 1946 to the extent that the single party made it possible "for the fragile plant of democracy to grow in soil that is not prepared for its reception" (Weiker, 1973: 301).

illusion that the state was above the classes and represented the common interests of various sections of society (Gülalp, 1985).

Frederick Engels presented a similar characterisation of Germany under Otto von Bismarck in a letter written to Karl Marx in 1866, saying, "Bonapartism really is the true religion of the modern bourgeoisie" (Engels, 1866: 266). In Bonapartism the core state apparatus, the military, can mutate into a special social power *only* under specific conditions (Şaylan, 1988: 449–459). A bureaucratised power, the military, rises above the society in precarious situations. In order to guarantee the reproduction of capitalist social relations, the state executive substitutes itself for the direct rule of the bourgeoisie in a form of Bonapartist capitalist state (Marx, 1972, 2000). In addition to its economic mission, a Bonapartist state can also assume a complementary role in "social transformation" of a society that did not complete its capitalist transformation (Şaylan, 1988).

It is vital to stress that the Bonapartist state does not mean the non-existence of a parliament. Instead, parliamentary power is reduced to the shadow of the executive power because the parliamentary regime is unable to maintain the social order that the capitalists need. Put simply, the bourgeoisie is too weak or has become too weak to rule in an effective manner. Thus, the Bonapartist capitalist state is a product of capitalist contradictions and of protracted political crisis of the ruling class in which the bourgeoisie as a whole is unable to properly maintain its social, ideological, and political hegemony over society through the smooth functioning of a parliamentary regime. That is to say, it emerges as a product of specific historical conditions (Şaylan, 1988: 454). An internal threat such as a civil war or uprising, or an external threat such as a war or territorial dispute, can necessitate the state power to assume additional roles in repressing any direct threats to national interests and consequent indirect threats to the capitalist order.

The concept of Bonapartism derives from Karl Marx's influential work *The Eighteenth Brumaire of Louis Bonaparte*. In the 1869 preface to this work, Marx mainly demonstrates "how the *class struggle* in France created circumstances and relationships that made it possible for a grotesque mediocrity to play a hero's part" (1972: 6). The important narrative of *The Eighteenth Brumaire of Louis Bonaparte* is to reveal how Louis Bonaparte's successful *coup d'état* overthrew bourgeois representatives in the National Assembly and installed in their stead a dictator at the head of an enormous bureaucratic and military organisation, and that "this appalling parasitic body ... enmeshes the body of French society and chokes all its pores..." (Marx, 1972: 104). Nonetheless, the all-intermeddling, parasitic Bonapartist body is in the service of bourgeois interests without being under their control (Marx, 1972).

Bonapartism, then, refers to the form of the capitalist state where "an economically dominant class is served by a government which is strong enough to crush opponents and autonomous enough for the bourgeoisie to be able to distance itself from the responsibility of rule" (Krygier, 1985: 60). By substituting itself for the direct rule of the bourgeois class, the state executive plays the role of the bourgeoisie and serves bourgeois interests. As Marx puts it "...in order to save its purse, it [the French bourgeoisie] must forfeit the crown, and the sword that is to safeguard it must at the same time be hung over its own head as a sword of Damocles" (1972: 55). In other words, while the Bonapartist state administers the interests of the ruling class, it is not obliged to do the latter's command (Krygier, 1985). On that point, history confirms this theory; when the French bourgeoisie failed to maintain its hegemony over society due to the economic crisis in 1851 it was the repressive French state apparatus that restored the hegemony and tranquillity in France. To the extent that the bourgeoisie tied itself to the maintenance of this military caste, "[the French bourgeoisie] apotheosised the sword; the sword rules it". (Marx, 1972: 101).

It is undeniable that successful economic development is attained under the supremacy of this "terrific parasitic body". In *The Civil War in France,* Marx clearly indicates that the Empire of Louis Bonaparte protects the propertied classes and assures their economic supremacy over the working class (2000: 586). "Under its [executive power's] sway, bourgeois society, freed from political cares, attained a development unexpected even by itself. Its industry and commerce expanded to colossal dimensions; financial swindling celebrated cosmopolitan orgies; the misery of the masses was set off by a shameless display of gorgeous, meretricious and debased luxury" (Marx, 2000: 586). Therefore, the Bonapartist state is not only a *form of the state* that refers to a strong and bureaucratised executive power. It also refers to an exceptional form of the capitalist state, which enables the continuation of capital accumulation in a country under specific historical conditions.

For example, as Colin Mooers (1991: 88) points out, "between 1852 and 1857, with the rapid extension of rail networks, financed through the new credit mechanisms pioneered by the state, France was able for the first time to sustain a rate of growth comparable to that of other industrialising countries". Under the Second Empire, Mooers claims that industrial expansion and economic modernisation became the religion of Bonaparte's advisors (Mooers, 1991: 89).

In *The Eighteenth Brumaire*, Marx (1972) also delineates the autonomy of the French state under Louis Bonaparte. "Only under the second Bonaparte", Marx writes, "does the state *seem* to have made itself completely independent" (1972: 105, *emphasis added*). Miliband (1965: 285) explains that "for Marx, the

Bonapartist State, however independent it may have been *politically* from any given class remains, and cannot in a class society but remain, the protector of an economically and socially dominant class". In other words, the independence of the Bonapartist state from all classes in society is a fictitious independence because Bonaparte represents a class.

Marx (1972: 105) plainly clarifies the historical function of executive power with its bureaucratic and military organisation both in the time of absolute monarchy and the decay of the feudal system in France. Marx argues that "... under the absolute monarchy, during the first Revolution, [and] under Napoleon, bureaucracy was only the means of preparing the class rule of the bourgeoisie" (1972: 105). As a corollary, by means of "vast and ingenious state machinery" of executive power "with is enormous bureaucratic and military organisation", "[t]he seigniorial privileges of the landowners and towns became transformed into so many attributes of the state power, the feudal dignitaries into paid officials, and the motley pattern of conflicting medieval plenary powers into the regulated plan of a state authority whose work is divided and centralised as in a factory" (Marx, 1972: 105). In other words, the centralised French bureaucracy had helped to accelerate the decay of the feudal societal formation.

On the other hand, in a capitalist social formation in France, the existence of the executive power and bureaucracy seems to be quite different. Marx (1972: 105) argues that "[u]nder the Restoration, under Louis Philippe, under the parliamentary republic, it [the executive power] was the instrument of the ruling class, however much it strove for power of its own". The French bourgeoisie instrumentalised bureaucratic centralisation to break the power of the feudal aristocracy, and then to establish and maintain bourgeois domination (Baehr and Richter, 2004: 3). This bureaucratic centralisation allowed Louis Bonaparte to play the role of the balancer of class forces, an arbiter of class struggle in France, and a benevolent dictator for all classes.

As an example of exceptional forms of the capitalist state, the Bonapartist state is relatively autonomous from the dominant classes and fractions, which is the precondition for the reorganisation of the hegemonic power bloc (Poulantzas, 1974: 313). Marxist theorist Nicos Poulantzas (1973: 284) claims that the inability of the bourgeoisie to achieve internal unity and to realise its political hegemony *vis-à-vis* the dominated classes allows the capitalist class state to take charge of the bourgeoisie's political interests. Second, in the exceptional forms of the capitalist state, there is a "strict control of the whole of the State system by one 'branch' or one apparatus in the hands of the class or class fraction which is struggling to establish its hegemony" (Poulantzas, 1974: 316). By referring to Marx's work on Bonapartism, Poulantzas (1974: 316, footnote 3) notes that "the greater the relative autonomy of the State from the hegemonic class or class fraction, the stronger is its internal 'centralisation'". Thirdly, the function of the exceptional state is to reorganise the ideological hegemony, which concentrates and increases repression against popular classes (Poulantzas, 1974: 316–318). That is to say, in these exceptional forms of the capitalist state a particular intervention of ideology is necessary to legitimise the increased role of physical repression (Poulantzas, 1974: 316). Fourth, Poulantzas claims that under Bonapartist conditions, the police state replaces the legal state. In other words, juridically the distinction between the public and private blurs. As such, the law no longer regulates and virtually everything falls within the scope of state intervention (Poulantzas, 1974: 322–323). In these exceptional forms of the state, the law is no longer the limit due to the unlimited exercise of executive power (Poulantzas, 1974: 322).

The Kemalist state, which emerged upon the complete dissolution of the Ottoman Empire in 1923, encapsulates the classic characteristics of the Bonapartist state (Başkaya, 2008; Tura, 1998). Clearly the physiognomy of the Kemalist state under Mustafa Kemal between 1923 and 1938 took a republican form, whereas the French states under Napoléon Bonaparte between 1804 and 1815 and Louis-Napoléon Bonaparte between 1852 and 1870 exhibited an imperial form. In other words, while Mustafa Kemal principally waged his struggle against the patrimonial rule of the Ottoman Empire and consequently declared the Republic of Turkey, the Bonapartes were officially declared Emperors of the French. However, these two divergent political forms in different territories and different centuries share common traits, which can be summed up as the concentration of power into the hands of an individual, and more importantly, the tendency toward the hypertrophy of executive power over legislative power. A tranquil socio-political environment, which these classes require to gain strength, can only be reached by a Savior of Nation. The Bonapartist Kemalist regime in Turkey, the Nasserist regime in Egypt, and the Boumediene regime in Algeria were long-lived and repressive due to the weakness of capital accumulation in those countries and the necessity to make the bourgeoisie stronger (Başkaya, 2008: 105). Therefore, the repressive Turkish state is the product of the objective and subjective weakness of the national-liberal bourgeoisie, which failed to produce its hegemony by consent *vis-à-vis* the dominated classes in the first quarter of the twentieth century.

Turkish Bonapartism covers a long period commencing with the ascension of Mustafa Kemal as the first president of the Republic of Turkey on 29 October 1923. Mustafa Kemal's trajectory to becoming president was the product of the gradual disintegration of the First Assembly, which functioned between its foundation on 23 April 1920 and dissolution on 16 April 1923. Besides, the domestic context that resulted in Mustafa Kemal's domination of the Assembly was situated in the precarious conditions of the National Struggle (Başkaya, 2008; Demirel, 2011).

From the beginning, the Constituent Assembly exercised both legislative and executive powers; Mustafa Kemal was elected as President of the Assembly and of the Committee of Executive Commissioners (*İcra Vekilleri Heyeti*) (Demirel, 2011: 160). The Assembly was also empowered with a judicial function on 29 April 1920 when the Grand National Assembly enacted the High Treason Law (*Hıyanet-i Vataniye Kanunu*) against deserters and opponents of the National Struggle (Demirel, 2011: 161; Zürcher, 2004: 152). Mustafa Kemal consolidated his grip when a law on 4 November 1920 granted him, as president of the Assembly, to appoint the executive commissioners (Demirel, 2011: 178). With the Greco-Turkish War threatening the fall of Ankara—where the Assembly was located—all of the Assembly's power was provisionally devolved to him on 5 August 1921 (Demirel, 2011: 178, 260–265).

In this historical context, the constituent role of the Kemalist army was brought into being in a political and economic setting in which none of the propertied classes were strong enough to establish hegemony over the other classes during the National Struggle period of 1919 to 1922 (Tura, 1998: 52). Consequently, the strong and repressive state and the power of bureaucracy in Turkey are the product of *necessity* of the nascent Turkish bourgeoisie in an underdeveloped country "where capitalism took root belatedly in the twentieth century" (Savran, 2002: 6).

Distinct from Western examples of Bonapartism, the Kemalist capitalist state rests not only on the *personal* control of state power. Thus, even though this book retains Fikret Başkaya's emphasis on the Kemalist state as a Bonapartist state in its theoretical framework, it also departs from Başkaya's analysis due to the fact that he only relates Bonapartism to the personal rule of Mustafa Kemal; at no point does Başkaya look at the institutionalisation of the Kemalist regime in Turkey through successive coups or legal means. In other words, while Başkaya posits that Turkey's Bonapartist regime ended with the demise of Mustafa Kemal in 1938, this book contends that Kemalist Bonapartism stretches from the *personal rule* of Mustafa Kemal between 1923 and 1938 to a long-lasting period of institutionalised military power over the parliament after the 1960 coup. The long existence of Kemalist Bonapartism mainly stems from the political decision-making process going on behind the scenes. In other words, the Kemalist military has usurped state power, but not for very long unlike what has been seen in Latin American cases, for instance, in Brazil between 1964 and 1985, in Spain between 1936 and 1975 and in South Korea in the series of military dictatorships from the 1960s up until the 1980s. Indeed, the Turkish military enjoyed sharing and controlling state power with the political representatives of the bourgeoisie, which created "a dual system of executive decision making" (Sakallioğlu, 1997: 158). This long period of Turkish Bonapartism was perpetuated by the ideological dominance of the military (Şen, 1996), which was successful in presenting itself as the supreme head of the nation and promoting the indivisibility of the nation from its own self-image. Conceivably, the military has not only been a repressive apparatus of the state but also an ideological apparatus for the reproduction of the regime and preservation of Kemalist modernity (Şen, 1996). This is mainly due to the fact that the Turkish armed forces, to a certain extent, substituted the prominent function of the ideological tools of capitalism in favour of the Kemalist Republic since the schooling was low and the communication tools were inadequate to accomplish the ideological struggle in rural areas (Şen, 1996: 33–35). Kemalism has been a state ideology, which is preserved and supported by means of administrative and criminal sanctions (Beşikçi: 2010: 17).[2]

The Turkish Bonapartist era reverberated with a tendency for Turkish armed forces to frequently migrate from their barracks to the forefront of Turkish politics, as seen in 1960, 1971, 1980, and 1997. The reproduction capacity and eagerness of the armed forces to intervene in political life have corresponded with the impotence and incapacity of the bourgeoisie to get its interests accepted by society within the framework of parliamentary sovereignty (Savran, 2010: 192). In short, the intervention capacity of the Turkish military is *inversely* related to the hegemonic governing capacity of the bourgeoisie through its parliamentary apparatus (Savran, 2010: 192).

Crucially, Bonapartist law was imposed in the convulsive founding period of Turkish Bonapartism, and used as an effective tool to reproduce the political regime. By declaring martial law and a state of emergency, the Kemalist Bonapartist state exerted its power for a long time. In the 75 years from the establishment of the Republic of Turkey on 29 September 1923 to the 75th anniversary of the Republic of Turkey in 1998, the total duration of martial law (wholly or partially proclaimed) was 25 years, 9 months and 18 days (Üskül, 1997: 71). Worse still, even though martial law, which had been put into effect in the wake of the 12 September 1980 coup, was lifted in July 1987, the Council of Ministers under the control of the National Security Council maintained an

---

2 For instance, the Law Concerning Crimes Committed Against Atatürk (Law No 5816), which was enacted in 1951, makes defamation of the memory of Mustafa Kemal a criminal act. In one of the recent cases in 2005, two young people under 18 were handed jail sentences over defamation of Atatürk when they wrote flippant words such as *mstık* (an abbreviation in Turkish for the word *Mustafa*) into the memorial book of Anıtkabir where the mausoleum of Mustafa Kemal is located (*Habertürk*, 28 January 2010).

official state of emergency in Kurdish region of Turkey's southeast until November 2002.[3] Following fluctuations in the extension and gradual nullification of the state of emergency declarations in some parts of Kurdish region of Turkey's southeast, the final one was abrogated in the Diyarbakır and Şırnak districts in November 2002. It would be far from exaggeration to say that an extraordinary governmental declaration turned into an ordinary rule in the Republic of Turkey. It is astonishing to note that until the complete abrogation of the exceptional rule of the state of emergency in Diyarbakır and Şırnak in November 2002, more than 42 years of the life of the Republic of Turkey had been under extraordinary rule, either in all or part of the country. Moreover, the entire country had been under the AKP-declared state of emergency since the July 2016 attempted coup, which continued two years (Table 1).

Characterised by a hypertrophied state apparatus coupled with capitalist economic objectives of developing bourgeois property relations and catching up with Western countries through national developmentalism (Başkaya, 2008), Turkish Bonapartism was perpetuated through institutional arrangements up until the 1980s, long past the death of Mustafa Kemal in 1938. During the institutionalisation period of Bonapartism between 1960 and 1983, Kemalism was the *political, economic,* and *ideological* force in Turkey. The *economic* pillar of Kemalism started to gradually dissolve after the 1980s, corresponding with the decline of nationalist and secular policies worldwide and a crisis in the popular ideology based on national-statist developmentalism. However, despite this fact, the ideological and political pillars of Kemalism—Kemalist nationalism and military tutelage—became more rigid. This is because of the perpetuation of the army's definition of Kurdish separatism and political Islam as internal threats in the 1990s (Cizre, 2011: 61).

The political pillar of Kemalism was narrowly challenged by limited political liberalisation under the rule of Turgut Özal between 1983 and 1993. Accompanied by the recommencement of the democratic transition in the late 1990s,

---

[3] One of the blind acts of violence which was unleashed upon Kurdish region of Turkey's southeast in the Republican period was just after the Mount Ararat Revolt of 1930. Law No 1850 protected civilians and military authorities who killed Kurds during the revolt. According to the Law, "Murders and other actions committed individually or collectively, from the 20th of June 1930 to the 10th of December 1930, by the representatives of the state or the province, by the military or civil authorities, by the local authorities, by guards or militiamen, or by any civilian having helped the above or acted on their behalf, during the pursuit and extermination of the revolts which broke out in Erciş, Zilan, Agridag (Ararat) and the surrounding areas, including Pulumur in Erzincan province and the area of the First Inspectorate, will not be considered as crimes. (Article 1)" (as quoted in Kendal, 1993: 56). The area of the first Inspectorate covered Diyarbakır, Elazığ, Van, Bitlis, Muş, Hakkari, Mardin, and Siirt (Kendal, 1993: 56).

TABLE 1 Martial law and state of emergency in Turkey and their durations

Event	Date	Duration
Sheikh Said Rebellion	23/24.2.1925–23.12.1927	2 years and 9 months
Menemen Incident	1.1.1931–8.3.1931	2 months and 7 days
Second World War	20.11.1940–23.12.1947	7 years and 1 month
Events of September 6–7	7.9.1955–7.6.1956	9 months
Student protests and the 27 May 1960 coup	28.4.1960–1.12.1961	1 year 7 months and three days
Attempted coup by Colonel Talat Aydemir	21.5.1963–20.7.1964	1 year and 2 months
Events of 15–16 June of the Workers' Resistance	16.6.1970–16.9.1970	3 months
12 March 1971 Memorandum	26.7.1971–26.9.1973	2 years and 5 months
Operation in Cyprus	20.7.1974–2.9.1975	1 year and 15 days
Civil War in Iraq	27.3.1975–27.3.1975	Not implemented
Widespread acts of violence	26.12.1978–12.9.1980	1 year, 9 months and 4 days
The 12 September 1980 coup	12.9.1980.19.7.1987	7 years 10 months and 7 days
The war between the Turkish Army and the PKK (the state of emergency)	19.7.1987–30.11.2002	15 years, 4 months and 11 days
Total duration (until the AKP)		42 years 2 months and 17 days
The coup attempt in 2016 (under the AKP)	20.07.2016–18.07.2018	Around 2 years

SOURCE: ÜSKÜL (1997: 70–71) AND MY CALCULATION FOR THE WAR BETWEEN THE TURKISH ARMY AND THE PKK, INCLUDING THE STATE OF EMERGENCY.

this political liberalisation eventually succeeded in allowing bourgeois interests to maintain control of the parliamentary branch, aided by the impact of the EU accession process on military's supervisory role. In other words, even though the economic aspect of the military-Bonapartist regime had completed its historical function during the national developmentalist era, it maintained its political hegemony in society as a political force through the ongoing military tutelage over the bourgeois parliament.

The AKP government has symbolised the culmination of a post-Kemalist/Bonapartist process which commenced in the 1990s. AKP rule has signified the completion of the historical function of Turkish Bonapartism until 2010/2011. The governing power of the party has corresponded to a situation of symbiosis among the different class fractions in Turkey, namely big finance capital and peripheral capital at the expense of the political omnipotence of the military. In other words, these fractions of the bourgeoisie managed to build their social, political and moral hegemony in the parliament, and thus eclipse the state's hard core or coercive apparatus: *the military*. Yet, the AKP is not the creator of this bourgeois democratic transition as in the cases of the third wave of democratisation (Huntington, 1991). On the contrary, the AKP government is the product of and has been carrier of this bourgeois democratic transition in Turkey until 2010/2011.

Procedural democratisation in Turkey until 2010/2011 has not been a product of mass popular struggles against the Kemalist state. Thus it differs from the 1974 Carnation Revolution in Portugal, which started as a military uprising and overthrew *Estado Novo*, an authoritarian regime in place since 1933; Solidarność (Solidarity), a Polish independent trade union federation in the 1980s; and the People Power Revolution in the Philippines that ousted the Marcos regime in 1986. Furthermore, it has not been the "long-term revolutionary process", as Gilbert Achcar (2013) puts it, like that of the Middle East since December 2010. The bourgeois democratic transition in Turkey is not comparable even with the revolutions of 1830 and 1848 in Europe, where struggle from below was decisive in overthrowing King Charles X in 1830 and Louis Philippe, the July Monarchy, in 1848. Nor is it possible to compare procedural democratisation in Turkey with the political mobilisation of the Levellers during the English Civil War between 1642 and 1651, which supported the extension of suffrage and popular sovereignty. Borrowing Adam Przeworski's concepts (1991), Turkey's democratic transition succeeded in achieving "extrication" from the Kemalist/Bonapartist regime, without constituting a democratic regime. While it empowered civilian rule and led the military to be subjected to civilian control, it failed to achieve democratic consolidation.

The *form* of democratisation is related to its various formal, procedural, and electoral aspects. Contrary to the classical notion of democracy as being a normative theory of means and ends, a realistic, procedural, and modern definition of democracy, which has been purified from ideals, refers to "the democratic method ... that institutional arrangement for arriving at political decisions in which individuals acquire the power to decide by means of a competitive struggle for the people's vote" (Schumpeter, 2003: 269). Therefore, competition by potential decision makers for the electorate's votes becomes the prime barometer of Schumpeter's procedural definition of democracy (Sørensen, 2008: 10–11). Conceptualising democracy as such, the importance of democratic rights to conduct competitive struggle is underlined. "If, on principle at least, everyone is free to compete for political leadership by presenting himself to the electorate", says Joseph Schumpeter, "this will in most cases though not in all mean a considerable amount of freedom of discussion *for all*" (Schumpeter, 2003: 272). He continues to say that "[i]n particular it will mean a considerable amount of freedom of the press" (Schumpeter, 2003: 272). This leads us to conclude that bourgeois liberal democracies fulfil the following characteristics: "...1. a representative government elected by 2. an electorate consisting of the entire adult population, 3. whose votes carry equal weight, and 4. who are allowed to vote for any opinion without intimidation by the state apparatus" (Therborn, 1977: 4). Democratic rights such as freedoms of speech, assembly, organisation, and the press are prerequisites associated with existing bourgeois liberal democracies (Therborn, 1977: 4).

Yet, there can be specific conditions in which *real power* is not held or conferred by parliamentary institutions, as in the case of Bonapartist regimes. This necessitates an expansion of the procedural dimension of the definition of democracy, so that a political system is deemed to be democratic "to the extent that its most powerful decision makers are selected through fair, honest, and periodic elections in which candidates freely compete for votes and in which virtually all the adult population is eligible to vote" (Huntington, 1991: 7). In this expanded definition of procedural democracy, the question revolves around the election of the "most powerful decision makers", leading us to go further in conceptualising "democratisation".

The electoral, procedural, and minimalist definitions of democracy are challenged by various scholars (Dahl, 2000; Grugel, 2002; Held, 2006; Kaldor and Vejvoda, 1997; Rueschemeyer, Stephens, and Stephens, 1992; Schmitter and Karl, 1991). Mary Kaldor and Ivan Vejvoda (1997) differentiate between formal and substantive democracy. According to them, substantive democracy is "a process that has to be continually reproduced, a way of regulating power relations in such a way as to maximize the opportunities for individuals to influence the conditions in which they live, to participate in and influence debates about the key decisions which affect society" (Kaldor and Vejvoda, 1997: 62). Philippe C. Schmitter and Terry L. Karl (1991: 78) draw attention to the fact that the contemporary meaning of democracy affirms the principle of accountability of rulers for their actions, which necessarily relates to not only procedures for forming government but also to power of civil society organisations in order for citizens to exert pressure on public policy. David Held develops his own model of democracy what he calls "democratic autonomy". In this model, an extensive range of political, social, and economic rights are legally entrenched for citizens to enable them to demand democratic rule and participation (Held, 2006: 277).

Moreover, the Marxist scholars emphasise that the *content* of this form indubitably corresponds to its bourgeois character (Draper, 1974; Therborn, 1977; Savran, 1987; Schwarzmantel, 1995; Wood, 1995). This particular *form* of democracy bears "a tension between the democratic idea of equal citizenship rights and the structure of inequality that exists in 'civil society', or rather in the capitalist economy within which [liberal] democratic political institutions are situated" (Schwarzmantel, 1995: 210). Empirical theories on democracy assume pluralism in society and therefore neglect to see structural power relations perpetuated by capitalism (Grugel, 2002: 20–22). In the context of the antagonistic relationship between labour and capital, the representative state tends to mean the representation in government of the political and economic interests of the different fractions of the capitalists, against labour. In the last analysis, as Friedrich Engels (1991: 553) puts it in *The Origin of the Family, Private Property and the State*, "...the modern representative state is the instrument for exploiting wage-labor by capital". Parliament becomes a political sphere where the capitalists can hide their class interests and make the class differences in society invisible to the extent that "[t]he class difference within civil society becomes a political difference" (Marx, 1970: 72). For instance, in the 19th century French Legislative Assembly,

> *The parliamentary republic* was more than the neutral territory on which the two factions of the French bourgeoisie, Legitimists and Orleanists, large landed property and industry, could dwell side by side with equality of rights. It was the unavoidable condition of their *common* rule, the sole form of state in which their general class interest subjected to itself at the same time both the claims of their particular factions and all the remaining classes of society (Marx, 1972: 82).

The representatives of the capitalists turn the parliament into a place where "the common denominator of the interests of the bourgeoisie could be determined" (Mandel, 1969: 15). Under capitalism, parliament becomes the political meeting place of the representatives of the ruling class where they "could be listed, groups opposed to one another by a multitude of sectional, regional, and corporative interests" (Mandel, 1969: 16). It is only in parliament that the superficial appearance of conflicting political parties can conceal the class struggle and the peculiar physiognomy of the period (Marx, 1972: 22).

It is the class content of bourgeois liberal democracy that inherently restricts the majority of the population from exerting effective control over their workplaces and lives (Roper, 2013: 238). Parliamentary cretinism "…holds those infected by it fast in an imaginary world and robs them of all sense, all memory, all understanding of the rude external world…" (Marx, 1972: 77). Purporting to represent the whole society by conferring political equality on labouring citizens who are otherwise unequal, the parliamentary republic neglects the basic contradiction between labour and capital in the form of exploitation. It passes over the fact that "vast areas of our daily lives—in the workplace, in the distribution of labour and resources—[…] are not subject to democratic accountability but are governed by the powers of property and the 'laws' of the market, the imperatives of profit maximisation" (Wood, 1995: 234). This had been referred to by Marx a century ago as "democratic swindle"; democratic forms of government are utilised to keep "the expression of popular opinion within channels satisfactory to its class interests" (Draper, 1974: 306).

These critiques of bourgeois/capitalist democracy do not necessarily mean that its value can be entirely dismissed (Savran, 1987: 57; Therborn, 1977: 5). It is true that under capitalism, it makes little sense to assert an absolute distinction between democracy and dictatorship, given that under specific conditions and class conjuncture in bourgeois politics, dictatorship may emerge out of liberal democratic institutions (Carver: 2004: 125). And indeed, while the French Assembly nearly abolished universal male suffrage in 1850, Napoleon III paradoxically re-established it albeit in a plebiscitary fashion, after the 1851 coup (Hazareesingh, 2004: 131). However, that being said, capitalist democracy is substantively if not absolutely distinct from certain exceptional forms of the capitalist state, as analysed by Poulantzas, such as fascism, Bonapartism, and military dictatorship "which override or smash the degree of pluralism and autonomy of civil society from the state" (Schwarzmantel, 1995: 208). In addition, it should be recalled that the development of representative democracy, which now encompasses universal suffrage and civil rights, is the product of popular struggles against exclusive and limited suffrage in which various qualifications enfranchised only the wealthy (Roper, 2013: 206–208). In other words, the bourgeoisie has not historically been a decisive and consistent promoter of democracy, as it has asked for democracy only in order to have a stake in the political process and guarantee its position thereafter. Moreover, the bourgeoisie's limited support for democracy does not stem from an inherent and structural relationship between capitalism and democracy, but rather from contingent factors that could be otherwise. The extension of political rights has become possible only when a politically organised working class challenge the property rights of the propertied classes (Huber and Stephens, 1999). As Rueschemeyer et al. (1992: 46) state:

> [I]t was the subordinate classes that fought for democracy. By contrast, the classes that benefited from the status quo nearly without exception resisted democracy. The bourgeoisie wrested its share of political participation from royal autocracy and aristocratic oligarchy, but it rarely fought for further extensions once its own place was secured.

When the bourgeoisie is challenged by *les classes dangereuses*, it directly or indirectly supports authoritarian regimes in order to protect its economic interests; Pinochet's regime in Chile between 1973 and 1990 is a good example of this (Rueschemeyer et al., 1992: 58). Therefore, Moore's classic formula "No bourgeois, no democracy" cannot be a universal framework for conceptualising democracy and democratisation (1966). As mentioned at the start of this chapter with reference to Marx on Bonapartism, the bourgeoisie can renounce its political power to save its economic interests and consecrate "the sword ... hung over its own head as a sword of Damocles" (Marx, 1972: 55).

Switching to the Turkish case, the book argues that the military-Bonapartist regime was a decades-long phenomenon, with the beginning of its dissolution coming in the post-Kemalist phase in the late 1980s and the 1990s. The democratic transition in Turkey under the AKP, which ran until 2010/2011, corresponds with the demise of the Bonapartist regime, in that a representative government was now able, to a large extent, to control the core pillar of the state apparatus. In other words, the AKP, as a Muslim conservative party, found itself taking charge of the completion of the liberal democratic transition, a process which was already underway and had gone through many ups and downs before 2010/2011.

Significantly, the AKP as a governing party was not solely an *actor* in the democratic transition but a *product* and *surrogate* of this process, which had already commenced under Turgut Özal in the late 1980s and the 1990s. The gradual march of Turkish bourgeoisie towards the political possession of the state after the late 1980s was the product of class alliance between the ruling classes. Concomitantly, the ruling classes were forced to adopt a new strategy to deal with ingravescent Kurdish problem and the Kurdish people's struggle in the 1990s, which meant getting rid of military rule. The EU process also played an external role, preventing the politically dominant fraction of the bourgeoisie from aligning with the military. Overall, the civilian supremacy over the military corresponds to the *transition to the democratic form of class domination* which shelters the common sovereignty of the different fractions of capital in the parliament. However, this does not mean that bourgeois rule necessarily leads to a transition to liberal representation in every case. The Turkish context provides very strong evidence to support the theory that the bourgeoisie's interest in liberal democracy is not linked to its essential and structural dependence on democracy, but rather on its political necessities. In other words, when the bourgeoise's political and/or economic interests are threatened or hegemony weakened, the bourgeoisie can easily support authoritarianism.

It is also important to point out that transition from the Bonapartist state to the functioning parliamentary republic has nevertheless manifested a neoliberal political atmosphere which "shrinks the scope of equality and democratic public life dramatically, in all areas of material production and distribution" (Duggan, 2003: 13). It is a fact that this democratic transition in Turkey takes place in an epoch of neoliberal globalisation in which the capitalists have more freedom to codify political power and ability to enact devastating neoliberal legislative programs due to the weakness of organised labour in Turkey, which had been crushed after the 1980 coup. The AKP period is, no doubt, the uninterrupted continuation of neoliberal globalisation in Turkey—through the transformation of work, the privatisation of state-owned enterprises, and the downsizing of the civil service—which inherently place limits on the democratic character of workplaces, social institutions and the state.

This introduction has outlined the main concepts used throughout this book. Following on, Chapter 1 presents the birth of the Kemalist/Bonapartist state and its institutionalisation in the apparatuses of the state through successive coups. Then, Chapter 2 lays out the construction of a new society after the 1980 military coup with emphasis on political liberalisation in the 1990s under a post-Bonapartist rule. This chapter suggests that the completion of the historical function of the Kemalist/Bonapartist state actually started with the neo-liberal economic policies of the 1980s. Referring to Antonio Gramsci's terminology, Chapter 3 argues that an Islamic fundamentalist party challenged the Kemalist/Bonapartist state in the 1990s; however, it failed to take control due to its inappropriate "war of manoeuvre" strategy. With this in mind, Chapter 4 suggests that the alternative "war of position" strategy adopted by the AKP has succeeded in ending Turkey's military tutelage through implementing democratising reforms in the first decade of the 2000s. Then, Chapter 5 highlights the reversal of the previous wave of democratisation and the expansion of the Gülen Movement in state apparatuses and sub-imperialist foreign policy. This chapter maintains the view that Turkey's sub-imperialist stage is the result of decades-long military and economic development. The chapter also highlights the 2016 attempted coup in arguing that the resurgence of war in Turkey's

Kurdish region and an AKP foreign policy that diverges from the imperialist order have decisively tipped the balance in the military's favour, which culminated in the 2016 attempted coup. The Conclusion of this book questions Turkey's potential for sub-imperialist expansion with respect to structural economic problems and problematises arguments that increasingly label Erdoğan a new Bonaparte. The book concludes that Turkey has been swinging between military rule and civilian authoritarianism throughout history, and the AKP is no exception.

CHAPTER 1

The Kemalist State

> The struggle of man against power is the struggle of memory against forgetting.
> Milan Kundera, *The Book of Laughter and Forgetting* (1979)

∴

1   The Historical Legacy

Kemalism rested on national developmentalism, which promoted state-led industrialisation and political modernisation (Esen, 2014). From the dissolution of the Ottoman Empire, Kemalist Turkey inherited an underdeveloped country in every sense (Başkaya, 2008, 2009). An agricultural society was bequeathed to the newly founded Republic. According to the 1927 census, some nine million people lived in agricultural areas out of a population of 13.6 million, equivalent to 67% of the total population. By the time of the 1935 census, the number of people living in agricultural areas had risen to 76.6% of the total population. Of the economically active population, the population working in agriculture, however, corresponded to a higher proportion of 81.6%. Even though nearly one third of land was arable according to the 1927 agricultural census, only about 5% was cultivated. Moreover, land ownership was based on pre-capitalist forms—a feudal landlord system (*ağalık*) and the rule of sheikhs—which aggravated the problem of low productivity in land, exacerbated further by backward production techniques (Başkaya, 2009: 32–34).

Underdeveloped manufacturing was no exception to this economic backwardness with Turkey having a scant dynamic industrial base (Başkaya, 2009: 42). Enterprises were small and insignificant, which translated into low capital intensity. According to the 1927 Industrial Census, only 155 enterprises out of 65,245 production units employed more than 100 workers. The structure of industry was also dominated by small-scale petty commodity production in small workshops. Manufacturing industry was concentrated in İstanbul, İzmir, Adana, and Bursa, which absorbed 75% of all manufacturing. According to the 1921 figures, the number of workers per enterprise stood at 2.3 in these centres. In addition, foreign capital mostly dominated the railway and commercial sectors. The ownership structure of the enterprises was also undeveloped and uncluttered: 55% of total enterprises were in the form of sole proprietorship whereas the rate of partnership and joint-stock companies accounted for 17% and 6% of all companies, respectively. Besides possessing an underdeveloped manufacturing sector, Turkey's foreign trade structure was based on exporting low value-added products. Turkey's main exports were tobacco, cotton, opium, raisin, dried figs, nuts and animal products, while the proportion of manufactured products that were exported was only 8.6% (Başkaya, 2009: 42–53).

This socio-economic condition substantially explains why Turkish Bonapartism tasked itself with pursuing the economic strategy of national developmentalism. Similar to typical nation-state building projects in the twentieth century, the Kemalist economic project was based on a belief that national independence and political sovereignty could only be fortified through attainment of economic sovereignty by rapid industrialisation. The Kemalist capitalist state—emulating the five-year plans of the Soviet Union, the first of which spanned from 1928 to 1932—initiated an economic programme based on five-year industrialisation plans in the 1930s, the first of which was implemented between 1933 and 1937 (Zürcher, 2004: 197). Therefore, the prevailing aspect of the Kemalist state's economic function lies in the fact that the state effectively and heavily stepped in as an *entrepreneur* for capitalist development. This occurred in the context of the *objective* and *subjective weakness* of the industrial bourgeoisie, which was unable to carry out its national-liberal tasks within the limits of bourgeois revolution. The state therefore played a role as a facilitator of the Turkish bourgeoisie's objectives.

In that regard, Kemalism continued capitalist development in the form of national developmentalist projects initiated by the Committee of Union and Progress (CUP, *İttihat ve Terakki Cemiyeti*), which was in power in the last days of the Ottoman Empire. For instance, under CUP rule, there was a tremendous increase in the number of joint-stock companies. While there were only 86 joint-stock companies in the Ottoman Empire in 1908, this had risen to 236 by 1918 (Toprak, 1982: 57). In addition, nationalisation and Turkification of the economy had commenced earlier with the adoption of the National Economy Policy (*Milli İktisat*) by.the CUP. This economic policy aimed to strengthen Turkish Muslim entrepreneurs while preserving Ottoman small-scale industry. In the wake of the promulgation of the Law on the Encouragement of Industry in 1914 before the First World War, the products of Ottoman industry were to be preferred even if they were as much as 10% more expensive than the imported ones. The law sought to build a strong national bourgeoisie by establishing entrepreneurial cadres which were recruited from among Muslim traders in provincial towns, guilds and even bureaucrats (Zürcher, 2004: 125–126).

However, this economic policy turned non-Muslim entrepreneurs and people in general into targets. During the implementation of the *Milli İktisat* policy, Greek and Armenian entrepreneurs faced discrimination and even exile.

A campaign of threats and intimidation drove at least 130,000 Greeks from the Western coastal regions into exile in Greece, transferring their wealth to new Muslim entrepreneurs. This was orchestrated by the İzmir CUP secretary, Celal (Bayar), who later became the president of the Turkish Republic (Zürcher, 2004: 126). This economic policy was systematic, multidimensional, and gradual. For instance, the deportation of Armenians in the East was catastrophic, resulting in the deaths of 600,000–800,000 people after 1915 (Zürcher, 2004: 115). The result was indeed an economic convulsion to the extent that this political atrocity took place in a *multi-ethnic Empire* where a huge number of private enterprises were in the hands of non-Muslim minorities. According to the Ottoman industry industrial census of 1913–1915, out of 264 enterprises only 42 (19.6%) of private firms, were owned by Muslims in the Ottoman Empire, whereas 172 (80.4%) were owned by non-Muslims.[1] The number of state-owned enterprises was 22, or less than 10% of all enterprises (Buğra, 1994: 38–39). Fatma Müge Göçek effectively illustrates the subjective weakness of the state-dependent bourgeoisie:

> Throughout Europe, the European Enlightenment and the ideas it fostered had advantaged the newly emerging bourgeoisie in spearheading the ensuring transformations. What distinguished the burgeoning Ottoman bourgeoisie from the European one, however, was its multi-ethnic character. The original Ottoman bourgeoisie comprised of the [non-Muslim] minorities whose access to economic capital (due to their structural restriction to urban commercial activities within the empire) and connections with Europe enabled them to establish many joint companies, banks and industrial enterprises. Yet, unlike their Turkish Muslim counterparts who specialized in either the military or the state bureaucracy, the Ottoman minorities did not have the social and political capital that would have enabled them to sustain and reproduce their economic transformation of the empire. In addition, the *millet* divide predicated on the dominance of the Muslim Turks structurally prevented the Ottoman minority bourgeoisie from uniting forces with their Muslim Turkish counterparts to instigate a bourgeois revolution. Instead, the newly forming Ottoman Turkish bureaucratic bourgeoisie gradually eliminated the Greek, Armenian and Jewish minority bourgeoisie under the banner of

---

1 The Ottoman industrial census of 1913–1915 targeted a limited geography, which covered İstanbul, İzmir, Manisa, Bursa, İzmit, Karamürsel, Bandırma and Uşak. Nevertheless, it gives a useful picture of Ottoman industry given that industry was concentrated in these areas at this time.

nationalism and, by doing so, destroyed the only chance it had not only of preserving empire, but also of sustaining its commercial and economic development. What instead emerged at the end of empire and over the life course of the republic was a state-dependent bourgeoisie robbed of its potential (Göçek, 2011: 19).

This long process of deportation of non-Muslim minorities, which peaked with the Armenian genocide during the First World War under the rule of the Committee of Union and Progress was instrumental in "the creation of a Muslim bourgeoisie" (Akçam, 2012: 361).[2] In one of the cables that was sent by the Interior Ministry to Ottoman provinces on 16 May 1916 during the First World War, it was instructed that the abandoned and confiscated Armenian properties were to be "rented or sold to Muslim applicants at low prices" and the "necessary assistance" and "all manner of facilitation" were to be provided (as quoted in Akçam, 2012: 361). This leads to the conclusion that while the objective weakness of the industrial bourgeoisie stemmed from the unequal integration of the Ottoman Empire to global capitalism as an exporter of raw materials and importer of manufactured goods, its subjective weakness stemmed from the systematic and continuous forced deportations and pogroms directed primarily at non-Muslim minorities during the dissolution of the Ottoman Empire.

2   The 1923 İzmir Economic Congress and National Developmentalism

The 1923 İzmir Economic Congress, which was organised between 17 February and 4 March during the interval between two sessions of the Lausanne Peace Conference gathered delegates who were selected on the basis of occupational representation (Finefrock, 1981: 376). Some of the prominent decisions that were taken related to:
1) The development of national and domestic industry;
2) The establishment of an industrial bank for granting loans to industrialists;
3) The inauguration of the chamber of industries in districts;

---

2   Vecdi Gönül, Minister of National Defense between 2002 and 2011, said that, "if Greeks continued to live in Aegean and Armenians continued to live in many parts of Turkey, would it be possible to have the same nation-state today? I don't know how to phrase the importance of this population exchange but if you look at bygone balances [in those years], its importance would very clearly show up..." (*Radikal*, 11 November 2008).

4) Removing import duties for the machines and machine components for industry;
5) The establishment of a national insurance company;
6) The protection of domestically produced commodities and products through heavy import tariffs;
7) Nationalisation of mines and utilisation of them according to national interests;
8) The abolition of the monopoly (*inhisar*) system which favoured foreign capital, while allowing collaboration with foreign capital on more equal terms to continue;
9) Scheduling the construction of railways;
10) Granting privileges only to the subjects (*tebaa*) of Turkey;
11) The abolition of tithe (*aşar*) tax;
12) The abolition of monopolies over tobacco production;[3]
13) ranting the right to perform trade and business in Turkish ports exclusively to ships and vessels flying Turkish flags and exclusive utilisation of cabotage right;[4]
14) Bestowing the right of association and to form trade unions;[5] and
15) The encouragement of mechanisation in agriculture (Afetinan, 1982).

Parallel with a decision taken in the Congress, a mixed economy was adopted as national policy, with state undertaking major investments in infrastructure (Zürcher, 2004: 195). Eight hundred kilometres of track were laid between 1923 and 1929, and by 1930, 3,000 kilometres of track had been bought while another 2,400 still remained in foreign hands. Eventually, the remainder would all be bought up by the Turkish state. Foreign monopolies over tobacco production were abolished. These enterprises were nationalised, and turned into a state monopoly integrated with other economic sectors in alcohol, sugar, matches, and explosives. İş Bank and Industrial Bank were established in 1924 and 1925 for commercial credits and industrial credits, respectively. Through the promulgation of the Law on the Encouragement of Industry in 1927, tax exemptions were provided for newly expanding industrial firms. Heavy import tariffs were put into effect in 1929 after the lapsing period of the Lausanne Treaty, which

---

3 Régie Company, the largest foreign investment in the Ottoman Empire, was founded by Ottoman Public Debt Administration (*Düyun-u Umumiye*) in 1883 with backing from a consortium of European banks. It was nationalised in 1925 and named TEKEL. TEKEL was privatised to British American Tobacco in 2008.
4 The cabotage law in Turkey was adopted in 1926.
5 The right of association and of trade unions was not granted until the introduction of the Law on trade Unions in Turkey in 1947. Türk-İş, for instance, was founded in 1952. However, the right to strike was acknowledged in the 1961 constitution.

had restricted the implementation of tariffs. In 1925 the tithe (*aşar*) tax, which was based on the traditional practice of in-kind tax from agricultural production, was abolished and replaced with a sales tax (Zürcher, 2004: 195–196). It is important to note that these economic initiatives had been implemented even before the introduction of the five-year industrialisation plans which came after the Great Depression in 1929.

Importantly, even though the construction of the national economy was the objective of the state elites, for economic development they also welcomed foreign capital and the collaboration of the domestic bourgeoisie with foreign capitalists. Nevertheless, it was stipulated by the state elites that political independence would be respected and quasi-capitulation privileges would not be given to foreign capitalists (Boratav, 2006: 52). However, foreign capital found a sound base in the newly founded republic through the establishment of joint ventures with Turkish capital or through organising itself within the joint-stock companies owned by Turks. The result was that between 1920 and 1930, out of 201 Turkish joint-stock companies, 66 had foreign capital. Yet the role of Turkish shareholders in those companies, which was to take dividends but not to participate in the capital formation, was planned as a protective façade (Boratav, 2006: 57–58).

On the other hand, the economic policies of the 1920s were interpreted by left-Kemalism—a socialist-leaning wing of the Kemalist intelligentsia—as a *deviation* from the *founding* principles of Kemalism. This is because this group considered "economic sovereignty" to be one of the fundamental principles of Kemalism. According to them, the economic policies pursued in the 1920s were innately incompatible with Kemalist principles because the 1920s was a period of concession to imperialism; this period was unavoidably shaped in accordance with the "pressure of the time" (Birgül Ayman Güler, 2013, personal communication). Otherwise, left-Kemalists believed Kemalism to be intrinsically "anti-imperialist". In their view, circumstances and virtual structures forced the Kemalist Republic principles in the 1920s to adopt more liberal economic policies which were in search of foreign capital. This aberration was unavoidable and very similar to what happened in post-revolutionary Soviet Russia:

> We are close to the experience in the Soviet Union. For instance, there was a period of 'war communism' in the Soviet Union. Then, it was followed with the NEP period—New Economic Policy. [Then], the first development plan came into force in 1928 and the kulaks [big land-owners] were eliminated from the economy with the help of *kolkhozes* [a form of collective farm in Soviet Union] and *sovkhozes* [state farms]. So, with

reference to us, the first period in the 1920s is a liberal period, [which is] similar to the NEP period [in Soviet Russia]. There has been nothing to do [in Turkey]. You can demand neither a statist economy nor a socialist economy. [In Turkey], everything is taken over from the Ottomans. Municipal Water Management is in the hands of foreigners. Terkos, for instance, is owned by foreigners. It is owned by French. Communication channels are in the hands of foreigners. You hold barely anything in your hand. If you knock [foreign capital] out, then you are left out in the cold. That is to say, the period of the 1920s is a concessional period. It is a period that is not only open to liberal politics but also to foreign capital (Birgül Ayman Güler, 2013, personal communication).

However, the significance of the 1923 İzmir Economic Congress does not lie in its national-developmentalist economic project, but in the creation of the conditions favourable to the establishment of an unchallenged political party—the People's Party—led by Mustafa Kemal (Finefrock, 1981: 384–386). In other words, the Congress was instrumentalised by Mustafa Kemal for his Bonapartist rule thereafter. About one month after the end of the Congress, on 8 April 1923, Mustafa Kemal announced his text called *Dokuz Umde* (Nine Principles), which was the nine-point programme of the People's Party (Zürcher, 2004: 195). However, these nine-points largely adopted the recommendations of the 1923 İzmir Economic Congress while the incorporation of different occupational groups' interests into the programme were quid pro quos for their electoral support (Finefrock, 1981: 385–386). This manoeuvre afforded Mustafa Kemal a political opportunity since "any attempt by [his] political foes to attack it could easily be labelled as opposition to the practical reforms and nationalist slogans identified therein" (Finefrock, 1981: 385).

In the Assembly, the Second Group (*İkinci Grup*), which was founded in July 1922 as an opposition force to the Defence of Rights Group (*Müdafaa-ı Hukuk Grubu*) challenged the exceptional powers exercised by Mustafa Kemal during the National Struggle (Demirel, 2011: 379). This group was mainly against the autocratic power of Mustafa Kemal and called for parliamentary supremacy (Demirel, 2011: 391–405). However, hardly any opposition was present in the Assembly subsequent to the elections in June-July 1923, when Mustafa Kemal controlled all candidates (Zürcher, 2004: 160). An amendment to the High Treason Law on 15 April 1923 put the Group in a position of treason and prevented it from taking part in the elections (Demirel, 2011: 530). With a final manoeuvre on 19 December 1923 when a law ended military involvement in politics, Mustafa Kemal eliminated his foes in the military (Başkaya, 2008: 109), thus rendering his Bonapartist rule largely unassailable.

3 The Statist and Ultra-nationalist Phase in the Kemalist Capitalist State

In the convulsive period of the Great Depression in 1929, the Kemalist capitalist state merged heavy industrialisation with a statist and national form under nation-state building. Statism, which found its full expression following the years of the Great Depression, was a typical characteristic of this military-Bonapartist regime in the sense that statist implementations were deemed to be for the general interests of the nation. In Mustafa Kemal's words:

> The statism that we pursue is to put the State into operation in order to make the nation prosperous and the country affluent as soon as possible in such a way that the state activities which predicate on individual labour and principally on the economic sphere include the general and high interests of the nation (Afetinan, 1982: 15, based on my translation).

Statism was incorporated in the CHP programme in 1931 and then became a constitutional principle in 1937 (Zürcher, 2004: 197). This phase in national-statist developmentalism facilitated the establishment of the SOEs through five-year plans as being an accelerator to capitalist development. Clearly, this was a specific *means* of capital accumulation in a capitalist system (Boratav, 2006: 24–25). The Soviet experience of the first five-year plan in 1927 was imitated and the Soviet Union supported the Turkish five-year plan (Zürcher, 2004: 197). In line with Turkey's first five-year plan, initiated in 1933, a number of state-owned enterprises were established in iron and steel, textiles, paper, ceramics, glass, and chemical products (Bayar, 1996: 775). Two state-owned banks, Sümerbank and Etiler, were established to provide finance for public enterprises (Bayar, 1996: 775). This big push strategy of the 1930s resulted in an annual average industrial growth rate of 10.3% between 1930 and 1939 (Boratav, 2011: 71).

The establishment of the SOEs was a characteristic of the Kemalist capitalist state and continued even after the partial economic liberalisation period following the 1950s. *Makine Kimya Endüstrisi Kurumu* (Machinery and Chemical Industry Institution, 1950), *Gübre, Et ve Balık Kurumu* (Fertilisers, Meat and Fish Institution, 1952), *Türkiye Çimento, Azot* (Turkey Cement, Azote, 1953), *Türkiye Petrolleri Anonim Ortaklığı* (Turkish Petroleum Corporation), *Devlet Malzeme Ofisi* (The State Procurement and Supply Office, 1954), *Selüloz ve Kağıt* (Cellulose and Paper, 1955), *Demir-Çelik* (Iron-Steel, 1955), *Türkiye Kömür İşletmeleri* (Turkey Coal Enterprises, 1957), and other SOEs were established to meet the expanding domestic demand for manufactured products. They contributed to the development of the private sector through the production of its input requirements. In line with the establishment of the SOEs, the proportion of public funds invested in industry showed an increasing trend: 57% in 1950, 60% in 1955, and 78% in 1962 (Kepenek and Yentürk, 2003: 110–111). In 1977, 31.4% of valued added in industry was derived from the SOEs (Başkaya, 2009: 145).

On the other hand, the statist phase in Turkey between 1930 and 1950 occurred in the context of a single party regime between 1925 and 1945 which, if not fascist in the strict sense, carried some fascistic elements. Fascism is "*a revolutionary form of right-wing populism, inspired by a totalitarian vision of collective rebirth, that challenges capitalist political and cultural power while promoting economic and social hierarchy*" (Lyons, 2008: 148). The fascist state emerges from a response to a specific political crisis in the imperialist stage of capitalism whereby the class representation of political parties breaks down and the transition to monopoly capitalism is fulfilled under the ideological state apparatuses controlled by the fascist party (Poulantzas, 1974). With respect to Turkey's military-Bonapartist regime, the fascistic dimension of Kemalism became prominent after the 1929 Great Depression; the single party consolidated itself in the 1930s and continued until 1945. The 1931 Party Congress of the Republican People's Party (*Cumhuriyet Halk Partisi*, CHP) declared Turkey to be a one-party state, while the 1936 Party Congress merged the state with the party in such a way that the governors became the heads of party branches in their provinces (Zürcher, 2004: 176–177). The unification of the state apparatus with the party was completed in 1937 when the party's six principles—or the Kemalist principles of republicanism, populism, nationalism, secularism, statism, and revolutionism—were stipulated in the constitution and institutionalised as state ideology (Zürcher, 2004: 182). Moreover, in the 1930s the Kemalist state reorganised the ideological apparatus by suppressing social and cultural organisations. In 1931, the Turkish Hearths (*Türk Ocakları*)—established in 1912 to disseminate nationalism, positivism and secularism—was closed down to be replaced in 1932 by a semi-official party organisation called People's Rooms (*Halkevleri*). In 1935 the Turkish Women's Union disbanded upon the request of the CHP since it was accepted that the Kemalist leadership fulfilled the proclaimed objective of the Union to grant women a right to vote. The same year, the Turkish Freemasons' lodges were closed down (Zürcher, 2004: 180). Similarly, the totalitarian tendencies of Kemalism were accompanied by promoting a palingenetic myth of the national history—"the Greek *palin* (again or anew) + *genesis* (creation or birth)" (Roger Griffin in Lyons, 2008: 140). In 1932 the first Turkish History Congress accepted the "Turkish History Thesis", which depicted the Turkish race as the creator of all ancient civilisations including Sumerians, Hittites, Egyptians and Greeks (Cagaptay, 2004: 87–88). The history courses in Turkey between 1932 and the late 1940s were based on this thesis (Zürcher, 2004: 191). Similarly, the third Turkish Language Congress in 1936 announced the "Sun Language Theory", which argued that all major languages could be traced to Central Asia and consequently to the Turkish language due to alleged phonemic similarities "such as that between ancient Turkish word *siliy* (sun) and the French word *soleil* (sun)" (Cagaptay, 2004: 91). This theory was also taught in the Arts Faculty in Ankara (Zürcher, 2004: 190).[6]

4 Industrial Upgrading (1960–1980)

Between 1960 and 1980, state policy predominantly gravitated towards the deepening of import substitution industrialisation (ISI). Under ISI, state intervention in trade and industrialisation policy involved "overvalued exchange rates, quantitative restrictions and direct prohibitions of imports, bilateral trade, a strict system of exchange control, high tariffs and guarantee deposits on imports, together with a variety of tax and credit incentives for manufacturing investment" (Şenses, 1994: 52). This inward-oriented capital accumulation model had a specific objective for the development of the bourgeoisie, which was to achieve the "conversion of the domestic merchant's capital into the industrial bourgeoisie" (Ercan, 2002: 23). In the second phase of the ISI, the first of which was experienced in the statist period in the 1930s, Turkish capitalism expanded its manufactured production. According to the 1979 TÜSİAD data the increase in industrial production in 58 countries of the middle income group was 7.6% between 1960 and 1970 and 7.2% between 1970 and 1976 (Ercan, 2002: 23). The increase in industrial production in Turkey exceeded these rates amounting to an increase by 7.8% and 9.5%, respectively (Ercan, 2002: 23). Overall, between 1962 and 1976, the average annual growth rate in Turkey was 6.8% (Boratav, 2011: 130).

---

6 The Kemalist Bonapartism of the 1930s diverged from fascism with respect to a different conjuncture of class struggles that led to the rise of these exceptional states (Poulantzas, 1974). While in the beginning of the rise of fascism a fascist popular movement was reacting "to the disruption of traditional society brought about by the industrial revolution and to the threat posed by the socialist movement to the middle class; the Young Turk regimes in Turkey imposed their policies from above on an indifferent population" (Zürcher, 2004: 186). In addition, while fascism in power relied on a permanent mobilisation of masses for propaganda, Kemalism was at odds with practices of rallying the people (Zürcher, 2004: 186).

With respect to wages, the increase in real wages from 1963 to 1976 was 220%, equal to an annual increase of 4.9% (Boratav, 2011: 139). Moreover, investment by the SOEs proceeded to be the main transmission belt for capital accumulation for the private sector. As a 1981 World Bank report indicated, investment by the SOEs constituted about one quarter of total fixed investment by the late 1970s, with public investment accounting for 59% of total investment and 10% of GNP in 1980.

This phase of the ISI model between 1960 and 1980 had distinctive characteristics in terms of the content of industrialisation, distribution of investment, and investment priorities. The import substitution of nondurable consumer goods which was initiated in the 1930s had already been completed in those years. The production of durable consumer goods and intermediate goods became the main target of industrial production in Turkey between 1960 and 1980. With regards to the internal dynamics of capitalism, the increase in the level of income of the urban and rural bourgeoisie generated a demand for the production of durable goods such as radios, televisions, washing machines, vacuum cleaners, automobiles, modern office furniture, kitchen utensils, and homeware. Owing to scant foreign currency, these goods were produced inside the country with a collaboration of foreign capital. The increase in the real wages of workers and the middle classes facilitated the purchase of these products by the middle of the 1970s (Boratav, 2011: 118–120).

The transition to the production of durable consumer goods and intermediate goods between 1963 and 1980 can be seen in Table 2. The table demonstrates that, on the one hand, the share of durable consumer goods in total manufacturing industries increased from 4.4% in 1963 to 10.1% in 1980 (Table 2). On the other hand, two decades of development in manufacturing resulted in the increase of the share of intermediate goods in total manufacturing industries from 20.5% in 1963 to 42.6% in 1980 (Table 2). In addition, the SOEs pioneered the production of intermediate goods while the period witnessed the decreasing share of non-durable consumer goods in production value. As Table 3 demonstrates, manufacturing in state-owned enterprises was predominantly geared towards the production of intermediate goods, the rate of which increased from 36.5% in 1963 to 64.5% in 1980 (Table 3). This clearly proves that the state manufacturing sector undertook the task of procurement of basic inputs to the private sector (Boratav, 2011: 134).

Not surprisingly, the value creation process by the working class for the private sector during the ISI phase clearly shows that the latter model predominantly contributed to the monopolisation of industry in Turkey (Sönmez, 1992). This monopoly capitalism was in line with the international division of labour

TABLE 2 Structure of manufacturing, share in production value (%), 1963–1980

Years	Non-durable consumer goods	Durable consumer goods	Intermediate goods	Investment goods	Total
1963	66.7	4.4	20.5	8.4	100
1980	39.8	10.1	42.6	7.5	100

SOURCE: BORATAV (2011: 133).

TABLE 3 Internal structure of state manufacturing, share in production value (%), 1963–1980

Years	Non-durable consumer goods	Durable consumer goods	Intermediate goods	Investment goods	Total
1963	53.3	0.4	36.5	9.8	100
1980	29.2	0.1	64.5	6.2	100

SOURCE: BORATAV (2011: 133).

between the centre and periphery capitalist countries in which peripheral countries played a *complementary* role for the industries in the centre countries (Başkaya, 2009). In other words, industrialisation in peripheral countries was not in competition with the big capitalist countries, rather it relied on importing their technologies for producing more. Turkey was no exception to this process (Başkaya, 2009: 146). In addition to its dependence on the core countries, the development of the manufacturing sector led to the concentration of capital in Turkey in private hands. Following the exhaustion of the ISI model and the transition to export-oriented capitalism, by 1985 406 out of the biggest 500 companies in Turkish industry already belonged to the private sector (Sönmez, 1992: 25). Capital was concentrated such that 126 out of these 406 private companies belonged only to 23 capital groups or families (Sönmez, 1992: 25). Table 4 shows that in 1985 the biggest 25 business groups accounted for more than half

TABLE 4   Concentration in manufacturing (1985)

Number of business groups	Number of owned companies	Sale (%)	Workforce (%)	Accounting profit (%)	Value added (%)
Biggest 25	126	53	48	58	53
Biggest 10	97	39	34.2	47	41
Biggest 3	60	23.8	21.5	27.4	26

SOURCE: SÖNMEZ (1992: 25–26).

of the sales, absorbed approximately half of the workforce, had more than half of the profits, and paid more than half of the taxes of the national total. Not surprisingly, the republican project from the 1920s was successful in preparing the conditions for the maturation of Turkish capitalism and its expansion to the international market, which would be possible with the shift to export-led growth after the 1980s. The 1980 coup was instrumental in the transition to export-led industrialisation.

5   Failed Democratic Transition under the Democrat Party (1950–1960)

The Democrat Party (DP, *Demokrat Parti*) was officially founded in January 1946 as an outcome of a political and economic split within the CHP. The split in the party was crystallised with the introduction of the Land Distribution Law for farmers (*Çiftçiyi Topraklandırma Kanunu*) in May 1945. The aim of the land reform was to end the political influence of landlords and war profiteers and to pave the way for independent peasant proprietors (Ahmad, 1993: 103).[7] Adnan Menderes, one of the founders of the DP was a big landowner in Aydın province and challenged the Land Distribution Law for farmers in 1945. Adnan Menderes, the business-banker Celal Bayar, the bureaucrat Refik Koraltan, and the famous historian Fuat Köprülü all submitted a memorandum known as *Dörtlü Takrir* (Memorandum of the Four) to the CHP asking for the

---

7   For more information on land reform in Turkey, see M. Asım Karaömerlioğlu. 2000. Elite perceptions of land reform in early republican Turkey. *The Journal of Peasant Studies*, 27(3): 115–141.

implementation of the Turkish constitution and the establishment of democracy (Zürcher, 2004: 210).

Political and economic factors paved the way for transition to a multi-party system. From a political point of view, political disintegration and the restructuring of the power bloc in the CHP coincided with the end of the Second World War and the defeat of Nazism, which precipitated the transition to a multi-party system in Turkey in 1945.[8] The post-war adjustment involved the intensification of Turkey's incorporation into the global capitalist system both in the field of economy and foreign policy. The Truman Doctrine launched in March 1947 by US President Harry Truman was to ensure military and financial support for Greece and Turkey upon the withdrawal of British assistance to these countries (Zürcher, 2004: 209; Satterthwaite, 1972: 75). The Truman Doctrine was welcomed by İsmet İnönü, the President and the leader of the CHP, as a vivid and hopeful sign from the US towards world peace (Gevgilili, 1981: 53). The military assistance programme involved modernisation and training of the Turkish army and the construction of all-weather roads for military aims which would also foster an agricultural revival (Satterthwaite, 1972: 80). In addition to that, in 1948 Turkey was included in the European Recovery Programme, known as the Marshall Plan, which aimed to revive Europe's post-war economies and ward off Soviet influence. Intensified relations with the US played a role in changing the institutional status of the Chief of Staff. In 1949, the Chief of Staff became tied to the ministry of defence rather than the prime ministry (Hale, 1994: 93).

From an economic point of view, the statist industrialisation in the 1930s, under the single-party regime between 1923 and 1945, reached saturation. The disintegration of the alliance between the military, landlords, and the bourgeoisie during the Kemalist period, however, made the maintenance of the status quo impossible (Ahmad, 1993: 102). In 1947, the implementation of the new five-year plan was unsuccessful. The CHP already redefined and liberalised the concept in the 1948 Economic Congress as "New Statism". The DP had indeed positioned itself against the statist economic implementation under the single-party period, which suggested a free market economy and the privatisation of SOEs (Barkey, 1990: 51–52). The post-war adjustment was to ensure the reintegration of the Turkish economy into the world capitalist economy

---

8   There were failed attempts under the single-party period by allowing the formation of opposition parties such as the short-lived Progressive Republican Party (*Terakkiperver Cumhuriyet Fırkası*) between 1924 and 1925 and the Free Republican Party (*Serbest Cumhuriyet Fırkası*) in 1930.

in conformity with the liberalisation of international trade relations, without sacrificing the objective of industrialisation (Yalman, 2009: 177).

In the 1950 general elections, the leadership under Adnan Menderes and Celal Bayar won 53.4% of the votes while the CHP acquired 39.8% of the votes (Zürcher, 2004: 217). The DP appealed to the masses and achieved popular legitimacy as the winner of consecutive general elections in 1954 and 1957 with vote shares of 58.4 per cent and 47.3 per cent, respectively (Zürcher, 2004: 223, 232). Indeed, the class representation of the bourgeois party constituted of an alliance of the agrarian bourgeoisie and the big landowners with the commercial bourgeoisie under the DP, and represented a disengagement from the Kemalist leadership (Savran, 2010: 159–160).

In terms of economic activity, agricultural growth and infrastructural investment came to prominence in the DP period between 1950 and 1960. These economic priorities were in line with the findings of official US reports on Turkey in the post-war adjustment period after 1945. A report in 1949 by Max Weston Thornburg, Graham Spry and George Henry Soule (1949: 254) for the Twentieth Century Fund concluded that "[t]he first necessity [for Turkey] for further advance is increased governmental activity in public works—roads, railroads, irrigation, drainage, expansion of local power stations—and progress in education, agricultural extension work, sanitation and health measures". The 1951 report of the International Bank for Reconstruction and Development, (IBRD), later the IMF, stressed the priority of agricultural development for Turkey and allocation of public resources to agriculture "because it provides the greatest opportunity for increased productivity and because it is an essential prerequisite for industrial development" (1951: 254). The report also suggested the training of personnel in the fields of public health and education (but not fixed investment in the construction of schools and hospitals), improvements in transportation, public works such as irrigation and municipal utilities and services, public power facilities, and a withdrawal of public investment for large-scale industry and mining (IBRD, 1951: 265–271).

The DP government relied on the state for investment owing to the objective weakness of the dynamic industrial base. The difference between the situation under the DP government and the previous single-party government was, however, the direction of investments. Under the DP, there were significant investments in highways and electrification, which procured the expansion of the domestic market and horizontal integration of different regions (Başkaya, 2009: 140). The second difference was in orientation towards the industrial activity. While the CHP in the single-party period focused on the production of investment goods, the DP turned towards the production of consumer goods (Singer, 1977: 264). These differentiated approaches to investment were understandably bound up with the DP's economic class representation. It was predominantly representing the interests of the commercial and landed bourgeoisie, and private manufacturing was largely associated with agricultural prosperity thanks to mechanisation in the countryside and the increase in agricultural productivity. The results were the increase of income in the agricultural sector, the expansion of the domestic market and the flow of surplus labour to urban areas, which provided a positive stimulus for industrialisation (Başkaya, 2009: 140–141). Close collaboration with foreign capital, US aid under the Marshall Plan and Turkey's accession to NATO in 1952 helped the DP government find foreign resources to finance its investment expenditure. As of June 30 1953, the US made contributions to Turkey consisting of $261,500,000 as grants and $140,200,000 as loans via the Marshall Plan and later through the Mutual Security Program and Foreign Operations Administration (McGhee, 1954: 629).

The industrial advance of the private sector was supported by the DP through the Industrial Development Bank (IDB, *Türkiye Sınai Kalkınma Bankası*), which was founded under the recommendations of the World Bank. The IDB aimed to provide long-term loans and technical assistance to private manufacturers, to satisfy the foreign exchange requirements in the import of equipment, and to assist the development of a private securities market (Singer, 1977: 256–257). The ISI model was pursued by the IDB to the extent that it credited projects which would decrease the balance of payment deficit by favouring import replacement rather than export promotion. Towards the end of the decade, IDB started to direct its loans from simple processing manufactures such as "ginning; cotton and wood spinning and weaving; bricks and tiles; flour and macaroni; rice decortication; extraction of vegetable oils and soap making; leather and leather goods" to the development of more advanced industries such as "textile dyeing, finishing and printing; pharmaceuticals; paint and varnishes; glue manufacturing; cables; metal ore smelting; foundries; machinery; metal goods; ceramics; fibre and chip boards; asbestos cement sheets" (The Industrial Development Bank in Singer, 1977: 262). The result was a sharp decline in the distribution of loans to simple processing industries, from 65% of the Bank's loans in 1951 to 6% in 1956, even though labour-intensive activities with low technology and less advanced business administration techniques were used by the entire private manufacturing sector (Singer, 1977: 262–263). The size of the public sector in industrial production also remained high; 219 public establishments produced almost the same amount of industrial output as nearly 5,300 private firms. Due to their scale, the SOEs were able to employ a larger number of workers. In 1956, the number of workers in the SOEs was on average 624, while it was only 31 among larger private enterprises (Singer, 1977: 302).

It is clear there was a restructuring of class power under Menderes's leadership, favouring the economic interests of a broad bourgeois coalition, especially through support of the agricultural and commercial bourgeoisie in credits, support purchase, and taxations. For instance, credits provided by the Ziraat Bank, a state-owned bank which provides financial support to farmers, were 270 million TL in 1948, which increased to 2.7 billion by the late 1950s. The notes receivable that were discounted to the Central Bank by the Turkish Grain Board (*Toprak Mahsulleri Ofisi*) increased from 200 million TL in 1950 to 1.3 billion TL in 1959, while the net credits of agricultural credit and sales cooperatives amounted to 500 million TL by the end of the 1950s (Savran, 2010: 163, fn. 8).

In the political arena, civil-military relations during the Democrat Party era between 1950 and 1960 meant an intermission, a period of democratic interim. It was clear that the loyalty of the army to İsmet Pasha, the leader of the CHP in those years, was the DP's main concern. In June 1950, just after the general elections where the Menderes government captured 52.67% of votes, it was easier to ward off any threat from the army. Thus the government purged the army in June 1950 by replacing the bulk of the military High Command, including Abdurrahman Nafiz Gürman, Chief of General Staff and the commanders of the army, navy and air force—in total 16 generals and 150 colonels (Hale, 2011: 197; Özdağ, 1997: 24–25). In 1954, the Menderes government increased its control over the bureaucracy by introducing a new law which made possible the early retirement and service suspension of civil servants with more than 25 years, including judges and university professors (Zürcher, 2004: 230). The attempts to control the military included the supervision of military spending. National defence expenditure declined from 1950 to 1960 under the DP government. Table 5 shows that in 1950, national defence expenditure accounted for more than 30% of general budget expenditures; this dropped to 23.4% in 1960. And while national defence expenditure stood at 44.2% of total investment in 1950, it constituted just less than one fifth of total investment in 1960 (Table 5). Under NATO influence, the DP government aimed to rationalise and modernise the army, putting it under the control of the government. Seyfi Kurtbek, ex-colonel and then DP parliamentarian, prepared a reform programme for the army in 1953, but Menderes opted for the loyalty and cooperation of officers so that the programme was never able to be implemented (Ahmad, 1977: 151–153).

TABLE 5 National defence expenditure, 1950–1960

Years	National defence expenditure (million TL)	% of GNP	% of total investment	% of general budget expenditures	% of general and annexed budget expenditures
1950	441.7	4.25	44.2	30.1	24.2
1951	468.0	3.81	37.1	29.4	23.1
1952	611.0	4.27	33.3	27.2	23.6
1953	711.1	4.23	34.1	31.0	28.3
1954	833.6	4.87	33.1	32.5	31.3
1955	1,160.8	5.51	38.6	35.1	34.2
1956	979.5	4.03	30.0	28.1	26.0
1957	1,060.1	3.47	26.4	25.5	24.6
1958	1,395.5	3.87	27.7	28.1	27.2
1959	1,736.1	3.88	24.8	25.8	25.0
1960	1,727.5	3.53	22.2	23.4	22.3

SOURCE: SINGER (1977: 414).

6 The 1960 Coup and 1971 Memorandum in the Context of the Cold War

The 1960 coup was instrumental in the transition to the state-planning era and in the institutionalisation of the social and national security state (Akça, 2010a). Nevertheless, one can observe that in the second half of the 1950s that the interest of the industrial bourgeoisie became gradually more prominent than the interests of the agrarian bourgeoisie and the big landowners, represented under the leadership of Menderes (Savran, 2010: 162–163). The dislocation in the power bloc surfaced in the parliament by means of a crackdown in the DP and the emergence of *Hürriyet Partisi* in 1955 (which merged with the CHP in 1958). The 1960 coup resolved the political spasm that would feature prominently in the economic interests of the industrial bourgeois' investment policy. The military takeover represented a forcible resolution of the contradiction between the industrial bourgeoisie and the other components of the power bloc, the agrarian bourgeoisie and big landowners, given that it was impossible to resolve the contradiction in a parliamentary way (Savran, 2010: 166). It was also instrumental in allowing the industrial bourgeoisie to upgrade itself to the hegemonic position in the power bloc, so that state planning became the hallmark of the two decades following the coup in 1960 (Akça, 2010a).

The necessity to transition to the state planning phase and channel investment activity through institutional arrangements came to the surface in the late 1950s, in conjunction with reports from the OEEC (The Organisation for European Economic Co-operation, later the OECD) and the IMF. While in 1957 the OEEC declared that "it is strongly to be hoped that the Government will be able to achieve the necessary degree of control in the near future, so that investment activity may be directed into the most appropriate channels and remain within the limits compatible with internal and external equilibrium" (as quoted in Sönmez, 1967: 32), tripartite negotiation with the IMF, OEEC and the US authorities in Paris in 1958 concluded that "It is of great importance that this Ministry [of Co-ordination, to be established] should exercise the necessary powers to ensure that, henceforth, there should be the necessary co-ordination of investment, within the framework of a development program" (as quoted in Sönmez, 1967: 32). The economic discomfort that was revealed in the 1958 devaluation and the payment crisis was coupled with steps towards further authoritarianism by the DP after winning the 1957 general elections with 47.3% of votes (Zürcher, 2004: 229–232).

In 1956, the press law was changed to increase government control over the media. Political meetings, except during an election campaign, were prohibited. In April 1960, the establishment of *Tahkikat Komisyonu* (Investigatory Commission) empowered the ruling party to investigate the activities of the opposition, which in turn augmented the discomfort of the masses. Riots, the suppression of student demonstrations by troops, and, restrictions of the press to report on the riots (Zürcher, 2004: 230–240) clearly marked the evaporation of the government's political hegemony. The combination of economic and political instability shattered the political hegemony of the power bloc, which had been united under the dominance of the commercial and landed bourgeoisie.

It was known that the army had been in any case uncomfortable with the electoral results, because the DP was perceived as a counter-revolutionary party that betrayed Kemalist principles. In December 1957, nine army officers were arrested for plotting against DP rule (Hale, 2011: 198; Zürcher, 2004: 238). The opposition to the ruling party was successful in gathering together a broad coalition in which urban elite, bureaucrats, intellectuals, and İstanbul-based bourgeoisie became prominent (Keyder, 1979: 25; 1987b: 45).[9]

---

9   Regional dynamics towards authoritarian rule encouraged anxiety in the DP. The overthrow of the Hashemite Dynasty by a military group led by General Abd al-Karim Qasim in Iraq in

The 1960 coup trumped the legitimacy of the student protests while spreading an illusion that the armed forces extricated the country from anarchy and prevented fratricide (Zürcher, 2004: 241). Not surprisingly, the 1960 coup was celebrated by the state in the "Freedom and Constitution Festival" from 1963 until 1981. The euphoric victory over the DP government was incorporated into the Constitution of 1961. The preamble of the Constitution of the Republic of Turkey celebrated the achievement of the Turkish nation in the Revolution of 27 May 1960 "by exercising her right to resist the oppression of a political power which had deteriorated into a state of illegitimacy through behaviour and actions contrary to the rule of law and the Constitution" (The Constitution of the Turkish Republic, 1961: 3). The military takeover was perceived to be a "revolution" by some writers (Harris, 1970; Karpat, 1970; Tunçkanat, 1996; Weiker, 1963). However, ironically enough the proclamation of the coup—read by Colonel Alparslan Türkeş, founder of the extreme nationalist party called *Milliyetçi Hareket Partisi* (Nationalist Movement Party, MHP)—clearly stated the army's loyalty to and reliance on NATO and CENTO. *Milli Birlik Komitesi* (the Committee of National Unity) abrogated the constitution of 1924 and endowed a commission to prepare the new constitution. In addition, the Committee of National Unity purged 147 prominent staff members from the universities (Kayalı, 2012: 65).

The 1961 Constitution of the Republic of Turkey introduced the bicameral parliament (Ahmad, 1993: 129). However, the main aim of the constitution was to prevent the monopoly of governments such as the DP and to counterbalance it with other institutions (Zürcher, 2004: 245). These constitutional amendments were institutional valves intended to preclude the rule of the rural majority over the urban minority,[10] and particularly to guard against any act incongruous with the interests of the industrial bourgeoisie (Savran, 2010: 176). Therefore, the political regime was based on "a form of the domination of the industrial bourgeoisie over the rural majority" (Savran, 2010: 177).

The new constitution of 1961 aimed to encompass the economic and political interests of the urban population, academia, the military, the bureaucracy, and the industrial bourgeoisie. The industrial bourgeoisie benefited from planning in economic, social and cultural development through the establishment of the State Planning Organisation, tasked with "the preparation and execution, and application and revision of the plan, and the measures designed to

---

1958 put the DP government on red alert for fear that it too could be overthrown by a similar coup.

10   According to the World Bank database, the rural population of nearly 19 million accounted for 68% of the total population in Turkey in 1960 (The World Bank, 2020).

prevent changes tending to impair the unity of the plan" (The Constitution of the Republic of Turkey, 1961, Article 129: 35).

The 1961 Constitution formally guaranteed freedom of thought, expression, association and publication. It also enshrined social and economic rights while giving the state a responsibility to plan economic development and preserve the right of individuals to property and inheritance and the right of freedom of work and enterprise. Full autonomy was given to universities and the mass media (Ahmad, 1993: 129; Zürcher, 2004: 245). Legal respite was given to workers with the right to strike. The relatively liberal constitution of 1961 also paved the way for an increase in political activity. The left benefited from this environment and *Türkiye İşçi Partisi* (TİP, Workers' Party of Turkey) was established in 1961 by trade unionists. Thanks to the proportional representation system, TİP was able to get 15 seats in the 1965 general elections even though they got only 3% of the votes. This period was also marked by the foundation of *Devrimci İşçi Sendikaları Konfederasyonu* (Confederation of Revolutionary Trade Unions in Turkey, DİSK) in 1967 and the further radicalisation of the working class and youth, which peaked in the 15/16 June upheavals in İstanbul and Kocaeli in 1970.

Nevertheless, the liberal-reformist environment and political polarisation ultimately served to undermine the political hegemony of the ruling classes. The armed forces had assumed the co-responsibility of fighting against communism after the 1960s. In 1966, Cemal Tural, the Chief of the General Staff, ensured that the book *Komünizmle Mücadele Metodları* (The Methods for Combating Communism) was read throughout the armed forces (Ahmad, 1977: 195). The manipulation of religion was also an integral part of the military's approach in the 1970s. It was scrupulously and gradually introduced as an ideological counter-weapon against the leftist currents in the country, while communism was seen as the primary threat in the Cold War period. A leaflet titled *Komünistler İşçilerimizi Nasıl Aldatıyorlar?* (How do communists deceive our workers?), which was published by the General Staff in 1973, shows the use of Islam against communism. In this leaflet, communism is defined as "a primitive regime that is unable to reach God, repudiates [private] property, uses people slavishly" (Genel Kurmay Başkanlığı Birinci Ordu ve Sıkıyönetim Komutanlığı, 1973: 3). It states that:

> Communism which is more perilous than cancer causes the death of a nation, not only of a person, through contamination from person to person. Thus, each person who has caught the malady of communism and each nation that is composed of those people start to lose the concepts of Allah, Nation, Morality, and Free Thought which are the highest

cognizance of humanity; and they turn into a living robot or community of robots which only obeys the rules of communist parties and implements them (Genel Kurmay Başkanlığı Birinci Ordu ve Sıkıyönetim Komutanlığı, 1973: 3–4).

In this leaflet, the military portrayed the Turkish workers as the ones who "have strong common sense even though they do not have a sufficient education pertaining to the general conditions of our country. Basically, they are nationalist, Atatürkist and attached to their customs". Any class conflict was rejected. The leaflet stated that "[Turkish workers] find great pleasure in using their labour as capital in order to live honourably. They are respectful to the rules. They don't believe that their rights will be exploited, as they enjoy all kinds of constitutional guarantees that would prevent it" (Genel Kurmay Başkanlığı Birinci Ordu ve Sıkıyönetim Komutanlığı, 1973: 6).

In addition, Major General Turhan Olcaytu's book, which was published in 1973 to be circulated in the military and national education system, exposed how "real religion" could be used against communists and Islamic fundamentalists. In his book, he aimed to "explain how Atatürk, indeed, saved and preserved our religion" and showed how revolutions were compatible with the Quran's verses and hadiths from the Prophet (Olcaytu, 1973: 13). Olcaytu condemned vehemently "the alleged intellectuals, certified traitors" who "masterfully exploited the high national sentiments of patriot workers and youths whose hearts throb for homeland love" (1973: 14). According to him, Atatürkism should be explained unilaterally not only in "the minbars of the mosques but also in school desks" to youths who "are sucked into the maelstrom of Maoist, Castroist, Marxist, Leninist, Right-wing, Left-wing, Nurist, Süleymanist, etc. beliefs which are not compatible with our national interests" (Olcaytu, 1973: 252).

Islamic fundamentalist forces also played a supporting role in assisting the fight against communism. When the radicalisation of the working class and youth between 1967 and 1971, which also manifested itself in growing anti-Americanism, reached its peak in the arrival of the Unites States' Sixth Fleet to Turkey in 1969, Islamic forces were alarmed and mobilised. 1969's Bloody Sunday was marked by a clear provocation and use of Islam against the left. As a consequence, two people were killed and 114 people were wounded (*Milliyet*, 17 February 1969). Mehmet Şevket Evgi, a well-known writer in Islamic circles, wrote an article in *Bugün Newspaper* on 16 February 1969 titled "Cihada hazır olunuz" (Be Ready for Jihad), which called for a total war between Muslims and "red infidels" and urged Muslims to arm against communism. The column represented the overt animosity of Islamic fundamentalist forces in those years towards communists and progressive forces: "…Let it be known that a big thunderstorm is brewing. A full-scale war between the Muslims and red infidels is unavoidable. The trial day has arrived. There is no possibility of escaping and avoiding fate…" (Kural, February 16, 2013). Eygi continued, calling Muslims to:

> Arm against the communist impiety. In Islam, recruitment and jihad are not arbitrary but compulsory. Do not forget even for a moment that jihad is also the obligation upon you for Allah and for your servitude to him. If the red rascals of Stalin and similar antichrists pour into the streets to demolish Turkey, all Muslims should encounter them. Do they have stones, batons, irons and molotov cocktails? We are not bereft of their deployment (Kural, February 16, 2013).

In addition, the regional balance of power turned out to be to the military's advantage for a possible intervention. Hafez al-Assad had seized power in Syria through a coup in November 1970, just four months before the memorandum in Turkey in 1971. There was no harmony within the Higher Command on the extent of the memorandum, in which General Muhsin Batur, the commander of the air force, had been arguing for radical social and economic reforms, including tax and land reform, nationalisation of foreign trade, and reform in the electoral system. Nonetheless, the memorandum was issued on 12 March, 1971 at the will of Higher Command of the army by Memduh Tağmaç, the Chief of the General Staff; Faruk Gürler, the Commander of the Land Forces; Celal Eyiceoğlu, the Commander of the Naval forces; and Muhsin Batur, the Commander of the Air Forces.[11] Without taking over the state administration, the

---

11   The Turkish left in the 1960s and 1970s was under the heavy influence of Doğan Avcıoğlu, who was an editor of *Yön* (Direction) magazine between 1961 and 1967 and the chief editor of weekly newspaper *Devrim* (Revolution) between 1969 and 1971 (Samim, 1981: 66; 1987: 153–154). Avcıoğlu criticised the parliamentary system by arguing that the multi-party system only served the interests of American imperialism with its local compradors in Turkey. Rather, an independent country under an authoritarian regime would pave the way for democratic and egalitarian society. Therefore, it was suggested that a "national democratic revolution" required the close collaboration between the army and civilians. Not surprisingly, he had in contact with the leaders of the 27 May 1960 coup, with ex-General Cemal Madanoğlu and ex-Colonel Osman Köksal. Avcıoğlu's position was also adopted by a faction in the army. Muhsin Batur, the commander of the air force, recounted in his memoirs that a group of officers proposed to him a military regime which would advocate the views of Avcıoğlu such as land and tax reforms, nationalisation of foreign trade, mineral resources and large institutions, educational and military reform, and the pursuit of independent foreign policy. He said he rejected this proposal (Hale, 1994: 186–190). In addition, the memorandum was perceived positively by a faction on the left. *Devrim* newspaper, in its first issue following the memorandum in 1971, ran the headline

army asked for a strong and credible government that would be able to end the disorder and carry out reforms in a Kemalist spirit. The Chief of the General Staff warned that if their demands were not met, the army would exercise its constitutional duty and take over power itself (Zürcher, 2004: 258).

The political effects of the memorandum were the resignation of the Demirel government and the holding of governmental power by a technocratic government under Nihat Erim, a right-wing CHP member. The political consequences of the military intervention highlighted the enduring antagonism between capital and labour. While TİP was dissolved after the military intervention, TÜSİAD was founded in 1971, just three weeks after the memorandum. The economic policies of the technocratic government between 1971 and 1972 also favoured the interests of big industrialists. The reform programme led by Atilla Karaosmanoğlu, who had worked for the World Bank, included "land reform, a land tax, nationalisation of mineral industry and measures to protect Turkish industry by demanding that joint ventures be least 51 per cent Turkish owned" (Zürcher, 2004: 258). Vehbi Koç and Nejat Eczacıbaşı, leading big industrialists in those years and afterwards, supported the proposals, which were important for Turkey if she was to join the industrialised countries' club in the future (Zürcher, 2004: 259).

Political instability intensified in the 1970s. An armed guerrilla struggle was carried out by various groups such as TİKKO (*Türkiye İşçi Köylü Kurtuluş Ordusu*—Turkish Workers and Peasants Liberation Army), THKO (*Türkiye Halk Kurtuluş Ordusu*—People's Liberation Army of Turkey), and Deniz Gezmiş and THKP-C (*Türkiye Halk Kurtuluş Partisi/Cephesi*—Turkish People's Liberation Party/Front) of Mahir Çayan (Zürcher, 2004: 256). The 1970s were also the years in Turkey in which the fascist groups, backed by the MHP and its paramilitary youth group "The Grey Wolves", adopted a strategy of tension to crush the scattered leftist groups.[12] By the end of the 1960s, the Nationalist Movement Party's 140 paramilitary commando camps in İstanbul, Ankara, İzmir, and Adana had

---

"Ordu Anti-Kemalist Gidişe Dur Dedi" [The Military Put a Lid on the anti-Kemalist Departure] (Kayalı, 2012: 187).

12   Former colonel Alparslan Türkeş, who served in Turkish military mission to NATO from 1955 to 1958, became the chairperson of Republican Peasants' Nation Party (*Cumhuriyetçi Köylü Millet Partisi*, CKMP) in 1965 and changed its name to the National Action Party (*Millliyetçi Hareket Partisi*, MHP) in 1969. Based on Pan-Turkism, the Grey Wolves functioned as a fascist armed youth force of the MHP against the "communist threat" during the Civil War. Some notorious civilian members of the Turkish "deep state" such as Abdullah Çatlı, Haluk Kırcı and Ali Ağca were recruited from the Grey Wolves. On the relationship between the NATO's stay-behind army in Turkey, Counter-Guerrilla, and the Grey Wolves, see Ganser (2005).

trained over one thousand young people against "communists and masonic-capitalist collaborators" (Alparslan Türkeş 1968 in Ağaoğulları, 2003).[13]

This political turmoil peaked in 1977 after the massacre of 34 people on May Day 1977. This was accompanied by successive fascist attacks and pogroms against students, such as the shooting of seven students in İstanbul University on 16 March, 1978, and against Alevis in Eastern and Central Anatolian provinces, such as in Malatya (1978), Sivas (1978), Maraş (1978), a seven-day massacre causing at least 100 deaths, and Çorum (1980). The years leading up to 1980 in Turkey, particularly 1977–1980, were marked by the intensification of fascist attacks on workers, students, leftist groups, and Alevis, after which the army staged its bloody coup in 1980.

7 Institutionalisation of "Kemalism without Mustafa Kemal"

Capitalist development in Turkey was backed by the hypertrophy of the executive power over the legislative power. To the extent that there has been a functioning assembly in Turkey in fits and starts, the military has frequently found ways to exert its power over the legislative branch. This makes the military in Turkey a "ruling but not governing" establishment (Cook, 2007). Kemalism is not solely limited to the personification of rule and the domination of an individual whose personality stands in for the validity of popular sovereignty. The political regime has predominantly relied on the autonomous institutional setting of the armed forces, which would limit popular sovereignty. In such a political regime, the Kemalist/Bonapartist legacy has been easily transmitted over the descendant governments.

That is to say, the political power of the regime is highly dependent on *the political autonomy of the armed forces vis-à-vis* the civilian governments, where the political autonomy of the armed forces can be defined as "its ability to go above and beyond the constitutional authority of democratically elected governments" (Sakallioğlu, 1997: 153). In such a political system, the military has tended to emancipate itself from the limitation of popular will. The ability to adopt the role of the sovereign emanates from favourable conditions granted by the reproduction and legitimisation of the official ideology—Kemalism. Unambiguously, the Turkish military perceives itself as the guardian of the Republic and the staunch proponent of the Kemalist principles: republicanism, nationalism, populism, secularism, statism, and revolutionism. This is a

---

13 For the original and English version of the book, see Schick and Tonak (1987: 113, fn. 113).

consequence of the fact that civil-military relations are power relations (Demirel, 2004); Bonapartist-Kemalist rule dominated the state executive, showing itself to be in favour of the reproduction of Turkish capitalism amid the convulsive changes taking place in society.

This Kemalist/Bonapartist rule in the state apparatus has been fortified by institutional arrangements in the wake of the coups. It can be said that it was a transition from the charismatic Kemalism, in Weberian terms, of Mustafa Kemal and İnönü to the routinisation of rule by the military through institutional arrangements. In other words, "Kemalism without Mustafa Kemal" was institutionalised after the 1960 coup. Following the 1960 coup, the military fortified its politically autonomous position via the establishment of the National Security Council (*Milli Güvenlik Kurumu*, MGK) under Article 111 of the Constitution of the Turkish Republic in 1961. The MGK performed a kind of dual power together with the civilian government. The composition and role of the MGK were stated in the Constitution of Turkish Republic in 1961 as such:

> The National Security Council shall consist of the Ministers as provided by the law, the Chief of the General Staff, and representatives of the armed forces. The President of the Republic shall preside over the National Security Council, and in his absence this function shall be discharged by the Prime Minister. The National Security Council shall communicate the requisite fundamental recommendations to the Council of Ministers with the purpose of assisting in the making of decisions related to national security and coordination (The Constitution of the Republic of Turkey, 1961: 30).

Through a bill in 1962, however, the MGK was endowed with having regular consultations and participation in the preparatory discussions of the cabinet (Ahmad, 1993: 130). Whereas the assigned task of the MGK in the Constitution of 1961 was decision-making related to national security and its coordination, this institutional task of the MGK was extended to the designation, determination, and implementation of national security policies and the procurement of the necessary coordination (Kardaş, 2009: 304). In addition to that, the 1973 constitutional amendments following the 1971 memorandum assigned the MGK the role of giving policy recommendations to the government. With institutionalisation and routinisation of Bonapartism through the MGK, the military could exert its influence on politicians without a direct usurpation of power.

Furthermore, the supremacy of the MGK over the parliamentary branch took its roots not only in the constitutional institutionalisation of this "bifurcated executive body" but largely from the broad definition of the concept of *national security* in the Cold War and post-Cold War era. The might of the military largely stemmed from its ability to use the national security concept interchangeably with public policy. According to Article 2a of the MGK, "*National Security means the protection of the constitutional order of the State, its nation and integrity, all of its interests in the international sphere including political, social, cultural and economic interests, as well as the protection of its constitutional law against all internal and external threats*" (European Commission, 2005). This comprehensive definition of national security was persistently approved by the higher echelons of the army. Orhan Erkanlı, the former Commander and member of the Committee of National Unity after the coup in 1960, clearly expressed this reality at the fourteenth anniversary of the 1960 coup:

> From the price of rice to roads and touristic sites, there is not a single problem in this country which is not related to national security. If you happen to be a very deep thinker, that too is a matter of national security (Orhan Erkanlı as cited in Ahmad, 1993: 130).

In addition to the formal arrangements, the army perpetuated its ideological dominance over society by presenting itself as an apolitical establishment. It represented itself as superior to the civilian governments. As expressed by the former Chief of General Staff General Doğan Güreş:

> Ministries, universities, the bureaucracy, the judiciary have all lagged behind. In the Turkish Armed Forces, we constantly renew appointments, promotions, registration standards. System engineering was first taught at the military schools. The private sector in Turkey looked at the army with admiration and employ[ed] its methods. The Armed Forces in the US, by contrast, look at the private sector and benefit from it (as cited in Demirel, 2004: 142).

The ideological power of the MGK was further strengthened through the enactment of Law No 2945 in 1983 on National Security and the Secretariat-General of the National Security Council. Under Article 4e of this law, the jurisdiction of the body was enlarged to include determining the necessary measures for preserving the constitutional order, maintaining national unity and integrity, and directing the Turkish nation to national ideas and values in accordance with Atatürkist thought and Atatürk's principles and revolutions (Kardaş, 2009: 301). In addition, the National Security Policy Document (*Milli*

Güvenlik Siyaset Belgesi), known as the Red Book, has functioned as the second and top-secret constitution of Turkey. In November 1997 National Security Council meeting, it was concluded that no laws, circulars, and regulations were to contradict the National Security Policy Document (*Hürriyet*, 4 November 1997). This meeting also agreed to facilitate economic initiatives, including privatisation, which aimed at Turkey's integration with the world economy (*Hürriyet*, 4 November 1997).

Even though the Council of Ministers is legally responsible for preparing against internal and external threats to the country, the Secretariat-General of the National Security Council is empowered with implementation. Doğan Güreş, the Chief of the General Staff of Turkey from 1990 to 1994, properly explained the supremacy of the National Security Council decisions:

> As defined in our constitution, the MGK sets the national security policies which are the God and the constitution of all policies. You cannot think to act in a manner which contradicts with these policies. For this reason, the 1982 Constitution states that 'MGK notifies the Ministry' rather than stating that 'MGK recommends to the Ministry'. This is a constitutional commitment ... (Bila, 1997).

Apart from the supremacy of the MGK over the parliament, the Kemalist/Bonapartist institutionalisation in the state executive reflected itself in the double-headed judiciary. The military succeeded in enlarging its jurisdiction regarding administrative and criminal laws. For instance, the decisions of the Supreme Military Council (*Yüksek Askeri Şura*, YAŞ), a body responsible for deciding promotion, retirement and expulsion from the army, were exempted from judicial oversight. Moreover, following the amendments in the 1961 Constitution, the military bureaucracy benefited in the scope of administrative jurisdiction from the establishment of the High Military Administrative Court. The judicial control of administrative acts and actions by the military body were then taken from the jurisdiction of the Council of State and given to the High Military Administrative Court. Furthermore, the 1982 Constitution extended the jurisdiction of the military administrative court to civilians, on the condition that the administrative acts and actions falling under its remit were related to military service (Kardaş, 2009: 297–301). According to Article 157 of the Constitution of Republic of Turkey in 1982,

> The High Military Administrative Court shall be the first and last instance for the judicial supervision of disputes arising from administrative acts

and actions involving military persons or relating to military service, even if such acts and actions have been carried out by non-military authorities. However, in disputes arising from the obligation to perform military service, there shall be no condition that the person concerned be a member of the military body (The Constitution of the Republic of Turkey, 1982: 82).

The institutionalisation of the Kemalist/Bonapartist regime is not only related to the extended executive and judiciary power of the Turkish armed forces. The president as the head of the state has predominantly been a tutelary power for the continuation of the Kemalist/Bonapartist regime. Traditionally, generals were the presidents of the Republic or, if civilian candidates were elected for this position, they would not be allowed to supersede the military (Sakallioğlu, 1997: 158). Contrary to the common belief that the role of the presidency in Turkey is symbolic, the reality is the exact opposite: The Turkish Constitution of 1982 endows the presidential office with substantive political powers in the legislative, executive, and judicial spheres. According to Article 104 of the Constitution of 1982, the most important powers include the power to send laws back to the Grand National Assembly of Turkey when necessary; to represent the office of Commander-in Chief of the Turkish Armed Forces; to decide on the use of the Turkish Armed Forces; and to appoint the members of the Council of Higher Education, the university presidents, the members of the Constitutional Court, one fourth of the members of the Council of the State, the Chief Public Prosecutor and the Deputy Chief Public Prosecutor of the High Court of Appeals, the members of the High Military Court of Appeals, the members of the High Military Administrative Court, and the members of the High Council of Judges and Prosecutors (The Constitution of the Republic of Turkey, 1982: 50–52).

Apart from the institutionalisation of Kemalist Bonapartism in the executive, the state ideology was empowered through Turkey's legal system. For instance, the legal framework prohibited the foundation of class-based associations and advocacy for religion-based government according to Articles 141,[14]

---

14   According to Article 141 of the Turkish Penal Code which was repealed in 1991, "Anyone creating, leading or inspiring associations, whatever their designation, which seek to ensure the domination of a particular social class or to overthrow the country's existing social and economic institutions, is liable to a period of imprisonment running from eight to fifteen years" (Kendal, 1993: 94, fn. 51).

142,[15] and 163[16] of the Turkish Penal Code, which had been imported from Mussolini's Italy in 1926 and was repealed in 1991. Articles 141 and 142 of the Turkish Penal Code were also used to punish Kurdish militants who dared make the slightest cultural or political demand (Kendal, 1993: 78). It can be argued that the longevity of the state ideology in the legal system was the product of socioeconomic instability in Turkey in which the big bourgeoisie could by no means find sufficient support in the masses, which were polarised towards the camps of the revolutionary and reactionary forces, particularly in the late 1960s and 1970s. The ultra-nationalist party of Colonel Alparslan Türkeş, the NAP (National Action Party, *Milliyetçi Hareket Partisi*) and its youth organisation, the Grey Wolves, were under the protection of the security forces and the police during the Nationalist Front governments between 1974 and 1977 (Zürcher, 2004: 263).

Not surprisingly, the Turkish Constitution of 1982 restricts the right to form political parties. Even though it is stated that "[p]olitical parties are indispensable elements of democratic political life", and shall be formed without prior permission, the Constitution restricts this political right "within the limits of the law" by Articles 68 and 69 of the Constitution. It is clearly stated that "[t]he statues and programs, as wells as the activities of political parties shall not be contrary to the independence of the State, its indivisible integrity within territory and nation, human rights, the principles of equality and rule of law, sovereignty of the nation, the principles of the democratic and secular republic; they shall not aim to promote or establish class or group dictatorship or dictatorship of any kind, nor shall they incite citizens to crime" (The Constitution of the Republic of Turkey, 1982: 30, Article 68).

The articles on the formation and dissolution of a political party have been broadly interpreted in order to punish Kurdish, Islamist and communist/socialist parties. Article 5 and Articles 78 to 90 in the Political Party Law detail the restrictions on the aims and activities of political parties. Communist parties, parties aiming at regionalism, religious distinctions and racial differences are excluded from the party system. In order to prevent the politicisation of citizens, Article 68 of the Constitution forbade political parties from forming auxiliary branches such as women's or youth branches, and other groups until

---

15   According to Article 142 of the Turkish Penal Code which was repealed in 1991, "Anyone spreading propaganda of any type which seeks to ensure the domination of one social class over another or seeks to overthrow any of the country's existing fundamental institutions, or aims to destroy the social and legal order of the state, will be liable to five to fifteen years imprisonment" (Kendal, 1993: 94, fn. 51).

16   Article 163 of the Turkish Penal Code prohibited the domination of the political structure of the State by religion.

1999. The Constitution also banned political parties from engaging in political cooperation with associations, trade unions, foundations, cooperatives, occupational and professional associations, and also from developing political ties and various modes of political co-operation with such existing organisations until 1995. Aside from restrictions on forming political parties, the Constitution banned political parties from receiving aid or financial support from these organisations. Freedom of association was prohibited for voluntary associations (Articles 33 and 34) and labour unions (Articles 52 and 54) to pursue political goals, engaging in "political activities", developing links with political parties, co-operating or co-ordinating their activities with them, and receiving or giving aid to them (Turan, 1988: 69–70). However, these articles in the constitution that aimed to depoliticise citizens through the restriction of elementary freedoms were eventually repealed in the process of political liberalisation by constitutional amendments in 1995.

According to the Constitutional Court data, as of 2020 49 political parties had been dissolved since the establishment of the Court in 1962. Following the transition to civilian rule in 1983, 19 political parties were dissolved; of these, seven were Kurdish parties, five were socialist parties and three were Islamic parties (Constitutional Court, 2020a).[17] Even the names of the dissolved political parties reveal the ideological biases of Bonapartist rule. These political parties and the year they were closed by the Constitutional Court since 1983 are demonstrated in Table 6.

Sami Selçuk, the honorary first president of the Court of Cassation between 1999 and 2002, openly summarised the legal political framework of Turkey in the inaugural speech of the 1999–2000 court year, where he criticised the functioning of political power in Turkey:

> ...The 1982 Constitution is not a normative constitution that guarantees human rights and freedoms. It is not preventive against the arbitrariness of political power and it is not protective of the essence of individual rights and freedoms. This is apparently a nominal, semantic constitution, a text. Because even on the position of the Directorate of Religious Affairs, it aims to protect the state while regulating the state organisation in detail. It fails to coalesce with social dynamics. It perceives rights and freedoms as exceptions. It converts them into a titular text. It is like a ball gown waiting in the wardrobe because it is not related to daily life and

---

17 As of 2020, the Constitutional Court has not yet verdicted on cases demanding the dissolution of three Kurdish parties—Democratic Party of Turkish Kurdistan, Kurdistan Freedom Party, Kurdistan Socialist Party.

TABLE 6   Political parties banned by the Constitutional Court since 1983

Kurdish parties	Socialist parties	Islamic Fundamentalist parties	Other parties
The People's Labour Party (*Halkın Emek Partisi*)-1993 The Freedom and Democracy Party (*Özgürlük ve Demokrasi Partisi*)-1993 The Democracy Party (*Demokrasi Partisi*)-1994 The Democracy and Change Party (*Demokrasi ve Değişim Partisi*)-1996 The Democratic Mass Party (*Demokratik Kitle Partisi*)-1999 The People's Democracy Party (*Halkın Demokrasi Partisi*)-2003 The Democratic Society Party (*Demokratik Toplum Partisi*)-2009	The United Communist Party of Turkey (*Türkiye Birleşik Komünist Partisi*)-1991 The Socialist Party (*Sosyalist Parti*)-1992 The Socialist Turkey Party (*Sosyalist Türkiye Partisi*)-1993 The Socialist Unity Party (*Sosyalist Birlik Partisi*)-1995 The Labour Party (*Emek Partisi*)-1997	The Tranquillity Party (*Huzur Partisi*)-1983 The Welfare Party (*Refah Partisi*)-1998 The Virtue Party (*Fazilet Partisi*)-2001	The Republican People's Party (*Cumhuriyet Halk Partisi*)-1991 The Democratic Party (*Demokrat Parti*)-1994 The Greens (*Yeşiller Partisi*)-1994 The Resurrection Party (*Diriliş Partisi*)-1997

SOURCE: CONSTITUTIONAL COURT OF THE REPUBLIC OF TURKEY (2020A).[a]

a   The Republican People's Party (CHP) was dissolved by the Constitutional Court in 1991 on the grounds that the CHP used the logo and the name of a banned party and the CHP claimed its continuity with this banned party (Constitutional Court of the Republic of Turkey, 2020b, Number: E.1990/2, K.1991/2). The Democratic Party was dissolved on the same grounds in 1994 (Constitutional Court of the Republic of Turkey, 2020b, Number: E. 1994/1, K.1994/3). The Greens Party was dissolved in 1994 on the grounds that it did not submit its account (*kesin hesap*) of 1988 in the statutory period to the Constitutional Court (Constitutional Court of the Republic of Turkey, 2020b, Number: E.1992/2, K.. 1994/1). The Resurrection Party was dissolved in 1997 on the grounds that it did not participate in two consecutive general elections in Turkey (Constitutional Court of the Republic of Turkey, 2020b, Number: E.1996/2, K. 1997/2).

rights. According to the Constitution, people and individuals are for the state. The state is not for the people and the individuals… Secularism is mentioned in the constitution. However, the constitution kills off secularism by the introduction of compulsory religious education. It is, therefore, anti-secular. Thus, if needs to be remarked by the concepts of constitutionalism, Turkey is today a "state with a constitution" but it is not a "constitutional state" (Court of Cassation, n.d.).

8 Bourgeoisification of the Military

All these institutional nexuses clearly show that TAF not only holds a politically autonomous position—in keeping with its Bonapartist character—but also finds an interest in the establishment and continuation of its economic empire. The armed forces economically benefited from the institutionalisation of Kemalist Bonapartism in the executive. In the deepening phase of the ISI discussed earlier, the armed forces founded OYAK (*Ordu Yardımlaşma Kurumu*, Turkish Armed Forces Assistance and Pension Fund) in 1961 following the 1960 coup, which provided social security privileges for them. It has functioned as a supplementary social security fund in addition to the state retirement fund (*Emekli Sandığı*) for members of the armed forces. In 1961 OYAK was designed to be a pension fund that would serve "members of the Turkish Armed Forces, members of the Gendarmerie General Command, Coastal Guard Command and … employees including members of public seeking to participate voluntarily" and has been operating in accordance with the article of law numbered 205 (OYAK, 2012). It is administratively and financially autonomous. According to Article 18 of the OYAK Law, the revenues of the fund are primarily based on a ten percent deduction from the salaries of the permanent TAF members and a five percent deduction from the salaries of the reserve officers (Military Personnel Assitance and Pension Fund Law, 1961: 6). This fund is not only "Turkey's first and most prodigious private pension fund" (OYAK, 2012: 1), but also a gigantic economic actor in production and consumption, with its 55 companies scattered in different sectors: 33 OYAK companies function in the industrial sector, 17 in the service sector and five in the financial sector (OYAK, 2012: 3). Industrial corporations running under OYAK Group conduct economic activity in sectors such as "iron and steel, energy, cement and automotive production" (OYAK, 2012: 3), with an oligopolistic economic structure in those sectors.

Through diversification of economic activity, OYAK corporations have been functioning in the service sector as well such as in the construction, foreign trade, logistics, and information sectors (OYAK, 2012: 3). According to the Annual Report of OYAK in 2012, OYAK served 275,990 members. In 2012 OYAK Group companies, employing 27,596 people, owned total assets which stood at US$20.005 billion, with total gross sales revenues of US$15.540 billion and total pre-tax profit amounting to US$918 million (OYAK, 2012: 7). The Annual Report testifies that total exports of OYAK companies stood at US$4.2 billion, accounting for 2.79% of Turkey's total exports in 2012 (OYAK, 2012: 3).

This is why OYAK whets the appetite of the retired members of the armed forces. The Board of Directors of OYAK gives us a clue to how this entity has been placed as a retirement office for the retired generals and bureaucrats. In 2012, six out of seven members of the Board of Directors were composed of four generals, one rear admiral, and one retired governor (OYAK, 2012: 11). Yıldırım Türker, the retired lieutenant general, was the Chairman of OYAK until May 2012, and was succeeded by Hasan Memişoğlu, the retired lieutenant general. This is not surprising, though. Since its establishment, the core state apparatus and the big capitalists have been in harmony through the convergence of the interests of the military elite and the big capitalists in OYAK. Since then, big capitalists have been integrated in the structure of OYAK. Vehbi Koç, industrial and commercial emperor of Turkey during his time, and Kazım Taşkent, baron of the private banking sector and founder of the Yapı Kredi Bank, were members of the first Board of Directors in OYAK and founding shareholders of OYAK-Goodyear and OYAK-Renault, respectively (Parla, 2009: 211).

This mutual relationship between the armed forced and the big capitalists helped OYAK benefit from the oligopolistic economic structure in the deepening phase of ISI in Turkey. Between 1960 and 1980, OYAK and Koç group, for instance, controlled the private car market in Turkey; Goodyear, Uniroyal and Pirelli were the sole producers of tires in the market. Goodyear produced 28.8% of tires in 1971 and its market share was 21% in 1982. OYAK also produced 23% of cement in Turkey in 1976 (Akça, 2009: 250–251). Between 1962 and 1970, the net value of OYAK increased phenomenally by 2400% (Parla, 2009: 202).

In a similar way, this oligopolistic structure continued in Turkey's period of export-led capitalism after the 1980s. OYAK produced 13.4% of cement between 1985 and 1998 on average and this ratio rose to 18.8% in 1998. Moreover, in the pesticides sector, Hektaş, one of its companies, owns 18–20% of the market. The share of OYAK-Renault in the automotive sector between 1992 and 2001 was 20% on average and this share rose to 27.7% in 2001. In the motor vehicles sector, one of its companies, MAİS, owned 23% of the sector in 2000 (Akça, 2009: 250–251). This oligopolistic structure in specific economic activities continues today. According to a report by the İstanbul Chamber of Industry,

OYAK-Renault is the fourth biggest industrial enterprise in Turkey in production-based sales, which stood at more than TL 20 billion, equivalent to US$4.2 billion in 2012 (ISO, 2017). The OYAK Group also maintains its leadership position in the cement industry with a market share of 15%. In the private car sector, the group manufactured 53.8% of Turkish cars with 311,000 cars, of which almost 227,000 were exported in 2012 (OYAK, 2012: 1–17).

Taking into account the oligopolistic industries that OYAK dominates, OYAK reaped the benefits of legal privileges to which it has been entitled since its establishment. Under Articles 35, 36, and 37 of the OYAK Law, it enjoys a variety of tax exemptions (Akça, 2010b: 11). Its properties, revenues, and debts are under legal protection, and its members enjoy housing benefits. In OYAK Law, Article 35 juxtaposes the exemptions of the Fund as such:

> ...a) The Fund shall be exempt from taxes on Corporations; b) Donations made to the Fund and benefits of any kind provided by the Fund to its members or to their legal heirs shall be exempt from Income Tax and Inheritance Tax; c) The Fund shall be exempt from stamp duty in connection with its transactions; d) Dues collected from permanent and temporary members shall be exempt from Income Tax; e) All kinds of revenues of the Fund shall be exempt from Expenditure Tax (Military Personnel Assisance and Pension Fund Law, 1961: 11).

While according to Article 36 the Fund is entitled to privileges with respect to the construction of housing for its members, Article 37 states "All of the property of the Fund as well as all of the revenues of and debts due to the Fund shall enjoy the same rights and privileges as State property. Offences against such property shall be subject to the same legal remedies as offences against State property" (Military Personnel and Assitance and Pension Fund Law, 1961: 11). According to a report by the Parliamentary Investigation Committee in November 2012, OYAK was immune from any institutional auditing until 2001 (TBMM, 2012a: 151). In addition, subsidiaries of OYAK are also under the state guarantee. For instance, when the Turkish Automotive Industry (TOE) and its subsidiary company Motor Vehicles Trade (MAT) went bankrupt, in 1984 they were taken over by Ziraat Bank, one of the state banks in Turkey (Sönmez, 1992: 230).

Therefore, an army playing this role in a late developing country like Turkey not only benefits by rewarding itself political power, but also serves to reproduce the system in its convulsive periods. The 1960 coup and 1971 memorandum temporarily resolved the political crisis of the bourgeoisie that was unable to bring political solutions in a classic bourgeois parliamentary way. While the 1960 coup was functional in upgrading manufactured production through a transition to the deepening of the ISI model and the planned economy, the 1971 memorandum functioned as the Sword of Damocles, targeting the radicalisation of youth in those periods.

CHAPTER 2

The Construction of a New Society after the 1980 Military Coup

The previous chapter explained the Bonapartist character of the regime, which pertains to a particular economic model, national developmentalism. This chapter looks firstly at the completion of the national developmentalist project. The Kemalist state's economic pillar had started to slowly decline with the erosion of national developmentalism. It was only in the 1990s that the political pillar of Kemalism began to weaken under limited political liberalisation. This chapter introduces the economic background for the "conservative coup" of 12 September, 1980. The military dictatorship as an exceptional form of the state between 1980 and 1983 was functional in transitioning to export-led capitalism and the suppression of labour. Export-led capitalism in Turkey after the 1980s increased the economic and political power of what Gumuscu and Sert (2009) call "the devout bourgeoisie" in the periphery. Importantly, religion has become the ideological cement, particularly for the second generation of Turkish capitalism.

1 The Completion of the National Developmentalist Project

The development of big monopoly capitalism in Turkey was a protracted process backed by the military through providing the necessary social conditions for its maturation. Yet, at a certain stage in the development of the means of production, the conditions for which national developmentalism served capital accumulation turned into fetters for its further expansion. In other words, the crisis of national developmentalism, the economic pillar of the Kemalist state, was decisively *structural*.

The incompatibility between reducing dependence of the Turkish economy on foreign resources and sustaining planned economic growth in the five-year development plans (1963–1967, 1968–1972, and 1973–1977) under the low levels of domestic savings and capital formation (Aydın, 2005: 34–35) produced an economic blockage to further capital expansion. This was mainly due to the fact that Turkish industry was unable to deepen the import-substitution model under national developmentalism for imported investment goods. Whereas the share of durable consumer goods and intermediate goods in industrial manufacturing increased from 24.9% in 1963 to 52.7% in 1980, the share of investment goods in industrial manufacturing decreased from 8.4% in 1963 to 7.5% in 1980 (Boratav, 2011: 133; Table 2 in the previous chapter).

The contradiction of the Turkish economy under the import-substitution industrialisation (ISI) model reflected itself in the increase of imports of intermediate and capital goods in manufacturing. Between 1950 and 1978, while the proportion of consumer goods in total imports declined from 20.6% to 2.9%, the proportion of raw materials in total imports rose from 33.4% to 62.4% (TÜSİAD's 1979 Report in Ercan, 2002: 24). On the other hand, the level of domestic savings, which could have balanced the scarce foreign currency, lagged behind the increase in investment. While the rate of investment rose from 19% of GDP in 1967 to 26% in 1977, savings stayed at an average of around 17% of GDP (The World Bank, 1981: 5). The World Bank warned that the gap between domestic savings and investment was increasingly financed by short-term and medium-term borrowing from abroad (The World Bank, 1981: 5).

Yet, the crucial contradiction was that the ISI model, which had aimed to reduce the dependence on foreign resources, resulted in the import dependence of industry. Whereas imports were US$2.1 billion in 1973, they rose to US$5.5 billion in 1980 (Başkaya, 2009: 165). By 1977 export revenues were able to cover only 30% of import costs and the foreign trade deficit exceeded $US4 billion (Boratav, 2011: 140). Figure 1 shows that the gap between the share of exports in GDP and the share of imports in GDP widened after 1973. In 1977, the share of exports was only 4% of the GDP while the share of imports in the GDP rose to 11% (Figure 1).

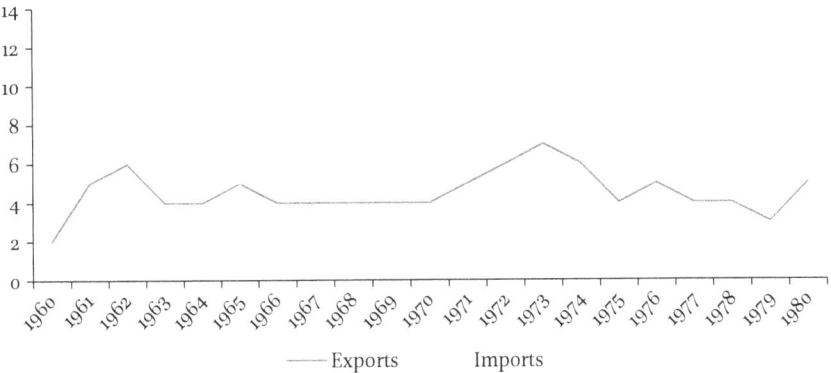

FIGURE 1   Exports and imports (% of GDP), 1960–1980
SOURCE: THE WORLD BANK (2015).

Even though the trade deficit problem was a common symptom of the Turkish economy since the post-war adjustment period in 1946, it was underlined by the increase in consumption between 1960 and 1980. The middle classes, which constituted the social base of Kemalist Bonapartism, largely benefited from the ISI period between 1963–1980 in the form of an increase in real wages and the consumption of durable consumer goods. However, the production of these goods were dependent on imports and their quality, unit costs and the scale of production fell behind Western products (Boratav, 2011: 119).

The exhaustion of national developmentalism under the ISI model—that successfully united the divergent interests of the proletariat, urban population, industrial bourgeoisie and bureaucracy—precipitated the dissolution of the historic bloc. National developmentalism under ISI made the implementation of populist distributive policies possible between 1962 and 1976 (Boratav, 2011: 123). This brought reconciliation between the ruling classes and mass population (Boratav, 2011: 123). Higher wages and workers' rights, the right to strike and collective bargaining, which was put into effect in 1963, facilitated the extension of the domestic market (Boratav, 2011: 123). However, trade union activism in the 1970s was seen as a barrier to capital accumulation by international financial organisations. The World Bank's 1980 report, *Turkey: Policies and Prospect for Growth*, acknowledged that trade union participation was high in Turkey compared to other developing countries (The World Bank, 1980: 141). Unionisation rates in the industrial labour force were 43% and 57% in 1967 and 1977, respectively (The World Bank, 1980: 141). Turkey was characterised as "an outliner [sic] amongst developing countries" with regards to the workdays lost per striking worker (The World Bank, 1980: 143). The report observed that an average of 57 days per striking worker were lost in 1973 in Turkey, whereas the closest developing country was India with 10 days (The World Bank, 1980: 143).

Not only national developmentalism but also Keynesianism was in crisis. The crisis of the Keynesian economic policies which had prevailed in advanced countries after the Second World War until the 1970s led to the neoliberal turn. The radical assault on Keynesian economic policies with full employment as the key objective was fundamentally carried out in October 1979 by Paul Volcker, chairman of the US Federal Reserve Bank under Carter, who was reappointed to his position under Reagan in 1980. The Volcker shock, known as a sudden and high increase in the nominal interest rate in the US in order to fight inflation, had a devastating effect on debtor countries. Following the OPEC oil price hike in 1973, the developing countries were seen as the safest and more profitable destinations for the New York investment banks to lend petrodollars of oil-producing states such as Saudi Arabia, Kuwait, and Abu

Dhabi. The abundance of foreign credit designated for developing countries pushed these countries into default by the sharp increase of the US interest rates as in the case of Volcker shock (Harvey, 2005: 23–29).

Turkey was no exception to this global debt crisis. The symptom of this economic contradiction crystallised itself in the perpetual balance of payment crises during the late 1970s (Başkaya, 2009: 170–172; Boratav, 2011: 139–144). Nevertheless, workers' remittances, which in 1974 reached US$1.462 million, played some role in the postponement of an imminent economic crisis (Zürcher, 2004: 267). Between 1971 and 1974, workers' remittances approximated 5% of the national income (Pamuk, 1984: 58). They equalled 93.1% and 93.6% of Turkish export earnings in 1974 and 1975, respectively (Başkaya, 2009: 175).

Industrialisation's high dependence on foreign resources compelled successive governments to steer the economy towards the prescriptions of the IMF and the World Bank. From 1978 onwards, the government of Bülent Ecevit negotiated with the IMF, WB, and OECD on stabilisation programme for new credits. However, even though an agreement for $US1.8 billion was reached in July 1979, it was conditional on the introduction of a reform package by the Turkish government which would include abolishing controls in trade, cutting subsidies to state-owned enterprises, freeing interest rates, raising prices and reducing government expenditure (Zürcher, 2004: 268). The implementation of this programme became the priority of the Demirel government in late 1979 and of the undersecretary in the State Planning Organisation, Turgut Özal (Zürcher, 2004: 268). Even though coalition governments were compelled to devaluate the Turkish Lira by 29.9% and 40% in 1978 and 1979 respectively (Öniş, 1998: 16), the resistance of the unions and especially of DİSK (*Türkiye Devrimci İşçi Sendikaları Konfederasyonu*—Confederation of Progressive Trade Unions of Turkey) to this programme—including factory occupations and strikes resulting in confrontation with the police and army—paralysed the implementation of the economic package (Zürcher, 2004: 268).

As a result of the unstable economic and political conditions, in 1979 the representational link between big monopoly capitalists and the Ecevit government was severely weakened. It culminated with a notice published by TÜSİAD (*Türk Sanayicileri ve İşadamları Derneği*—Turkish Industry & Business Association) declaring "the only realistic solution" for Turkey to be "free enterprise" and "the encouragement of the individual in competition" while criticising the government for "increasingly moving away from the market economy" (*Milliyet*, 15 May 1979: 3). While this proclamation of big monopoly capitalists was evaluated by the government as a "memorandum" (*Milliyet*, 16 May 1979: 13). Nejat Eczacıbaşı, then president of TÜSİAD, declared his "suspicion" toward Ecevit after the latter denounced private corporations as exploiters on state television (*Milliyet*, 17 May 1979: 8). The Ecevit government fell in November 1979, and was replaced by a minority government under Demirel. This political situation confirms the fact that the bourgeoisie was politically weak in Turkey, unable to overcome the economic contradictions and political crisis. This led to a political spasm in the leadership of the bourgeoisie in which only the military dictatorship, as an exceptional state form, could overcome the political and economic crises once again (Savran, 2010: 182–183).

However, the increasing geostrategic role of Turkey in the Cold War period meant the US administration was obliged to take into account the exigency of stability in the country, which helped to strengthen the army's position. It should be stressed that as a NATO country since 1952, Turkey has always been one of the main recipients of the US military assistance programme. For instance, according to a 2012 report by the Security Cooperation Agency, part of the United States Department of Defence, Turkey ranked second in Europe, after the United Kingdom, in Foreign Military Sales (FMS) deliveries of the US from 1950 to 2012 receiving more than US$16 billion (Security Cooperation Agency, 2012: 14–21).[1] Nevertheless, the gradual success of Necmettin Erbakan (the leader of the Islamic parties in Turkey since 1970) in the coalition governments with the CHP in 1974 and in the consecutive National Front (*Milli Cephe*) governments led by Demirel in 1975–1977 and 1977–1978, together with the emergence of pro-Khomeini para-military groups in Turkey, ruffled the US. This was due to the fear of losing of Turkey as a "buffer zone" not only for the Middle East but also for Europe (Birand, 1987: 67). Fundamentally, the political and economic crisis in Turkey that politicians were unable to resolve ran counter to the interests of the US. The coup was therefore welcomed by the US administration (Birand, 1987: 185).

2   The Absorption of Kemalism into Neoliberalism

On the morning of 12 September 1980, Kenan Evren, Chief of General Staff, explained that the army was fulfilling its "duty of protecting and safeguarding the Turkish Republic as laid down under its Internal Service Code in an orderly

---

1   Turkey ranked seventh in the world in FMS (Foreign Military Sales) acquisitions from the U.S. between 1950 and 2012. The top ten in FMS of the U.S. between 1950 and 2012 were Saudi Kingdom, Israel, Egypt, Taiwan, Korea, United Kingdom, Turkey, Germany, Australia, and Greece. The amount of the FMS of the U.S. for these countries were $72.3 billion, $30.2 billion, $29.6 billion, $28 billion, $17.3 billion, $16.4 billion, $16 billion, $15.3 billion, $15.2 billion, $12 billion, respectively (Security Cooperation Agency, 2012: 14–21).

manner within the chain of command" as such had "taken over the complete administration of the country" (General Secretariat of the National Council, 1982: 221). The purpose of the coup was described as being "to preserve the integrity of the country, to restore national unity and togetherness, to avert a possible civil war and fratricide, to re-establish the authority and existence of the State and to eliminate all the factors that prevent the normal functioning of the democratic order" (General Secretariat of the National Council, 1982: 221–222).

In some respects the form of the 1980 coup was different from the previous ones in 1923 and 1960. Adopting Gilbert Achcar's categorisation of coups in Arab history, one could say that Turkey witnessed a "revolutionary coup" in 1923, a "reformist coup" in 1960 and, a "conservative coup" in 1980. According to Achcar (2013: 177–178), "revolutionary coups aim radically to transform the political regime and call themselves 'revolutions'" such as anti-monarchical coups in Egypt in 1952, Tunisia in 1957, Iraq in 1958, Yemen in 1962, Libya in 1969 as well as in Sudan in 1969 with Nasserite inspiration and in 1989 with Islamic inspiration. "Reformist coups", on the other hand, look for the correction or rectification of an already established regime without effecting a radical break such as coups in Algeria in 1965 by Houari Boumediene, Iraq in 1968 by Ahmed Hassan al-Bakr and Saddam Hussein, Syria in 1970 by Hafez al-Assad, Tunisia in 1987 by Zine el-Abidine Ben Ali, and "palace revolutions" in the oil monarchies (Achcar, 2013: 178). "Conservatives coups", however, respond to political instability and seek to preserve the established order or restore it in a transitional period such as most of the repetitive coups in Mauritania (Achcar, 2013: 178).

Therefore, the establishment of the Turkish Republic in 1923 under Mustafa Kemal followed a form of a revolutionary coup which abolished the Ottoman Sultanate in 1922 and radically transformed the country in line with Western modernisation. The 1960 coup was rather a reformist coup which set out the institutionalisation of Bonapartist rule via the establishment of the National Security Council. The 1980 coup was, on the other hand, a conservative coup which brutally reacted to political and economic convulsion of the 1970s and re-established the state order between 1980 and 1983.[2] Unlike the 1960 coup when middle-rank army officers seized power, the military hierarchy was preserved in the 1980 coup and the leader of the coup, Kenan Evren,

---

2 Gilbert Achcar also describes a fourth category of coups: reactionary coups which "sets out to repress a movement for a radical change that has come to power or is about to" such as the 1992 Algerian coup (2013: 178). In this regard, the 1980 coup shares more similarities with a conservative coup than a reactionary coup. Even though the left was brutally repressed after the coup in 1980, the left was politically feeble to come to power in the pre-coup period of the 1970s.

became the president. The military body of the 1980 coup did not necessitate expulsing existing military officers whereas in the 1960 coup, Rüştü Erdelhun, Chief of General Staff during the coup, was removed (Hale, 1994: 248). Aside from the expulsion of the civilian members in the National Security Council, there was no purge of military officers after the 1980 coup. The 1980 coup was, therefore, the reflection of "the collective will of the high command" (Hale, 1994: 248–249). Importantly, whereas the 1960 coup established the National Security Council which sometimes replaced the cabinet as a locus of power and decision-making, the 1980 coup had a firm effect on controlling every aspect of society through, for instance, the promulgation of a new Law on Political Parties and the establishment of YÖK (*Yüksek Öğretim Kurulu*-Higher Education Authority) which was responsible for directly appointing all rectors and deans (Zürcher, 2004: 241, 280–281).

The class character of the 1980 coup was obvious. In his inaugural speech for the Second Economic Congress of Turkey which was held in İzmir on 2–7 November 1981 and imitated the First Economic Congress of Turkey held in 1923 in İzmir by Mustafa Kemal, Kenan Evren stressed that the pre-1980 period of "anarchy and terrorism" had been a threat to the national economy. Indeed, his speech reflected the economic rationale of his coup:

> ...the conditions created by anarchy and terrorism spreading throughout the country before 12 September, had brought our State to the brink of collapse, and our country to a stage of dismemberment. These conditions were exercising an increasing pressure over the social and economic life of our people. As a result of such pressure, production was declining, investments were decreasing, unemployment was growing, and all these factors were further imperilling the atmosphere of unrest and insecurity developed by anarchy and terrorism. The most evident example of this can be noticed in factories. Their outputs that had fallen down to 15 per cent have subsequently increased up to 80 and 90 per cent, following the arrest of many notorious subversive gang leaders, the prevention of partisanship, the securing of an impartial rule, and the resumption of peace and security that was the right of the Turkish worker. In the agricultural sector, armed rural gangs were seizing at gun point a share of the produce [*sic*] harvested by the Turkish farmers at the price of a whole season's toiling and sweat; agricultural workers were being held up, threatened and prevented from working; and sometimes produce [*sic*] and farming machinery like tractors and combines, which represent the national wealth and the labour of the farmer, were being burnt and destroyed (Evren, 1983: 10).

Owing to the necessity to preserve the social order of capitalism and overcome the political impasse of the pre-1980 period, the military indubitably acted to protect the Turkish capitalists. The suspension of the parliamentary regime and the instalment of the military dictatorship in Turkey between 1980 and 1983 was applauded by Turkish capitalists, recalling the Marx's observation in 1852 on the attitude of the French bourgeoisie to the demise of the parliamentary republic in France, which had effectively been to say *"Rather an end with terror than terror without end!"*.

Complaining about the inability of political parties, despite all warnings, to form stable governments between 1973 and 1980, Vehbi Koç, industrial and commercial emperor of Turkey during his time, defended the coup on the grounds of the sharp decrease in anarchic movements after the intervention. While Koç claimed that people felt relieved after the coup, he also asked the military government to introduce the "necessary laws and Constitution" and to allow the liberal democratic parliamentary system to function in a normal way (*Milliyet*, 18 December 1980: 6).

It goes without saying that the "conservative coup" mercilessly pursued the eradication of political activities and dissidents. A state of emergency was declared throughout the country and no one was allowed to leave. By the end of 1981, 30,000 people had been arrested and by September 1982, 80,000 were in prison, 30,000 of them awaiting trial (Zürcher, 2004: 278–279). The Grand National Assembly of Turkey's (*Türkiye Büyük Millet Meclisi*-TBMM) 2012 report summarised the balance sheet of the coup as follows: 650,000 people were taken into custody, of which 210,000 were prosecuted in martial courts, and 65,000 were sentenced. 6,353 people were tried under the threat of capital punishment; more than 500 people were condemned and of these 50 people were executed. Hundreds of thousands of people were blacklisted, 388,000 people were forbidden to travel abroad, and 4,891 public officials were fired. Four thousand five hundred and nine public officials were deported and more than 20,000 public officials were forced to retire or resign. Thirty thousand people fled abroad, and the citizenship of 15,000 people was cancelled. Speaking Kurdish was banned. With this regulation, Turkey became the first and only country in the world to legally ban the speaking of a language. Newspapers, magazines, periodicals and non-periodicals were forbidden; journalists and authors were given heavy prison sentences. Tens of thousands of books were burned, 937 movies were banned, all political parties were dissolved, and trade unions and non-governmental organisations were closed down (TBMMb, 2012: 916–917). The transitional period and the military dictatorship between 1980 and 1983 was a substitute for the direct rule of the bourgeoisie.

Meanwhile, "the necessary laws and the Constitution" were introduced. The Constituent Assembly, composed of the Consultative Assembly and the National Security Council (NSC), replaced the parliament to prepare a constitution in which Evren and his colleagues would have the final say (Hale, 1994: 256). A referendum was conducted for the constitution and it was accepted in November 1982 by a majority of 91.4% with a 91.3% turnout (Hale, 1994: 256). The Higher Education Law, Political Parties Law, Trade Unions Law, and Law on Collective Labour Agreements were passed under the military regime (Hale, 1994: 251–259). Indeed, from September 1980 to December 1983 when power was handed down to the civilian government, the military regime passed 669 laws (TBMMa, 2012: 74).

Allowing major changes in the state structure, the military played a key role in shifting Turkey's economic trajectory from a state-controlled to a market economy. It was crucial because the civilian government led by Demirel, which confronted the militant working class, had certainly failed to fully implement the stabilisation programme. The coup regime's decisions involved "[t]he reduction of direct government intervention in the productive sector, and instead greater emphasis on market mechanisms, competition, private initiative and indirect government incentive schemes, [t]he replacement of an inward-oriented development strategy with a substantial increase in exports and gradual import liberalisation, [and] some lowering of barriers to foreign direct investment, even in sectors from which it had previously been barred" (Wolff, 1987: 99). These policy measures were evaluated by the OECD as representing "a courageous attack on the serious economic problems facing the economy" (OECD, 1980: 29). "Greater reliance of market forces" and "reduction of direct government intervention in guiding the economy", along with "exposing Turkish enterprises, including most State-owned firms, to more competition" constituted the pillars of the structural adjustment programme in a mixed economy where the SOEs provided 40% of valued added and employment in industry in 1979 (OECD, 1980: 5, 19). The structural adjustment programme became "the new hegemonic strategy of the post-1980 era" aiming to integrate Turkey into the world market (Yalman, 2009: 250). The target was to open up the Turkish economy by relying on market forces (Başkaya, 2009: 189). The new paradigm in the economic model was based on the increase of export and foreign currency, in which industrial production would serve the demands of the competitive international market rather than the protected domestic market. In this way, exposure to "international competition" was regarded as the path to increased industrial production. The structural adjustment programme opened a new economic reform period in the post-1980s which included flexible exchange rates, austerity and export drive, public enterprise reform and privatisation, financial liberalisation, import liberalisation and the promotion of direct foreign investment (Arıcanlı and Rodrik, 1990: 1343–1350).

This new hegemonic strategy was put into practice under conditions of military dictatorship. While fully implementing the stabilisation programme and paving the way for the transition to export-led capitalism in Turkey, the military prepared the socio-political conditions for competition in the world market by disciplining the working class. The left-wing trade union confederation DİSK was closed down along with the extreme right-wing confederation MİSK (*Milliyetçi İşçi Sendikaları Konfederasyonu*, Nationalist Trade Union Confederation) and their leaders were jailed (Sayarı, 1992: 31). The military only permitted the continuation of the centrist trade union organisation Türk-İş (*Türkiye İşçi Sendikaları Konfederasyonu*, Turkish Trade Union Confederation) whose leader was appointed as Social Affairs Minister in the military government (Sayarı, 1992: 31; Wolff, 1987: 120). Measures taken by the military regime included suspension of trade union activities, the trial of the DİSK leaders, banning strikes, and the replacement of collective bargaining by the determination of wages by *Yüksek Hakem Kurulu* (High Board of Arbitration) (Boratav, 2011: 150). In the "counter attack of capital against labour", borrowing the phrase from Korkut Boratav (2011), the post-1980 period, notably between 1980 and 1988, saw a setback for the rights of the working class. Real wages dropped 29% from 1978/1979 to 1988 relative to wholesale prices, and by 32% with relative to consumer prices. Moreover, the ratio of wages to the value-added in the manufacturing industry dramatically fell to 15.4% in 1988 from 37.2% in 1978/1979 (Boratav, 2011: 163–165). Real wages were repressed in the export-led capitalist period, a trend initiated after 1976, in order to increase the competitiveness of the industry, which was accompanied by a rapid decrease of real salaries (Figure 2).

3   Islamisation of Society after the 1980s

The military regime also had an interest in the Islamisation of society. The fusion of religion with nationalism appeared in the post-1980 period, with Islam used to complement the formulation of Turkish national identity. The military drew ideological legitimisation from a nationalist and conservative institution called *Aydınlar Ocağı* (The Hearth of the Enlightened) which was founded in 1970 to counter the monopoly of leftist circles in the political, social and cultural fields (Zürcher, 2004: 288). This organisation worked out a system called *Türk-İslam Sentezi* (Turkish-Islamic Synthesis) which has been used as an official state ideology ever since. Pioneered by İbrahim Kafesoğlu, *Türk-İslam*

FIGURE 2 The development of real wages and salaries (TL/day), 1963–1988
SOURCE: KEPENEK AND YENTÜRK (2003: 429).
Note: Data are in local currency.

Sentezi held that Islam had been attractive to Turks because of the remarkable similarities between the pre-Islamic Turkish culture and Islamic civilisation; these include justice, monotheism, a belief in the immortal soul and attachment to family and morality. The Turkish mission was determined to be acting as "soldier of Islam", with the two main pillars of Turkish culture built on a 2500-year-old Turkish element and a 1000-year-old Islamic element (Zürcher, 2004: 288).

These views were also adopted by the state bureaucracy. The State Planning Organisation (SPO) prepared a *Report on National Culture* in 1983 which attacked the "divisive foreign ideologies" that were seen as the cause for the moral and cultural deterioration of Turkish people during the 1970s (Atasoy, 2005: 155). While criticising the republican education system for adopting a materialist and positivist view, the report suggested a "faithful, knowledgeable and moral" generation (Eligür, 2010: 106). The family, the mosque, and the military constituted the three basic institutional pillars of the Turkish-Islamic synthesis view for accomplishing social cohesion and discipline (Yavuz, 2003a: 73). The Presidency of Religious Affairs (*Diyanet İşleri Başkanlığı*) expanded its tasks beyond the organisation of religious activities; it supported Turkish nationalism while defining its institutional aims as the protection and preservation of Turkish national identity and confrontation with communist and atheistic ideologies among the youth (Yavuz, 2003a: 70). Religious courses and ethics were also offered to more than 80,000 prisoners in 1982 by the Minister of Justice (Geyikdağı, 1984: 141). In addition, religious courses were made compulsory in primary and high schools under the military dictatorship, as stipulated in Article 24 of the 1982 Constitution.[3] The Chief of General Staff Kenan Evren (1991: 309) explained the reason for this regulation in Erzurum on 26 October 26 1982:

> ...When the exploiter of religion and, above all, ignorant politicians say, mingling freely with the crowd, that "this is the case in our religion that is the case in our religion", there have been no people around who had enough religious knowledge to say to him frankly that this is actually the true one... Turkish children were completely unable to learn the religion of the Turkish nation, of their family, of their mothers and fathers, of themselves *in propria persona*. This religious knowledge cannot be given by each family at home. If they attempt to teach it, this would not be in good taste. Because they can teach it wrongly, teach it faultily or they can teach it according to their views... I asked you not to send your children to illegal Quranic courses... [T]he religion [and] piety will be taught to our children in the state schools by the state. In this way, are we acting against the clause of secularism as some people who are inimical to religion argue? Or, on the contrary, are we serving secularism? Of course we are serving secularism. Because secularism does not mean that through being deprived of religious knowledge, Turkish youth and Turkish citizens would be exposed to the people who exploit religion so that they could be deceived [and] cheated.

The control over Islam by the military developed in a particular context of socio-transformation in the domestic and international environment after the mid-1970s. The crisis of national capitalists in the developing countries and the triumph of market economy and individualism challenged traditional state-society relations. The Turkish state increasingly needed to control religion "as the main vehicle through which the state reshaped modernity in line with ideology of marketisation while also resolving the problem of legitimacy" (Sakallioglu, 1996: 245). The political and ideological vacuum left by the secular and left forces to confront the assertiveness of Islamic fundamentalism was immediately filled by the manipulative power of the state over Islam (Sakallioglu, 1996: 246). In addition, the interests of the business world were also in line

---

3   Article 24 of the 1982 Constitution stipulates, "...Religious and moral education and instruction shall be conducted under state supervision and control. Instruction in religious culture and morals shall be one of the compulsory lessons in the curricula of primary and secondary schools. Other religious education and instruction [Quran courses and Quran summer courses] shall be subject to the individual's own desire, and in the case of minors, to the request of their legal representatives" (The Constitution of the Republic of Turkey, 1982).

with the incorporation of religion within state as the best way to curb the power of Islamic fundamentalism (Sakallioglu, 1996: 246). In a letter by Vehbi Koç, the leading industrialist in Turkey, submitted to Kenan Evren on 12 October 1980, it was proposed that "A nation with no religion is not possible. This time religious affairs should be regulated in such a way that as not to allow the political parties to exploit it" (as cited in Sakallioglu, 1996: 246; *Milliyet*, 23 December 1990: 9).

In this way, the institutionalisation of Islam in the state—and a particular branch of it, Sunni Islam—gained momentum after the coup. The personnel of *Diyanet* increased tremendously.[4] Whereas there were 50,765 personnel in *Diyanet* in 1979, this number rose to 84,172 in 1989. An average of 1,500 mosques was built annually and the number of mosques rose from 54,667 in 1984 to 62,947 in 1988, equivalent to one mosque for every 857 people.[5] Building mosques in Alevi districts has been a part of the assimilationist state policy towards Alevis (Bulut, 1997: 81). Brigadier Kenan Güven who was appointed in 1982 as the governor of Dersim, an Alevi populated district, praised the "ascension of call for prayer" in a Kızılbaş region.[6] In addition, the expansion of lower grade Quran schools after the 1980 coup, which increased from 2,610 before 1980 to 4,715 schools in 1989, went hand in hand with that of imam-hatip schools (religious vocational schools). The number of students going to imam-hatip schools increased incrementally from 68,486 to 155,403 in the same period, of whom 58,350 were female (Ahmad, 1993: 220–221).

It was also under the military regime between 1980 and 1983 that the salary of official Turkish imams sent for Turkish people living Belgium and West Germany by the Directorate of Religious Affairs was paid by World Muslim League (*Rābitat al-ʿĀlam al-Islāmī*, known as *Rabıta*) between 1982 and 1984 (Mumcu, 1993: 171–173). In addition, *Rabıta* financed a mosque, an Islamic centre on the campus of left-wing Middle East Technical University, and a major portion of the university's Arabic language program (Akin and Karasapan, 1988: 15; Mumcu, 1993).

Furthermore, religion has increasingly been used as a tool for the adaptation of Turkish foreign policy to establish close economic and political relations

---

4   With its 107,206 personnel in 2018, this bureaucratic machine has been administering 88,681 mosques and 16,159 Quran courses that 1,032,834 people attended by the end of schooling year 2017/2018 (Diyanet İşleri Başkanlığı, 2020).

5   The number of mosques in Turkey was 88,681 in 2018 (Diyanet İşleri Başkanlığı, 2020) and the population of Turkey was 82,003.822 by the end of 2018. This means that there was approximately one mosque for every 925 people.

6   Kenan Güven was later appointed to the general directorate of a municipal company called *Belko* by Melih Gökçek, the major of Ankara from the Welfare Party in 1994 (Hür, 2013).

with the Muslim world without deviating from the main goal of membership of the European Economic Community. At the Fourth Islamic Summit Conference held in Casablanca, Morocco in 1984, Kenan Evren was elected as the Chairman of the Standing Committee for Economic and Commercial Cooperation of the Organisation of Islamic Cooperation (COMCEC), the main multilateral economic and commercial cooperation platform of the Islamic world, which is one of the four standing committees of the Organisation of Islamic Cooperation (OIC) founded in 1969. He suggested that "improvement of our relations with the Middle Eastern and Islamic countries has gained a special political and economic content. We are in the endeavour of elevating our relations with the Middle East and Islamic countries by developing and strengthening the existing historical, cultural, and spiritual ties and by achieving [a] productive cooperation in all areas that serve the interests of all sides. We see the positive results of various contacts both in the dual-plan and in the framework of the Islam Conference" (as cited in Eligür, 2010: 116).

4 Turgut Özal in Power (1983–1989 and 1989–1993): Post-Kemalist Rule

After establishing "peace and security" through their exceptional form of state rule, the military junta only allowed three political parties to participate in the general elections in November 1983. These were the Motherland Party (*Anavatan Partisi*, MP) led by Turgut Özal, the People's Party (*Halkçı Parti*, PP) led by Necdet Calp, and the Nationalist Democracy Party (*Milliyetçi Demokrasi Partisi*, NDP) led by an ex-general Turgut Sunalp. Although the military supported Turgut Sunalp's Nationalist Democracy Party, the MP under Turgut Özal won the elections with over 45% of the votes (Zürcher, 2004: 282). The first MP term spanned from 1983 to 1987. In the 1987 elections, Özal was able to acquire 36.3% of the votes. Later, he became the 8th president of Turkey in 1989 and died of a heart attack in 1993. After Özal left the MP to become the president in 1989, the party lost its charismatic leadership. In the 1991 elections, the MP under Mesut Yılmaz acquired 24% of the votes, and was replaced by the True Path Party (*Doğru Yol Partisi*, TPP) under Süleyman Demirel.

Özal was a bureaucrat well-known for working in the interests of big business (Acar, 2002). As a protégé of Demirel, he worked in the State Planning Organisation (SPO) as an undersecretary between 1967 and 1971. In 1972, he went to the World Bank in Washington, D.C. and worked there about two years. At the same time, he continued his links with the representatives of big capitalists and business groups in Turkey that he was connected to through the

SPO. Özal also provided some Turkish firms with technical advice on industrial and mining projects when he was in the US. After returning to İstanbul, he worked as a top-level manager in private firms for six years and conducted business by establishing partnerships with friends and family members. Following the coup of 12 September 1980, he was appointed as deputy prime minister in charge of economic affairs and stayed in this position until 1982, when he successfully implemented the January 24 Decisions (Acar, 2002: 164–167). The January 24 Decisions combined a stabilisation programme including devaluation, an increase in the price of state-owned enterprises' products and the removal of price controls, within a structural adjustment programme including several measures to strengthen domestic and international capital against labour (Boratav, 2011: 147–148).

As a follower of monetarist economic policies, Özal was a staunch supporter of the stabilisation programme. He declared in the government programme of 1983 that the government's foremost target was to combat inflation. Anti-inflationary policies were presented as a means to achieve income redistribution and to combat poverty (The Government Programme, 1983: 9). Second, in line with the transition to export-led capitalism, Özal declared his dedication "to market economy based on competition" (The Government Programme, 1983: 9). The main function of the state was deemed to be regulatory; it should not take part in industry and trade (The Government Programme, 1983: 10). In his own words:

> We find it imperative to abandon the long prevailing import substitution mentality and switch to an industrialization policy which would be export-oriented and would integrate with world industry and trade. The import substitution policy which as a general rule envisaged the production of everything by [us] only pushed the cost up and neglected the element of quality. As a result a structure emerged whereby the entire burden was placed on the shoulders of the consumers and industries, with no export capability [resulting] (The Government Programme, 1983: 26).

The abandonment of "the long prevailing import-substitution mentality" and transition to export-led capitalism as a prominent result of the stabilisation programme necessitated a strong leadership, embodied in Özal's prime ministerial position (1983–1989). The support of the transnational community for this transition, establishing trust for domestic and international capital for necessary investment performance, and the ability to get the consent of the people became possible only under a strong and effective leadership (Öniş, 2004: 118). Yet, this aggravated the political calamity in Turkey caused by the fact that Özal preferred to rule by governmental decrees rather than by laws, in order to circumvent parliamentary rules and pressures (Öniş, 2004: 114). The violation of the rule of law was the most damaging economic legacy of Özal (Öniş, 2004).

The post-1980 period under Özal was marked by a rapid increase in the export of goods and services as a percentage of GDP. While Turkish exports amounted to 3% of GDP in 1979, it increased to 16 % in 1989 (The World Bank, 2015). Merchandise exports rose considerably from $2.3 billion in 1979 to $11.7 billion in 1988 (Arıcanlı and Rodrik, 1990: 1347). Özal pursued a dual strategy of encouraging foreign investment and promoting Turkish exports. On the one hand, he passed a decree in 1983 which legalised the establishment of special financial houses to administer Islamic banking (Moore, 1990: 247). Saudi and Kuwaiti capital flowed into Turkey through Al-Baraka and Faisal Finance, both of which "financed Turkish oil imports—in the respective amounts of $150 million and $50 million annually—with which Korkut [Ö]zal [the brother of Turgut Özal] was alleged to have had an interest" (Moore, 1990: 248). On the other hand, Özal submitted an official application for membership of the European Community in April 1987 (Zürcher, 2004: 323). According to him, Turkey's membership of the EC would be a win-win situation for both parties. He said that:

> ...we [Turkey] shall represent a vast market for its [European] high technology products, and we shall offer enormous opportunities for productive investment for its enterprises, because we have many major projects to undertake. You have in large measure completed your infrastructure: you are in position to help us. Your companies will be able to invest in this area and create a great deal of employment, both in your [European] countries and in ours. Bearing in mind the differing wage costs of Europe and Turkey, you will be able to employ Turkish labour more economically in Turkey. Turkey will be able to play for the Community the role which the 'sun-belt' played in the economic development of the United States (Özal, 1991: 314).

Even though Özal was hostile to state dominance of the economy, the transition to neo-liberalism actually necessitated omnipresent state involvement in the economy in order to provide a fertile ground for the private sector. The state assumed an active role in the increase of public fixed investment in the share of total fixed investment in Turkey until 1988. While public fixed investment accounted for nearly half of total fixed investment in 1979, this increased to 58.1% in 1985. The value of private fixed investment exceeded that of public fixed investment only in 1988 (Table 7).

TABLE 7 Relative share of the public and private sectors in total fixed capital investments, 1973–1988

Year	Total fixed investment (% of GDP)*	Public fixed investment (% of total fixed investment)	Private fixed investment (% of total fixed investment)
1973	15.7	47.0	54.9
1974	14.8	47.9	52.1
1975	16.1	50.4	49.6
1976	18	51.5	48.5
1977	19.2	55.4	44.6
1978	17	48.2	51.8
1979	15.6	49.7	50.3
1980	15.9	55.8	44.2
1981	15.1	62.2	37.8
1982	15.1	61.5	38.5
1983	14.8	56.2	43.8
1984	14.4	54.0	46.0
1985	15.3	58.1	41.9
1986	17.1	58.1	41.9
1987	24.7	54.4	45.6
1988	26.1	47.5	52.5

SOURCE: NAS AND ODEKON (1992: 50).
* Data on total fixed investment as ratio to total GDP are taken from The World Bank (2015).

When the composition of fixed capital investment is analysed in the first decade of the transition to export-led capitalism, it can be easily seen that there was a structural division of labour in the orientation of public and private investment. According to TÜSİAD's 1992 report, private fixed investment was concentrated in the housing and manufacturing sectors in 1990 and 1991, while the public sector played a crucial role in providing infrastructure and energy investment for the private sector (Table 8). This clearly shows that the capitalist state under neoliberalism does not necessarily mean the minimisation of state, but rather signifies the redefinition of the role of the state.

With respect to civil-military relations, the Özal period between 1989 and 1991 was a post-Bonapartist phase in Turkey. Özal took advantage of the

TABLE 8 Distribution of fixed capital investment (as % of total)

Sectors	Public		Private		Total	
	1990	1991	1990	1991	1990	1991
Agriculture	9.5	10.7	4.8	4.5	6.9	7.3
Mining	3.4	3.4	1.2	1.3	2.2	2.3
Manufacturing	4.5	5.1	27.5	26.4	17.5	16.7
Energy	21.4	19.4	1.6	1.8	10.2	9.8
Transport and communications	34.1	36.5	12.7	13.7	22.1	24.1
Tourism	1.3	1.5	6.2	6.1	4.0	4.0
Housing	4.0	1.6	41.1	40.5	25.0	22.8
Education	7.0	5.6	0.6	0.7	3.4	2.9
Health	2.8	2.7	0.9	1.5	1.7	2.0
Other	12.1	13.5	3.4	3.4	7.2	8.0
Total	100.0	100.0	100.0	100.0	100.0	100.0

SOURCE: TÜSİAD (1992: 36).

transition to the post-Evren period in terms of military control by counterbalancing the political factions in the army. General Necdet Üruğ planned to retire in July 1987 and then choose General Necdet Öztorun, commander of the land forces, as his successor for Chief of General Staff. So, Üruğ wanted to control the military by opening a space for his political faction in the army and then become president after Evren's term expired in 1989 (Ahmad, 1993: 215). However, Özal overruled the senior military command and appointed Necip Torumtay to succeed General Necdet Üruğ (Evin, 1994: 32–33; Özbudun, 2000: 118; Zürcher, 2004: 285). According to Feroz Ahmad (1993: 217), "[i]n the future, Özal wanted by his side a chief of staff who shared his views on Turkey's defence needs". Özal also planned to make the Chief of General Staff directly responsible to the Minister of Defence rather than the Prime Minister (Karabelias, 1999: 137).

However, the fissure between Özal and Torumtay on the Gulf crisis in 1990 led to the resignation of the latter in December 1990. Özal was eager to benefit from the Gulf Crisis in 1990, saying that "Many things have changed in Turkey… In foreign policy the days of taking cowardly and timid position are over. From now on we'll pursue an active policy based on circumstances. This is a totally political choice" (as cited in Ahmad, 1993: 201). In terms of holding power in the executive, Özal declared his candidacy for the presidency to succeed Evren. He was elected by the assembly as the eighth president of the Republic of Turkey in 1989, becoming the first civilian president since the toppling of Celal Bayar by the military in 1960 (Özbudun, 2000: 118).

Even though Özal sought to hold sway over the military, he continued the Turkish-Islamic Synthesis put into effect by the military. The 1983 Government Programme (1983: 13) stated that, "...it is necessary to take measures in order to ensure religious education in the primary and secondary schools so that generations with stable minds and moral values could be raised". Recognising the family as "the foundation of the nation", Özal put special emphasis on the training and education of children and youth to have "perfect national, moral and cultural values" (The Government Programme, 1983: 35,38). As Hakan Yavuz (2003a: 75) notes, Özal followed a policy of Islamising the educational system. A new curriculum prepared by Vehbi Dinçerler, the Minister of Education and a follower of the Nakşibendi order, rewrote national history and culture. In this new curriculum, the term "national" (*milli*) included and made reference to a religious sense (Yavuz, 2003a: 75). Religion gradually complemented Kemalist nationalism, which was in decline, in the latter's role as the ideological basis of Turkish Bonapartism.

It is not surprising that the military incorporated religion into the general aims of "national power" following the dissolution of communism in the Eastern Bloc between 1989 and 1991 and the Republics of the Soviet Union in 1991. Religion was characterised by the military as a necessary component of "psycho-social and cultural power". By doing so, the Turkish state not only fortified social integration in society, but also gained more room to manoeuvre in the Republics of the Soviet Union. In *Devlet'in Kavram ve Kapsamı* (The Concept and the Extent of the State), published by the General Secretary of the National Security Council in 1990, psycho-social and cultural power (socio-cultural power in short) is defined as "the sum of thoughts, faith and behaviour which develop through culture and play a driving and decisive role in improving and preserving the national entity" (Milli Güvenlik Kurulu Genel Sekreterliği [Secretariat-General of the National Security Council], 1990: 230). In this sense, religion was seen as a necessary institution that would contribute to "national morality, patriotism, defence of motherland, brotherhood and national unity, and integrity and thereby to the development of social power" (Milli Güvenlik Kurulu Genel Sekreterliği [Secretariat-General of the National Security Council], 1990: 239). However, it was deemed that religion should be interpreted in a modern way (Milli Güvenlik Kurulu Genel Sekreterliği, 1990). It was noted that:

As long as religion is interpreted in a modern, rational, and realistic way, as long as it is not used as a 'tool' by a community or a group that would provide them any political and social interest, but rather [religion is] appraised as an 'aim' in order to develop into a perfect person and perfect society; as long as it does not allow fundamentalism and bigotry, as long as it is invoked not simply for a proper departure to the hereafter but rather for future orientation to live in modern and advanced conditions without sticking to the past, religion benefits not only its believers but the whole of humanity ... (Milli Güvenlik Kurulu Genel Sekreterliği [Secretariat-General of the National Security Council], 1990: 240).

5   Political Liberalisation in the 1990s under Post-Bonapartist Rule

"[Political liberalisation] refers not to *liberalism* in its two modern senses but to the oscillation toward a "soft" internal policy instead of a "hard" one on the part of a despotic government which does not thereby give up its power to decide on one or the other" (Draper, 1977: 276). One could say that limited liberalisation in Turkey under post-Bonapartist rule in the 1990s was the extension of "the third wave of democratisation" in the late twentieth century (Huntington, 1991). In addition to the general factors that created conditions favourable to democratisation in the 1970s and 1980s such as the development of democratic norms, the demise of authoritarian regimes, the increase in economic wealth, and the spread of democratic transitions and of democratic social movements (Huntington, 1991: 106–107), the rapid development of information and communication technologies (ICTs), together with the availability of television weakened authoritarian regimes, since the ICT revolution played a key role in disseminating information about human rights violations, thus creating alternative sources that challenged the state's information monopoly (Selian, 2002). The development of ICTs made access to the alternative sources of information possible. While there were only 1 billion Internet subscribers in the world in 2005, corresponding to 16,8% penetration rate, this rose to 4.1 billion subscribers by 2019 with an estimated penetration rate of 53.6% (International Telecommunication Union, 2020). The increase in the rate of individuals using the Internet in the developing countries was also been high over the past fifteen years. While only 9% of households in the developing countries were Internet subscribers in 2005, this rose to an estimated 46.7% by 2019 (International Telecommunication Union, 2020).

Turkey followed the same global pattern in the development of ICTs. Figure 3 demonstrates the development of ICTs of the past two decades. While there were only 81,276 mobile telephone subscribers in Turkey in 1994, this rose to 71,888,416 subscribers in 2014. The Internet users also incrementally increased in the 2000s. While there were only 229,885 internet users in Turkey in 1998, this rose to 41,272,940 in 2014 (Figure 3).

Similar to the dynamics of third wave democratisation, a combination of both external and internal dynamics contributed to the weakening of Kemalist/Bonapartist rule in Turkey in the 1990s. First, as an external force, the end of the Cold War brought EU pressure on the Eastern Bloc for democratisation and free markets, and US foreign policy under the Clinton administration (1993–2001)—from containment to enlargement—produced a snowballing effect that reached Turkey. In September 1993 National Security Advisor Anthony Lake declared the US's strategy of enlargement: "enlargement of the world's free communities of market democracies" (Lake, 1993/1994: 71).[7] This put pressure on Bonapartist rule in Turkey to partially liberalise its political regime. Second, those bourgeois interests who desired accession to the European Union (EU) pushed the Turkish state to make reforms, particularly the 1995 constitutional amendments, which were then followed by the Customs Union between the EU and Turkey, put into effect in December 1995. The Decision of the EC-Turkey Association Council to implement the Customs Union between

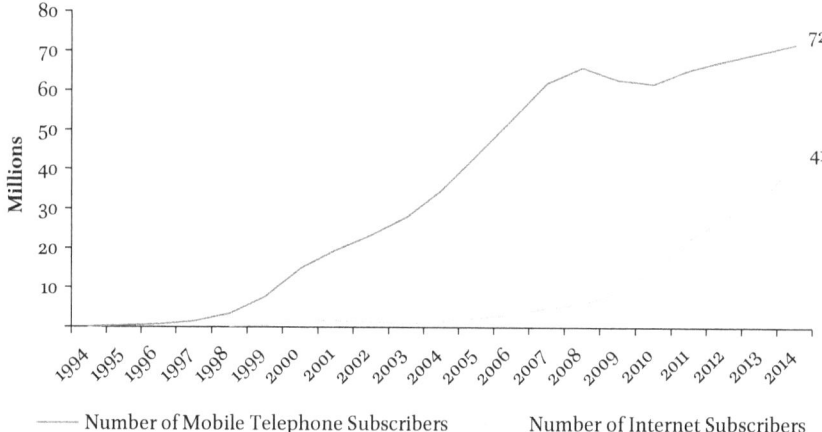

FIGURE 3   Number of mobile telephone and internet subscribers in Turkey, 1994–2014
SOURCE: TÜİK (N.D.).

---

7   Even after the end of the Cold War, the US and Western governments continued to back despotic regimes in the Middle East mainly due to the control of oil and for the fear of Islamic fundamentalism. (Achcar, 2013: 108–118).

the European Community and Turkey in December 1995 was the final phase of the Association Agreement, known as Ankara Agreement, which was signed in September 1963 between the European Economic Community and Turkey. The conclusion of the Customs Union was conditioned by the EU upon further liberalisation (Zürcher, 2004: 297).

Indeed, to shift from a state-controlled to a market economy the Turkish bourgeoisie needed more political space. It can be argued that this is why they then pushed for constitutional amendments for political freedom. An important aspect of liberalisation was realised with the 1993 constitutional amendment which put an end to the state monopoly on television and radio broadcasting (Özbudun, 2007: 184; Zürcher, 2004: 297). This contributed to the increase of private radio and television stations together with the development of social and political pluralism in Turkey (Özbudun and Gençkaya, 2009: 35; Özbudun, 2007: 184). It was, nevertheless, the 1995 constitutional amendments that were the most comprehensive in the realm of political liberalisation (see Box 1). These amendments contributed to the development of political participation while nonetheless failing to improve the rule of law and fundamental rights and liberties (Özbudun and Gençkaya, 2009: 40).

The relaxation in Bonapartist rule was illustrated by the publication of a report written in 1989 by a commission headed by Deniz Baykal, the General Secretary of the Social Democratic Populist Party (*Sosyal Demokrat Halkçı Parti*, SHP), titled *Sosyal Demokrat Halkçı Parti'nin Doğu ve Güneydoğu Sorunlarına Bakışı ve Çözüm Önerileri* (Social Democratic Populist Party's View on Eastern and South-Eastern Problems and its Recommendations). For the first time, a mainstream Turkish party challenged the official ideology regarding the Kurdish problem and recognised the Kurdish people as a separate ethnicity. It was emphasised that citizens living in some places in Eastern and South-Eastern Anatolia are of predominantly Kurdish origin with respect to ethnicity. The report recommended that the citizens who accept their Kurdish identity and say "I am of Kurdish origin" should be able to express this identity freely in every area of their life (SHP, 1989).[8]

The parliament enacted the "Law for Suppression of Terrorism" in April 1991 which deleted Articles 141, 142, and 163 from the penal code so that establishment of association based on class and religion was no longer an offence

---

8 Similar reports on the Kurdish situation followed over the years. Most remarkable were those of Adnan Kahveci "who warned in 1992 of civil war if a democratic solution was not applied, and Doğu Ergil, an Ankara University professor, whose 1995 report showed that although not all Kurds supported the PKK, they did want respect for a separate Kurdish cultural identity" (Pope and Pope, 1997: 265).

BOX 1   Constitutional amendments in 1995

Amendments accepted

- Abolition of the paragraphs of the preamble referring to the necessity and legitimacy of the 1980 coup
- Lifting restrictions on trade unions, associations, foundations, cooperatives, and public professional organisations engaging in political activity and granting political cooperation between political parties and these civil society institutions
- Lowering the voting age to 18
- Increasing the number of parliamentarians to 550 from 450
- Granting Turkish citizens living abroad the right to vote
- Recognition of the right to unionise for public employees
- Allowing university instructors and students to become members of political parties
- Lowering the age of party membership from 21 to 18
- Permission for political parties to form auxiliary bodies such as women's and youth branches, foundations, and organisations in foreign countries
- Concerning the suspension of activities of associations and public professional organisations, the requirement that a competent judge review within 24 hours and make a decision within 48 hours
- Relaxation of restrictions on changing party membership, which had been a cause for loss of parliamentary membership
- Restricting the loss of parliamentary membership to those whose words or deeds caused the banning of a political party
- Limiting the grounds for prohibition of parties
- Limiting the ban to five years for those who caused the prohibition of the party by their words or deeds

SOURCE: ÖZBUDUN AND GENÇKAYA (2009: 39–40).

(Hale, 1994: 289–290; Zürcher, 2004: 292). As Şevket Kazan (2012, personal communication) claims, since the 1950s, while Articles 141 and 142 of the penal code prohibited communism, Article 163 targeted religious movements in Turkey. Laws on political parties and press, however, limited the repercussions of the withdrawal of Articles 141, 142, and 163 of the penal code (Hale, 1994: 290).

The writing and speaking of Kurdish in public, which had been banned since 1983, became legal in 1991 (Hale, 1994: 290). In 1991, Demirel publicly stated official recognition of the "Kurdish reality" (Hale, 1994: 286; Pope, 1997: 271). As Hale (1994: 286) notes, "For the first time in the history of the republic, Kurdish-language books and newspapers began to appear in Turkey, and government even began a dialogue with the Kurdish leadership in Iraq, which now enjoyed virtual autonomy under Western protection". Nevertheless, because the concept of terrorism was broadly defined in the newly enacted anti-terror law, verbal or written statements could fall under the concept of terrorism, which resulted in the persecution of many trade unionists, lawyers, human rights activists, journalists, and writers (Zürcher, 2004: 292).

Nonetheless, the army continued to rule from behind-the-scenes both in the post-Evren period and in the 1990s even though the provisional Article 4 of the constitution, which prevented the leaders of the pre-1980 parties to engage in political activities for ten years, was repealed with a referendum in 1987 (Hale, 1994: 279). The army was still controlling the state apparatus, if not formally ruling the country, through institutional routes and mechanisms such as the National Security Council, the presidency, martial law, and the military courts (Evin, 1994: 25–26). In this period, repression in Kurdish region of Turkey's southeast and political liberalisation occurred simultaneously. The Turkish armed forces reasserted themselves in Kurdish region of Turkey's southeast with the foundation of the Regional State of Emergency Governorate (*Olağanüstü Hal Bölge Valiliği*, OHAL) and of state of emergency in 13 cities from 1987 to 2002. This left behind high social and economic costs in the forms of underdevelopment, high unemployment, forced migration, and low levels of investment in education (Kayaoglu, 2014). While the official statistics declared that by the mid-1990s there were a total of 329,916 displaced people from 12 South-Eastern provinces (Pope and Pope, 1997: 274), it was estimated that around 1.1 million people in the OHAL region were forced to migrate between 1985 and 2000 due to the war (Mutlu, 2011: 68). In terms of total economic costs, the war with the PKK between 1984 and 2005 imposed an economic burden on the economy which amounted to between $100 billion and $170 billion depending on different valuations (Mutlu, 2011: 73).

Mehtap Söyler (2015: 143) labels the 1990s as "the transformation of the deep state into *the* state, i.e. the emergence of the informal state, hence, the shift of the state to the boundary between democracy and autocracy, where the difference between an authoritarian regime and defective democracy is nominal". This period saw a stern repression of the Kurds especially in Kurdish region of Turkey's southeast. During the Newroz celebration of March 1992, more than 90 people were killed in the South-East (Pope and Pope, 1997: 269). Successive

Kurdish parties were banned one after the other in 1993, 1994, 1996, and 1999 (see Table 6). In this period murders by unknown assailants were widespread. The following list outlines some of the murders during the 1990s: the assassination of intellectuals and public figures such as Muammer Aksoy, Çetin Emeç, Turan Dursun, Bahriye Üçok in 1990, Uğur Mumcu in 1993 and Ahmet Taner Kışlalı in 1999; the assassination of several military officers throughout the 1990s; the assassination of Kurdish politicians such as Vedat Aydın in 1991, Musa Anter in 1992, Mehmet Sincar in 1993; the unexpected death of Eşref Bitlis, Commander of the Turkish Gendarmerie Forces, in 1993; the Sivas Madımak massacre in 1993 in which a mob of Islamic fundamentalists set fire to the Madımak Hotel, causing the death of 33 Alevi people; the Gazi Quarter incident in 1995 in which a vehicle opened fire on coffee houses, causing clashes between Alevis and the police and the death of 22 people; the assassinations of Kurdish businessmen in Bolu, Düzce, and the Sapanca triangle between 1993 and 1996; the assassination of Özdemir Sabancı, a prominent Turkish businessman, in 1996 (TBMMa, 2012: 164–165).

6 Second-generation Devout Turkish Bourgeoisie[9]

The shift from a state-controlled to a market economy contributed to the emergence of the second-generation Turkish bourgeoisie, known as the Anatolian bourgeoisie, as an economic and political force after the 1980s. This faction in Turkish capitalism mainly consists of the second generation of business groups in Turkey (Cokgezen, 2000). Among the second-generation Turkish bourgeoisie, economic activity is overwhelmingly performed by small and medium-sized enterprises that are predominantly active in labour intensive industries with low technology such as textiles, construction, and food. Contrary to the big monopoly capital—the sovereignty of which crystallised under the state-controlled economy with the foundation of TÜSİAD in 1971—Anatolian capitalists converged their scattered interests under the banner of MÜSİAD in 1990 in the period of export-led capitalism.

Nevertheless, divergence within the Anatolian bourgeoisie is clearer than that of the big capitalists. Three main groups can be identified within the Anatolian bourgeoisie. First, the "devout bourgeoisie" (Gumuscu and Sert, 2009), which flourished within export-led capitalism under Özal after the 1980s; its interests in the continuation of political and economic liberalisation led it to

---

9 This classification is based on the Cokgezen's article titled "New fragmentations and new cooperations in the Turkish bourgeoisie" (Cokgezen, 2000).

support Erdoğan in the 2000s. The devout bourgeoisie refers to a new faction within the ruling class in Turkey which broke away from the Islamic economic programme that has highlighted social justice, state intervention, and redistribution in the realm of economy (Gumuscu and Sert, 2009). MÜSİAD has been the economic representative of this rising devout bourgeoisie, of which the AKP has been the political reflection. The second group comprises a small number of companies owned by the religious sects (*tariqats*) or religious communities. They also have a vested interest in economic liberalism and mostly engage in the service sector such as education, publishing/media, and health. Server Holding under the *İskenderpaşa* community is the classic example of a *tariqat* company. This holding does business in various sectors such as education (*Asfa Eğitim Kurumları* [Educational Institutions] and Server Publication), media (*Server İletişim* [Server Communication] and *Akra FM*), construction (*Necat İnşaat* [Necat Construction]), tourism (*Seyran Turizm* [Seyran Tourism]), technology (*Halas Technology*) and foreign trade (*Vera İç ve Dış Ticaret* [Vera Domestic and Foreign Trade]) (Server Holding, 2019). The third group is the Anatolian Holding Companies, which "followed the Islamic finance principle of profit and loss sharing or partnership finance through selling issued bonds of companies and investors to individuals, families and businesses" (Ozcan and Çokgezen, 2003: 2070). They first emerged in the 1970s to control small family savings and workers' remittances from Germany but became popular in their second wave in the 1990s, a period in which Islamic fundamentalism was ascendant (Ozcan and Çokgezen: 2003). Well-known Anatolian Holding Companies include Kombassan, Yimpaş, İttifak, Jet-Pa, Endüstri, Kimpaş, Büyük Anadolu and Investment Holding.

Importantly, the second-generation devout bourgeoisie takes its name from the spatial concentration of particular capital groups in Anatolia even though the headquarters of MÜSİAD and ASKON, the prime organisations of the second generation of Turkish capitalism, are located in İstanbul. The second generation of Turkish capitalism refers to a specific dependency relationship with big finance capital. Regardless of their spatial concentration, this capital faction has emerged in the orbit of monopoly capitalism in Turkey. In other words, their peripheral position in the circuit of production has been the necessary condition for the development and advancement of big monopoly capitalism. Big capitalism benefits from the existence of the second generation of Turkish capitalism for the maintenance of a relatively low cost of labour reproduction and surplus extraction. To the extent that this second-generation Turkish capital develops, the members of this capital faction are predisposed to the echelons of the big capital group. Examples can be seen in the TÜSİAD membership of Ahmet Çalık from Çalık Holding, Ethem Sancak from Hedef Alliance

Holding and Memduh Boydak from Boydak Holding. Ideologically, Islam, which gradually complemented Kemalist nationalism in the form of a Turkish-Islamic synthesis for social cohesion, has been the ideological cement unifying the scattered second-generation Turkish capitalists.

The particular nature and composition of this capital faction is the result of the unequal distribution of state loans in favour of big capital under national developmentalism. Due to the structure of the holding banking system, in which big business groups have controlled the main sources of money capital, SMEs were excluded from the credit system (Öztürk, 2014: 199). Subcontracting relations with big capital and being unprotected by the state made these small and medium-sized enterprises prone to exploitation by larger ones (Gülalp, 2001: 439). The dynamics of Anatolian enterprises were neglected by the state. Moreover, they were excluded from state investment funds and other privileges granted to big capital symbolised by TÜSİAD (Buğra, 1998: 525). Even though SMEs constituted approximately 99% of the total enterprises and 45% of employment in Turkey, the loans extended for SMEs were limited to 3.5% in 1996 (TÜSİAD, 2002: 144).[10]

However, the shift to export-led capitalism increased the economic force of the peripheral cities. For instance while the proportion of total private manufacturing value added accounted for by five selected Anatolian cities (Gaziantep, Denizli, Kayseri, Konya, and Kahramanmaraş) increased from 3.55% in 1983 to 8.5% in 2000, this ratio in five metropoles, (İstanbul/Kocaeli, Ankara, İzmir, Bursa, and Adana) decreased from 80% to 66% over the same period (Buğra and Savaşkan, 2014: 95). Only fourteen companies from five selected cities made the İstanbul Chamber of Industry's 1980 survey of Turkey's *Top 500 Companies*. Denizli and Kayseri were represented by only five and nine companies, respectively (Buğra and Savaşkan, 2014: 111). The number of big companies in these five selected cities had more than quadrupled by 2012, according to a survey conducted by the İstanbul Chamber of Industry. *Turkey's Top 500 Industrial Companies in Turkey-2012* showed that these five cities absorbed the 62 biggest companies in Turkey in 2012. It also revealed that Gaziantep, Kayseri, Denizli, Konya and Kahramanmaraş included 23, 12, ten, nine and eight companies in 2012, respectively (İSO, 2012). Nevertheless, it is still hard to say that the distribution of economic power is skewed towards the second-generation Turkish bourgeoisie. According to a calculation, 38 of the 50 private enterprises that had highest revenues in 2002 before AKP rule increased their

---

10 According to the OECD report titled *Small and Medium Size Enterprise Outlook 2002*, they accounted for 99.5% of establishments, 61.6% of employment and 27.3% of value added in the manufacturing sector in Turkey (OECD, 2002).

value added share in total industry from 10.1% to 14.2% during a decade between 2002 and 2012 (Onaran and Oyvat, 2015: 30).

6.1 MÜSİAD (*The Independent Industrialists' and Businessmen's Association*)

An offshoot of TÜSİAD, MÜSİAD was founded on 5 May 5 1990 by 12 entrepreneurs.[11] Erol Yarar was the first chair of the organisation.[12] Ömer Cihad Vardan, the fourth chair of MÜSİAD, perceived the establishment of MÜSİAD in 1990 as the revival of a forgotten potential of Anatolia (Vardan, 2012). In his autobiography, he argues that

> MÜSİAD was the name of an outcry, opposition, and awakening. We can say that Anatolia woke up with MÜSİAD; Turkey rose to her feet. Indeed, MÜSİAD contributed to the termination of unilateralism, monologism [the reduction of multiple voices to a single version of truth], and the sovereignty of a specific layer in the business world. After the 1990s, it initiated a transformation in the business world from a point where businessmen were marginalised, weren't credited, and their self confidence wasn't developed, to a point where they achieved the will which will rule the country afterwards (Vardan, 2012: 63).

This association saw itself as the representation of the "periphery" and claimed it had always been excluded from the "centre" (Selçuk Mutlu, 2012, personal communication). According to MÜSİAD, the "periphery", which burst through its shell only after the 1990s, had been represented neither in local governments, state administration nor the business world since the establishment of the Republic. Arguing that "the economic opening in the 1980s led to a change in the country's destiny", the import-substitution industrialisation model was discredited since it claimed that import prohibitions created the emergence of monopolies in Turkey that favoured TÜSİAD (Turkish Industry & Business Association) members (Selçuk Mutlu, 2012, personal communication).

As one of the representatives of the second-generation of Turkish capitalism, MÜSİAD is an umbrella business organisation of small and medium-sized

---

11 The founders of MÜSİAD are Erol Mehmet Yarar, B. Ali Bayramoğlu, Abdurrahman Esmerer, Natik Akyol, Sekib Avdagic, Mehmet Gönenç, Mahmut Ekrem Ensari, Arif Gülen, Cihangir Bayramoğlu, Mehmet Turgut, and Ahmet Yıldırım (MÜSİAD, *Müstakil Sanayici ve İş Adamları Derneği*, Independent Industrialists' and Businessmen's Association, 2012: 13).

12 Erol Yarar father, Ali Özdemir Yarar, was a member of the board in TÜSİAD between 1974 and 1975.

enterprises (SMEs) that mushroomed following the export-oriented industrialisation model in Turkey after the 1980s. The basic underlying difference from TÜSİAD was said to be the size of member enterprises—mostly SMEs—and the representation and embracement of Anatolia (Selçuk Mutlu, 2012, personal communication). It is also accepted that the SMEs are more effective in putting pressure on governments due to their high number of members. A middle-ranking MÜSİAD official eloquently sumps up the representational link between the AKP and the capital group:

> The views of MÜSİAD on constitution and laws are very important, effective and real [on government]. They are even more effective than those of TÜSİAD in this period ... We annually issue an Economic Report on Turkey and inside it, there is a part called 'suggestions, views and evaluations' from a wide range of issues such as education and constitution. When you look at them, all that we had said one or two years ago was translated into constitutional change or sometimes into law amendments one or two years later. [These economic reports] are highly effective (Selçuk Mutlu, 2012, personal communication).

MÜSİAD provided a platform for the Anatolian capitalists. For instance, businessmen in Konya had the chance to go abroad to do business only after the 1990s with the help of MÜSİAD (Selçuk Mutlu, 2012, personal communication). This has been reflected in the MÜSİAD biennial international business fairs occurring since 1993. Around 150,000 visitors and 5,140 foreign businessmen from 92 countries participated in the 14th MÜSİAD international fair in İstanbul in 2012 (MÜSİAD, 2014).

The fair was supported by various state institutions such as the Ministry of Economics, Ministry of Development, Small and Medium Enterprises Development Organisation (KOSGEB), and Turkish Airlines. It is worth noting that even though the motto of the 14th International Fair was "The Islamic World is in this fair", the only noticeable Islamic element was the conversion of a large area in the Expo Centre into a temporary mosque for Friday prayers.[13]

According to the provisional data gathered from MÜSİAD, the organisation represents more than 11,000 members, employing approximately 1.8 million workers in nearly 60,000 companies in Turkey. It has 89 domestic contact offices and four foreign representatives together serving 225 destinations in 95 countries (MÜSİAD, 2020). Even though MÜSİAD members are ostensibly more

---

13 The observation was based on a participant observation in the 14th MÜSİAD International Fair and 16th International Business Forum in İstanbul on October 11th–14th, 2012.

homogenous with respect to members' common religious sensitivities than TÜSİAD members, the most important material difference between MÜSİAD and TÜSİAD was said to be different attitudes towards international creditors such as the IMF (an economist in MÜSİAD, 2012, personal communication). It was argued that TÜSİAD had become "accustomed" to a particular type of economic model based on crony capitalism in Turkey in the 1980s and 1990s. TÜSİAD members have relied on foreign resources because enterprises with foreign currency debts are overwhelmingly TÜSİAD members (an economist in MÜSİAD, 2012, personal communication). It was further argued by MÜSİAD that the state always worked for TÜSİAD members, because in the period of scarcity and oil crisis in Turkey in the 1970s, the state did not open up the economy for competition, instead selling oil to members of TÜSİAD at subsidised prices to support their domestic production. The result was that while South Korea, for example, took off, the wealth and prosperity of TÜSİAD members became the price for which Turkey kept going in circles (an economist in MÜSİAD, 2012, personal communication).

The sectoral distribution of MÜSİAD members seems to be divergent. Table 9 shows that the members encompass printing, publication, packaging and advertisement, information technologies, durable consumer goods and furniture, energy and environment, food and agriculture, services, construction, chemistry-metal and mining, logistics, machinery, automotive industry, health, and textiles and leather. Construction companies account for 5,606 out of 27,657 companies in the organisation, or more than one fifth of the total, holding influence over a large proportion of firms in the business organisation in 2014. These construction companies specialise in infrastructure, elevator/escalator, bathroom/kitchen equipments, glazing, landscaping, fittings, service, constructional service, fine construction material, building construction machinery and equipment, bulk material, hardware, installation, and insulating products.[14] The textile and leather sector is represented by 3,605 companies, accounting for 13.02% of the total (Table 9).

Not surprisingly, in the second-generation of Turkish capitalism the sectoral power of the financial sector in the organisation is marginal when compared to TÜSİAD members. Only 19 companies in MÜSİAD are engaged in financial services, out of which four companies engage in participation banking (Islamic banking) (e-MÜSİAD, 2014). These four participation banks are AlBaraka Türk, Asya Katılım, Kuveyt Türk, and Türkiye Finans. According to the data of the

---

14   The biggest overseas contracting Turkish companies such as Rönesans, Enka, Polimeks, TAV, Çalık, Gama, Yüksel, Gap, Nurol, Limak Companies are still TÜSİAD members.

TABLE 9   Sectoral distribution of MÜSİAD members (2014)

The sectors (MUSIAD)	Number of companies/members	(%)
Construction	5,606	20.26
Textiles and leather	3,605	13.02
Durable consumer goods and furniture	3,430	12.39
Food and agriculture	3,110	11.24
Chemical substances, metal, and mining	2,329	8.41
Printing, publication, packaging, and advertising	2,164	7.82
Services	1,827	6.60
Machinery	1,679	6.06
Energy and environment	1,576	5.69
Automotive	830	2.99
Information technologies	802	2.89
Health	414	1.49
Logistics	295	1.06
Total	27,667	~100

SOURCE: OWN CALCULATIONS BASED ON E-MÜSİAD (2014).

Participation Banks Association of Turkey, these four banks only held 5.55% of the total assets of the banking sector in Turkey in 2013 (n.d.: 84).

On the other hand, in 2013 TÜSİAD had 67 out of 606 members operating in the financial sector. Manufacturing is the constitutive sector of big capital in Turkey in which 212 companies account more than one third of total TÜSİAD members (Table 10). Yet, even though the number of TÜSİAD members is just above 600, TÜSİAD *dominates* the Turkish economy. According to TÜSİAD figures in 2013, TÜSİAD's contribution to the Turkish economy includes 50% of value added in the non-public sector, 65% of industrial production, 80% of the volume of foreign trade (excluding energy), 50% of registered employment in the non-agricultural and non-public sectors, and 85% of corporate tax (TÜSİAD, 2011, 2013).

TABLE 10 Sectoral distribution of TÜSİAD members (2013)

The sectors (TUSIAD)	The number of members	(%)
Manufacturing	212	35
Wholesale and retail sale	79	13
Financial services	67	11
Construction	67	11
Transportation	61	10
Energy	36	6
Agriculture and food	24	4
Education	6	1
Mining	6	1
Other	48	8
Total	606	100

SOURCE: OWN CALCULATIONS BASED ON TÜSİAD (2011: 88–95; 2013).

MÜSİAD has a vested interest in liberalising the economic system for a competitive economic environment and overcoming the omnipotence of the bureaucracy in Turkey. One of its first publications in 1993 titled *Orta Ölçekli İşletmeler ve Bürokrasi* (Medium-sized Enterprises and Bureaucracy) affirms these vested interests.[15] The first chair of MÜSİAD, Erol Yarar, contends in this publication that bureaucracy, which he compares to cancer with its self-growing structure and a structural illness paralysing the organs one by one, is one of the biggest factors hampering the implementation of common ideas (MÜSİAD, 1993a: 111).

Bureaucracy, according to Yarar, is the primary obstacle to development in Turkey. In this report, MÜSİAD offers to reduce the burden of the bureaucracy. It includes a number of recommendations: The foundation of a Small and Medium Sized Industry Promotion Department in the State Planning Organisation and of entrepreneurship development and a small enterprises ministry; curtailing the ability of big enterprises to take part in small tenders; ensuring that 30% of government tenders go to small enterprises; a five-year tax

---

15 The report was written in 1993 by Hüner Şencan and Ömer Dinçer, who was elected as a member of parliament from the AKP in 2007 and served as Minister of Labour and Social Security between 2009 and 2011 and Minister of National Education between 2011 and 2013.

exemption for newly formed enterprises; and an obligation for the banks to credit small and medium-sized enterprises (MÜSİAD, 1993a: 22–25). In another report in 1993, SOEs are attacked. Privatisation is seen as a *tool*, not an *aim* in itself, to strengthen the free market economy, to increase efficiency, update technology levels, disseminate wealth to the masses, ensure public utilisation, enable a minimal state and support private enterprises while restricting the share of foreign investors in SOEs (MÜSİAD, 1993b: 77–78). In a report in 1996 titled "A New Perspective of the World at the Threshold of the 21st Century", a dual economic development policy that would combine import substitution with export promotion is proposed. The competitiveness of Turkish corporations in global markets should in any case be secured. Otherwise, "[t]he one-dimensional import-substitution [would transform, as it did in the past] our large industrial enterprises into domestic parasites" (MÜSİAD, 1996: 48).

Furthermore, an Islamic focus fails from view when one considers that MÜSİAD has gained from the share of wealth under export-led capitalism and facilitated the new practice of global voracious consumption. The result is that the "devout bourgeoisie" have successfully combined the Islamic way of life with luxury consumption, ostentation, and intemperance by commodifying Islamic culture. Fashionable Islamic attires for women, five-star alternative halal vacations or holiday villages in which swimming pools are segregated, deluxe hajj and umrah packages, Islamic personal care products which have halal certification, and the establishment of luxury shisha cafes and non-alcoholic restaurants in major cities help the devout bourgeoisie to articulate global consumerist patterns while leading to "discursive tension" (Madi, 2014: 151). The Islamist writer Mehmet Şevket Eygi (July 2, 2013) teases in *Milli Gazete* this new form of fusion of Islamic identity and individualism by labelling new rich Muslim women as *Süslüman*[16] who wear stiletto heels, colourful non-traditional veils, and tight and short dresses. In this "discursive tension", the founding president of MÜSİAD, Erol Yarar, on the other hand, disagrees with the Islamic values of sobriety and modesty. He says,

> Allah wants to see his blessing on his subjects. The garments of the Ottoman sultans do not look like those of Karacaoğlan.[17] If the calibre is to dress as little as possible, then, how will we explain Abu Hanifa? His house was the most beautiful house in Baghdad. If I give alms, then,

---

16   *Süslüman* is a modified word which combines two words, *Süslü* (Fancy) and *Müslüman* (Muslim). It was used by Mehmet Şevket Eygi to refer to the fancy Muslim women.

17   Karacaoğlan was the 17th century Anatolian folk poet (*âşık*) whose poems were on the nomad life of Turcomans, nature, love, and death.

nobody has the right to ask in Islam why I behave so. The prophet too does not allow the whole disbursement (*infak*) of property. It is supposed that a man despite the fact that he is becoming rich should live like the poor. There is no such thing (Özkan, July 20, 2009).

Significantly, this economic acquisition threatens to break down worldly asceticism by calling the devout bourgeoisie to fulfil a duty in worldly affairs, which is "a struggle for profit free from the limits set by needs" (Weber, 2005: 27). Money-making is valued "as the highest means to asceticism, and at the same time the surest and most evident proof of rebirth and genuine faith" (Weber: 2005: 116).

6.2 ASKON (*The Anatolian Tigers Business Association*)

To the extent that the new Islamic ethos—framed by the idea "Allah wants to see his blessing on his subjects"—is articulated by the devout bourgeoisie, the pursuit of wealth as an end in itself ceases to be reprehensible. However, the interest (*faiz*), which inhibits the release of acquisitive activity, is a significant constraint on a particular section of the devout bourgeoisie, namely ASKON (The Anatolian Tigers Business Association). Founded in 1998 from a split in MÜSİAD, ASKON states that it does not exclusively affirm an economic target but maintains "a claim and identity" (ASKON, n.d.: 3). The name Anatolia references more than the geographical area; it corresponds to a "deep value" in a heritage and in future which stretches "from Baghdad to Bukhara, from Caucasia to Bosnia and from Africa to Asia" (ASKON, n.d.: 3). Supporting the perspective of Rightful Wealth (*Haklı Zenginli*k)—that "the right (*hak*) and the rightness (*hakkaniyet*) are defined by reference to Islam which is an alternative to the system of Adam Smith and to the system of Marx"—this faction of the devout bourgeoisie remains together not only through specific conditions of production but also through a political commitment (Sıtkı Abdullahoğlu, 2012, personal communication). ASKON is under the control of the Felicity Party which continues to embrace the views of Erbakan.

ASKON greatly benefited from the diversification of the domestic entrepreneurial groups under export-led capitalism. The number of companies in ASKON was boosted from 72 in 1999 to 2,350 in 2011 (ASKON, n.d.: 7). These companies are mostly in the small-scale manufacturing and commercial sectors for domestic consumption, such as apparel, ready to wear, furniture and home textiles, leather and shoes, construction and construction materials, services, finance, jewellery, machinery and replacements, and the food and agriculture sectors (ASKON, n.d.: 20–21). Even though ASKON companies employed 250,000 employees and had US$25 billion business volume in 2010 (ASKON,

2010), only nine ASKON export companies were in the top 1000 Turkish export companies in 2011 (ASKON, n.d.).

While proscribing interest as an illicit source of undeserved wealth (Sıtkı Abdullahoğlu, 2012, personal communication), ASKON encourages a corporate identity which adopts the view that "the commercial life of our Prophet is the best example for ASKON members" (ASKON, n.d.). It argues that in addition to advocating morality and not cheating people, the system of the Prophet provides the regulation of the market. In order to prevent monopolisation in the market, the Prophet did not allow the price to be set before it was determined in the market; implementing fixed prices was not allowed. In other words, it is said that the Prophet organised the free market in such a proper way that he averted the systems and schemes such as hoarding (*ihtikar*) that would manipulate the market (Sıtkı Abdullahoğlu, 2012, personal communication). ASKON suggests the adoption of this system and supports "an economic freedom that is compatible with righteousness" (Sıtkı Abdullahoğlu, 2012, personal communication) and against financial speculation and monopoly capitalism.

6.3 TUSKON (*Turkish Confederation of Businessmen and Industrialists*)

Composed of seven different business federations and representing 211 business associations, TUSKON had been the biggest business association in Turkey by membership, involving over 55,000 entrepreneurs, until its closure following the attempted coup in 2016 (TUSKON, n.d.). Even though TUSKON had risen under the second-generation Turkish bourgeoisie, it involved big holding companies including Fernas Group, Boydak Holding, Orkide Group, Alfemo Group, Kaynak Holding, and Sanko Holding.[18] Established in 2005, TUSKON had been organising business forums called Turkey-World Trade Bridge since 2006. These business forums brought together Turkish businessmen with their foreign counterparts where they can engage in one-to-one bilateral business matching.

Correspondingly, TUSKON had four foreign representatives' offices in New York, Brussels, Beijing and Moscow and partner organisations in 140 countries (TUSKON, n.d.). It is important to note that the confederation was close to the Fethullah Gülen community and the Hizmet movement, which has been active notably in Central Asia after the dissolution of the Soviet Union (Hendrick, 2009). The Gülen community is known for opening schools and cultural centres all over the world but particularly in Central Asia and Africa. The significance of these schools and cultural centres is that they generate a kind of

---

18   It is important to note that Fernas Group and Boydak Holding are also TÜSİAD members.

social capital.[19] Accordingly, Fethullah Gülen, the Islamic preacher, acknowledged the economic function of these schools by stressing

> These institutions [schools and cultural centres] in all places but notably in Central Asia create material, cultural, and social sources of honour for our nation and the state...In the near future, many people who are ready and enthusiastic to engage in every kind of dialogue on behalf of our nation and the state will be trained in all such places... Wherever [these] schools exist, people who go there for education and culture also create opportunities that will develop economic relations; they develop business and commercial relations. This will certainly provide fruitful development in the future (Gülen, October 18, 2005).

Within this framework it can be concluded that a new capital accumulation strategy, namely export-led growth based on private initiative and competition, was successfully implemented in Turkey under military rule. As shown, export-led capitalism in Turkey after the 1980s increased the economic and political power of the devout bourgeoisie in the periphery. Nevertheless, even though decomposition and necrosis of the economic pillar of the Kemalist State slowly started with the erosion of national developmentalism after the 1980s, the political supremacy of military tutelage eroded until the rise of the AKP. The military coup on 12 September 12 1980 was functional in shifting the economic trajectory of Turkey to export-led capitalist growth. However, at a certain stage, notably after the second half of the 1990s, the interests of the devout bourgeoisie are found to undermine military rule in Turkey. This resulted in the convergence of the interests of the devout bourgeoisie with those of the big capitalists, which precipitated a move to control the core state apparatus. The bourgeoisie as a whole concurrently demanded to control political power as Bonapartist state power became costly and began to act as fetters, politically. The process was completed in the 2000s under AKP rule, belatedly resulting in a continuous power struggle between the bourgeoisie as a whole and the military elite. Therefore, it is important to underline that AKP rule is the product of Turkey's neoliberal transition that was steered by Özal (1983–1993). The AKP completed this democratic transition that had already

---

19 Social capital refers to "the aggregate of the actual or potential resources which are linked to possession of a durable network of more or less institutionalised relationships of mutual acquaintance and recognition—or in other words, to membership in a group—which provides each of its members with the backing of the collectivity-owned capital, a 'credential' which entitles them to credit, in the various senses of the word" (Bourdieu, 1986: 248–249).

commenced in the 1990s. The political, economic, and ideological transformation of the Kemalist pillars mostly benefited the second-generation Turkish bourgeoisie. For this reason the second-generation devout Turkish bourgeoisie has been able to constitute themselves as social force that challenged Bonapartist rule together with the big capitalists.

CHAPTER 3

War of Manoeuvre by Islamic Fundamentalism against the Kemalist State

The term Islamic fundamentalism is used throughout this chapter in order to refer to a political-religious ideology which seeks a return, recuperation, or revival of the foundations of Islam, the Quran and the Prophet's Sunna, for practical guidance to resolve any social problems. The return to or revival of these Islamic fundamentals is accordingly instrumental in "(a) ... organizing people for radical socio-political action, (b) ... mobilizing the masses for the coming struggles and fights against internal and external enemies, and (c) ... providing a lasting and authentic solution to all the ills and problems plaguing present-day Muslim societies" (Al-Azm, 1993). Therefore, "Islam is the Solution", the political motto of the Muslim Brotherhood (founded in Egypt 1928 by Hassan al-Banna), is the classic example of the political signifier of an Islamic fundamentalist movement/party.

Given the heterogeneity of Islamic movements in the MENA region, which have adopted various brands of this religious-political ideology—some revolutionary, some reactionary, some gradual or moderate—Islamic fundamentalism is distinguished by its *political* character, rather than its *ecclesiastical* nature. Maxime Rodinson, a prominent French Marxist historian in Islamic studies, characterises Islamic fundamentalism as a political-religious ideology: A glorious and peaceful "Muslim community in Medina between 622 [the era of the *hijra*, meaning emigration, from Mecca to Medina] and 632 [the year when Prophet Muhammad died]" would be reproduced for the Muslims or for the whole world by the complete imposition of "Islamic dogmas and practices" in politics and society (Rodinson, 2004: 2–4).

By defining a political-religious ideology using the term and concept "fundamentalism", this chapter aims to show that Islamic fundamentalism should not be conflated with Islam *per se*. Orientalists frequently commit this misrepresentation by attributing an essence to Islam and reinforcing the peculiarity and exceptionalism of the "Islamic world" while explaining the historical circumstances through reference to an "immutable culture" of MENA (Achcar, 2013b; Bayat, 2007; Said, 2003). Here the term and concept fundamentalism emphasises a political-religious ideology influenced by past social and political schemes while suggesting an all-embracing religious dogma for society and politics. In this sense, the term "fundamentalism" can equally be used to refer to movements within Christianity, Hinduism, or Judaism. In other words, Muslim societies are not unique in witnessing the resurgence of fundamentalist movements. Indeed, the term fundamentalism was originally used to designate a distinct version of American evangelicalism which developed in the US in the late 19th and early 20th centuries.[1] The real issue, as Asef Bayat puts it, is to examine the *social conditions* of agents—for instance Muslim societies—or social forces which "render a particular a particular reading of the sacred texts hegemonic" (Bayat, 2007).

Islamic fundamentalist social forces in Turkey grew in the context of the Cold War by means of Saudi Arabia's economic power, which challenged the progressive nationalism embodied by Gamal Abdel Nasser's Egypt (Dreyfuss, 2005). This led to the successive Islamic fundamentalist parties led by Necmettin Erbakan[2] from the late 1960s to the late 1990s waging a war of manoeuvre

---

[1] It referred to "a movement among American 'evangelical' Christians, people professing complete confidence in the Bible and preoccupied with the message of God's salvation of sinners through the death of Jesus Christ" (Marsden, 1980: 3). Alarmed with the radical forms of theological liberalism and cultural crisis of American civilisation following the First World War, fundamentalists were "evangelical Christians, close to the traditions of the dominant American revivalist establishment of the nineteenth century, who in the twentieth century militantly opposed both modernism in theology and the cultural changes that modernism endorsed" (Marsden, 1980: 4). Published in a set of 90 essays in 12 volumes from 1910 to 1915 and funded by a Southern California oil millionaire, Lyman Stewart, *The Fundamentals* became a referencing point for recognising a fundamentalist movement in the U.S. (Marsden, ibid. pp. 118–119). *The Fundamentals* "was meant to be a great "Testimony to the Truth" and even something of a scholarly *tour de force*" (Marsden, 1980: 118). This set of essays was an attempt to defend the faith and to emphasise overwhelmingly personal experience, soul-saving, and individual prayer while combining various traditional theological questions to attack the frailties of modern ideologies of that time. These ideas were mainly rooted in theology and politics such as Protestant liberalism, Mormonism, Eddyism, Modern Spiritualism Romanism, modernism, Darwinism, Russellism, communism, and anarchism. *The Fundamentals* championed criticism only to the extent that they could be used as a tool for discovering the plain facts of God evident in Scripture, consequently proving the compatibility of the theological text with scientific "common sense" (Marsden, 1980: 120–123).

[2] Necmettin Erbakan was born in 1926 in Sinop, a city on the Black Sea coast in Turkey. Erbakan had a completely secular education in state schools. He graduated in 1948 with a degree in mechanical engineering from İstanbul Technical University. He was sent to Aaachen Technical University in Germany to conduct scientific research. After his return to Turkey, Erbakan played a key role in the establishment of the Gümüş Engine Factory in 1956, which produced local and national engines. In 1966, he became president of the Industrial Division of the Union of Chambers and later the General Secretary of the Union. He was elected president of the Union of Chambers in 1969 but was removed from office by the government of Süleyman Demirel. He applied to join the Justice Party under Demirel to become a parliamentarian in 1969, but after being refused, he became an independent parliamentarian for Konya, a central Anatolian city known for its reputation for being the most conservative city

against the Kemalist state by challenging the secular and national character of the state. All these successive Islamic political parties were the same party, only under different names. The parties were closed down and had to recreate themselves in this manner due to Kemalist pressure and interruptions in the democratic process (Yavuz, 2003: 208). They shared uniform economic and social bases and came under the generic title of the National View (*Milli Görüş*) parties. The term "nation" (*millet*) does not stand here for ethnicity or civic nationality. It points to "the Qur'anic notion of "Millet" which often appears in association with the Prophet Abraham... [It] denotes a community that gathers around a prophet and the values he conveys" (Islamische Gemeinschaft Milli Görüş, n.d.; Yükleyen, 2012: 57–58). The term indirectly alludes to the *millet* system of the Ottoman Empire, referring to "the organized and legally recognized religious communities, such as the Greek Christians, the Armenian Christians, and the Jews, and by extension also to the different 'nations' of the Franks" (Lewis, 1961: 329).

Another commonality that the Islamic fundamentalist parties in Turkey shared is that their economic bases mostly consisted of small and medium-sized enterprises, which were in confrontation with big and monopoly capital in terms of accessibility to state resources such as credits and loans (Gülalp, 2001, 2003). The fundamentalist political parties found their social base in the traditional petty-bourgeois segments of society, including the lower middle classes, manufacturers, shopkeepers, artisans and peasants. From the late 1980s, this came to include professionals, students and intellectuals (Gülalp, 2001, 2003). The Islamic fundamentalist parties also successfully appealed, under the "Just Economic System", to the impoverished new middle classes

---

in Turkey. He founded his first political party, the National Order Party (*Milli Nizam Partisi*, MNP), in 1970 with the encouragement of Sheikh Mehmet Zaid Kotku, leader of the Nakshi-bendi order. After its closure following the military coup in 1971, Erbakan went to Switzerland, which was referred to by his supporters as *Hegira* (holy emigration) (Özdalga, 2002: 130). In 1972, Erbakan founded another party, the National Salvation Party (*Milli Selamet Partisi*, MSP), which took part in the coalition governments between 1974 and 1978. After the coup in 1980, the party and Erbakan himself were banned from politics. He returned to politics in 1987 as part of the Welfare Party (*Refah Partisi*, RP), which had been founded in 1983. Following the general elections in 1995, he formed a coalition government with the True Path Party (led by Tansu Çiller) in June 1996 and served as prime minister for only 11 months. After the military intervention in 1997, he was again banned and his party disbanded. The Virtue Party (*Fazilet Partisi*) was established in 1998 as a successor of the RP. However, Erbakan controlled the Virtue Party from behind the scenes until its dissolution in 2001. Erbakan died in February 2011 as the leader of the Felicity Party (*Saadet Partisi*, SP) (Erbakan, 2013a: 5–12; Elizabeth Özdalga. 2002; Saadet Partisi [The Felicity Party]. 2010a).

and to the proletariat whose living standards were deteriorating in the age of neoliberal globalisation. To a great extent, the Welfare Party had been instrumental in unifying petty entrepreneurs' and peripheral small capitalists' political interests, which were in opposition with the Kemalist state. However, the party only found room for manoeuvre in the late 1980s in the crisis of Turkey's state-led development under globalisation (Gülalp, 2001). After the 1990s, the small and medium-sized business sector, the lower middle classes, and a large portion of the working class were steadily mobilised through Islamic politics. This Islamic politics was able to boldly challenge elements of Kemalist principles of secularism and nationalism.

1 The Political Trajectory of Islamic Parties Led by Necmettin Erbakan in Turkey

1.1 *The National Order Party (1970–1971)*

Divergent class interests between the big bourgeoisie (which was tied to the import-substitution industrialisation model) and the peripheral small bourgeoisie, small merchants, craftsmen, and small farmers intensified within the Justice Party under Demirel in the late 1960s. This prompted a search for a new party with Islam as its unifying ideology (Gülalp, 2001: 435–436). Erbakan led the initial search for an alternative establishment in the interest of the peripheral capitalists by capturing a high-ranked position in the Union of Chambers. As the representative of small and medium-sized merchants, Erbakan was elected to the presidency of the Union of Chambers in 1969. The İstanbul and İzmir-based bourgeoisie responded by prompting the Minister of Commerce in the AP not to recognise his presidency, which was as a result suspended. This was the first confrontation between peripheral merchant capitalism and monopoly capitalism. Erbakan characterised this cleavage explicitly in terms of competition over access to state resources in the import-substitution industrialisation period:

> The economic system has been operating in favour of big urban merchants; thus the Anatolian merchants perceive themselves to be stepchildren. The lion's share in import quotas has been reserved for three to four urban merchants... The deposit in the Anatolian banks is deposited by Anatolian people but this money has been given to the big urban merchants in the form of credit. The union of chambers completely works via a comprador-masonic minority. Huge chambers are under the control of comprador commerce and industry. Thus, first of all, we claimed to join

the administrative board and put it at the disposal of Anatolian merchants and industrialists as well (as cited in Sarıbay, 2005: 576).

The National Order Party (*Milli Nizam Partisi*, MNP) was founded out of this economic cleavage by Erbakan and 17 companions on 26 January 1970. Even though the party promoted Islam, there was only one theologian, Hasan Aksay, among the founders. The founders were mainly middle class. Five were lawyers, four were merchants, three were constructors, two were engineers, and the remaining included a peasant, a retired state officer and a doctor (Çakır, 2012: 229–230).

The political principles embodied by the MNP were not perceived as right-wing policies by its key figures, although successive Islamic parties in Turkey embraced right-wing conservative agendas in the social arena. As Şevket Kazan (2012, personal communication) explains, the parties headed by Erbakan, which sharply differentiated themselves from right-wing and left-wing parties, had an explicit all-embracing Islamic ideology:

> The parties based on an ideology started in Turkey after the '60s. Previously, the parties were catch-all parties (*kitle partisi*). They were talking about some ideologies but they didn't know what these ideologies were. They claimed to be populist (*halkçı*) but they didn't know what populism was…Erbakan Hodja's National Order Party, however, was a party of an ideology (*fikir partisi*) … When he talked about the Justice Party, he nicknamed them "colourless people". Of course, colourless people mean the right-wing people… On the other hand, *Milli Görüş* (National View) was different. Indeed, our youngsters generated a slogan: "We are neither right nor left. We are on the path of right, on the path of right" (*Ne sağdayız ne solda. Hak yolundayız, hak yolunda*). This slogan was continuously repeated. After all, our position as a political party turned into *Milli Görüş*. It became a party of an ideology.

The party was also supported by the Islamic Orders (Tariqas), particularly by the İskender Pasha Order.[3] Mehmet Zahid Kotku, the leader of the Naqshbandi

---

3   Islamic orders have always been in politics since the transition to the multi-party system in 1945. During the single-party regime between 1923 and 1945, state persecution of the Islamic Orders led them underground. After 1945, religious orders such as Naqshbandi, Süleymancı, and Nurcu found an opportunity to increase their political influence in the elections by providing votes for the centre-right parties from the rural areas (Eligür, 2010: 52). The Democrat Party (*Demokrat Parti*, DP) under Adnan Menderes between 1950 and 1960 was a channel for Islamic groups to voice their demands. After the 1950 elections, the DP lifted some Kemalist

Order,[4] spoke pejoratively of politics and political power: "The Real Muslim is the one who annihilates the desire for power and leadership. Without annihilation of this desire, it is impossible for a Muslim to reach maturity" (as cited in Yaşar, 2005: 330). Despite this, he openly supported the establishment of the MNP:

> In the aftermath of the deposition of the Sultan Abdülhamid II, the country's governance has been taken over by masons, who are imitating the west. They are a minority. They cannot represent our nation. It is a historical duty to give the governance of the country to the real representatives of our nation by establishing a political party. Join this already belated endeavor (Eligür, 2010: 66).

The "Principal Objective" section of the party programme emphasised the fulfilment of a national temperament of high morality and virtue together with the development of morality which would bring order, peace, social justice, and happiness and salvation for the citizens. The party claimed to achieve the synthesis of material and spiritual development in the democratic legal order without vitiating national and moral values. It also proposed to reestablish a superior global civilisation (Sarıbay, 2005: 577). The party programme also underlined the importance of educational policy, which it claimed it could overcome underdevelopment and help the nation reach a point where it would be a model for humanity. Therefore, it was emphasised that the new generation should be "faithful, hardworking, patriotic, spirited in national morality, family order, and historical consciousness, righteous, devoted, and determined to scientific, technical progress for illuminating all of humanity" (as cited in Sarıbay, 2005: 578). In addition, the programme emphasised that an education system

---

bans on Islamic practices such as the call for prayer in Turkish and ban on Quran schools (Yeşilada. 2002b: 63). The party also stopped the persecution of Said-i Nursi, the leader of the Nur community, which in turn led to the dissemination of his ideas by his followers (Yavuz, 1997: 63). The followers of Nursi gathered around a "reading public" or "textual community" that "evolved into a major social movement, the Nur movement, with powerful economic, cultural and political capital" (Yavuz, 1997: 33). After the military intervention in 1960 and the closure of the DP, the support of Islamic orders in Turkey was channelled to the Justice Party (*Adalet Partisi*, AP) under Demirel (Yavuz, 2003a: 33). Appealing to the Nur movement vis-à-vis the Erbakan movement and using religion as an antidote to the increasing leftist movements in Turkey, Demirel tried to amalgamate personal religiosity with political secularism and the market economy (Yavuz, 2003a: 65).

4   Necmettin Erbakan, Korkut Özal, Hasan Aksay, Fehmi Adak and the ministers in various coalition governments during the 1970s were notable followers of İskenderpaşa Order before their rise in politics (Atasoy, 2005: 82).

based on morality and morals would be the primary strategy for the prevention of anarchist events and communism in Turkey (Erbakan, 1975: 30).

The party programme envisaged state intervention in the economy. It proposed that the state should establish economic and industrial institutions where the private sector cannot. However, once the economic efficiency of the institutions increases, they would be transferred to the private sector. By defending the enactment of a new Law for Encouragement for Industry (*Sanayii Teşvik Kanunu*), the party also supported the development of heavy industry for the whole country, as this was seen as a symbol of economic and political independence (Erbakan, 1975: 30).

However, the political life of the MNP was short. The Constitutional Court disbanded the party two months after the military coup since it was judged that the party violated the secular principles of the state. According to the unanimous 1971 Constitutional Court decision, the speeches of the party leaders, which included such statements as "the religion and the state are the same, they go hand in hand, it is impossible to separate them" (Anayasa Mahkemesi Kararlar Dergisi, Journal of Constitutional Court Decisions, 1972: 67) and the anthem for the youth "The only solution is Islam" (Anayasa Mahkemesi Kararlar Dergisi, Journal of Constitutional Court Decisions, 1972: 68) were considered to violate constitutional principles and the law on political parties.

1.2   The National Salvation Party (1972–1981)

The army was dissatisfied with the closure of the Islamic party in the anticommunist era. The state was able to control the Islamic brotherhoods through the MNP and aimed to use it against the left and communism in Turkey. According to Süleyman Arif Emre, former secretary general of the MNP and founder of the subsequent National Salvation Party (*Milli Selamet Partisi*, MSP), Rafet Ülgenalp, the general Secretary of the National Security Council, objected to the closure of the MNP and advocated religious education in order to launch a counterattack against "leftist anarchy" (Eligür, 2010: 68).

The MSP, successor to the MNP, was founded by Süleyman Arif Emre on 11 October 1972. The party immediately took part in the general elections. The 1973 election was actually a success for the party, which received 11.8% of the votes and 48 parliamentary seats thus becoming the third largest party after the CHP (186 seats) and the AP (150 seats). Erbakan became chairperson of the party in 1973 following the elections. The party participated in a coalition government in February 1974 with the Kemalist party, the CHP, headed by Bülent Ecevit. This enabled the party to hold the office of Deputy Prime Minister and the Ministries of State for Religious Affairs, Internal Affairs, Justice, Commerce, Food, Agriculture and Livestock, and Industry and Technology (Alkan, 1984:

82–83; Çakır, 2005: 547; 2012: 232). During their ten months' tenure in government, the most important political development was the 1974 Turkish invasion of Cyprus, which resulted in the partition of the island. According to Erbakan, the MSP was firmly determined to launch the operation despite the hesitations of the CHP, and succeeded in mobilising the government for the operation (Erbakan, 1991a: 59–77). He further suggested that the objective of the MSP in this military operation was to control the whole of the island (Erbakan, 1991a: 72).

In addition, Erbakan did not refrain from forming coalition governments headed by Demirel, despite having previously accused him of being "colourless", and a supporter of exploitation and usurer capitalism (Şevket Kazan, 2012, personal communication). Erbakan served as a Vice Prime Minister in the National Front governments led by Demirel between 1975 and 1977, and 1977 and 1978. In the June 1977 elections, the MSP only managed to get 8.56% of the vote with 24 seats (Alkan, 1984: 84).

Indeed, the period between 1973 and 1980 was a window of opportunity for the *political socialisation* of the Islamists with regard to the preparation and development of alternative state staffs. During that period, Erbakan prioritised the removal of the blockage against devout segments by Republican elites in the bureaucracy by assigning his supporters to key civil service posts. He also established civil society organisations such as associations for lawyers, crafts, local administrations, health, Islamic sciences, teachers, contractors, and businessmen to support his party. These institutions were, in one sense, alternative ministries (Çalmuk, 2005: 567).

During the 1970s, the visibility of Islamic organisations went hand in hand with Saudi influence in Turkey. Under the National Front governments, Turkey was eager to form an alliance with the Saudi Kingdom. In 1976, the country participated in one of the conferences led by the Saudi-based Muslim World League (*Rabıta al-Alam al-Islami,* or *Rabıta*), the Seerat Congress in Pakistan, and was represented by the state minister of the MSP, Hasan Aksay. Salih Özcan, owner of the Islamic magazine, *Hilal* (Crescent), and later MSP parliamentarian for Şanlıurfa and founder of the Islamic bank Faisal Finance,[5] was the Turkish representative in the constituent assembly of *Rabıta*, which was composed of 41 delegates.[6] Ahmet Gürkan, a parliamentarian between 1950 and

---

5 Tevfik Paksu with Salih Özcan was involved in the foundation of Faisal Finance (Atasoy, 2005: 151).
6 In his well-researched article, Hakan Köni traces the Saudi influence in Turkey in the 1970s. According to a book published by Rabıta, *A World Guide to Organizations of Islamic Activities in Cooperation with Rabıta*, some important associations and foundations of that time were the branches and representatives of Rabıta *in* Turkey. They included the Turkish National Student Union, Eastern Turkestan Immigrants Foundation, Istanbul University Islamic

1957 in the DP, later the Konya representative for AP between 1961 and 1965 and the President of the Turkish-Saudi Arabian Friendship Association, was also a founding member of *Rabıta* (Mumcu, 1993: 173). Korkut Özal, a former NSP parliamentarian and minister of agriculture and brother of Turgut Özal, was a consultant for the Islamic Development Bank. He established Al-Baraka Turk as a joint venture with Eymen Topbaş (Atasoy, 2005: 151; Mumcu, 1993: 180).

Besides the Saudi influence in Turkey, Turkish workers living in Europe, and Germany in particular, contributed to Erbakan's political movement from the 1970s (Sunier and Landman, 2015; Yükleyen, 2012). In 1976, the "Türkische Union in Europa" was founded. In 1985 it was renamed European National Vision Organisations (*Avrupa Milli Görüş Teşkilatları*, AMGT), whose headquarters was in Cologne (Sunier and Landman, 2015: 73–74; Yükleyen, 2012: 60–61). Since 1995, it has been referred to as *Islamische Gemeinschaft Milli Görüş* (IGMG), the Islamic Community of Milli Görüş, which "incorporates 514 mosque communities [in Europe], 323 of which are in Germany" (Islamische Gemeinschaft Milli Görüş, n.d.: 21). According to the Islamic Community of Milli Görüş, "[T]he teachings of the Qur'an and the Sunnah ... constitute the guiding principles for both the community and its [around 87,000] members" (Islamische Gemeinschaft Milli Görüş, n.d.: 3).[7]

The 1973 MSP election manifesto opposed integration with the European Community via the common market, arguing that the national industry together with merchants, craftsmen, and artisans would be destroyed by European competition (Milli Selamet Partisi 1973 Seçim Beyannamesi, 1973: 37–38). The party basically favoured industrialisation, the establishment of organised industrial districts and small industrial areas by the state, and the creation of a heavy military industry (Milli Selamet Partisi 1973 Seçim Beyannamesi, 1973: 44–51). The MSP proposed an "expanded private sector" (*yaygın özel sektör*), identified with the joint-stock company. A joint-stock company, which was composed of at least 100 shareholders and with no one having a share more than 5% of the company stock, could connect small businessmen to heavy industry under state control (Gülalp, 2003: 64).

Research Institute, Izmir National Turkish Foundation for Building and Sheltering Islamic Institutes, Cyprus Turkish Islamic Association, Turkish-Saudi Arabian Fellowship Foundation, Turkish-Saudi Arabian Parliament Fellowship Association, and Radio Turkish Voice in Australia (Köni, 2012: 106).

7 IGMG also built a "personal link" with the Islamic Community in Germany (IGD) known as the Muslim Brotherhood in Germany. Ibrahim al-Zayat, the head of the IGD since 1997, is married to the sister of Mehmet Sabri Erbakan, the head of the IGMG between 2001 and 2002 and the nephew of Necmettin Erbakan (Steinberg, 2010: 150).

The party programme championed moral and material development in its first article but proposed that moral development preceded material development (Alkan, 1984: 85). In fact, in his speech at the Turkish Grand National Assembly in 1973 regarding the third Five-Year Plan (1973–1977), Erbakan argued that even economic development depended on the advancement of morality (Erbakan, 2013f, Vol.5: 50). "Morality and Morals" were seen as an antidote to the threat of communism and materialism (Erbakan, 2013f, Vol.5: 54). It was believed that interest as a capitalist notion should be abolished and the poor should not be taxed (Erbakan, 2013f, Vol.5: 68–69).

The party was disbanded after the military coup in 1980 and Erbakan was banned from politics until 1987. It was with the Welfare Party (*Refah Partisi*, RP), a pro-Islamist party, that Islamic politics in Turkey reached its peak in the era of neoliberal globalisation.

1.3 *The Welfare Party (1983–1998)*

The municipal elections of 27 March 1994 and the general elections of 24 December 1995 marked a tremendous victory for the RP. In the former, it managed to capture 28 municipalities out of 75 provincial centres, including the metropolitan municipalities of İstanbul and Ankara, with a voting share of 19% (Ayata, 1996: 40). The RP more than doubled its vote share from the previous 8.74% in the municipal elections in 1989 (Figure 4) and more than tripled its number of constituents from 1.175 million in 1989 to 3.785 million in 1994 (Yerel Yönetimler Portalı [Local Administrations Portal], 2014).

The victory of the RP signalled an unmitigated failure for the Social Democratic Populist Party (*Sosyal Demokrat Halkçı Parti* SHP); in the municipal elections of 1989, the pro-Islamic party won the sizable municipalities of İstanbul, Ankara, Kayseri, and Diyarbakır (Yerel Yönetimler Portalı [Local Administrations Portal], 2014). With more than 5.3 million votes, the Islamic party received almost one fifth of the total votes in 1994 local elections. İstanbul and Ankara were taken over from Social Democrat municipality mayors. Likewise, the general elections in 1995 created the opportunity for the RP, which won 21.4% of the votes with 158 seats (Figure 5), to lead the country. The 1991 and 1995 general elections, which increased the votes of the Welfare Party (*Refah Partisi*, RP), revealed that crisis of Kemalism's modernist ideology and the failure of state-led development in the 1980s had created a vacuum, ready to be filled by just such an Islamic fundamentalist party. This was reflected in a zero-sum game between the social-democratic parties associated with Kemalism and the Welfare Party, in which the latter replaced the former in big cities in the 1990s (Gülalp, 2001: 442).

WAR OF MANOEUVRE BY ISLAMIC FUNDAMENTALISM 107

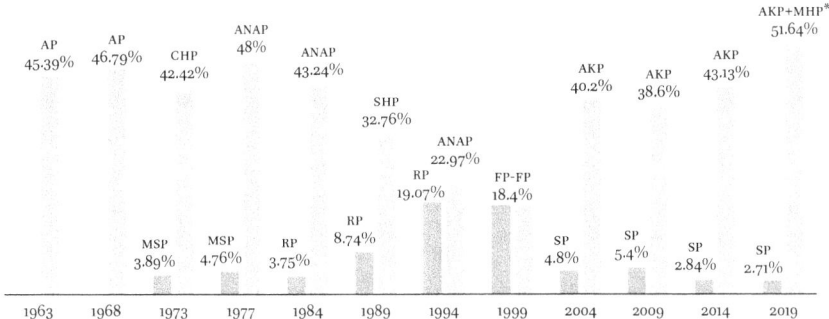

FIGURE 4 *Milli Görüş* parties and the party that won the municipal elections, 1963–2019
SOURCE: *YEREL YÖNETIMLER PORTALI* [LOCAL ADMINISTRATIONS PORTAL], (2014); TÜİK, (2005; 2009); YSK, (2014); SEÇIMHABERLER (2019).
* For 2019 local elections, AKP was in alliance with MHP under the name of People's Alliance (*Cumhur İttiakı*).

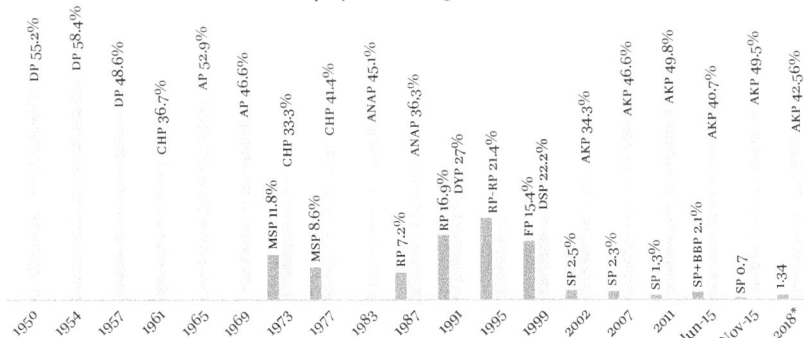

FIGURE 5 *Milli Görüş* parties and the party that won the general elections, 1950–2018
SOURCE: TÜİK (2012: 25; 94–95), YÜKSEK SEÇIM KURULU [THE SUPREME ELECTORAL COUNCIL], (2015); SEÇIMHABERLER (2019).
* For 2018 general elections, AKP was in alliance with MHP under the name of People's Alliance (Cumhur İttifakı), whereas SP was in alliance with Republican People's Party and Good Party under the name of Nation Alliance (Millet İttifakı).

The successive electoral victories of Refah revealed that a pro-Islamic party found fertile ground in Turkey during a *particular* time span between the late 1980s and throughout the 1990s (Figures 4 and 5). There were several causes for this Islamic revivalism. Neoliberal globalisation altered employment relations through the declining power of working class politics, the rise of small entrepreneurship, sweatshops and sub-contracting, which in turn provided a basis for Islamic fundamentalism (Gülalp, 2001: 437; 2003: 47). Precarious employment relations were coupled with the decreasing role of the state in providing for the social needs of the poor. As a result, Ziya Öniş, a Turkish political economist, suggests that

> The increasing incapacity of the nation state, especially the failure of the social democratic movements within the individual nation-state to cater explicitly for the needs of the poor, the disadvantaged or the excluded, has created a vacuum in political space. This vacuum has provided a gateway for the proliferation of political movements organised on the basis of extreme nationalism and religious fundamentalism (Öniş, 1997: 746–747).

The failure of state-led development in Turkey in the late 1970s and the intense process of globalisation had social costs. The effects of neoliberal globalisation on Turkey began to be experienced in the mid-1980s. According to a study by Michael Förster and Mark Pearson published by the OECD in 2002, Turkey witnessed a significant increase in income inequality—more than 12 per cent, similar to Italy—from the mid-1980s to the mid-1990s (Förster and Pearson, 2002: 9). Among the 21 OECD countries selected, Turkey ranked 20th with a 0.49 Gini coefficient value, before Mexico with a 0.53 coefficient value in the mid-90s (Förster and Pearson, 2002: 9; 38). Furthermore, real wages deteriorated in line with the structural adjustment programme. While labour productivity increased after the 1980s, this was not accompanied by an increase of real wages: "While value added made by the labour in the manufacturing industry increased 2.5 times between 1980 and 1997, increases in real wages have always fallen behind. In fact, wages in the manufacturing industry in 1997 were at 1980 levels" (Aydın, 2005: 130).

The reaction to the social consequences of neoliberal economic transformation was marked by mass protests led by organised labour between the late 1986 and 1991, commonly known as the Spring Demonstrations of 1989 and the Great Miners' March (Doğan, 2010). In 1990 there was an explosion in the number of strikes and of workers participating in strikes, with 458 strikes in 861 workplaces and 166,306 workers going on strike (Akkaya and Çetik, 1999: 155). In 1995 there were strikes in 3,369 workplaces with approximately 200,000 workers going on strike (Akkaya and Çetik, 1999: 155). As mass resentment reached its apex, the change in *Refah*'s political approach—from conveying an Islamic message (*tebliğ*) to concerning themselves with people's worldly affairs—played an important role in its electoral success. The party no longer proclaimed that "their rivals are 'bad Muslims'" but could now say they were "bad leaders/politicians" (Çakır, 1994: 81).

The rise of Refah coincided with the search by the impoverished masses for a new party to channel their discontent using Islamic rhetoric. Mainstream centre-left and centre-right political parties throughout the 1990s were unable to gain the public's trust in their ability to find solutions to social problems such as corruption, poverty, and unemployment (Delibas, 2015). In such a political environment, Refah gained the support of a wide range of economic and social bases, including the peripheral segment of the capitalist class, which consisted of small and medium scale and mostly provincial businesses, the professional middle class, and lastly the working class (Gülalp, 2001: 444–445; 2003: 59). In addition to the established working class who supported Refah, Gülalp (2001: 444) contends that the working class who had recently immigrated to the cities and had most difficulty finding secure jobs were influenced by the populist propaganda mobilised by this Islamic party.

The "global crisis of modernism and the rising challenges against the universal myths of Western civilization" also popularised an Islamic post-modernism (Gülalp, 2001: 442–443). Contemporary Islamist intellectuals such as İsmet Özel, Ali Bulaç, İlhan Kutluer, Ersin Gürdoğan, and Rasim Özdenören utterly rejected modern science, technology, and industry and proposed a return to the "Golden Age of the Prophet" (Toprak, 1993).[8] For instance, İsmet Özel, the most notable Marxist-turned-Islamist intellectual in Turkey, made the following criticism: "Commodities are sacred; brands and designer names have a special spiritual force; advertisement has replaced prayer" (as cited in Toprak,

---

8 The depiction of the past as an ostensible "Golden Age" is not only narrated by Turkey's Islamists but also by elderly Republicans. In *Nostalgia for the Modern: State Secularism and Everyday Politics in Turkey*, Esra Özyurek explains how the elderly Republicans recounted the early Republic as a "past utopia in which people were too innocent ... to look after their private interests, which could conflict with the collective goal" (Özyürek, 2006: 48). The representation of the past as such, Özyürek (2006) argues, is then used as a way to challenge the arguments that the early Republic was an authoritarian regime. Özyurek's book (2006) illustrates the way in which state ideology and Kemalist symbolism permeated the domestic and intimate worlds of individuals in the 1990s through their voluntary acts and market-based choices without any state imposition. The articulation of state ideology through the intimate worlds of individuals was the outcome of a process that commenced when neoliberal ideology "privatised" state ideology and imaginary and political Islam started to become visible in the public arena in the 1990s (Özyürek, 2006).

1993: 250). In his 1978 book, *Üç Mesele: Teknik-Medeniyet-Yabancılaşma* (Three Problems: Technology-Civilisation-Alienation), Özel argued that technology and civilisation are inseparable in as much as technology inevitably goes hand in hand with the civilisation it stems (Toprak: 1993: 253). "Alienation only comes into question with a civilised lifestyle; civilisation only exists with technology. Technology reproduces a civilisation in order to continue its presence. It is impossible to be civilised without being alienated. The relationship between these three issues is completely intrinsic" (İsmet Özel as cited in Aktay and Özensel, 2005: 785–786).

The economic base of the pro-Islamic party included small and medium-sized enterprises with MÜSİAD (The Independent Industrialists' and Businessmen's Association) as their umbrella organisation.[9] 1994 MÜSİAD's research report titled "Economic Cooperation Among Islamic Countries", pointed out the importance of cooperative actions among Islamic countries. Erol Yarar, the founding President of MÜSİAD (1990–1999), argued that Muslim countries lag far behind the industrialised nations (MÜSİAD, 1994a: 3). The report contended that Islam pays special attention to human problems and their solutions from a unique angle of brotherhood and cooperation. The inclusion of Quranic words such as *taawun* (cooperation) and *jem'ia* (society) and Hadiths reflected this endeavour (MÜSİAD, 1994a: 9).[10] Yarar (n.d.: 8) put a particular emphasis on a conservative social agenda, highlighting the characteristics of pre-industrial and agricultural societies such as family values, small- and medium-sized enterprises, and non-profit voluntary associations. Yarar (n.d.: 49) also stressed that economic development should not be the main objective of a Muslim. Economic development could only be a tool for God's sake (*Allah rızası*).

Another report that same year in December, titled *İş Hayatında İslam İnsanı* (Men of Islam in the Business World), offered an Islamic challenge to contemporary capitalism, albeit not to capitalism itself, and to its inevitable product—the modern capitalist man. This report, which provided an alternative societal

---

9   However, to the extent that small and medium-sized enterprises expanded and integrated with the world economy, they came to conflict with the economic agenda of Refah. An executive officer in MÜSİAD argued that The National Economy model was indifferent to direct integration with the world. Unless this transformation of the National View had taken place, it would have been impossible to attract foreign capital. (Selçuk Mutlu, 2012, personal communication).

10 Islamic references in the research report were quite visible in 1994. However, it is interesting to see that the organisation published a report with the same title "Economic Cooperation Among Islamic Countries" in 2008 in which direct reference to Islam and Islamic civilisation were less prominent.

programme, can be considered the political manifesto of ascendant small capital in the 1990s in Turkey. It suggested that an Islamic paradigm should be established and social relations should be based on *Homo Islamicus*. *Homo Islamicus* refers to servitude to Allah (*el-abd*) and being His successor on earth (*halifetullah fi'l-arz*) (MÜSİAD, 1994b: 21).

The outline of the individual paragon was complemented with a vision of the desired relations between, and attitudes of, employees and employers in the workplace. Sabahattin Zaim, in his article, idealised the attitudes and behaviours of employees and employers by urging that an employee should be proud of working physically and intellectually for his living (MÜSİAD, 1994b: 103). He suggested that:

> A Muslim man works in his job according to these principles: He is clean, his appearance (his dress) is nice, he is easygoing, he obeys the rules and instructions, he is swift. He enjoys his work performs his work thoroughly, controls and corrects it, he goes the whole hog, he works fast, he does a good job, he cooperates, he is open to criticisms, he works properly in the workplace ... he takes care of the equipment, raw material and stock as required, he properly uses the equipment and engine, he implements productive working methods, he complies with health and safety measures (MÜSİAD, 1994b: 103–104).

According to the report, an employer also had some responsibilities. By ensuring that the right of possession was guaranteed by the state, he could bequeath his legitimate wealth to his children and to the extent that the state would not interfere in economic activity, he was confident about the future and knew he would make his living from honest earnings (MÜSİAD, 1994b: 104).

MÜSİAD's 1996 report prefigured for the political aims of the Welfare Party when it came to power. Titled "A New Perspective of the World at the Threshold of the 21st Century", the report proposed the rebirth of Islamic civilisation. It questioned the causes of backwardness in the Islamic civilisation. Yet, contradictory views on wealth acquisition were present in the report. Presenting something of an Islamic version of Max Weber's Protestant work ethic, Erol Yarar was critical of the Islamic ascetic motto "living on very little" (*bir lokma, bir hırka*) because this resulted in the complete deterioration of business motivation (MÜSİAD, 1996: 39). On the other hand, the report offered subordination to God as a means to economic acquisition.

> For a Muslim individual, the main goal in this life is to get the consent of the Creator ... In this respect, economic development is not an end in

itself, but simply a means to this end. Our goal is to reach a high morality, by which we can make the world a happy and prosperous place where men and the whole creation can live in peace and harmony (MÜSİAD, 1996: 45).

The report argued that the decline of Western civilization was inevitable. Western civilisation was based on a rational, Cartesian philosophy and the rejection of value and existence (MÜSİAD, 1996: 50). Secularisation was strictly criticised by stressing that "[t]his overturning of religious values and their replacement by a secular 'morality'", transformed *homo sapiens* into "*homo brutalitas*" (brutal man) (MÜSİAD, 1996: 50–51). *Homo economicus* in the capitalist system had "transformed endless accumulation of capital into the sole goal of individual life" resulting in wars and the deterioration of ecological balance (MÜSİAD, 1996: 51).

2 The Just Economic System: a Petty-bourgeois Utopia in the Era of Neoliberalism

The Just Economic System (*Adil Ekonomik Düzen*) concept is essentially an expression of specific socio-political interests; it manifests the utopia of an "egalitarian petty-bourgeois society composed of individual entrepreneurs" (Gülalp, 2001: 440). Therefore, it provided a platform for the social classes and groups challenging their resentment of the Kemalist state while also tapping into their desire for an alternative state, society, and world order. The Just Economic System was a very influential doctrine in Turkey in the 1990s when the masses were searching for an alternative.

The booklet titled *Adil Ekonomik Düzen* (The Just Economic System) by Erbakan (1991b: 1) starts with a diagnosis of the economy stating that there is a "Slave Order" in Turkey. However, this order is not self-created; it is the result of "Modern Colonialism" in which Imperialism and Zionism are intentionally, deliberately, and systematically enforced. The booklet employs biological language to comment on the "slave order" in Turkey where "five microbes" in the usurious capitalist system exploit the masses. These microbes are (1) the interest microbe; (2) the unduly collected tax microbe; (3) the bank note microbe; (4) the foreign exchange microbe; and (5) the credit system microbe (Erbakan, 1991b: 3–4).

Following the diagnosis of the economic system in Turkey, it observed that the contemporary economic system nurtures world imperialism, Zionism, Israel, and comprador allies (Erbakan, 1991b: 4). The principal cure for the malady requires wiping these microbes out of the system; without this the healing of the body and the end of suffering are impossible (Erbakan, 1991b: 12).

The Just Economic System is in contradiction with Western civilisation, since the latter is the product of a mentality which praises force. This civilisation oppresses the masses through the twin brothers of communism and capitalism. According to Erbakan, both systems, which praise force, are basically the same. They are based on an oppressor-oppressed system. The only difference is that in communism the oppressive force is the political power while in capitalism the oppressive force is the economic power of a minority that controls capital (Erbakan, 1991b: 16).

The Just Economic System discusses the pros and cons of the capitalist and communist systems, highlighting itself as an alternative to both. On the one hand, the capitalist system includes profit, which is an incentivising factor. It nevertheless also includes interest (*faiz*), which is an instrument for cruelty and oppression. The capitalist system also includes free market competition; however, it cannot prevent the development of monopolies and trusts. On the other hand, the communist system opposes interest in principle; however, its rejection of profit and the right to property is in contradiction with human nature (Erbakan, 1991b: 18). By contrast, the Just Economic System is an ideal order—an amalgam of these two economic systems where the useful sides of capitalism and communism exist together (Figure 6).

The most significant principle of the Just Economic System is its rejection of interest, which is described as an unduly collected tax paid to imperialism and Zionism (Erbakan, 1991b: 43). It is proposed that the Salam contract (*selem senedi*)—an agreement in Islamic economics in which an advance payment is made for a specified commodity to be delivered on a specified future date—substitutes the interest gained. This substitution, according to the Just Economic System, is crucial for wiping out imperialism and Zionism. It is said they can be destroyed not by "the atomic bomb" but by "the Salam agreement" (Erbakan, 1991b: 41). It is further suggested that when the Salam agreement replaces the bonds of the usurious capitalist system, unjust exploitation will be prevented and cheapness will prevail over expensiveness (Erbakan, 1991b: 41–42). Ruşen Çakır, a leading researcher in Islamic politics in Turkey, suggests that the Just Economic System is an "intermediary stage for the transition to the "Order of Happiness", which emulates an Islamic order in the Golden Age (*Asr-ı Saadet*) of Prophet Mohammed and the Four Caliphs" (1994: 149).

The Constitution of the Just Order System proposes that "there shall not be interest gain", "the state shall not release fiat currency", and "the state shall not pass a tax law" (Erbakan, 1991b: 55). In this economic system, there will

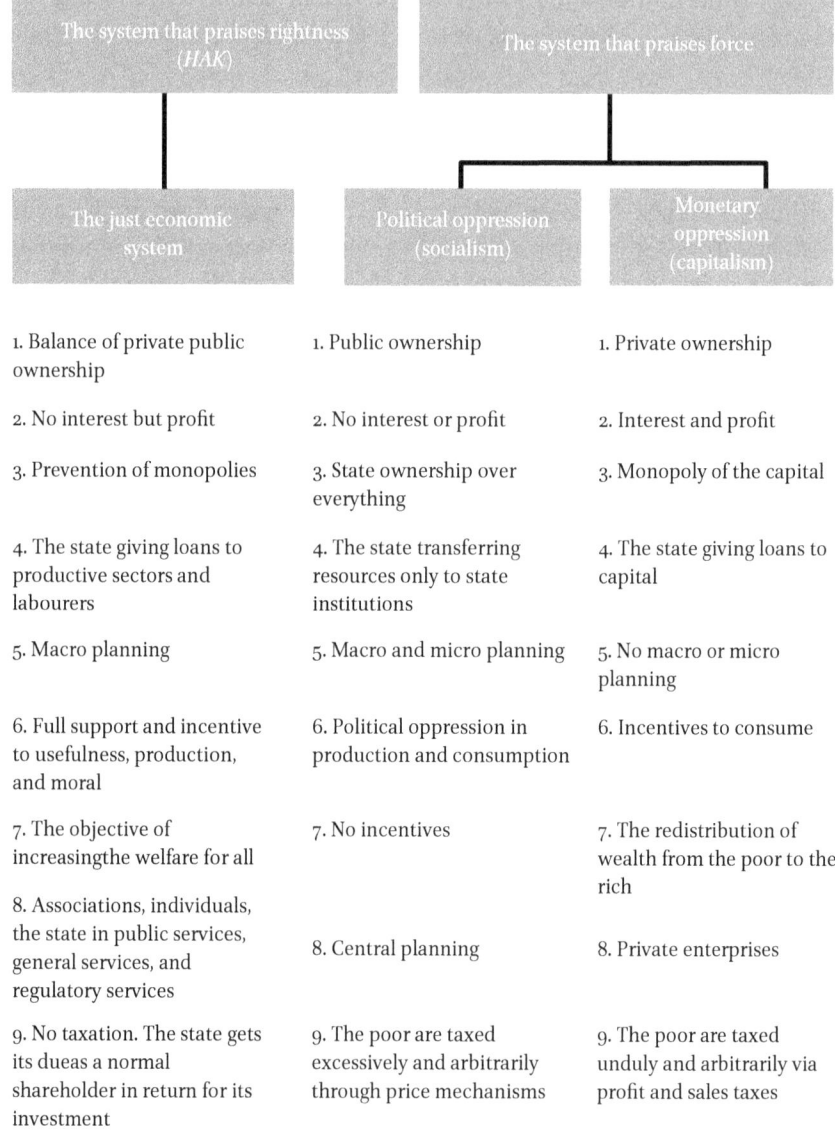

FIGURE 6   The characteristics of economic systems according to *Milli Görüş*
SOURCE: ERBAKAN (1991B: 79).

ostensibly be only one uniform tax and it will be taxed in terms of the type of production (Erbakan, 1991b: 59). The state, which is also a shareholder in production, claims its stake, equivalent to 20% of production (Erbakan, 1991b: 60).

The Just Order System divides the role of the state in the economy into two categories. First, the state carries out General Public Services such as security, administration, the courts system, energy procurement, water, construction and maintenance of roads and other public infrastructure, health, education, transport, and communication services. Second, the state carries out "Regulatory Services" for essential economic goods. For instance, a Wheat Waqf would replace the Turkish Grain Board so consumers and producers would buy and sell goods via this *waqf*, which does not aim make profit (Erbakan, 1991b: 22–23).

Under the Just Economic System, there would be no need for strikes and lockouts (Tuğal, 2007: 13); Erbakan paints a rosy picture of an economy which only produces prosperity and welfare:

> Because the economy keeps progressing and develops, the real problem will be to find an unemployed person. Because in the Just Order, there will be no person without a job. Because the economy develops in the Just Order, everybody will receive recompense for their work, which will serve for a decent life. As soon as the Just Order is adopted, the unemployed people who hang around in the coffeehouses consequently will have the opportunity and potential to gain higher wages. Contrary to a situation where unemployed people are looking for a job, entrepreneurs will in fact look for new employees in order to get credit [from the state] (Erbakan, 1991b: 36).

The Just Economic System is not only concerned with the economy. It is concurrently presented as a cure for any problems in moral development of human beings and society. It is claimed that interest gain leads to moral corruption since it makes the rich richer and the poor poorer (Erbakan, 1991b: 84–85). It is argued that if a person has not been morally edified, he is easily pushed to drugs, alcoholism, gambling, and other moral corruption (Erbakan, 1991b: 85). In the capitalist order, bribes, squandering of money, drug use, alcoholism, gambling, mafia, criminality, general moral corruption and AIDS all proliferate (Erbakan, 1991b: 85). However, the following five points were proposed to counter the "five microbes": (1) "The Just State Order" should replace "the Order of Slavery" which Imperialism and Zionism established and have maintained; (2) The "exploitative system" of the usurious capitalist order should be replaced by the "Just Economic System"; (3) A "national, powerful, rapid, and expansive development" should be implemented, (4) The "devout personnel" are a prerequisite for this development; and (5) "A wise person" knows how to discipline his or her desires (Erbakan, 1991b: 90–92).

3   The National View (*Milli Görüş*) as Common Ideational Ground for Islamic Parties

According to Erbakan (1975: 27), *Milli Görüş*, arising from the glorious Ottoman legacy, is "the spirit and essence of our nation which conquered İstanbul, thus ushered in a new age and brought the old one to an end, surrounded Vienna, won the Battle of Gallipoli, waged a War of Independence, and most recently made miracles again in Cyprus in 1974". This glorious legacy reminded people of wars and started "when the community confronted a thousand years ago the deceitful character of the Crusaders which constituted the overall might of the West" (Erbakan, 1975: 18). In order to repulse Western attacks on Muslim soil, the power of faith was an instrument to mobilise the emboldened Muslims against external aggression. Erbakan (1975: 17) agreed on the special attributes of the Islamic community (*Ummah* in Arabic) boasting that "Our community is the precious and immaculate chosen community of Allah in the track of supporting rightness (*hak*), attaining goodness, and preventing evil".

> It is such a community which established admirable civilisations, illuminated humanity, taught them what morality and virtue mean, controlled and regulated the world order. Until the modern age, it fought with the world nations not one to one but as a whole and prevailed over the whole. In gaining these victories, it was surely beyond doubt that faith constituted the preeminent source of its power. At the same time, in the material field, it outranked the whole world, guided humanity. It was the flag of civilisation. It was advanced in knowledge, science, technology, and education. Specifically, moral and spiritual supremacy was the reason for its success in every field. In addition to its supremacy for a long time in the field of divine sciences, it guided the whole of humanity in the material sciences by its constructive, exploratory, and constitutive faculty. It is our community that founded the material sciences of which the West is now able to take better advantage than we who established them as sciences and were the owners of them (Erbakan, 1975: 17).

That this community unacceptably lagged behind Western civilisation, according to Erbakan (1975: 18), was mainly due to the fact, that after the enemy failed to defeat our nation by external attacks, a different strategy was adopted in which "non-communal movements" led to the material and spiritual decay of the empire. This distinct strategy was embodied in the Westernisation process in the Ottoman Empire, which led to the neglect of the authentic laws, institutions, and customs of the nation. Imitation of the West was severely criticised in Erbakan's book *Mukaddesatçı Türk'e Beyanname* (Declaration to the Religious Turk), published in 1969. It argues that the Westernisation process since the 19th century resulted in the abandonment of the Muslim Turks' personality and nobility, "thus bringing to [European] knees the Turk who for centuries could not be defeated by the crusaders and external blows" (as cited in Ahmad, 1991: 14–15).

The remedy, it was argued, can only be found in *Milli Görüş* since the latter represents "the national fabric" (Erbakan, 1975: 28). "The liberal view" and "the leftist view" in Turkey were, according to Erbakan, based on external sources and do not fit Muslim Turks' body. That is to say, while the CHP's leftist view took its sources from inefficient socialist views in the West which restricted freedoms, the AP's liberal view was inspired by the exploitative, usurer capitalist views (Erbakan, 1975: 28). In order to realise "All-Powerful Turkey Again" (*Yeniden Büyük Türkiye*), a spiritual development, which would pursue material development in technology and science, was to guide Turkey with a motto of "First of all, Morality and Morals" (*Önce Ahlak ve Maneviyat*) (Erbakan, 1975: 17–29).

Another rigid issue in *Milli Görüş* is its undeniable obsession with "Jewish-Masonic institutions", wrapped in anti-Semitic rhetoric where the "terms Jew-Zionism-Israel were intermixed freely" (Bali, 2013: 184).[11] Zionism is frequently portrayed as a transcendental power, which manifests itself in every turning point of history against Islam. Zionism, for instance, is seen as preventing the Islamic world from reviving:

> As an ideology, Communism is one arm of Zionism, and capitalism is the other. Actually, Zionism wants to rule the world and manipulates these two arms according to its will… The purpose of the Yalta Conference was to divide the world in the name of Zionism; since then some new forces have appeared and they want to consolidate this division in Vladivostok. However, the revival of the Islamic world in the last ten years has changed the situation. Then what happened? The rhetoric of détente and rapprochement between East and West in Helsinki appeared. What does it mean? It means 'there is a revival in the Islamic world, let's stop fighting each other and find a solution to this problem (as cited in Alkan, 1984: 94).

---

11 Anti-Semitic views were more obvious in the case of Cevat Rifat Atilhan, the founder of *İslam Demokrat Partisi* (the Islamic Democratic Party) in 1951. Showing a personal interest in Nazi Germany, he translated anti-Semitic classics such as *The Protocols of the Elders of Zion* and several books such as *Zionism and the Danger of Surrounding Islam, Turkish Son: Know Thine Enemy!, Jewish Spies on the Palestinian Front*, and *Freemasons: How They Have Conspired to Destroy Turkish Nationalism and Islam* (Brockett, 2009: 446).

The obsession with "Jewish-Masonic" institutions is still a hot issue for *Milli Görüş* followers. For instance, Şevket Kazan, Refah's Minister of Justice in between 1996 and 1997, vividly mentioned a "Jewish focus" in the USA which controls elections and ultimately US foreign policy through a Jewish-Zionist lobby group, the Washington Institute, whose aim is to establish a "Greater Israel" stretching from the Nile to the River Euphrates (Şevket Kazan, 2012, personal communication). Not surprisingly, Erbakan (1991b: 1) said that the centre of Zionism is Wall Street, New York.

4 The Islamic Alternative to the Kemalist State

Erbakan waged a frontal attack on the Kemalist state, which had historically led Turkey on the path of Westernisation. Erbakan's political strategy concentrated on reversing Westernisation and rejecting the liberal euphoria of the 1990s. According to Erbakan, using the West as a reference point was a major mistake. In his book, *Türkiye'nin Temel Meseleleri* (The Fundamental Problems of Turkey), he states that even though the nation sought remedies in the West over the past 200 years, by adopting Western education, family structure, state organisation and judicial system, it neither became European nor was it able to protect its Muslim identity (Erbakan, 1991a: 27–28). This Westernisation process, he claimed, continued in modern Turkey, its application to the European Community in 1987 being the "last chain of the endeavour of the Republic to become a European country" (Erbakan, 1991a: 28). In terms of its economic relations with the West, Erbakan objected to integration with the European Community, seeing it as a manifestation of the "denial of our Muslim identity and hypothecating of our past, history, culture, art, and economy to the European Community" (Erbakan, 1991a: 28).

Erbakan (1991a: 42) attributes to the European integration process a religious plot, arguing that the only objective of the European Union is the victory of the Crucifix over the Crescent. In one of his speeches in the Turkish Grand National Assembly, he presented economic integration with the European Community via the common market as a Zionist trick. Echoing the anti-Semitic work *The Protocols of the Elders of Zion*, he speculated that European integration was the consequence of an insidious plan by Theodor Herzl[12] in

---

12   Theodor Herzl (1860–1904) is known as founder of modern political Zionism who organised the First Zionist Congress in Basel in 1897 and forthwith founded the Zionist Organisation. He wrote a book *Der Judenstaat*–meaning "state of Jews" which was published in 1896 and commonly known in its English version "The Jewish State" (Achcar, 2011: 9).

which Zionists aimed to rule the world and establish a system of usury, which Masonic institutions pushed to implement (Erbakan, 1971: 65). The criticism of the European integration in 1971 was that

> In its illusionary form, the common market is supposed to commence with the integration of six Catholic countries. However, in reality, the common market is an institution that relies upon Zionists. Despite their low population, Zionists established capital and a usury rule in order to sovereign the world. They have aimed to make the masses of the world work in their Zionist capital, and they developed it in the West (Erbakan, 1971: 64).

Antipathy to the West was a ubiquitous issue for Erbakan in the 1990s. In his book *Adil Ekonomik Düzen* (Just Economic Order), he proposes the establishment of an Islamic Customs Union against the Catholic European Community. He notes that

> There two basic faults in the pillars of the Treaty of Rome. One is that its cultural pillar is based on the ancient Roman civilisation, in other words, the mentality "that praises oppression". The second fault is that the economic system is taken from capitalism. This pillar does not bring felicity. It brings oppression, crises, and social explosions for the masses (Erbakan, 1991b: 93).

Another alternative political project targeting the Kemalist state and its tutelary democracy pivoted around the criticism of Western representative democracy. It is undeniable that Turkey had never been a fully-fledged representative democracy under the Kemalist state, but rather a tutelary democracy in which the military controlled the key pillars of the state. Nevertheless, Erbakan's perception of representative democracy was as problematic as the military's. Even though Erbakan tentatively attacked the principle of Western representative democracy, his vision of representative democracy had little to do with the Schumpeterian procedural model but was more related to a meritocratic rule in the pursuit of rightness (*hak*). The party programme and the charter of the National Order Party, described one aspect of democracy as the way in which the most wise and competent people, who are the most respectful to the right (*hak*), would serve the nation (*millet*, in the sense of "community") (TBMMc, n.d.: 5). Another aspect of democracy was regarded as having opportunities that would lead to the pursuit and fulfilment of the rightness (*hak*) for the most just, appropriate, and scientific ways (*ilmi usuller*) of administration

(TBMMC, n.d.: 5). According to Erbakan, democracy should be understood as "the product of the development of people on the path of virtue" and "bodily, rambling freedoms should not be aimed for" (TBMMC, n.d.: 5). Democracy, according to the party's view, can only be established and developed in a community where virtue and morality dominate; otherwise; democracy is degenerated and becomes a tool for anarchy (TBMMC, n.d.: 6). In *Türkiye'nin Meseleleri ve Çözümleri* (Problems of Turkey and Their Solutions), published in 1991 as the party programme of Refah, Erbakan (2013c: 384) continued his views on representative democracy by claiming that "Democracy is a tool. It is not an objective. The objective is to establish the Order of Happiness (*Saadet Nizamı*)". This is due to the potential of democracy to elect an unexceptional person would lead to an "Order of Oppression" (*Zulüm Nizamı*) (Erbakan, 2013c: 384). Ruşen Çakır argues that this instrumentalist view of representative democracy shows "Refah is neither a follower of Sharia nor a democrat because Refah is both a self-styled follower of Sharia and a self-styled democrat" (1994: 129). Çakır uses the term "theo-democracy" to specify the symbiosis of theocracy and democracy in Refah (1994: 129).

Indeed, theo-democracy is used by Maudūdi, founder of the Jamaat-e-Islami, and subordinates popular legitimacy for the suzerainty of Allah. In *The Islamic Law and Constitution*, first published in 1955, Maudūdi coined the phrase as describing a kind of popular vicegerency. According to Maudūdi's explanation, the Islamic theo-democracy is

> a divine democratic government, because under it the Muslims have been given a limited popular sovereignty under the suzerainty of God. The executive under this system of government is constituted by the general will of the Muslims who have also the right to depose it. All administrative matters and all questions about which no explicit injunction is to be found in the *shari'ah* are settled by the consensus of opinion among the Muslims. Every Muslim who is capable and qualified to give a sound opinion on matters of Islamic law, is entitled to interpret the law of God when such interpretation becomes necessary. In this sense the Islamic polity is a democracy… [I]t is a theocracy in the sense that where an explicit command of God or His Prophet already exits, no Muslim leader or legislature, or any religious scholar can form an independent judgement, not even all the Muslims of the world put together, have any right to make the least alteration in it (1967: 148).

The theo-democratic position of *Milli Gazete* (the National Newspaper), the semi-official newspaper of the party since 1973, on representative democracy turns out to be more radical than Erbakan's views. The motto of the newspaper since its foundation has been "The Rightness (*Hak*) has come and the Wrongness (*Bâtıl*) has passed away"; this was also used as one of the main slogans of the National Salvation Party. A closer look reveals that this is a direct quotation from the Surah *Al-Isra* of the Quran (Qur'an, 17:81).

Correspondingly, some hardliners in the newspaper such as Necdet Kutsal discredited democracy as a heretical regime antithetical to the order of Islam. As the newspaper put it, Islam's order of salvation argues against the follies of people such as communism, capitalism, socialism, and democracy (Alkan, 1984: 92–93). Others followed the same logic on democracy: The hardliners asked for the rule of the Quran, since the principle of the sovereignty of the people contradicts Islam (Alkan, 1984: 92–93). Even though popular sovereignty was a contested issue for *Milli Görüş* parties, the democratic aspirations of the Kurds and the impact of liberalisation after the end of the Cold War in Turkey compelled Refah to address the Kurdish problem. A Kurdish report prepared by the İstanbul Provincial Administration of the party in 1991, which was headed by Recep Tayyip Erdoğan, proposed to use the word "Kurdish" and articulate their agonies and problems (Çakır, 1994: 153). The report further suggested challenging the official ideology which had implemented "denialist, assimilationist, oppressive" policies with regards to the Kurdish problem for 75 years (Çakır, 1994: 153).

The pragmatic articulation of the Kurdish problem was blended with an Islamic vision in which the solution was said to be the establishment of an Islamic Unity led by Turkey and the fulfilment of a Just System (Çakır, 1994: 157). The reason for the protracted Kurdish problem in Turkey was attributed to the renouncement of "our national and religious values" and adoption of "denialist, racist, and materialist politics", against which the "Islamic brotherhood" binding Turkish and Kurdish people was frequently stressed (Erbakan, 2013b: 169).

During a rally in 1994 in Bingöl, a city in Kurdish region of Turkey, Erbakan attacked Turkish nationalism, one of the pillars of the Kemalist state. He was tried in the Diyarbakır State Security Court in 2000 and was sentenced to prison for one year for violating Article 312 of the Turkish Penal Code, which forbids "inciting hatred based on ethnic, religious, regional or linguistic differences" (*Ntvmsnbc*, 17 July 2000). In this rally, he said that

> When starting school in the morning assembly, the children of this country used to begin with "in the name of God". You changed that and made them say: "I'm Turk, I'm brave, I'm hard-working". On the other hand, when you said that, a Muslim of the Kurdish origin may feel it is within

his right to say: "Oh really, in this case I am a Kurd, I'm braver, I'm more hardworking". In the near future, when the Turkish Grand National Assembly is controlled by Muslims, everyone will get his equal right without any bloodshed (as cited in Cook, 2007: 112).

Another line of criticism of the Kemalist state concerned its statist-secular form. As his alternative, Erbakan offered a completely pragmatic and one-sided form of secularism in which he championed "freedom of thought, freedom of conscience, [and] freedom of worship. [Secularism] means that no one could oppress anybody due to his/her faith" (Erbakan, 2013b: 171). In the party programme of the MNP, secularism was succinctly defined as the guarantee of freedom of thought and faith. It stated that the party is against the use of secularism as oppression of religion and disrespect of the devout. Secularism was also supported in the party programme of the MSP, since it was a guarantor of freedom of thought and belief. However, it was noted that it should not be used as a means for suppressing people on the grounds of their thoughts and beliefs (Alkan, 1984: 85).

Erbakan juggled the concept of secularism by ignoring the crucial element in *Laiklik* (*laïcité* in French): the separation of religion and state. *Laiklik* has been comparably practiced in Islamic jurisprudence in order to set out "the existence and acceptance of divergent Islamic schools and sects" which implement particular forms of worship in different ways (Erbakan, 2013b: 171). Therefore, according to Erbakan (2013b: 172), *laiklik* refers to "acceptance of the existence of others" and the presence of people who think differently. However, he claimed, the implementation of secularism in Turkey went against this principle, because *laiklik* had been implemented as "hostility to Islam" and a "tool for oppression".

Erbakan never explicitly stated a desire for the establishment of a political party based on Sharia. This was, indeed, impossible because of the existing laws in Turkey. However, the youth organisation The Raiders (*Akıncılar*), which was founded in 1976, chanted for the abolition of the irreligious state and the establishment of an Islamic government (Ozgur, 2012: 124). Erbakan stated that he sought to give secularism its "real meaning"—freedom of thought, conscience and faith. In 1972, MSP offered to make a "scientific description" of secularism in which the related articles in the "Universal Declaration of Human Rights" recognising freedom of thought, conscience and religion would be embedded into the constitution (Erbakan, 2013e: 351).[13]

---

13   For Erbakan, science refers to science (*ilim*) stemming from the recognition of *Allah* (2013b: 49).

Despite Erbakan's ambiguous views on secularism, he directly criticised Article 163 of the Penal Code of Turkey. According to the 1999 Human Rights Watch report, "Violations of Free Expression in Turkey", Article 163 of the Penal Code of Turkey was used to prosecute Islamists until its abolition in 1991 after the passage of the Anti-Terror Law (Human Rights Watch, 1999).[14] In *Milli Görüş*, Erbakan (1975: 54) proposed to annul Article 163 of the Criminal Code and replace it with a Law on the Protection of Human Rights in order to implement freedom of thought, conscience, and worship.

Similarly, when questioned in a 1991 interview on the possibility of establishing a Sharia party Erbakan stated that the imitators of the West and imperialism would never provide the full implementation of freedom of thought and worship in Turkey (Erbakan, 2013d: 15). In addition, according to Erbakan, Islam had not been fully implemented in some Muslim countries such as Pakistan and Sudan because Islam is all-embracing; it encompasses a whole system of justice and right (*hak*). It is impossible to implement Islam, he stated, "under the exploitative and servile system" by enforcing only a small number of penalty clauses as implemented in Sudan under Nimeiri (Erbakan, 2013d: 17).[15,16]

---

14 Before its abolition, Article 163 was in use to penalise those who, "contrary to secularism, make propaganda or suggestions with the purpose of adopting, even partially, the basic social, economic, political, or judicial structures of the State based on religious principles or beliefs or with the purpose of obtaining political benefits or personal influence by making use of religion or religious sentiments or sacred things…" (Human Rights Watch, 1999).

15 Gaafar Niemeiri took power in Sudan after a military coup in 1969 and ruled the country until 1985. He initially pursued socialist and Pan-Arabist policies in the 1970s, but in the 1980s he formed an alliance with the Muslim Brotherhood and invited Hasan al-Turabi, the leader of Sudan's Muslim Brothers, and later the founder of National Islamic Front (NIF), into his government. In 1983, he enforced Sharia and Sudan was declared an Islamic state. In the following years, "decisive justice courts" were established, Islamic criminal punishments such as amputations (*hudud*) were applied, income tax was replaced with *zakat* (an alms tax), and banks were "Islamised" (Hale, 1997: 236–237).

16 Democracy and secularism continue to be a debated issue in *Milli Gazete*. Mehmet Şevket Eygi, one of its prominent Islamist writers, juggles with the concepts of democracy and secularism, giving the example of the UK, where religion and state are not separated and the ruler is also the head of the religious and national church. The UK is praised since even though it is not a secular state, it is the most democratic state in the world where Muslims live freely, dauntlessly, and comfortably. It is further stated that secularism is not a condition of democracy and republicanism since none of the universal and fundamental human rights declarations, agreements, and texts have advertised secularism as a value, duty or right (Eygi, November 26, 2012b). On the other hand, democracy is only acknowledged to the extent that it can be used as a tool for a smooth transition from a non-Islamic order to an Islamic one (Eygi, March 28, 2012a).

5 The Military Intervention of 28 February 1997

In the general elections of December 1995, Refah won 21.4% of the votes and became the leading party in the parliament. The anti-Western attitude and petty-bourgeois utopian economic programme of the Just Economic System intimidated the big capitalists. Just three days after the elections, TÜSİAD invited the centre-right parties to reconcile and form the government (*Milliyet*, 27 December 1995). The army, whose interests were closely tied to the big capitalists, were from the very beginning determined to hold off the popular majority under the pretext of opposing Islamic fundamentalism. As Güven Erkaya, the Commander of the Turkish Naval Forces the time, said in an interview in *Milliyet* in January 1996 that the military would not turn a blind eye to the transformation of the country's secular regime into a system based on Sharia by a political party which exploits democracy even if it achieves a majority of the votes. It was threatened that, if needed, this would be prevented by circumvention of the rules of democracy; because indeed, the people wanted and asked this of the army (TBMMb, 2012: 946).

For all that, the Refah-Yol cabinet was formed in July 1996 between Refah and the True Path Party (*Doğru Yol Partisi*, DYP), led by Tansu Çiller. This followed the failure of a short-lived (three months) centre-right coalition government formed by ANAP and DYP. During the Refah-Yol government, which lasted only about one year, a serious political scandal, the *Susurluk* Scandal, erupted in a car crash in November 1996. This incident uncovered the intricate relationship between the state (Hüseyin Kocadağ, the former deputy chief of İstanbul Police Department), the government (Sedat Bucak, a parliamentarian from DYP) and the convicted fugitive Abdullah Çatlı, as all three were revealed to have been in the same car (TBMMb, 2012: 950). In the context of the existence of the "deep state" tradition in Turkey, Deputy Prime Minister Tansu Çiller said that both people who killed others on behalf of the state and people who were killed on behalf of the state are honourable (*Milliyet*, 27 November 1996). The Susurluk Scandal prompted nation-wide protests popularised with the slogan "One minute's darkness for perpetual light" (*Sürekli Aydınlık İçin Bir Dakika Karanlık*) (TBMM, 2012: 952).

The military was able to overcome the Susurluk Scandal "by calling the social base of political Islam a danger to internal security" (Söyler, 2013: 318). In practice, the military had the power to define what "internal security" meant as it saw fit in its role as the "ultimate guardian of the republic", which allowed it to intervene in politics to varying degrees (Cizre, 2003). The army tried to eliminate the state's hegemonic crisis by designating Refah a national threat. Güven Erkaya, the Commander of the Turkish Naval Forces at that time, stated that "extreme religious currents do pose an important threat to the future of the country. İrtica [reactionism] has become a more particular threat than the PKK" (Milliyet, 12 August 1997). However, the Kemalist state, in all respects, was at the peak of its hegemonic crisis in the 1990s (Kurkcu, 1996). This crisis was compounded by the disintegration of Kemalist nationalism—"No other nation but Turks exist in Turkey"—especially after 1991 when approximately one million Kurds arrived in Turkey following Saddam Hussein's crushing of a popular uprising in Iraqi Kurdistan. A further problem was the weakening of Kemalist secularism, which first manifested itself after the coup of 1980 in the transition to a conciliatory approach of the military towards Islam; this occurred through a political project called Turkish-Islamic Synthesis and finally in the rise of Refah in 1996 (Kurkcu, 1996).

In addition, the traditional ally of the military, big capital was opposed to the economic policies of Refah, which aimed to block it from lending money to the state through government debt securities. This also sparked political tension within the coalition, particularly between Necmettin Erbakan and Ufuk Söylemez, the treasury secretary in the DYP. While Erbakan exhorted that the Treasury should not issue government debts, Söylemez insisted that government borrowing is the requirement of the market and would continue (İnan, 1997). Erbakan's position was supported by the Refah Minister of Justice Şevket Kazan, and explained in his four-volume book *Refah Gerçeği* (The Refah Reality). He argued that Refah's economic initiatives to reduce domestic borrowing threatened the interests of the big capitalists (Kazan, 2003, Vol.3: 28). According to the "pool system" (*havuz sistemi*), all the autonomous incomes of public institutions would be pooled in one account and capital would be used as needed; in this way the dependence of the Treasury on loans offered by rentiers at high interest rates would be reduced (Toker, 2008: 214). The Minister of Finance in the Refah-Yol cabinet Abdüllatif Şener argued:

> The attacks against the government and the developments succeeding the February 28 events were essentially attacks by a group of capitalists, since we implemented an [economic] policy in which the group of capitalists, especially the rentier sectors, would be disturbed... [The policy meant that] interest rates were perpetually decreased. Before February 28, interest rates nearly equalled the inflation rate... We achieved this with the pool system (as cited in Toker, 2008: 213–214).

The clash of interests between Refah, favouring small and medium-size enterprises, and big business turned into open hostility. Şevket Kazan (2003, Vol.3: 31) declared that

TÜSİAD is the main actor in the commercial exploitative order in Turkey. Koç [Holding] sits in the pilothouse of this order… You realise from a short investigation that the ones who hold the reins are the Doğan, Bilgin, and Uzan groups.

TÜSİAD was named the "Duchy of İstanbul" due to its relationship with the state. Şevket Kazan (2003, Vol.3: 31) stated that approximately 400 businessmen of the association could develop their enterprises by lending money to the state in the continuing economic crisis, and thereby become the country's "House of Lords". Even Özal's period was severely criticised:

> In Turkey, the architect and the first implementer of domestic borrowing is Turgut Özal. Özal started the domestic borrowing through the 24 January decisions, even in the 1980s. The owners of the big capital, who had become the economic duchy before [the 1980s] through the incentives and excessive loans they got from the state, gained more than they dreamed of in this new path to making easy money… Since 1995, it was seen that the percentage of interest revenues of the biggest 500 industrial enterprises in Turkey to their net accounting profits has risen by 87% [and] these establishments have neglected industrial production and leaned towards the rentier economy which was more profitable (Kazan, 2003, Vol. 2: 195).

On 28 February 1997, after a meeting of the National Security Council (NSC), the military issued an 18-point list of policy recommendations to the government. The list included extending compulsory education from five years to eight years and curbing the activities of religious schools and private Quran courses, which were believed to foster anti-secular values (Narli, 2000: 115). Unlike the former military interventions of 1960, 1971, and 1980, the military increasingly felt it necessary to have public consent and support rather than initiating a direct, brutal and sudden appropriation of political power. Therefore, direct appeals to the organised segments of urban-secular groups such as business, academia, the media, the judiciary, and civil society organisations—even holding briefing meetings with them to elucidate the extent and the magnitude of the Islamic threat (Cizre-Sakallioglu and Cinar, 2003: 322)—aimed at garnering public legitimacy for the military's intervention. Güven Erkaya describes the new political tools of the military in galvanising the public:

> We hold briefings to inform the public. The great part of our essential efforts is to persuade the deputies. They should principally realise that the

regime is under threat... We expected that the members of the parliament would politically resolve the issue. [However] they didn't get the messages we gave, they didn't want to get it. Now, we implement the second alternative. We create a public opinion in civil society. (as cited in Bayramoğlu, 2009: 99, fn. 57).

Nonetheless, the reason why the military decided against seizing power through a coup was that they had reckoned with the possible political and social costs, having taken into account the Algerian scenario.[17] In addition, the US administration opposed a military coup. Madeleine Albright, United States Secretary of State between 1997 and 2001 under the Clinton administration, warned the Turkish military to stay within constitutional limits and resolve the problems with the civilian government (Çongar, 1997).

The political strategy of mobilising civil society instead of staging a coup was successful to the extent that the "Civil Solidarity Group", composed of *Rıdvan Budak*, the Head of DİSK (Confederation of Progressive Trade Unions of Turkey), *Derviş Günay*, the Head of TESK (Confederation of Chamber of Merchants and Craftsmen of Turkey), and *Bayram Meral*, the Head of Türk-İş, sent a letter to all deputies stating their adherence to "the Republic of Turkey established by Grand Atatürk" and the principles of the secular and social state governed by the rule of law (*Milliyet*, 7 March 1997). In May 1997, TİSK (Turkish Confederation of Employer Associations) and TOBB (The Union of Chambers and Commodity Exchanges of Turkey) participated in the "Group", making a joint declaration stating their commitment to the principles and revolutions of Atatürk, the gains of the Republic and their preservation at any cost. They determined that the country was headed towards internal disorder and called to form a new government that could establish unity, solidarity and friendship (*Sabah*, 22 May 1997).

6 The Rupture in Islamic Politics

According to Hüseyin Kıvrıkoğlu, the Chief of the Turkish General Staff between 1998 and 2002, *irtica* was the "first prominent threat" for Turkey, and the

---

17 When the Islamic Salvation Front (*Front Islamique du Salut*, FIS) party won the first round of Algeria's first multi-party elections in December 1991, the military cancelled the electoral process, forced President Chadli Bendjedid to resign, and instituted a military junta, the State High Committee. The FIS was banned and several FIS senior members, including its leader Hachani, were arrested. A bloody civil war then began (Volpi, 2003).

February 28 process would last a thousand years, if necessary (*Milliyet*, 4 September 1999). During this process, Refah was closed down in January 1998 and Erbakan, along with senior party leaders, was banned from politics for five years. The dissolution of the Welfare Party in 1998 by the Constitutional Court was unanimously approved by the European Court of Human Rights (2003). In addition, MÜSİAD Chairman Erol Yarar and Deputy Chairman Ali Bayramoğlu were brought before the State Security Court (*Hürriyet Daily News*, 23 May 1999).

The Virtue (*Fazilet*) Party subsequently replaced Refah by toning down their political discourse by reconfiguring it towards democracy, human rights, and political freedoms. This was coupled with an economic break in "The Just Economic System" (Gülalp, 2003: 83–84). This was all essentially a democratic façade, since the party was in favour of repealing Article 312 of the Turkish Penal Code which restricted freedom of thought and expression *only when* Recep Tayyip Erdoğan was sentenced due to publicly reciting an Islamic poem (Gülalp, 2003: 113). With this new settlement, Fazilet won 18.4% of the votes in the 1999 municipal elections, keeping two big cities, İstanbul and Ankara. Its share of the vote in the 1999 general elections, however, declined to 15.4% from the previous 21.4% attained in the 1995 general elections (Figures 4 and 5).

The rupture in Islamic politics in Turkey surfaced with the first congress of Fazilet in May 2000. Divided between Traditionalists (*Gelenekçiler*), backed by Erbakan and led by Recai Kutan, and Reformists (*Yenilikçiler*) led by Abdullah Gül, the congress ended up with a narrow margin of victory for the Traditionalists; Kutan got 633 votes and Gül 521 (Yeşilada, 2002: 69). Gül and his reformist followers were dismissed from the party and the Constitutional Court disbanded Fazilet on the grounds that it was the continuation of Refah (Yeşilada, 2002). The split embodied itself in the establishment of two different political parties. The Reformists in the Justice and Development Party (*Adalet ve Kalkınma Partisi*, AKP), broke away from Erbakan's *Milli Görüş* doctrine, and the Traditionalists in the Felicity Party (*Saadet Partisi*, SP) adhered to Erbakan and *Milli Görüş* (Gumuscu and Sert, 2009).

The programme of the SP is the continuation of *Milli Görüş* in a more moderate form. From an economic perspective, a radical tone is put forward against "racist imperialism [and] financial capitalism" as characterised by the rentier economy. The transition to the "real economy" for development with the target of just redistribution is proposed, and a free market economy is endorsed. However, the monopolies and privatisation that favour foreign and domestic monopolies are disparaged, while the programme offers support for SMEs and craftsmen and artisans. IMF and global capitalist policies are to be abandoned in favour of national ones. On foreign policy, the party declares itself to be against the EU, and favours instead cooperative organisations with neighbours. The D-8 (Developing Eight)[18] is portrayed as an alternative bloc to establish "a new world" (Saadet Partisi, 2010b).

The political strategy of Erbakan in confronting the Kemalist state was radical. Only by ideologically separating itself from Erbakan's parties and "taking off the *Milli Görüş* shirt", as Erdoğan put it, could the AKP carry out a democratic transition in Turkey until 2010/2011. The AKP has so far accepted the principle of "actually existing Turkish secularism"—the control of religion by the state and the existence of the Presidency of Religious Affairs as a state body—but has pursued the Islamisation of society as a political agenda especially since 2010/2011. The democratic transition and the dismantling of the Bonapartist state in Turkey will be the theme of the next chapter.

---

18   D-8 (Developing Eight) instigated by Erbakan in 1997 is a development initiative for eight Muslim countries as a counter to the G-8. The D-8 consists of Bangladesh, Egypt, Indonesia, Iran, Malaysia, Nigeria, Pakistan and Turkey (Erbakan, 2013b: 202–203).

CHAPTER 4

War of Position by the AKP against the Kemalist State

This chapter elucidates the international conditions following the end of the Cold War that pre-date the rise of the AKP, before examining the economy under the AKP. It argues that the assurance of political and economic stability for Turkish capitalism by the AKP in the aftermath of the severe economic crisis of 2000/2001 enabled the party to settle accounts with the military over the latter's political influence over the following decade. This period was sealed with the approval of the constitutional referendum in September 2010 and rounded off with mass resignation of top military brass ahead of the Supreme Military Council (*Yüksek Askeri Şura*, YAŞ) of July 2011, all without spawning any considerable political crisis. This chapter analyses how the AKP successfully united the general interests of the devout bourgeoisie with those of the big bourgeoisie. Further, it examines the political strategy through which the AKP neutralised an army faction that opposed Turkey's European integration, co-opted the liberals, and entered into an alliance with the Islamic community of Fethullah Gülen for a pool of bureaucratic staff. The Gülen movement, which established a strong presence in the judiciary and the police force during the AKP's time in power, was instrumental in undermining the military's political power in Turkey. The chapter contends that the end of the Kemalist state and the democratic transition under neoliberalism have been a common interest for Turkish capitalism since the late 1990s, which the AKP carried out until 2010/2011. In order to give a full account of this democratic transition, the chapter explains external facilitators, such as the influence of the EU, and highlights the limits of democratisation and Turkey's authoritarian drift. Lastly, it is shown that following the AKP's third term in 2011, Turkey's democratic transition did not lead to a consolidated democracy, but to competitive authoritarianism.

1 The Restructuring of the State after the End of the Cold War

During the Cold War, the military allies of the US worked to suppress leftist and progressive forces within their territories and fend off Soviet threats as part of a "containment policy". It was feared that economic problems in these countries could pave the way for a strengthening of leftist forces. This necessitated the institutionalisation of the "national security state" in peripheral countries, which worked as an instrument of the hegemonic foreign policy of the US. The characteristics of these regimes were conditioned and implemented in accordance with a specific security perspective. In other words, these national security states hinged on a "specific security anxiety" (Uzgel, 2009: 326–328).

This "specific security anxiety", coupled with a fear of potential invasion by the Soviet Army, led to the establishment of secret stay-behind armies in some NATO countries (Ganser, 2005). In order to counter a possible Soviet invasion of Western Europe, these armies composed of clandestine soldiers under NATO command who would have carried out operations in enemy-controlled zones, formed local resistance groups, and conducted sabotage against enemy's logistic supplies (Ganser, 2005: 2). In November 1990 the European Parliament passed a resolution called "Operation Gladio" acknowledging the involvement of these secret military forces in acts of terrorism and crime; it is said that these organisations operated out of civilian control (Taş, 2014: 165). In January 2006, the US Department of State also admitted the existence of stay-behind forces in Europe as resistance forces against a possible Soviet occupation (Taş, 2014: 166).

Turkey was no exception for establishing stay-behind forces. After joining NATO in 1952, a stay-behind force known as Counter-Guerrilla was set up under the official name of the Special Warfare Department (*Özel Harp Dairesi*) and was tied to the General Staff (Söyler, 2013: 316; 2014: 9; 2015: 101). It was financed through the "Joint American Military Mission for Aid to Turkey" (JAMMAT) as a part of the US Armed Forces and it was renamed to the "Joint US Military Mission for Aid to Turkey" (JUSMMAT) in 1958 (Söyler, 2015: 101). During the Cold War, it functioned as the Tactical Mobilisation Council (*Seferberlik Tetkik Kurulu*) between 1952 and 1967 and Special Warfare Department (*Özel Harp Dairesi*) between 1967 and 1991 (Söyler, 2015: 101). Following the end of the Cold War, its operations were taken over by Special Forces Command (*Özel Kuvvetler Komutanlığı*) (Ganser, 2005: 226; 2015: 101), and since 1994 it has been operating as part of the Special Forces (*Özel Kuvvetler*) (Söyler, 2013: 316; 2014: 9; 2015: 101).

Despite the long-time denial of its existence, Chief of the General Staff between 1990 and 1994, Doğan Güreş, confessed in 1992 to the existence of a counter-guerrilla force aiming to "organise people for a resistance" (Yalçın, 1992). As part of the "deep state", this clandestine body was not subject to any parliamentary control. In fact, when Bülent Ecevit learned in 1974 of the existence of the Special Warfare Department, he started to investigate its funding resources but failed to go further. The prosecutor Doğan Öz started to investigate the links between the MHP, Counter-Guerrilla forces, the Special

Warfare Department and terror activities in Turkey in the 1970s. However, he was assassinated by a member of Grey Wolves, İbrahim Çiftçi in 1978 (Ganser, 2005: 236–237).

This body was "made up of elements from the military, security and judicial establishments wedded to a fiercely nationalist, statist ideology who, if need be, are ready to block or even oust a government that does not share their vision" (as cited in Gunter, 2008: 109; 2014: 20). The 1993 Parliament Fact-Finding Commission Report on Political Murders by Unknown Assailants acknowledged that "Such organizations cannot be overseen by bodies elected to lead the state, nor can they be questioned by judicial bodies. They control the bodies leading the state as they please and have the capacity to use the state for any and all of their own purposes" (as cited in Avşar, Özdil, Kırmızıdağ: 2014: 8).

The end of the Cold War rendered the functionality of "The Rule of the Pretorians"—a phrase from Marx's 1858 article in the *New York Daily Tribune* under the same title—and these clandestine organisations defunct. The euphoria for liberal democracy mobilised idealist neo-conservative ideologists to argue that democracy innately leads to peace. The triumph of liberal democracy was seen as the evolutionary culmination of humanity's social progress and the end of antagonistic history. In his 1989 article, "The End of History?" Francis Fukuyama hailed the "total exhaustion of viable systematic alternatives to Western liberalism". He argued that "[w]hat we may be witnessing in not just the end of the Cold War, or the passing of a particular period of postwar history, but the end of history as such: that is, the end point of mankind's ideological evolution and the universalisation of Western liberal democracy as the final form of human government" (Fukuyama, 1989) Criticising the extreme pessimism of the 20th century due to destructive wars, the rise of totalitarianism, manipulation of scientific knowledge in favour of nuclear weapons and ecological damage, Fukuyama suggested a Hegelian recognition of a universal and homogeneous history. Liberal democracy was portrayed as a global phenomenon under which nations can coexist with each other (Fukuyama, 1991, 1992).

On the other hand, these ideas were challenged by the realist Samuel Huntington. He rejected the universality of Western culture while objecting to the notion that Western civilisation fits all humanity (Huntington, 1993: 40). Instead, he argued that even though Western culture has permeated the world at a superficial level, the concepts of Western civilisation such as individualism, liberalism, constitutionalism, human rights, equality, liberty, the rule of law, democracy, free markets, and secularism are alien to Asian societies. Imposing such concepts in these societies would lead to a religious fundamentalist reaction (Huntington, 1993: 40–41). This is what he termed the "democracy paradox".

According to Huntington (1996: 94), the adoption of Western democratic institutions by non-Western societies leads to the triumph of indigenous forces, which are hostile to these values.

When the third wave of democratisation started in Southern European countries such as Portugal, Spain, and Greece in the 1970s before moving on to Latin America, the Asia Pacific region, and finally Eastern Europe in the late 1980s (Huntington, 1996), it was only the Arab-speaking countries, which were still under the "anomaly of Arab despotism" (Achcar, 1997). The "democracy paradox" was put forward as an explanation for the Middle East. In fact, the predominant long-standing US strategy in the Middle East—the control of oil reserves—necessitated the support of despotic regimes in order to achieve "stability" in this region before and *even after* the Cold War. The fact that Saudi Arabia owns one of the largest oil reserves in the world[1] and the existence of anti-Western Islamic fundamentalism in the region were significant reasons for Western governments to align with despotic regimes in the Middle East (Achcar, 2004, 2013).

Nevertheless, when Islamic fundamentalist movements, especially the Muslim Brotherhood, dissociated themselves in the 1990 Gulf War from the sponsorship of Saudi Arabia, the Western powers then favoured despotic regimes against anti-Western Islamic fundamentalism. This also explains why the US allowed Saddam Hussein to crush insurgents in Northern and Southern Iraq in 1991, the West's tacit endorsement of the military coup in Algeria against the Islamic Salvation Front (FIS) in the 1992 elections, and its acquiescence to repression in Tunisia and Egypt, which silenced the Islamic fundamentalist movements (Achcar, 1997, 2004: 73–74).

Western powers also had hypocritical attitudes towards Turkey. Unlike Middle Eastern countries, Turkey was not under a long-standing despotic regime; rather, it was a guided democracy in which the military held real political power. However, due to intensified Kurdish guerrilla movements and increasing anti-Western Islamic fundamentalism in Turkey in the 1990s, democratisation, if not liberalisation, was postponed for roughly a decade after the end of the Cold War. In this period, the US backed the Turkish military in its fight against Kurdish guerrillas. As Noam Chomsky points out, in 1997 alone, Turkey received more US weapons than the entire period between 1950 and 1983 (Chomsky in Chomsky and Achcar, 2007: 124).

---

1   Venezuela, which surpassed Saudi Arabia in 2010 with respect to oil reserves, owned a little over one fourth of proven oil reserves in the world at the end of 2018 while Saudi Arabia had nearly 22.5% (OPEC, 2020).

In the aftermath of the 9/11 attacks, the Bush administration adopted the slogan of the "War on Terror" and enhanced its military presence in Central Asia by establishing military bases in Uzbekistan[2] and Kyrgyzstan[3] after the invasion of Afghanistan in 2001 (Achcar, 2004: 38–41; Achcar in Chomsky and Achcar, 2007: 44; Achcar, 2013: 112). It was only *after* the 2003 invasion of Iraq that the US discursively endorsed "democracy promotion" when the pretext that Iraq owned weapons of mass destruction had been disproven (Achcar in Chomsky and Achcar, 2007: 44; Achcar, 2013: 113). At that point, the "Turkish model" of the AKP—a successful blend of neoliberal market fundamentalism with Islamic conservatism in social affairs and formal democratisation— coincided with the US pressure on its allies in the Middle East. This pressure also produced in 2005 the Iraqi, Palestinian, Saudi Arabian elections as well as the extension of political rights for Kuwaiti women and liberalisation in Egypt for the 2005 elections (Achcar, 2013: 115–117).

Importantly, the US administration was disenchanted with the Turkish military, upon the rejection by parliament of a bill on 1 March 2003 to station US troops on Turkish territory for the Iraqi invasion. The Turkish military was held responsible for this rejection. Deputy Secretary of Defence Paul Wolfowitz lashed out saying that the Turkish military "did not play the strong leadership role" for pressing government that it should have (Lacey, 2003). All these international and domestic conditions strengthened the AKP's hand against military omnipotence in politics. Still, it was predominantly the political and economic stability in the aftermath of the 2000/2001 economic crisis that played a key role in the strengthening of the liberal democratic institutions. It can be argued that the 2000/2001 economic crisis put an end to the historical function of Turkish Bonapartism. Turkish capitalists felt strong enough to hold real political power after long decades of military tutelage.

2 The Rise of the AKP in the Post-crisis Period and Continuation of Neoliberal Economic Policies

> "The cost for me of [my workers] praying is 20 minutes". *A conservative entrepreneur in Kayseri* (Emre, August 7, 2008)

---

2 US military forces withdrew from Karshi-Khanabad Air Base (K2) in November 2005 due to tense relations after the Andijan massacre in Uzbekistan in May 2005 (Wright and Tyson, July 30, 2005).

3 US military forces were evicted from Manas Air Base in Kyrgyzstan in June 2014 (Dzyubenko, June 3, 2014).

2.1 The 2001 Economic Crisis

Turkey drastically changed its state-led economic development policy to export-led development under the military dictatorship between 1980 and 1983. In this period, the dissidents and organised left were smashed. In this political vacuum, the implementation of neoliberal reforms encountered little opposition; Islam was elevated to a more prominent level by unearthing the "Turkish-Islamic Synthesis". Turgut Özal continued this neoliberal economic programme with export-led growth, as analysed in the previous chapter.

The AKP was the product of this economic shift. The devout bourgeoisie benefited from export-led growth and formed the main economic base of the party. However, the political and economic situation which paved the way for the rise of the AKP stemmed from the 2000/2001 economic crisis. This economic crisis mutated into a political crisis by shattering the decade-long hegemony of centre-right political parties in Turkey.

It is important to stress that the integration of Turkey into global capital markets and the liberalisation of capital accounts in 1989 set the stage for severe economic crises in the 1990s and 2000/2001 (Cizre and Yeldan, 2005; Öniş, 2003). This prompted an increase in the number of banks from 25 in 1990 to 36 in 1997 (Kazgan, 2008: 273). Crony capitalism made it possible to easily acquire banking licenses through links with politicians and hushing up inspection reports. Turkish banks increasingly relied on profitable high interest rates in treasury bonds, rather than supporting capitalist production (Kazgan, 2008: 273–274). Alongside political cronyism, increasing risk and uncertainty and increasing rates of return gap in favour of financial assets diverted portfolio choice of the non-financial corporations to the short-term reversible financial investments in the 1990s (Demir, 2009). While the average annual real GDP growth was only 3.4% between 1990 and 2000, the real rate of growth of banking assets was more than 13% per year (in Cizre and Yeldan, 2005: 391).

Correspondingly, these banks allowed Turkish companies to easily earn money in the 1990s. Some companies increasingly entrusted their liquid assets on repurchase, investment funds and treasury bonds instead of investing in production (Boratav, 2011: 191). The state also contributed to this organic link between companies and banks by pumping money into the banking system. It increasingly relied on borrowing from domestic agents; Turkey's domestic debt stock reached 25–30% of GDP before the 2001 crisis, while it was close to zero in 1987 (Öniş, 2003: 7).

The public sector was increasingly indebted and in need of funds; interest expenditure was a significant burden on the budget. Following a steady increase from 1990, the interest payment of the public sector reached over 50%

of total expenditure of the consolidated budget in 2001 (Figure 7). This is an important indicator that the public sector needed funds mainly in order to pay its interest expenditure, not because of an increase in public investment or expenditure of SOEs.

Between 1997 and 2002 the burden on the public was further aggravated when the wrecked banks were taken over by the Savings Deposit Insurance Fund (SDIF)—a government body which guarantees the protection of deposits—since the state was to guarantee to pay the creditors' receivables (Kazgan, 2008: 273–275). By early 2004, twenty-one domestic private banks were taken over by the SDIF (Steinherr, Tukel and Ucer, 2004: 6). The Treasury undertook commercial and public banks' debts, which amounted to $21.9 billion on duty losses and recapitalisation for the state banks and $21.8 for the private banks taken over by the SDIF. In other words, the total cost of the banking crisis to the Treasury amounted to $43.7 billion or 29.5% of GNP in 2001. The private sector, however, only spent $9.5 billion or only 6.4% of GNP in 2001. All in all, the cost of the banking crisis to Turkey came to over $53 billion or nearly 36% of GNP in 2001 (Steinherr, Tukel and Ucer, 2004: 5). Put simply, this was a "state-led banking rescue" on the basis of the socialisation of costs, with the benefits going to the financiers (Marois, 2012: 175).

The crisis also severely affected labour. The official statistics show that 600,000 enterprises were closed down and 2.3 million workers lost their jobs between August 2000 and August 2002 (Şenses, 2003: 99). According to the results of the Household Labour Force Survey, the unemployment rate increased from 6.3% in the last quarter of 2000 to 10.6% in that of 2001 (Şenses, 2003: 100). The urban non-agricultural unemployment rate also increased from 11.9% in

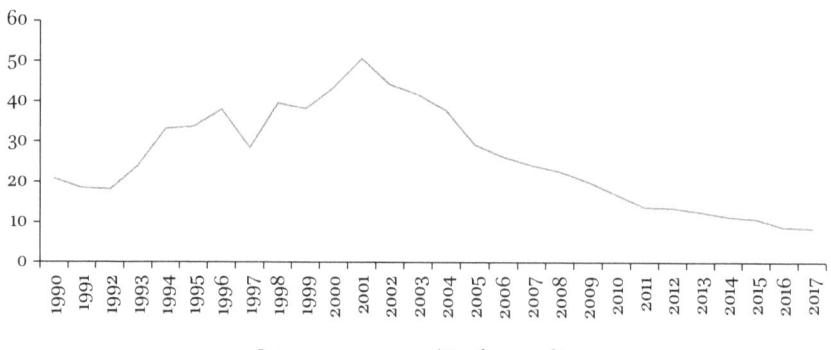

FIGURE 7 Interest repayments/total expenditure, 1990–2017
SOURCE: PRESIDENCY OF TURKEY, PRESIDENCY OF STRATEGY AND BUDGET (2018).

2001 to 14.6% in 2002 (Onaran, 2009: 252). The rate of decline in real wages in the manufacturing sector reached an average of 14.4% (Şenses, 2003: 101). The wage share fell continually for the eight years following the crisis in 2001, estimated by Onaran and Oyvat (2015: 18) as a cumulative fall of 22% from the pre-crisis level in 2000 to 2008. Regarding the poorest segment of society, applications to Social Assistance and the Solidarity Fund increased by two million from September 2000 to December 2001, while those holding a Green Card, the instrument to give the poorest access to health service, increased by 2.5 million from September 2000 to December 2001 (Şenses, 2003: 103–104).

The unemployment rate, first exceeding and then remaining at 10% in the post-crisis period, played a crucial role in lowering labour's bargaining power vis-à-vis industrial capital. This was further aggravated by the decline in the ratio of wage and salary earners that belonged to a trade union to 16.6% in 2003 from 20% in 1999 (OECD, 2020),[4] and the decline of labour's share in income to 26.3% in 2002 from 29.2% in 2000 (Dufour and Orhangazi, 2009: 116).

The economic crisis was to be overcome by the "Programme for the Transition to a Strong Economy". Initiated by Kemal Derviş, who worked in the World Bank as Vice-President for Poverty Reduction and Economic Management before being appointed plenipotentiary Minister for Economic Affairs and the Treasury under the Ecevit government in Turkey, the programme involved neoliberal restructuring of the economy and banking sector. This financial restructuring included increasing the petroleum consumption tax and value added tax; decreasing state support of cereal purchases; stabilisation of support-price increases; privatisation of public banks and the telecommunications, electricity, natural gas, tobacco and sugar sectors; operational independence of the Central Bank; reduction of government borrowing requirements; and sustainability of public debt (Nas, 2008: 100–101). The IMF also backed the programme by providing an extra $8 billion of credit, increasing Turkey's debt to the IMF to $19 billion (IMF, May 15, 2001).

2.2 The Economy under AKP Rule

It was this severe economic crisis that led to the rise of the AKP. On 3 November 2002 the AKP achieved a victory in the general elections, receiving 34.3% of the votes with 363 seats in the 550-member Parliament, while CHP received 19.4% of the votes with 178 seats. The AKP's electoral victory was welcomed by the different factions of the capital groups due to the urgent need for the political stability that a single party government could bring. Sakıp Sabancı, the

---

4 It should be stated that under AKP rule, trade union density in Turkey further declined to 9.2% in 2018 (OECD, 2020a).

Turkish industrial tycoon, commented that Turkey had paid a high cost for coalition governments, and with the victory of the AKP, Turkey could "hop on the second Özal train" (*Hürriyet*, 3 November 2002). Ali Bayramoğlu, the head of MÜSİAD between 1999 and 2004, shared similar views to Sabancı regarding the merits of a single-party government, and also pointed out the resemblance of this process with the era of Özal. Bayramoğlu noted:

> We haven't experienced the single party government since approximately 1987. When we think that political instability very much disturbs Turkey, I predict that stability will be positive for Turkey... I think that we should return to the successful line of Turgut Özal between 1983 and 1990 (*Hürriyet*, 3 November 2002).

Tuncay Özilhan, the chairman of TÜSİAD, the umbrella organisation of big capital, promoted the AKP to European leaders as a "conservative, democratic and secular party" (*Milliyet*, 5 November 2002a), while the leader of the main opposition Republican People's Party (CHP), Deniz Baykal, backed Erdoğan to cooperate in Turkey's EU accession process (*Milliyet*, 5 November 2002b). Defining itself in the *2023 Political Vision* as "a conservative democratic mass party that situates itself at the center of the political spectrum" (AK Party, n.d.), the AKP has been a Muslim conservative party which has equivalent in Christian Democrat parties in Europe and within the Republican Party of the USA. It distances itself from Islamic fundamentalism (Axiarlis, 2014). However, a reversal of democratisation since 2011 and the exclusionary politics of the AKP placed the latter under the umbrella of right-wing populist parties.

The AKP continued the neoliberal "Programme for a Transition to a Stronger Economy", an extension of the 1999 deflationary IMF-led programme (Nas, 2008). Ali Babacan, who was Minister of Economy (2002–2007) and of Foreign Affairs (2007–2009), then Deputy Prime Minister for Economic and Financial Affairs since 2009, played a key role in the implementation of this programme. The AKP first continued to lower the annual inflation rate from 45% in 2002 to 16.3.9% in 2018 (Figure 8). This was important considering the fact that the 1990s were years of high inflation—peaking at 106% in 1994—with damaging effects on the population (Figure 8).

Secondly, the "Programme for the Transition to a Strong Economy" aimed at restructuring Turkey's "debt management". The implementation of this programme made Turkey shift its growth and debt management model from one based on budget deficit and public debt to another model based on current account deficit and private debt (Eğilmez, 2013). Before 2005, the public sector relied more on external debt than the private sector except for a short period

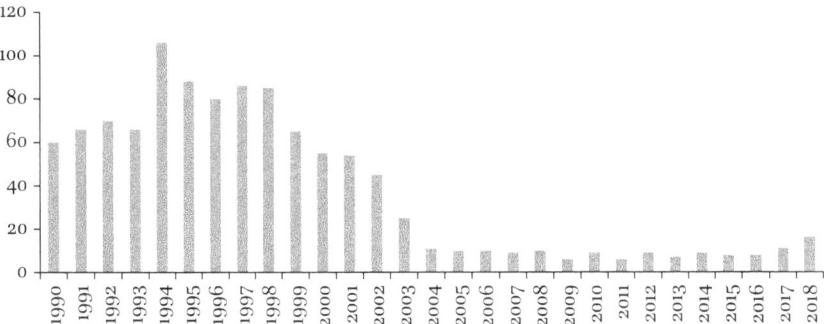

FIGURE 8   Annual inflation in consumer prices (%), 1990–2018
SOURCE: THE WORLD BANK, WORLD DEVELOPMENT INDICATORS (2020).

between 1998 and 2000 (Figure 9). Since 2005, the private sector has surpassed the public sector with respect to the external debt of Turkey (Figure 9). In 2019, the gross external debt of the private sector reached $283 billion, almost 65% of Turkey's gross external debt, whereas in 2000 it was about 45% (Figures 9 and 10). Nevertheless, Turkey's foreign debt has exceeded 50% of its national income since 2017 (Figure 10).

The IMF-led programme initiated by Derviş in 2001 and substantially adopted by the AKP adhered to fiscal discipline. The budget deficit decreased to 1.8% of GDP in 2019 from 11.2% of GDP in 2002 (Figure 11).

Another pillar of this neoliberal economic programme was privatisation. Privatisation revenues between 2003 and 2017 marked their highest level during the course of the Republic of Turkey. It is important to highlight that privatisation revenues in 2005 alone were nearly equal the entire 18 years between 1986 and 2003 (Figure 12).

Gross fixed capital formation[5] showed an upward trend during 2002–2006 after hitting bottom in 2001 (Figure 13). It declined throughout the three years following 2006, falling to a level of 22% in 2009. This was accompanied by a rise in the ratio of gross fixed capital formation to GDP during 2010–2011. However, it stagnated during 2012–2014, at a level of 28% (Figure 13). In 2018, the share of investment in total production in Turkey is similar to other emergent countries

---

5 According to World Bank Data (2020), "[g]ross fixed capital formation (formerly gross domestic fixed investment) includes land improvements (fences, ditches, drains, and so on); plant, machinery, and equipment purchases; and the construction of roads, railways, and the like, including schools, offices, hospitals, private residential dwellings, and commercial and industrial buildings".

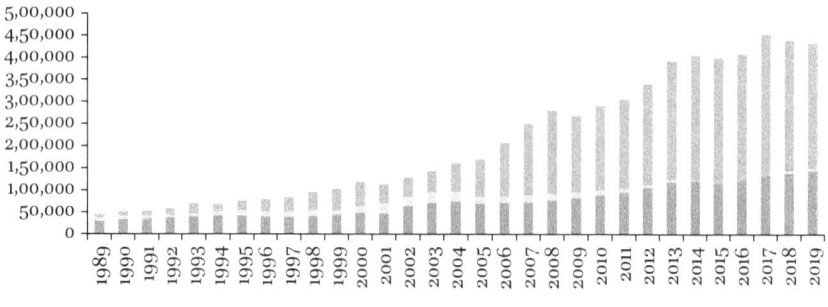

- Gross external debt of private sector
- Gross external debt of Central Bank
- Gross external debt of public sector

FIGURE 9   Turkey's gross external debt (million $), 1989–2019
SOURCE: REPUBLIC OF TURKEY, MINISTRY TREASURY AND FINANCE (2018).
Note: Gross external debt refers to the sum of total short-term and long term debts of public sector, private sector and Central Bank.

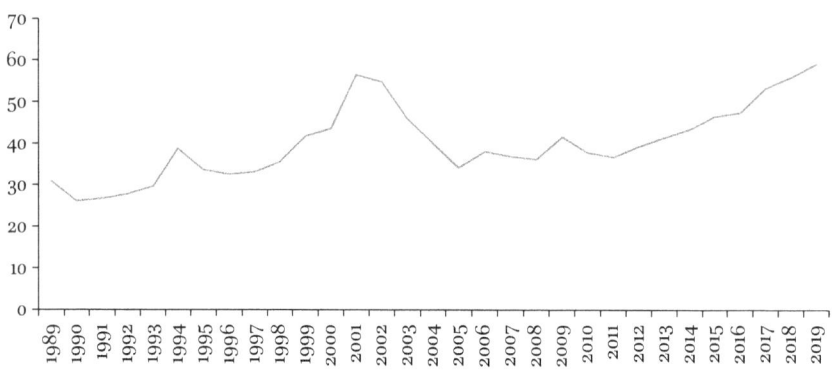

FIGURE 10   Turkey's gross external debt to GDP (%), 1989–2019
SOURCE: REPUBLIC OF TURKEY, MINISTRY TREASURY AND FINANCE (2018).

V as India, and Malaysia, which invested 29.3% and 24.2% of their respective GDPs in gross fixed capital formation in 2018.

Figure 13 also highlights the significance of political and economic stability in Turkey for private capitalist investment. For instance, the 1990s were a period of fluctuating investment, mostly due to the war between PKK guerrillas and the army focused in Kurdish region of Turkey's southeast. The declining trend of the rate of investment to GDP in Turkey during 1998–2002 was the outcome of the convergence of the several factors: the 1998 Russian crisis, which led to a relative deterioration in Turkish exports and a capital outflow at

WAR OF POSITION BY THE AKP   141

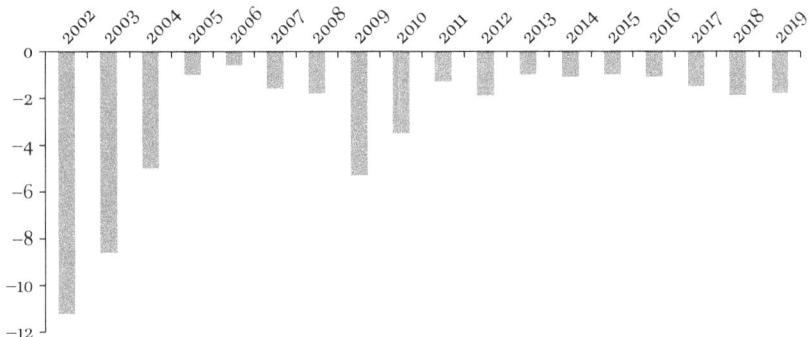

FIGURE 11 Budget balance to GDP (%), 2002–2019
SOURCE: REPUBLIC OF TURKEY MINISTRY TREASURY AND FINANCE (2019).

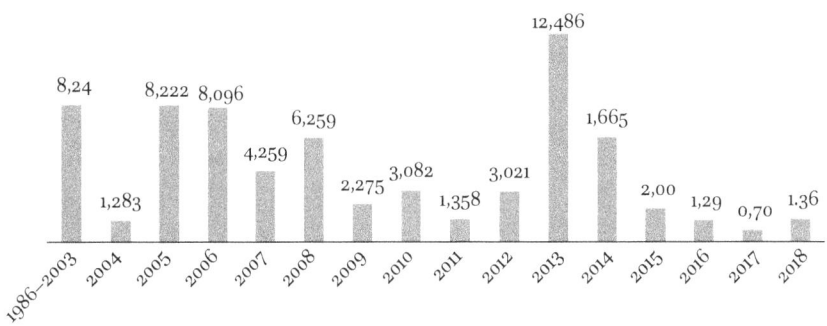

FIGURE 12 Privatisation revenue by years (million $)
SOURCE: PRIVATISATION ADMINISTRATION (2018: 54).

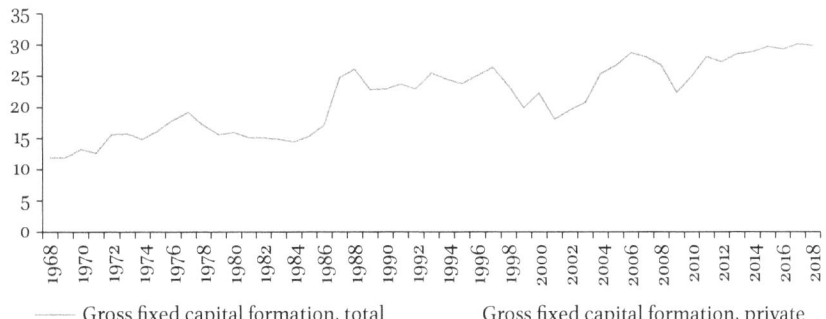

FIGURE 13 Gross fixed capital formation to GDP, total and private sector, (%), 1968–2018
SOURCE: THE WORLD BANK (2020).

$7 billion in the second half of 1998 (OECD, 1999: 4); a political crisis after the toppling of the Erbakan government by the military in 1997; the 1999 İzmit earthquake; and the 2000/2001 economic crisis. It can also be argued that political stability under AKP rule between 2002 and 2006 and the EU accession process played a role in stimulating gross fixed capital formation as a percentage of GDP, which increased from 18.1% in 2001 to 28.7% in 2006. On the other hand, the increase of gross fixed capital formation in Turkey since 2009 global financial crisis can be explained by the increase of state's invervention into the housing market in an authoritarian and neoliberal form though Mass Housing Administration, TOKİ (*Toplu Konut İdaresi*) (Dogru, 2016; Figure 13).

However, it should be emphasised that the AKP era showed a corresponding growth pattern since the liberalisation of capital accounts in 1989, which was based on speculative capital inflows, leading to the boom-bust cycles (Onaran and Oyvat, 2015). For instance, in the 1994 currency crisis following the liberalisation of capital accounts in 1989, the percentage of the depreciation of the Turkish Lira was 23.9 in 1994, leading international investors to benefit from deflated asset prices in financial markets (Onaran, 2009: 244; Onaran and Oyvat, 2015: 5–6). On the one hand, capital flows to Turkey increased during a five-year period after the 1994 currency crisis. On the other hand, the adoption of the currency peg in 2000 with a view to combatting inflation failed to prevent the appreciation of the currency and the current account deficit stood at 3.7% of GDP in 2000 (Onaran and Oyvat, 2015: 6). When Turkey plunged back into an economic crisis in 2000/2001, a rise in interest rates triggered the capital inflows again, which then financed Turkey's annual high growth rate of 7.2% between 2002 and 2006 (Onaran, 2009: 246; Onaran and Oyvat, 2015: 8). However, international financial investors again benefited from the deflated prices in the financial markets and the depreciation of the currency after the 2001 crisis. While Turkey was able to attract FDI thanks to the EU process, privatisation, and the high rates of the depreciation of the currency, local currency continued to appreciate and the current account deficit peaked at above 6% of the GDP in 2006, leaving the Turkish economy fragile in the wake of global economic instability (Onaran, 2009: 247; Onaran and Oyvat, 2015: 8–9). Put simply, the Turkish economy fell back into a boom-bust cycle.

Indeed, the pace of increase in GDP per capita (measured in constant local currency unit) between 2002 and 2014 was higher than the previous decade, which rose to TL1,660.5 in 2014 from TL1,113.5 in 2002, equivalent to an increase of slightly less than 50%. In 1990, GDP per capita was TL939.3 whereas it rose to TL1,145.4 in 2000, only an increase of approximately 22% in a decade (The World Bank, 2020). In contrast to the low GDP per capita annual growth in the 1990s—which witnessed three years of GDP per capita contractions in 1991 during the Gulf War, the 1994 economic crisis and the 1999 earthquake in İzmit, an industrial hinterland of İstanbul—the post-2001 period under the AKP resulted in high GDP per capita growth especially between 2002 and 2007 (Figure 14). The 2008 global economic crisis negatively affected Turkey in that GDP per capita decreased by 1% in 2008 and 6% in 2009. However, it was compensated by a higher increase in GDP per capita in 2010 and 2011, at 8% and 7% respectively (Figure 14).

This high GDP per capita growth between 2003 and 2012 under AKP rule can only be compared with two separate decades of high growth in Turkey: a period between 1963 and 1972 and another between 1983 and 1992. The "planned development" era commenced in Turkey with the 1963 First Five-Year Development Plan, which aimed at a high growth rate through the import-substitution growth model coupled with relatively high wages. The period between 1963 and 1972 had a record 3.61% GDP per capita average annual growth (Figure 15). In this period, Bonapartist rule consolidated its legitimacy over the popular masses. On the other hand, the 1970s were a recessionary period in Turkey where GDP per capita growth declined over the three consecutive years 1978, 1979 and 1980 (Figure 15). These years also saw an unabating polarisation of society and perpetuation of fascist attacks on the left and students. The 1980 coup crushed the left and created a vacuum, but it took until 1990s for Islamic fundamentalism to fill this vacuum.

The rise of Islamic fundamentalism in Turkey in the 1990s was not surprising, though. In the 1990s Turkey's GDP per capita growth was at its lowest with an average of 1%, far below middle income countries, OECD countries and the world average (Figure 15). Turkey's average GDP per capita annual growth rate

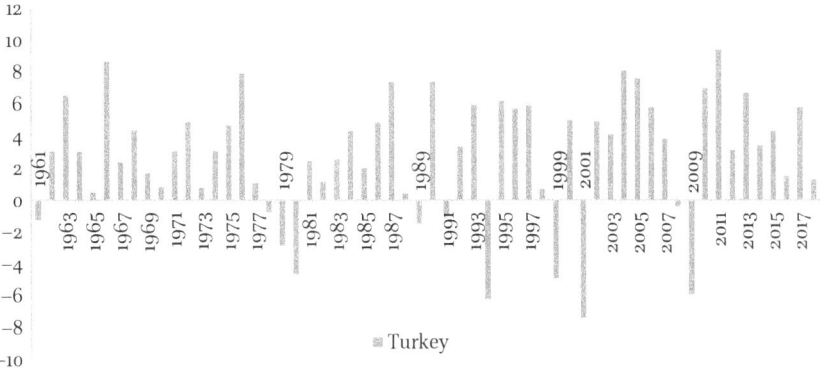

FIGURE 14   GDP per capita annual growth rate (%), 1961–2018
SOURCE: THE WORLD BANK (2020).

in the 1990s was very low: at 1%, it slipped below the world average of 1.44% (Figure 15). It was under these economic conditions that the Just Economic Order publicised by Erbakan became popular among the masses. It is fair to say that Islamic fundamentalism in Turkey found a wide cross-class alliance in two decades: first in the 1970s by participating in National Front governments and in the 1990s by winning the 1995 general elections, a common denominator of the two periods being that the GDP per capita growth was comparatively low. The rise of the AKP in 2002 was shaped by a period of low GDP per capita annual growth of the 1990s. Between 2003 and 2012, Turkey's GDP per capita increased by 3.71% annually under export-led capitalism (Figure 15). This ratio was above the OECD and world averages but below the GDP per capita average annual growth of middle-income countries.

Relatively high GDP growth in Turkey between 2002 and 2013 can be compared with the economic performance of emerging countries such as China, India, Malaysia, South Korea, Brazil, and Mexico. Between 2002 and 2013, GDP annual growth of Turkey was nearly 6%, ahead of South Korea, Brazil, Mexico, and Malaysia and falling behind China and India (Table 11).

On the other hand, high GDP per capita growth and neoliberal economic development in Turkey have been achieved at the expense of domestic labour. Longer working hours than those in OECD countries have been instrumental in achieving this economic development. According to OECD statistics, Turkish workers worked on average 1855 hours in 2012, compared to 1765 hours on average in OECD countries, a difference of over 90 hours annually (OECD, 2013). That said, Mexico (2226), Chile (2029), and Greece (2034) had the longest working hours of OECD countries (OECD, 2013). On the other hand, economic

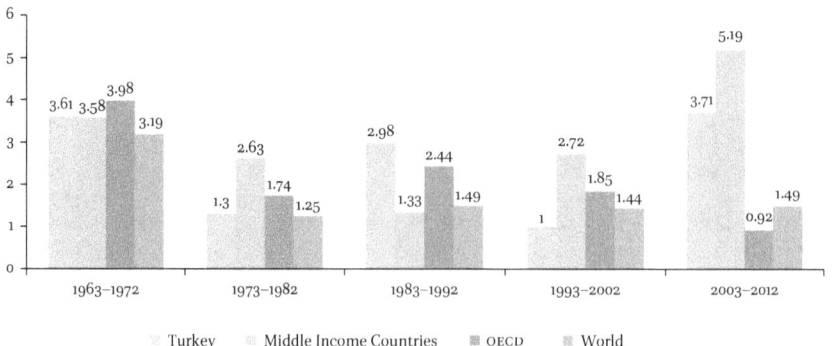

FIGURE 15   GDP per capita average annual growth rate in comparison (%)
SOURCE: OWN CALCULATIONS BASED ON THE WORLD BANK (2015).

TABLE 11 Annual GDP growth in some selected emerging countries and Turkey (%), 2002–2013

	2002	2003	2004	2005	2006	2007	2008	2009	2010	2011	2012	2013	Av.
China	9.1	10	10.1	11.4	12.7	14.2	9.7	9.4	10.6	9.6	7.9	7.8	9.4
India	3.8	7.9	7.9	7.9	8.1	7.7	3.1	7.9	8.5	5.2	5.5	6.4	6.6
Malaysia	5.4	5.8	6.8	5.3	5.6	6.3	4.8	-1.5	7.4	5.3	5.5	4.7	5.1
Turkey	6.4	5.6	9.6	9	7.1	5	0.8	-4.7	8.5	11.1	4.8	8.5	5.9
S. Korea	7.4	2.9	4.9	3.9	5.2	5.5	2.8	0.7	6.5	3.7	2.3	2.9	4
Brazil	3.1	1.1	5.8	3.2	4	6.1	5.1	-0.1	7.5	4	1.9	3	3.5
Mexico	0	1.4	3.9	2.3	4.5	2.3	1.1	-5.3	5.1	3.7	3.6	1.4	2.2

SOURCE: THE WORLD BANK (2020).

growth is not followed by a decrease in the unemployment rate. According to the Turkish Statistical data, the overall unemployment rate was around 9 % in 2005, while it reached to 13.2% in November 2019 (TÜİK, n.d.).

The "lower labour cost and lower average wages together with increasing labour productivity" in comparison to rival countries was highlighted by the Investment Support and Promotion Agency (2010: 12). This state body, which is under the control of the Prime Ministry, actively advertises Turkey to potential foreign investors by drawing attention to the "efficiency" of the labour force and employment relations in the country. To illustrate, between 2002 and 2009, the annual average of labour productivity growth was 4.4% in Turkey—compared to 9.6% in China and 6.0% in India. The average increase in real wages between 2002 and 2009, meanwhile, was one of the lowest among developing countries, with an increase in real wages of only 0.4%; this ratio was 11.6% and 14.7% for the same period for China and India, respectively (Investment Support and Promotion Agency, 2010: 12–13). The state agency (2010: 8) also boasts about the "labour force's dedication to work via low absenteeism" by comparing the annual average number of sick days per employee in Turkey (4.6 days in 2008) with those in other countries such as Bulgaria (22 days), Portugal (11.9 days), Czech Republic (10.8 days), Poland (9.7 days).

Not surprisingly, the social cost of neoliberal economic development reflected itself in lethal "occupational accidents" for the workers. Under AKP rule between 2002 and 2014, at least 14,555 workers died on "occupational accidents" (*Bianet*, 3 November 2014). Faruk Çelik, Labour and Social Security Minister, confessed that "[i]n 2002, the number of occupational deaths was 872, but by 2010, the number rose to 1444" (Gürgen, 2011). In 2019, 1,736 workers died on occupational homicides, 112 of whom were migrant workers (*Bianet*, 14 January 2020).

Occupational conditions have been strongly affected by the worsening organisational unity of the working classes. The AKP has been benefiting from the unorganised and defenceless position of the workers born of diminished trade union density in the neoliberal epoch. By July 2014, out of a total 12.3 million workers, only 1.2 million—9.68% of total workers—were unionised in Turkey according to statistics from the Ministry of Labour and Social Security. This was a tremendous regression, down from 57.54% in July 2003 (Republic of Turkey Ministry of Labour and Social Security, n.d.). On the other hand, percentage of employees with right to bargain is extremely low in Turkey. In 2002, collective bargaining covered only 11.9% of workers, down from 15.6% in 1998. This ratio hit rock bottom at 5.4% in 2012, being the lowest unionisation rate among OECD countries with a 33.9% average rate of unionisation in 2012 (OECD, 2020b).

It is this paradoxical condition of neoliberal economic development in Turkey since 2002, which partly explains the electoral success of the AKP. The AKP so far has been able to achieve a politics of class compromise between the poorest and the richest segments of population. On the one hand, the ratio of minimum wages to average wages of full-time workers increased from 0.28 in 2002 to 0.40 in 2018, while the ratio of minimum wages to median earnings increased from 0.53 to 0.71 in the period under consideration (OECD, 2020c). The share of the wage income held by the poorest two quintiles rose to 12% in 2013 from 10.7 in 2006, while the share in the top quintile within the total wage income also rose to 53.1% in 2013 from 51.7% in 2006. However, the class compromise was achieved at the expense of the organised blue collar and professional working class—rather than taxes levied on net profits—leading to a reduction in the wage income share of the middle 40% to 34.9% in 2013 from 37.6% in 2006 (Onaran and Oyvat, 2015: 25–26).

Moreover, while the AKP has been pursuing neoliberal policies on employment, in the process causing sub-contracting in all sectors and precariousness among workers,[6] it has also pursued a social policy based on social transfers. According to a June 2012 Social Assistance Statistics Bulletin published by the Ministry of Family and Social Policy, the ratio of social assistance and service to GDP rose from 0.5% in 2002 to 1.42% (including the compensation payments by the Social Security Institution) in 2011 (Republic of Turkey Ministry of Family and Social Policy, 2012: 18). In 2014, slightly more than 3 million households benefited from regular and/or non-regular social assistance (Republic of Turkey Ministry of Family and Social Policy, 2015: 74).[7] The estimated amount of total social assistance in 2014 was equivalent to nearly NTL 20.4 billion, or $8.95 billion (Republic of Turkey Ministry of Family and Social Policy, 2015: 74).[8] The bulk of this social assistance was dedicated to pensions for handicapped people in need of care, old-age pension, fuel assistance, free textbooks for students, free lunch assistance for poor students, conditional cash transfers on pregnancy, child health and education, and conditional cash benefit for needy

---

6   A 2011 constitutional proposal relating to the economic and commercial provisions by İstanbul Chamber of Commerce suggested that the concept of "public interest" (*kamu yararı*) be removed from the constitution, natural resources contribute to economic activity, and minimum wage be deregulated (Goncagül Avcı, 2012, personal communication). Murat Yalçıntaş, founding member of the AKP in 2001, was the chairman of the İstanbul Chamber of Commerce between 2005 and 2013.

7   Nearly 2.3 million households in Turkey benefited from regular social assistance in 2014 while approximately 1.9 million households benefited from non-regular social assistance (Republic of Turkey Ministry of Family and Social Policy, 2015: 74).

8   On 10 October 2014, 1 USD was equal to 2,2789 NTL according to the Central Bank of Turkey.

women whose spouses passed away (Republic of Turkey Ministry of Family and Social Policy, 2015).

High economic development had a significant effect on putting absolute poverty rates in decline in Turkey (Figure 16). According to official statistics, while nearly a third of the population (30.3%) lived on less than $4.3 (at purchasing power parity) per day in 2002, this decreased to 1.58% in 2015 (Figure 16). The OECD (2014b: 34, Box1) stated that "Turkey is one of the few OECD countries where inequality of household disposable incomes declined in the 2000s, even if some of the progress achieved was reversed following the onset of the global crisis". Nevertheless, with a relative poverty rate[9] of 19.3% Turkey had the 3rd highest level of relative poverty in the OECD in 2010, after Mexico (20.4%) and Israel (20.9%) (OECD, 2014a: 113). In addition, OECD (2014c) found out that there was an increase in the share of people who reported that they could not afford food from 26.6% in 2006/2007 to 32.7% in 2011/2012.

Neoliberalism has negatively impacted wealth distribution. It has been revealed that it was largely the top percentile of the population that could reap the benefits of economic growth under the AKP since the wealth was unequally distributed and concentrated in this percentile (Güney, 2015). The *Global Wealth DataBook 2014* indicated that Turkey contained more individuals with wealth over $1 billion in 2014 (37) than Japan (15), France (31), Italy (29), Canada

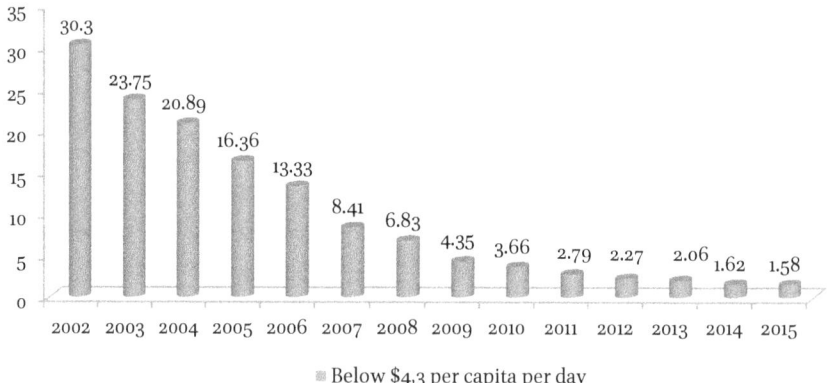

FIGURE 16   Poverty rates according to the international threshold of 4.3 dollars per day, 2002–2015
SOURCE: TÜİK (N.D.), THE POVERTY RATES ACCORDING TO POVERTY LINE METHODS.

---

9   Relative poverty rate refers to the percentage of people living with less than 50% of median income.

(25), and Korea (35) (Credit Suisse, 2014: 112). According to this databook, the wealth share of the top percentile of adults rose sharply from 38.1% in 2000 to 54.3% in 2014 (Credit Suisse, 2014: 125), thus making Turkey the sixth most unequal country in the world in terms of wealth inequality (Güney, 2015).

To sum up, the economy under AKP rule became the major parameter in broadening its mass electoral base. According to the Supreme Court of Appeals Prosecutor's Office data from November 2014, the AKP is the largest political party in Turkey with 8,698,551 members, followed by the CHP with 1,012,412 members; the DP with 715,399 members; the MHP with 374,430 members; and the SP with 210,521 members (*Milliyet*, 27 November 2014). The AKP managed to increase its share of the vote to 46.6% in 2007 and 49.8% in the 2011 general elections. In absolute terms, it doubled its votes from 10.8 million in 2002 to 21.4 million in 2011 (TUİK, 2012: 93). This electoral success, in turn, has helped carry out a relatively smooth democratic transition until 2010/2011. External factors such as the EU anchor and the USA facilitated this transition. Bonapartist rule, which was to reinforce social order and maintain bourgeois economic power under the grip of the military, was superseded by the AKP rule. As has been shown, the AKP represented the symbiosis of big capitalists and peripheral capitalists for holding state power.

3 Procedural Democratisation under the Influence of the EU

Procedural democratisation in Turkey until 2010/2011 has not been a product of mass popular struggles against the Kemalist state, as contrasted in Chapter 1. Moreover, the socio-economic context of procedural, formal and Schumpeterian democratisation undermines the realisation of democratic deepening. As Roper (2013: 238) argues that even in the most developed democratic countries, democratic control of workplaces, distribution of labour and resources remain under rule of market forces. Therefore, Turkey's democratic transition was a process of establishment of civilian rule in a neoliberal era in which the power of business outstrips that of labour. Neoliberal hegemony indubitably restricts and devalues democracy as a system of political representation by converting citizens into consumers (Munck, 2005: 65–66). In the Turkish case, the symbiosis of different bourgeois fractions to produce capitalist democracy—a process influenced by the EU and also supported by popular masses—extricated the country from long-lasting Bonapartist rule.

Indeed, the emphasis on civil and political rights and the rule of law has been straightforwardly vocalised by TÜSİAD since the intensification of Turkey's integration with the European Union after the conclusion of the Customs

Union in 1996. The fulfilment of the Copenhagen Criteria, which recommend that democracy and free market economy go hand in hand, have been prioritised by the big capitalists. According to the Criteria,

> Membership requires that the candidate country has achieved stability of institutions guaranteeing democracy, the rule of law, human rights and respect for and protection of minorities, the existence of a functioning market economy as well the capacity to cope with competitive pressure and market forces within the Union. Membership presupposes the candidate's ability to take on the obligations of membership including adherence to the aims of political, economic and monetary union (European Council, 1993: 13).

For TÜSİAD, the increasing economic relations of Turkey with the EU necessitated broadening of political freedoms. TÜSİAD's 1997 report, entitled *Türkiye'de Demokratikleşme Perspektifleri* (Democratisation Perspectives in Turkey) underlined that the permanence of a free market economy in Turkey can only be sustained in a pluralist democratic political structure (TÜSİAD, 1997). The report suggested amending the Political Parties Law. One of the bold proposals was even to repeal the clause that "political parties operate in accordance with Atatürk's principles and revolutions". The report proposed lowering the election threshold to 5% and expanding freedom of expression. It further suggested that the General Staff should be responsible to the Minister of Defence rather than the Prime Minister. The report proposed a motion for judicial independence, requesting that military courts should not try civilians. The National Security Council, as a constitutional body, was criticised and the report proposed to replace it with High Council of National Defence. It proposed ending compulsory religious courses. With regard to the Kurdish issue, even though the report rejected changing Article 66 on citizenship in the constitution, which stipulates that "Everyone bound to the Turkish State through the bond of citizenship is a Turk", it proposed using Kurdish as a mother tongue in schools in Kurdish areas (TÜSİAD, 1997).[10]

In addition, MÜSİAD's 2000 report, entitled *Anayasa Reformu ve Yönetimin Demokratikleşmesi* (Constitutional Reform and Democratisation of Power)

---

10   The content of the report resulted in serious controversy when TÜSİAD led members to declare that the report was "open to debate and does not bind TÜSİAD members" (TÜSİAD, 1999). TÜSİAD members were not alone in distancing themselves from the report. The Turkish armed forces declared that the real objective of the report was "to discredit the General Staff and dismantle the Turkish Armed Forces" (*Cumhuriyet*, 26 January 1997 in TÜSİAD, 1999: 47).

suggested that the Chief of Staff be tied to the Ministry of Defence and the structure of the National Security Council be amended in such a way that the army be represented only by the Chief of Staff (MÜSİAD, 2000: 14). MÜSİAD's 2011 constitutional text, entitled *Türkiye Cumhuriyeti Anayasa Önerisi* (Constitutional Proposal for the Republic of Turkey) maintained the secular character of the state but replaced reference to the state's loyalty to the "nationalism of Atatürk" with "nation state" (MÜSİAD, 2011: 60). MÜSİAD did not incorporate in its proposal the National Security Council and Supreme Military Council as constitutional bodies. Similar to TÜSİAD's 1997 report, MÜSİAD's 2011 constitutional text suggested that the General Staff be responsible to the Minister of Defence rather than the Prime Minister (MÜSİAD, 2011: 95).

Therefore, the role of the EU in applying pressure on Turkish governments to diminish the role of the military in politics and initiate constitutional human rights reforms started *before* AKP rule. At the December 1999 Helsinki Summit, Turkey was granted full membership candidacy status in the EU (Table 12). The EU's views on "progress made by Turkey in preparing for EU membership" have been annually recorded in Progress Reports since 1998. In the progress reports, called "Regular Reports" before 2005, the lack of civilian control of the army and the political influence of the National Security Council through its "recommendations" were prioritised by the EU with respect to the fulfilment of the Copenhagen political criteria.

The European Commission (EC) enunciated in Turkey's 1998 Regular Report "certain anomalies in the functioning of the public authorities, persistent human rights violations and major shortcomings in the treatment of minorities" (European Commission, 1991: 21,53). The European Commission (1991: 21,53) expressed

> The lack of civilian control of the army gives cause for concern. This is reflected by the major role played by the army in the political life through the National Security Council. A civil, non-military solution must be found to the situation in south-eastern Turkey, particularly since many of the violations of civil and political rights observed in the country are connected in one way or another with this issue.

The Copenhagen political criteria, together with economic ones,[11] have been included in the 2001 Accession Partnership Document for Turkey by the

---

11   Copenhagen economic criteria for candidate countries include "the existence of a functioning market economy as well as the capacity to cope with competitive pressure and market forces within the Union" (European Council, 1993: 13).

TABLE 12   Chronology of Turkey-EU relations

1959	Turkey's first application to join the European Economic Community (EEC)
1963	The signature of the agreement creating an association between The Republic of Turkey and the European Economic Community (the Ankara Agreement)
1970	Agreement between Turkey and the EEC on Additional Protocol
1982	Suspension of relations between Turkey and EEC
1987	Turkey's application for full membership of the European Community
1996	The completion of Customs Union between Turkey and the EU
1997	Failure to mention Turkey among candidate countries at the Luxemburg Summit
1998	Publication of first Progress Report for Turkey by the European Commission
1999	Official recognition of Turkey as a candidate state at the Helsinki European Council
2003	Establishment of EU Harmonisation Commission for Turkey in the General Assembly of Turkish Republic
2004	Refusal of Annan Plan in a referendum conducted in Cyprus
2005	The launch of Turkey's Accession Negotiations with the EU
2006	Admission that eight chapters of EU legislation shall be opened and none of the chapters of EU legislation shall be closed temporarily (due to the refusal of Turkey to open its ports and airports to Cyprus)
2007	Opening of negotiations on chapters of EU legislation relating to Policies of Enterprises and Industry, Financial Control and Statistics, Health and Consumer Protection on Trans-European Transport
2008	Opening of negotiations on chapters of EU legislation relating to Company Law, Intellectual Property Law, Free Movement of Capital and Information Society, Media
2009	Opening of negotiations on chapters of EU legislation relating to Taxation and Environment
2010	Opening of negotiations on chapters of EU legislation relating to Food Safety, Veterinary and Phytosanitary Policy
2013	Opening of negotiations on chapters of EU legislation relating to Regional Policy and Coordination of Structural instruments, launching a dialogue on visa liberalisation, and signing the Readmission Agreement

TABLE 12　Chronology of Turkey-EU relations (*cont.*)

2015	Opening of negotiations on chapters of EU legislation relating to Economic and Monetary Policy
2016	The European Parliament's decision to freeze Turkey's EU membership talks
2018	General Affairs Council Conclusions that "no further chapters can be considered for opening or closing"
2019	The Foreign Affairs Council's decision to adopt some measures regarding Turkey's activities in Eastern Mediterranean

SOURCE: REPUBLIC OF TURKEY MINISTRY OF FOREIGN AFFAIRS, DIRECTORATE FOR EU AFFAIRS, (2019).

European Council, which was revised in 2003, 2006, and 2008. Turkey responded by announcing its 2001, 2003 and 2008 National Programmes for the Adoption of the Acquis (NPAA). The 2001 Accession Partnership Document for Turkey listed strengthening of "legal and constitutional guarantees for the right to freedom of expression" as a short-term objective, and alignment of "the constitutional role of the National Security Council as an advisory body to the Government in accordance with the practice of EU Member States" as a medium term objective (Council of the European Union, 2001).

In Turkey's 2000 Regular Report, the EC (2000: 14) warned that the National Security Council (NSC) spontaneously interfered in political processes, by giving its "recommendations" "over the dismissing of the civil servants suspected of links with radical Islamic and separatist movements". As a response, and to harmonise Turkish legislation with the EU's requirements, the 2001 constitutional reform package on the structure of the NSC (Article 118), which had been the cornerstone of Turkish Bonapartism, arrived as the first blow against the army's position. Turkey's 2001 Regular Report welcomed the package, which increased the number of civilian members of the NSC from five to nine while the number of military representatives in the Council remained at five. The advisory character of the NSC decisions was emphasised, with its role limited to giving "recommendations". With these amendments, the government is only required to "evaluate" the NSC decisions instead of being obliged to give "priority consideration" to their implementation (European Commission, 2001: 19). Following the decreasing formal influence of the NSC, the European Commission (2004: 23) warned against the influence of the military in the political process through "informal channels" such as "public speeches, briefings or statements to the media and declarations".

The 2004 constitutional amendments were, indeed, more comprehensive. They included complete abolition of the death penalty; the precedence of international agreements concerning fundamental rights and liberties, which were to be duly put into effect, over domestic laws; permission to extradite Turkish citizens, stemming from being party to the International Criminal Court; abolition of the State Security Courts; elimination of the army's privileged exemption from the control of the Court of Accounts; removal of the military representative from the Board of Higher Education; reinforcement of equality between men and women by stating their equal rights and obliging the state to take action to ensure this equality (Hale and Özbudun, 2010: 55–57; Özbudun and Gençkaya, 2009: 66).

Nine harmonisation packages entered into force between February 2002 and July 2004. While three of these were enacted by the coalition government led by Bülent Ecevit, the AKP continued these packages as part of the EU candidacy (Hale and Özbudun, 2010: 57). With respect to freedom of expression, the third Harmonisation Package in August 2002 limited the severity of the criminal offense of "insulting Turkishness and the Republic" (Hale and Özbudun, 2010: 58). It was only in 2008 when vague words such as "Turkishness" and "the Republic" were replaced with "Turkish Nation" and "the State of the Turkish Republic". Importantly, it was specified that criminal investigations relating to Article 301 of the Turkish Penal Code shall only be commenced upon the approval of the Minister of Justice (Hale and Özbudun, 2010: 58).

Under the Sixth Harmonisation Package, which entered into force in July 2003, Article 8 of the anti-Terror Law was abrogated, which had prohibited "written, oral or visual propaganda, as well as meetings, demonstrations and marches carried out with the purpose of destroying the indivisible integrity of the state with its territory and nation". With the sixth package, the use of force or violence was made a prerequisite for the definition of terror. With the second, third, and fourth packages, a court decision was made a prerequisite to the confiscation of printed material (Hale and Özbudun, 2010: 58). In July 2004, a new Law on Associations was enacted, and freedom of association was expanded, while the power of provincial governors to postpone or ban meetings and marches was limited with the seventh harmonisation packages. The rights of non-Muslim communities in acquiring and disposing of property was enlarged but put under the permission of the General Directorate of Foundations with the fourth package. Under the permission of administrative authorities, they were allowed to build places of worship. While the third package permitted use of "different languages and dialects traditionally used by Turkish citizens in their daily lives" such as Kurdish in radio and television broadcasting, the sixth package enlarged this right to public radio and television channels

(Hale and Özbudun, 2010: 57–60). In January 2009, the government introduced TRT 6 (*TRT Şeş*), a 24-hour Kurdish TV station broadcasting on state-run television.

Meanwhile, the EU appreciated the appointment in 2004 of the first civilian chairman of the Secretary General of the NSC, Mehmet Yiğit Alpogan, and the reduction in the number of NSC staff from 408 to 305. Yet, the political influence of the military members of the NSC and senior members of the armed forces in foreign and domestic matters via public briefings continued to be an important issue (European Commission, 2005: 12–14). Turkey's Progress Reports in 2006 and 2007 noted delays in reforms concerning civilian control of the military. These stated that the Turkish Armed Forces Internal Service Law[12] and Article 2a of the Law on the National Security Council, which provided a broad definition of national security, had yet to be reformed.

The preparation of the defence budget was brought into question by the European Commission. The Commission (2002: 25) pointed out the "substantial degree of autonomy in establishing the defence budget" by the armed forces, highlighting the existence of two extra-budgetary funds available to the military. The problem of transparency and accountability of defence expenditures was pointed out by the EU with regards to restrictions on the Court of Accounts "under Article 160 of the Constitution under which the confidentiality of the national defence is foreseen" (European Commission, 2003: 19). Although the clause of Article 160 of the Constitution, which exempted state property owned by the Turkish armed forces from being audited, was repealed in the 2004 constitutional amendments, a new Law on the Court of Accounts (no. 6085) was only adopted in 2010 after waiting six years in the Parliament.

The law that was finally introduced reflected a political consensus between the government and the military. Under its terms, auditors would only audit the results of activities of public administrations, i.e. whether or not the objectives and indicators determined by them had been carried out. The Court of Accounts is unable to conduct "efficiency auditing" on military expenditures, i.e. whether or not the purchase of that amount of military arms is in compliance with the needs of the army. Article 35 of the law states that the "Turkish Court of Accounts shall not undertake propriety audit and shall not render decisions that limit or remove the discretionary powers of administrations" (Turkish Court of Accounts, 2011).

---

12   Enacted in 1961 and amended in 2013, the Turkish Armed Forces Internal Service Law granted the army to guard and protect not only the homeland but also the Republic of Turkey (*Hürriyet*, 14 July 2013).

In addition, the auditing of the Military Pension Fund (*OYAK*) and the Turkish Armed Forces Support Foundation (*TSKGV*) would now require a request by the Parliamentary Petition Committee, thereby circumventing the Court of Accounts (TESEV, 2013: 19).

A protocol on Security, Public Order and Assistance Units (*Emniyet-Asayiş-Yardımlaşma*, EMASYA), which allowed the military to intervene in domestic security incidents without permission from civilian authorities (European Commission, 2006: 7–8; 2007: 9), had been signed between the General Staff and the Ministry of Interior after the 28 February 1997 military intervention. During domestic security incidents, the EMASYA protocol permitted that "provincial police units, and governors are attached to the military in matters of intelligence, analysis, and planning. This structure enables the military to collect all social and intelligence-related information" (TESEV, 2009: 22). This protocol was abrogated in February 2010.

In January 2006, The Council of the European Union urged Turkey to "abolish any remaining competence of military courts to try civilians" as a short-term priority to be completed in one or two years (Council of the European Union, 2006). This was further emphasised in a revised 2008 Turkey Accession Partnership Document that advocated limiting the jurisdiction of the military courts to offenses committed by military personnel whilst on duty (Council of the European Union, 2008). In return, Turkey adopted its third National Programme for the Adoption of the EU Acquis (NPAA) in 2008. On civil-military relations, Turkey reassured the EU by preparing a Judicial Reform Strategy in which the tasks and competencies of the military courts were defined (National Programme for the Adoption of the EU Acquis, 2008: 7). Amendments in the Code of the Criminal Procedure in 2009 lifted the power of the military courts to try civilians in peacetime (European Commission, 2009: 10).

The EU welcomed two important developments in 2012: the removal from secondary school curricula of a national security course taught by military officers; and the trial of two non-commissioned officers and a PKK member turned gendarmerie informant for the 2005 bombing of a bookstore in Şemdinli, in Kurdish region of Turkey's southeast (European Commission, 2012: 12). The Şemdinli incident brought the Turkish deep state into the spotlight when two members of the gendarmerie intelligence service, Ali Kaya and Özcan İldeniz, and an informer, Veysel Ateş, were apprehended by local people for the bombing of the Umut bookshop in Şemdinli district on November 9, 2005 (Human Rights Watch, 2007: 18). The prosecutor of the Van Third Heavy Criminal Court, Ferhat Sarıkaya, prepared an indictment that sentenced these suspects to 39 years in jail and specified that the investigation should extend to the senior military officers. In March 2006, the General Staff accused Ferhat Sarıkaya of undermining the armed forces while the High Council of Judges and Prosecutors (HSYK) debarred Sarıkaya from the legal profession for "abuse of his duty and exceeding his authority" (as cited in Human Rights Watch, 2007: 18). The case was forwarded to a military court, which released the suspects. After the enactment of the constitutional referendum in September 2010, which allowed the civilian courts to try military personnel, the retrial process started. The Van Third Heavy Criminal Court handed down prison sentences to these three officers and charged them of forming a criminal organisation, which was overruled by the Supreme Court of Appeals in October 2012. The Supreme Court of Appeals however confirmed the prison sentences of these officers (*Hürriyet Daily News*, 11 October 2012).

4   The AKP Tactics towards the Military: the Modern Capitalist Prince and a "War of Position"

The crucial question still remains to be answered: *How did the AKP find popular support to defang the army and to decrease its role in politics?* The answer lies in the AKP's creation of a strategic alliance between peripheral capitalists and big capitalists in order to consolidate capitalist democracy. This was achieved through the party's capacity to organise the collective will. The AKP government assumed the historical task of carrying democratic transition after the main centre-left and centre-right parties were defeated in the 2002 elections in the aftermath of the major economic crisis of 2000/2001. The accompanying political crisis allowed the AKP to express the popular collective will with the objective of reducing military tutelage over the parliament.

This historical task that the party undertook was the embodiment of the "capitalist Modern Prince" in the Gramscian sense. In *The Prison Notebooks*, the modern prince "can only be an organism, a complex element of society in which a collective will, which has always been recognised and has to some extent asserted itself in action, begins to take concrete form" (Gramsci, 1971: 129). Two tasks of the "Modern Prince" are the "formation of a national-popular collective will" and being "the proclaimer and organiser of an intellectual and moral reform" (Gramsci, 1971: 133).

With regard to attenuating the pre-eminence of the military in politics, the strategy of the AKP was quite different from that of Refah. The Refah Party with a small Islamic fundamentalist force initiated a direct frontal attack on "actually existing Turkish secularism" and Kemalist nationalism. This resulted in the complete defeat of the party. Learning from this especially, the AKP pursued a low profile conflict against the "political autonomy of the military". This strategy consisted of pullbacks, entrenchment, sacrifices, and temporisation since this effective strategy—a war of position—necessitated "an unprecedented concentration of hegemony" in the form of alliances between classes in a historical bloc (Gramsci, 1971: 238–239).

First, the AKP benefited effectively from the division within the army between a "tutelary tendency" and a "controllable change tendency" (Demirel, 2010). The former tendency staunchly supports the "supervisory role of the Turkish Armed Forces of the Republic", believing that since Turkey's transition to a multi-party system in 1946, there have been concessions on Republican values, which peaked during the AKP government. The latter believes that these values can be better protected in a democratic regime (Demirel, 2010). On the other hand, those who advocate "controllable change" nonetheless ask for a continuation of the political and judicial prerogatives of the Turkish armed forces (Demirel, 2010: 19). This faction also supports Turkish integration with the EU (Aydinli, 2009; Demirel, 2010). According to this classification, while National Security Council Secretary General Tuncer Kılınç, General Chief of Staff Doğan Güreş (1990–1994), General Chief of Staff Hüseyin Kıvrıkoğlu (2000–2002) and Commander of the Turkish Army Aytaç Yalman (2002–2004) are more Euro-sceptic and favour conservative tutelary tendencies (Aydinli, 2009; Demirel, 2010), Chief of the General Staff Hilmi Özkök (2002–2006) and Chief of the General Staff İlker Başbuğ (2008–2010) endorse the EU and demand "controllable change" (Demirel, 2010).

The former faction, known as Eurasianists, developed an alternative political discourse to Turkey's Western orientation in foreign policy. They advocated "a cultural, military, political and commercial alliance with Turkey's eastern neighbours, notably Russia, Iran, the Turkic countries of Central Asia, and even Pakistan, India and China" (Akçali and Perinçek, 2009: 551). The "creation of a non-Western 'Eurasian space'" under the leadership of Russia had become the political objective of this faction (Akçali and Perinçek, 2009: 560). This was illustrated at the 2002 War Academy in İstanbul, when the National Security Council Secretary General Tuncer Kılınç highlighted the need for Turkey to explore new strategic allies "that would include Iran and the Russian Federation" (*Hürriyet Daily News*, 3 August 2002). In 2009, he also suggested exiting NATO (Küçük, 2009). Former General Chief of Staff Doğan Güreş (1990–1994) also stated in a 2007 interview his distrust towards the USA and EU since he believed that their objective had been to divide Turkey for the benefits of Kurds (Bila, 2007). In the retired General Suat İlhan's book *Why "No" to the European Union?*, European integration, which was deemed to jeopardise national interests and challenge national integrity, was perceived to be incongruent with Atatürkist thought (Kösebalaban, 2002: 140). The AKP gradually brought this faction within the army under control.

Second, the AKP achieved the "absorption" of Islamic fundamentalism "into secular neoliberalism more or less successfully at all levels of the hegemonic formation" under its moral and political leadership (Tuğal, 2009: 148). The AKP, as an organiser of political society, was able to constitute hegemony in linking civil society and the state through the "integration of antisystem cadres and strategies into the system" (Tuğal, 2009: 148). According to a survey conducted in 2006 by Ali Çarkoğlu and Binnaz Toprak (2007) as a follow-up to a study conducted in 1999, although there had been an increase in religiosity in Turkey during the seven years between 1999 and 2006, the support for a Sharia-based state declined from 21% in 1999 to 9% in 2006.[13] By integrating those segments of society who reflected these evolving views into the political system, the AKP departed from the Welfare Party, effectively neutralising, defusing, and demobilising the radical insurgency of Islamic fundamentalism in Turkey (Tuğal, 2009). The AKP's party programme provides a framework for coexistence of religious freedoms with secularism while rejecting the use of religion for political aims. While it suggests that the AKP "considers religion as one of the most important institutions of humanity, and secularism as a pre-requisite of democracy, and an assurance of the freedom of religion and conscience", the party "also rejects the interpretation and distortion of secularism as enmity against religion" (AK Party, n.d.). For instance, during the revolutionary process in Egypt, Erdoğan even called on the adoption of a secular constitution for Egypt and was criticised for interfering in Egypt's local affairs by the Muslim Brotherhood (*Al Arabiya News*, 14 September 2011). By no stretch of the imagination could Erbakan have called on the Muslim Brotherhood of Egypt to a secular constitution.

This transformation of Islamic radicalism into a US type of conservatism (Tuğal, 2007) has been instrumental in overcoming the Kemalist/Bonapartist regime. This is why the AKP could wage a war in the form of a "reciprocal siege", which necessitated "an unprecedented concentration of hegemony" and "a more 'interventionist' government" (Gramsci, 1971: 238–239), against the Kemalist state. In the initial phase of confrontation, the pro-status quo forces had a dominant position in balancing the political leadership of Erdoğan. He had been sentenced to ten months of incarceration and a life-time ban from

---

13 According to the research in 2006, people perceived themselves more religious as compared to 1999. While only a quarter of the respondents identified as "very religious" and only 6% as "extremely religious" in 1999, this percentage rose to 46.5% and 12.8%, respectively, in 2006 (Tuğal and Toprak, 2007: 41).

participation in elections by the State Security Court, which charged him with "inciting religious hatred" and asking for the "overthrow of the government" (Yavuz, 2009: 67). This is why even though Erdoğan was the leader of the AKP, Abdullah Gül formed the cabinet and became prime minister following the general elections of 2002. The AKP government under Gül immediately executed an effective strategy to enable Erdoğan to be elected, cooperating with the CHP in the Parliament to abolish the clause of the Constitution that hindered his election. Even though the incumbent President Ahmet Necdet Sezer sent back the constitutional amendments, arguing that laws cannot be issued for personal purposes (*Hürriyet Daily News*, 21 December 2002) he was constitutionally obliged to approve the amendment. This was followed by the AKP's claim of irregularities in the 2002 general elections in Siirt. The Supreme Election Board (*Yüksek Seçim Kurulu*) cancelled the elections there and prompted by-elections in March 2003. Consequently, Abdullah Gül swapped his post with Erdoğan's, who formed the new cabinet in March 2003. During the first tenure of the AKP between 2002 and 2007, the AKP passed major EU-led reforms on civil liberties and civil-military relations, as described above.

The last stage of this "reciprocal siege" unfolded when Turkey's political turmoil deepened during 2006–2007. The ultra-nationalist organisations that had close connections with former soldiers and right-wing party representatives were encouraged by the perceived crisis of the Turkish state in the context of Europeanisation (Jacob, 2011). Andrea Santoro, a Catholic priest, was killed in Trabzon in February 2006. A top judge in the Council of State, Mustafa Yücel Özbilgin, was assassinated and four judges were wounded in May 2006, with protests at the funeral of the slain judge. Chief of General Staff General Hilmi Özkök welcomed the protests, adding "it must not remain the reaction of just one day, a one-off event.... It must gain permanence, as something continuous. It must be pursued by everyone" (*Hürriyet Daily News*, 21 May 2006).

The death of Hrank Dink, a socialist Armenian journalist and chief editor of the weekly newspaper *Agos* on 19 January 19 2007 was a blatant assassination; Dink had been receiving death threats from Turkish nationalists due to his statements on Armenian identity and the Armenian Genocide. He was also under prosecution for denigrating Turkishness according to Article 301 of the Turkish Penal Code. At his funeral hundreds of thousands of people marched chanting "We are all Armenian, we are all Hrant Dink". Nevertheless, this political murder was followed by another murder of three Protestants in Malatya in April 2007. Meanwhile, in March 2007 *Nokta* magazine published excerpts of the diary of former Commander of the Turkish Naval forces Özden Örnek, which allegedly revealed two coup plans (*Sarıkız* and *Ayışığı*). The claims were challenged by Chief of General Staff Hilmi Özkök. Founded in 1983, the 24-year old magazine was closed down under "pressure" (*Radikal*, 21 April 2007).

The peak of the war, in the form of a "reciprocal siege" between the AKP and the civil-military bureaucracy, came when the term of the tenth President of the Republic of Turkey Ahmet Necdet Sezer (2000–2007) was about to expire in May 2007. This was the last stage of an institutional battle between the AKP and the presidency. After that, the political struggle mutated into a judicial struggle between the AKP and the pro-status quo forces. Since the AKP dominated the Parliament in the aftermath of the general election in 2002, it obtained a sufficient number of parliamentarians to elect any of its candidates for president. Kemalist nationalists, on the other hand, were very alarmed by Erdoğan's possible holding of presidential office, claiming that the secular character of the state would be under threat. As a conservative attack, Republic Protests (*Cumhuriyet Mitingleri*) were rallied under the initiative of the Atatürkist Thought Association (*Atatürkçü Düşünce Derneği*) whose head was the former Commander of the Gendarmerie General Şener Eruygur. Former Commander of the First Army General Hurşit Tolon (2004–2005) also participated in the protests.[14]

The AKP held off announcing its candidate until the last minute. Three days before the presidential elections, Foreign Minister Abdullah Gül was nominated. However the nomination of Gül, although not Erdoğan, did not put the secular/nationalist elites at ease, since Gül's spouse was veiled. At that point, former Chief Public Prosecutor of the Court of Cassation Sabih Kanadoğlu (2001–2003) "formulated" that a two-third majority (367 votes) was required for quorum to elect the president. This was, indeed, openly against the constitution. Even though Gül received 357 votes in the first round, the main opposition party applied to the Constitutional Court for the annulment of elections. In due course, on 27 April 2007 Chief of the General Staff Yaşar Büyükanıt (2006–2008) issued a statement on his website, dubbed an "e-memorandum". It stated that the military was following the debate over secularism in the presidential election with "concern" and would "openly display its position and attitude when it becomes necessary" (*Hürriyet*, 29 April 2007).

---

14 For nurturing the secular sentiments of the masses, *Cumhuriyet*, the daily hard-line secularist newspaper founded in 1924, run successive TV advertisements, which said: "Are you aware of the danger? Own up to your Republic", "On May 2007, the presidential elections are taking place. Are you aware of the danger? Own up to your Republic", "On May 16, the clocks are being set back 100 years. Are you aware of the danger?" The last one put an unveiled woman on the background who was then shown wearing *çarşaf* (black attire that conceals whole body) while the voiceover demanded "Own up to your Republic".

Not surprisingly, the Constitutional Court adopted Kanadoğlu's "367 formula" and annulled the first round of the presidential elections. When the Parliament was unable to assemble for the election of the President for the second round, the election process was paralysed. As a response by Erdoğan, the AKP, which believed it had public support behind it, called early elections in July 2007. The AKP also called a constitutional referendum, believing the president could be elected by a direct popular vote in order to block the military's intervention in the elections. Rather than discharging the generals, the AKP adopted a strategic move by transferring the locus of the struggle to the "popular will". The early elections in 2007 resulted in the AKP's landslide victory with 46.6% of the popular vote, an increase from 34.3% in 2002, and the control of the Parliament with a majority of 341 seats out of 550 (TÜİK, 2012: 93). Abdullah Gül was elected as the 11th president of the Republic of Turkey in August 2007.

Alongside this extended political feud ran the ongoing political struggle between Kemalist forces and the AKP over the headscarf, dubbed the "hijab wars". With a constitutional amendment in February 2008 supported by the AKP and the MHP, the ban on headscarves in universities was lifted. However, the secular establishments were alarmed that the AKP had a hidden agenda to change the secular nature of the Republic. They argued that lifting the headscarf ban in universities, which had been a zero-sum game between hard-line secularist forces and Islamic forces for a long time, was one step towards the Islamisation of society. Deniz Baykal, the leader of the CHP, described it as a "clear challenge to secularism" (*Hürriyet Daily News*, 6 February 2008). Following the appeal by the CHP and DSP to the Constitutional Court, the Court ruled to annul the constitutional changes on the grounds that they violated Article 2 of the Constitution on the secular character of the state.

The continuation of the political struggle between the AKP and the high judiciary came to a head in 2008. In March the judiciary struck again, harsher than before, with a file by the Chief Public Prosecutor of the Supreme Court of Appeals Abdurrahman Yalçınkaya to close the AKP and ban its 71 leading members for five years, including President Gül and Prime Minister Erdoğan. This case signalled possible political instability. The party was indicted as becoming the "centre of anti-secular activities" by Abdurrahman Yalçınkaya. The demand for the closure of the AKP was rejected with six votes to five while a verdict was rendered for partial cutting of public funding for the party (*Milliyet*, 30 July 2008).

The most important round of democratic struggle with pro-status quo Kemalist forces occurred in June 2009 when Parliament, by amending Article 250 of the Code of Criminal Procedure, passed legislation providing for civilian courts—actually "specially authorised heavy penal courts"[15]—to try military personnel in peacetime for crimes such as attempted coups d'état, crimes affecting national security and organised crime (European Commission, 2009: 10). By amending Article 3 of the Code of Criminal Procedure, the power of the military courts to try civilians in peacetime was totally abrogated (European Commission, 2009: 10). Upon the appeal in January 2010 by the CHP under Deniz Baykal to the Constitutional Court to annul legislation making amendments to the Code of Criminal Procedure, the Constitutional Court overturned it (*Today's Zaman*, 22 January 2010).

This prompted the last round between the AKP and the high judiciary through the 12 September 2010 Constitutional Referendum, strategically held on the 30th anniversary of the 1980 military coup. The AKP promised to enlarge, strengthen, and diversify fundamental rights and freedoms and enhance democratic standards (AK Party, 2010: 14). Therefore, the governing party was able to get the consent of liberals and some socialists who gathered under the banner of "Not Enough but Yes" (*Yetmez ama Evet*). It can be said that the AKP successfully implemented a strategy of a war of position by turning itself into a source of "moral and political leadership" of the liberal intelligentsia against the Kemalist monopolisation of the state. The AKP also made clear that one of the objectives of the constitutional referendum was to strengthen the rule of law and judicial independence (AK Party, 2010: 14). By modifying the composition of the Constitutional Court and the High Council of Judges and Public Prosecutors[16] the referendum broke the judicial monopoly of the Kemalists. However, it filled the vacancies with the followers of the Gülen movement.

---

15   These "specially authorised heavy penal courts" had been included in the Code of Criminal Procedure in June 2004 and equipped with special powers after the abolition of "state security courts" and became instrumental in trying military personnel in the Ergenekon and Sledgehammer cases. Their abolition was decreed in July 2012 but not completed until March 2014.

16   According to these constitutional amendments in 2010, the Constitutional Court was composed of 17 members. They were sourced from Parliament (3 members), President (4 members), Court of Appeal (3 members), the Council of State (2 members), the Military Court of Appeal (1 member), High Military Administrative Court (1 member), and the Council of Higher Education (3 members). However, the structure of the court also changed after the 2017 constitutional referendum. The court is composed of 15 judges.

The High Council of Judges and Public Prosecutors was composed of 22 members, made up of the Minister of Justice (1 member), Undersecretary of Minister of Justice (1 member), regular judges and public prosecutors of the first degree (7 members), administrative judges and public prosecutors of the first degree (3 members), Court of Appeal (3 members), Council of State (2), the Justice Academy (1 member) and President (4 members). However, the structure of the council also changed after the 2017 constitutional referendum. The council is composed of 13 members.

(Çakır and Sakallı, 2014: 28–32). The alliance between the AKP and the Gülen movement also worked in the Ergenekon and Sledgehammer (*Balyoz*) trials (Çakır and Sakallı, 2014: 28–32). The rapid expansion of the Gülen movement after Turkey's neoliberal turn in the 1980s has coincided in some ways with the AKP's struggle against the state establishment. On that point, it is crucial to outline the expansion of the Gülen movement.

CHAPTER 5

Authoritarian Turn, Sub-imperialist Foreign Policy, and the Failed Coup of 15 July 2016

1   The Expansion of the Gülen Movement

Fethullah Gülen, the leader of the movement, was born in Erzurum, a conservative city in Eastern Turkey, in 1938. There he received a Sufi education from Sheikh Muhammed Lütfi (Yavuz, 2003b: 20).[1] He graduated from a *madrasa* in Erzurum in 1958 (Ünal and Williams, 2000: 1) and in 1966 was appointed to the Kestanepazarı Quranic school in İzmir, Turkey's third biggest city located in the West of the country (Yavuz, 2003b: 20). As a sympathiser of the *Nurcus*, which "has been the major pro-NATO and pro-American Muslim group in Turkey" (Yavuz, 2003: 22), Gülen founded the Erzurum branch of the "Turkish Association for Struggle against Communism" in 1963 (Çetin, 2010: 31; Yavuz, 2003b: 22).

The 1980 coup was supported by Gülen himself, not only because he was in favour of a strong state as a buttress against anarchy but also because the political and social project propagated by the military, the Turkish-Islamic Synthesis, aligned well with his objective to cultivate a "golden generation" (Yavuz, 2003b). Inspired by the reading circles (*dershanes*) developed by Said-i Nursi (1873–1960) who authored a Quranic exegesis known as *Risale-i Nur* (the Epistle of Light), Gülen had formed the lighthouses (*ışık evleri*) where "university students stay, study, and develop a sense of identity to protect their Muslim personality from other temptations" (Yavuz, 2003b: 33). According to Gülen, the "golden generation" (*altın nesil*) and "people of service" (*hizmet insanları*) would be "faithful to the cause to which they have devoted themselves, that deeply in love with it, they willingly sacrifice their lives and whatever they love for its sake" (Gülen as cited in Hendrick, 2013: 90).

Gülen's ideas—integration of Islam into the formation of national identity and promotion of loyalty to the state—were seen as an antidote to Islamic fundamentalist forces after the 1980s (Yavuz, 2003b: 37–38). While in 1986 Turgut Özal lifted the ban on Gülen on delivering sermons (Yavuz, 2003b: 37), the Presidency of Religious Affairs elevated his official status to an Emeritus

---

1   According to Fethullah Gülen (2004), Sufism is a path that enables an individual to renounce his/her material ambitions and desires through a spiritual self-discipline, a strict religious observance, and an understanding of the religious and gnostic sciences.

Preacher in 1989, meaning that he was allowed to deliver sermons in any mosque in Turkey (Çetin, 2010: 46).

The Gülen movement capitalised on two important developments in the 1980s and 1990s. On the one hand, Gülen's trust networks benefited a lot from the neoliberal transformation of Turkey's education system; they set up private schools, supplemental tutoring centres such as lesson houses (*dershaneler* in Turkish), and dormitories. These institutions have provided a refuge for poor students struggling in a highly competitive university entrance examination system (Hendrick, 2013). On the other hand, the collapse of the Soviet Union, more specifically, the ideological vacuum that the Soviet Union left in the Central Asia after 1991, provided another window of opportunity for the Gülen movement. Unlike the *Milli Görüş* movement which provided religious services to Turkish migrants abroad, the Gülen movement concentrated on building schools and cultural centres (Balci, 2014). By means of building networks with the Turkish embassies there, the number of the Gülen-affiliated schools abroad increased exponentially during the 1990s. By 2003, 149 Gülen-affiliated schools all over the world, but mainly concentrated in Eurasia, served approximately 28,000 students with more than 3,000 teachers (Balci, 2003: 156). The Gülen-affiliated schools and especially the "dialogue" centres set up in virtually all countries fulfil a two-fold mission. They both establish solidarity networks (*hemşehrilik*) among Turkish people abroad and provide a platform for academics, researchers, and an "elite strata" (Hüseyin Gülerce, 2013, personal communication).[2]

By 1997, the Gülen movement had already established a strong presence in the media with a newspaper (*Zaman*); magazines (*Sızıntı, Ekoloji*, and, *Aksiyon*); a journal (*Yeni Ümit*); a periodical (*The Foundation*); a television channel (*Samanyolu TV*); a radio station (*Burç FM*) combined with a growing power in economy with a financial institution (*Asya Finans*) and a business organisation (The Business Life Cooperation Association, *İŞHAD*) (Yavuz, 2003b: 36). The expansion of the Gülen movement abroad during the 1990s was also instrumental in strengthening Turkey's soft power and it was supported by President Turgut Özal (Balci, 2014).

Despite Gülen's close relationship with Turkey's political establishment and his pro-state discourse, he could not avert the direct attack on him by the media and the military after the military coup in 1997 (Yavuz, 2003b: 43). The Ankara state security court requested an arrest warrant for Gülen in 2000, which was lifted later (*Hürriyet Daily News*, 29 August 2000). The pressure on the

---

2 Hüseyin Gülerce was a former columnist in the *Zaman* newspaper and an important figure in the Gülen Movement. He is now a staunch opponent of Gülen.

Gülen movement in the aftermath of the 28 February process eased off the AKP coming to power in 2002. The movement continued to expand in finance, media, and business. In 2005, a Gülen-affiliated business association (Turkish Confederation of Businessmen and Industrialists, TUSKON) was formed. In 2008, Gülen was acquitted of a charge in 2000 of forming an illegal organisation by a unanimous vote of the Supreme Court of Appeals (*Today's Zaman*, 8 March 2008).

The Gülen movement had an influence on the police institution and judiciary and had been backing the AKP since 2002, providing human resources to overcome the common enemy, the military (Çakır and Sakallı, 2014; Söyler, 2015: 171). According to Gülen's followers, the well-educated "golden generation" would be the only potential carrier of democratisation contrary to Turkey's intolerant and aggressive contemporary political figures (Hüseyin Gülerce, 2013, personal communication). Vis-à-vis the state establishment, the Gülen community claimed that the "Ergenekon mentality" was not limited to the military, but also fused into the judiciary, media, the business circles, and the university therefore the trials should be expanded to these zones of influences (Hüseyin Gülerce, 2013, personal communication).

2   The Ergenekon and Sledgehammer (*Balyoz*) Trials

The Ergenekon and Sledgehammer cases emerged as the last phase of a tug of war between the AKP and the Bonapartist tendency within the military *after* the balance of power shifted in favour of the AKP which challenged the e-memorandum by the military in April 2007. The AKP called for early elections in July 2007 and won a comfortable victory with 46.6% of the votes (TÜİK, 2012: 93). The Ergenekon trial between 2008 and 2013 and the Sledgehammer trial between 2010 and 2013 by "specially authorised courts" basically worked to paralyse a clique in the army—a clique which saw itself as saviour of the Republic and would not hesitate to intervene in politics since they deemed the AKP to be the facilitator of the decay of Republican ideas, secularism and national unity.

Few cases in the history of the Turkish Republic have so deeply polarised the public and been as baffling as the Ergenekon and Sledgehammer cases. From their initial phases, these inquiries were highly politicised. The CHP leader Deniz Baykal accused Prime Minister Erdoğan of being "the prosecutor of Ergenekon" and named himself as "the lawyer of Ergenekon" (*Radikal*, 5 July 2008). Erdoğan responded that he was a prosecutor in the name of the nation (*Yeni Şafak*, 16 July 2008).

On the one hand, the Ergenekon trials were deemed to be political trials aiming for suppression of the AKP's prosecular critics (Eligür, 2010: 266) by the Gülen movement supporters. The Ergenekon investigation was alleged to rest on a "largely fictionalized construct"(Rubin, 2008), which was "full of contradictions, rumors, speculation, misinformation, illogicalities, absurdities and untruths" (Jenkins, 2009: 11). It was also put forward that the Sledgehammer indictment was, similarly, based on fabricated evidence and conspiracy (Doğan and Rodrik, 2010). The Ergenekon trials were argued to be the product of a power struggle between "an inner core of unelected, self-appointed and often state-employed arch-nationalists" and "an imperfectly democratic, illiberal, but nonetheless electorally popular new elite of Anatolian populists" (Park, 2009).

On the other hand, it was suggested that the Ergenekon affair marked a crucial point in the democratisation of Turkey since the government could embrace a reformist-liberal agenda—for instance on the Kurdish issue—once it got rid of military tutelage (Cizre and Walker, 2010). Only then did the government feel strong enough to eliminate the autonomy of the military in internal security operations by abolishing the Police-Public Security Cooperation (EMASYA) protocol in early 2010 (Gürsoy, 2012: 748–749). This was a further step for a "regime with consolidated democratic control of the military" (Bardakçi, 2013: 425). In addition, by revealing internal divisions within the army—between absolutists and gradualists—the Ergenekon affair contributed to the evolution of society towards a more liberal democratic mindset with respect to civil-military relations, according to Ersel Aydinli (2011). In response to the legal/procedural flaws in trials, such as long pre-trial detentions, lack of secrecy during the investigation, the hurrying off of suspects from their homes at early hours, and awkward indictments, Necati Polat (2011: 214) reminded that judicial inadequacies were results of the accumulation of problems with a "long-standing, inefficient system that [was] simply oblivious to international standards". H. Akin Ünver (2009: 16) rightly warned that the polarisation in Turkish society hid a debate on democratisation and transparency of the state.

Named after the mythical birthplace of the Turkish nation in Central Asia, the "Ergenekon" investigation was launched upon the discovery in June 2007 in a shanty house in Ümraniye, İstanbul of 27 hand grenades, having serial numbers that matched those used in an attack against the pro-secular *Cumhuriyet* newspaper offices (Aydinli, 2011: 232). Following the investigation, several retired army officers, officers in active duty, mafia leaders, journalists and writers linked with the military, and prominent figures were arrested one after the other.[3] The charges of the suspects included "membership in an armed terrorist

---

3 In the 2,455-page first Ergenekon indictment, which was presented on 10 July 2008, 86 suspects were charged. Some of the prominent defendants in the first Ergenekon indictment

group, aiding and abetting an armed terrorist organisation, attempting to destroy the government of the Republic of Turkey or to block it from performing its duties, inciting people to rebel against the Republic of Turkey, being in possession of explosives, using them, and inciting others to commit such crimes, acquiring secret documents on national security, recording personal data, encouraging soldiers to disobey superiors and openly provoking hatred and hostility" (Park, 2008: 56). The Ergenekon process lasted six years from June 2007 to August 2013 and merged 23 indictments, charging 275 suspects, including former Chief of Staff General İlker Başbuğ (2008–2010).

On 5 August 2013, İstanbul's 13th High Criminal Court announced its punishments, which included consecutive life sentences, aggravated life imprisonment, and lengthy sentences for high-ranking officers and prominent figures (*Hürriyet Daily News*, 5 August 2013). After the Constitutional court decided that İlker Başbuğ had been "unlawfully deprived of his freedom", he was released in March 2014, followed by other convicts (European Commission, 2014: 12).

Unlike the heterogonous make-up of the suspects in the Ergenekon trials, all the suspects in the Sledgehammer (*Balyoz*) trials were military officers. The trial started after a liberal newspaper, *Taraf*, revealed in January 2010 the averted coup plan drafted between late 2002 and March 2003 by Çetin Doğan, who was Commander of the First Army at that time (*Taraf*, 20 January 2010). In the

---

were retired brigadier general and founder of gendarmerie intelligence and anti-terror unit (*JİTEM*) Veli Küçük, retired lieutenant Muzaffer Tekin, mafia leaders Sedat Peker and Sami Hoştan, the head of National Forces Association (*Kuvayı Milliye Derneği*) Bekir Öztürk, the leader of the Workers' Party Doğu Perinçek, former rector of İstanbul University Kemal Alemdaroğlu, lawyer and the head of The Great Jurists Union (*Büyük Hukukçular Derneği*) Kemal Kerinçsiz, Orthodox Patriarchate spokeswoman Sevgi Erenerol, chief editor of Workers' Party-linked TV channel (*UlUsAl Kanal*) Ferid İlsever, journalist in *Cumhuriyet* İlhan Selçuk, the president of the National Forces (*Kuvayı Milliye*) Association retired Colonel Fikri Karadağ (*Hürriyet*, 26 July 2008). A 1,909-page second Ergenekon indictment was presented on March 8, 2009, charging 56 suspects of being members or founders of "an armed terrorist organisation". The defendants included former General Commander of the Gendarmerie and later head of Atatürk Thought Association (*Atatürkçü Düşünce Derneği*) Şener Eruygur, former Commader of the First Army Hurşit Tolon, former General Levent Ersöz, columnist in newspaper *Cumhuriyet* Mustafa Balbay, journalist Tuncay Özkan, head of Ankara Chamber of Commerce Sinan Aygün and Commander Arif Doğan (*Radikal*, 25 March 2009). The third Ergenekon indictment of 1,454 pages charged 52 suspects of the same offence, which included socialist writer Yalçın Küçük, internationally renowned surgeon Mehmet Haberal, academician Erol Manisalı, rectors Fatih Hilmioğlu and Ferit Bernay, former head of Higher Education Board (YÖK) Kemal Gürüz, former Secretary-General of the National Security Council Tuncer Kılınç, former head of Police Special Operation Department İbrahim Şahin and head of trade union Türk Metal since 1975 Mustafa Özbek (*Radikal*, 5 August 2009).

Sledgehammer trials, the generals were charged with "attempting to hinder the operations of the executive body of the Republic of Turkey by force" (*Hürriyet Daily News*, 21 September 2012).

On 21 September 2012, a total of 331 serving and retired members of the military out of 365 suspects were convicted to 20 years' imprisonment, including the retired Air Force Commander General İbrahim Fırtına, retired First Army Commander General Çetin Doğan and retired Navy Commander Admiral Özden Örnek (*Hürriyet Daily News*, 21 September 2012). By March 2011, one tenth of the generals and admirals of the Turkish armed forces were arrested and charged with plotting a coup (İnce, 2011). However, in June 2014, the Constitutional Court ruled for the release of all convicts in the Balyoz trials and opened the way for retrial, since it concluded that the rights of the convicted suspects were violated concerning digital data used as evidence and the failure by the court to hear the testimony of witnesses, including Commander of the Turkish Army Aytaç Yalman (2002–2004) and Chief of the General Staff Hilmi Özkök (2002–2006). (*Zaman*, 18 June 2014). On 31 March 2015, all suspects in the Balyoz case were acquitted in the retrial and they vowed to pinpoint those behind the "plot" (Ergan, 2015).

The sudden change for the retrial of suspects in the Balyoz case was due to the fact that when the specially authorised courts started to question National Intelligence Organisation (MIT) chief Hakan Fidan in February 2012 over talks with the PKK in Oslo (*Hürriyet Daily News*, 9 February 2012), the alliance between the AKP and the Gülen movement broke down (Söyler, 2015: 172). After Erdoğan ensured that the military tutelage was over, the AKP sided with the military against his old ally, the Gülen network, and the government started to be critical of the trials. The AKP, first, partially abolished the specially authorised courts in July 2012 (*Hürriyet*, 5 July 2012). The Gülen movement was opposed to the abolition of the specially authorised courts due to the persistence of a "pro-coup mentality" in the military, judiciary, media, business circles, and universities (Hüseyin Gülerce, 2013, personal communication). Erdoğan, then, declared his discontent with the allegation that Başbuğ was a "member of a terrorist organisation", and asked for his trial without incarceration (*Today's Zaman*, 6 August 2012). In addition, in November 2013, Erdoğan sought to dismantle the Gülen network by shutting down all private preparatory schools, which were predominantly run by Gülen sympathisers (Akyol, 2013). The response to this attempt revealed in December 2013 one of the biggest corruption and bribery cases of Turkey, which extended to Erdoğan's family members (*Today's Zaman*, 4 September 2014). It was clear that the tug of war between the AKP and the military that started in 2007 had evolved into a war between Erdoğan and the Gülen movement. Fethullah Gülen (February 3, 2015) wrote in

The New York Times that the AKP leaders "are leading the country towards totalitarianism".

The Ergenekon and Sledgehammer (*Balyoz*) trials created growing public discontent not only because of the legal improprieties or *modus operandi* of the prosecutors but also because of the inclusion of some irrelevant figures in the trials, persons who had distanced themselves from the Gülen movement. The first serious blunder was that Prof. Türkan Saylan, a staunch defender of the modern way of life, and chairwoman of the Association for the Support of Contemporary Living (*Çağdaş Yaşamı Destekleme Derneği*, ÇYDD), a secular civil society organisation mainly working for girls' education, who was interrogated and her house and offices raided in April 2009 (*Hürriyet*, 13 April 2009). Whilst Türkan Saylan was among the people who organised the Republican Rally in 2007 against the AKP's nominee for the presidency, she had distanced herself from the secularist-nationalist camp by adopting the slogan "No to Sharia no to a Coup". This raised doubts on a retaliation of these trials since her initiative to foster education of girls and insistence on secular education disturbed the Gülen-affiliated civil society organisation in Turkish Kurdistan where ÇYDD had worked (Karaveli, 2009). In addition, the incarcerations in March 2011 of Nedim Şener, a well-known journalist critical of the Gülen movement, and Ahmet Şık, a leading journalist and the author of a book entitled *İmamın Ordusu* (The Imam's Army), which investigated the Gülen network in the police force, raised doubts on the real motivation behind the Ergenekon investigations.

Gareth Jenkins goes as far as to argue that the indictments did not give any evidence supporting the verdict that the Ergenekon as such does exist and that the trials were based on "fabricated evidence". He believes that "[t]he Ergenekon organisation as portrayed in the investigation is the product of a conspiracy theorist's imagination" (Jenkins, 2009: 80), referring to the description of the Ergenekon in the indictments as an "armed terrorist organisation". However, the problem lies in the broad and ambiguous definition of "terror" in Turkish laws, which allowed for frequent and excessive subsuming of acts of political opposition under the label "terrorism" (Law 3713 on Fight Against Terrorism, 1991). It is ironic that the law (Law 3713 on the Fight Against Terrorism) was in effect used against a political stratum that had effectively used it against every progressive and oppositional force in Turkey in the 1990s. However, the Ergenekon and Sledgehammer trials failed to mark the clearance of the "deep state tradition" in Turkey. They were mainly limited to military officers who wished to topple the AKP government.

Moreover, the AKP refrained from opening the way to try the military for their atrocities against the Kurds in the 1990s. It rather preferred to try the military for an "incomplete attempt to stage a coup" in the Sledgehammer trials or for being a member of an "armed terrorist organisation" in the Ergenekon trials. This shows that the government is willing to exculpate the military of their crimes against the Kurds, Armenians, socialists, and human rights activists in the history of the Turkish Republic. Overall, it can be suggested that while the Ergenekon case paradoxically sealed the end of the Kemalist/Bonapartist regime in Turkey and "represented a powerful blow against elements of the original Deep State" (Gunter, 2014: 33), the Balyoz case demonstrated that the principle of the rule of law, even if flawed, was circumvented in the process of investigation and trials. Both trials, nevertheless, showed that the higher echelons of the military were not immune to judicial punishment.[4] The abatement of the military's omnipotence is an indication of "the civilianisation of the Turkish landscape" (Axiarlis, 2014: 191). It is also certainly true that the acute polarisation of public opinion and failure to unite for a common purpose (Jacoby, 2014) eventually resulted in perpetuating the problem of "unconsolidated democracy" (Gürsoy, 2012).

3   Authoritarian Wave in Domestic Policy

Turkey's illiberal system, a political outcome of long decades of Kemalist/Bonapartist rule, crystallised once the AKP fully consolidated its electoral base in 2010/2011 after the constitutional referendum on 12 September 2010 and the 12 June 2011 general election. In *The Future of Freedom: Illiberal Democracy at Home and Abroad*, Fareed Zakaria (2003: 91) says that illiberal democracy corresponds to hybrid regimes "that mix elections and authoritarianism". It is a regime that backslides "toward an elected autocracy with more and more of its freedoms secure in theory but violated in practice, with corruption embedded into the very system of politics and economics" (Zakaria, 2003: 92).

Another categorisation for hybrid regimes—a more accurate rubric for understanding the AKP's third term since 2011—is the "competitive authoritarian regime", which combines the existence of democratic institutions with authoritarianism such as seriously violating the principle of fair competition by creating an uneven playing field (Levitsky and Way, 2010). According to Levitsky and Way (2010: 5), these regimes are

---

4   For various interpretations and critique of Ergenekon trials by Turkish socialists, see Yanardağ (2009).

civilian regimes in which formal democratic institutions exist and are widely viewed as the primary means of gaining power, but in which incumbents' abuse of the state places them at a significant advantage vis-à-vis their opponents. Such regimes are competitive in that opposition parties use democratic institutions to contest seriously for power, but they are not democratic because the playing field heavily skewed in favour of incumbents. Competition is this real but unfair.

"Croatia under Franjo Tudjman, Serbia under Slobodan Milošević, Russia under Vladimir Putin, Ukraine under Leonid Kravchuk and Leonid Kuchma, Peru under Alberto Fujimori, and post-1995 Haiti, as well as Albania, Armenia, Ghana, Kenya, Malaysia, Mexico and Zambia through much of the 1990s" fall into the category of competitive authoritarianism (Levitsky and Way, 2002: 52). Turkey perfectly fits in with this characterisation of its actual political system.

There is evidence to suggest that following the AKP's third term in 2011, Turkey's democratic transition did not lead to a consolidated democracy, but to competitive authoritarianism. While this hybrid regime includes important characteristics of democratic institutions in the sense that opposition parties use democratic institutions to contest for power, continued and serious violations of civil liberties render the regime authoritarian. As a case in point, despite political efforts to curb the power of the recalcitrant state establishment, the downsizing of the Kemalist military state gave way to a proliferation of police forces. Indeed, the increase in the power of police force started before the end of the military tutelage in Turkey. Through the legal changes under Law 2559 on Police Powers and Duties (*Polis Vazife ve Salahiyetleri Kanunu*) in 2007 and Law 3713 on the Fight Against Terrorism (*Terörle Mücadele Kanunu*) in 2006, discretionary police power was expanded at the expense of civil liberties. According to the changes in the Law on the Fight against Terrorism in 2006, police forces were endowed with the right to use weapons directly and without hesitation against those who disobey the call for surrender or intend to use their weapon (*Resmi Gazete [Official Gazette]*, July 18, 2006). According to a 2007 change in the Police Powers and Duties Law, the police force was authorised to use firearms even if the police officers did not face a threat to their lives (TESEV, 2013: 31).[5] The 2015 amendments in the Laws pertaining to the

---

5 According to an amendment in Police Powers and Duties (*Polis Vazife ve Salahiyetleri Kanunu*) in 2007, the police can use firearms "[(a) within the context of using the right of self-defence] (b) vis-a-vis resistance which cannot be rendered ineffective by way of using bodily physical and material force, with the objective of and proportional to breaking such resistance, (c) in order to capture individuals for whom there is an arrest warrant, a decision to detain, be captured or apprehended; or in order to capture the suspect in cases where he/

security and police powers, known as the "Internal Security Law Package", included articles that would be a sign of the usurpation of the roles of the prosecutors and judges. The police chiefs under the permission of provincial governors and district governors were authorised to search people and vehicles without a court order. Under "a serious disruption of public order or crime", the police were also authorised to detain people for up to 48 hours without getting a court order. When needed, governors were also allowed to dispatch the police to pursue suspects. The "Internal Security Law Package" allowed police forces to use firearms against those who attack public buildings with a gasoline bomb (Molotov cocktail) or similar inflammable materials (Human Rights Watch, December 11, 2014).

There was a sharp increase in the total number of convicts and detainees after the legal changes in the Law on the Fight Against Terrorism were put into effect in 2006. For instance, while there were 70,277 detainees and convicted people kept in penal institutions in 2006, this number more than doubled to 158,837 in 2014 (Figure 17). The Associated Press reported that since 9/11, "Turkey alone accounted for a third of all [terrorism] convicts, with 12,897" (in Mendoza, 2011). Interestingly, the total number of convicts and detainees by the end of 2018 was three times more than it was under the military dictatorship between 1980 and 1983 (Figure 17). The Ministry of Justice declared in June 2019 that 114 new prisons are being constructed (*Hürriyet Daily News,* 19 July 2019).

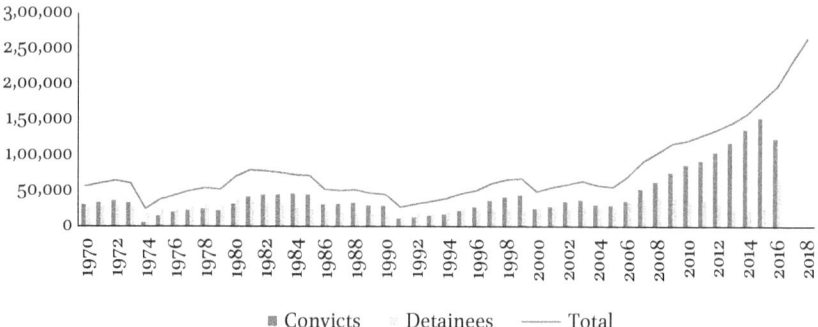

FIGURE 17 Total number of convicts and detainees in penal institutions, 1970–2018
SOURCE: REPUBLIC OF TURKEY, MINISTER OF JUSTICE, GENERAL DIRECTORATE OF PRISONS AND DETENTION HOUSES (2016) AND FOR 2017 AND 2018 STATISTICS SEE, TÜİK (N.D.), PRISON POPULATION.

    she is apprehended while the crime is in progress, and the extent proportional for that purpose" (TESEV, 2013: 31).

Apart from the hypertrophy of the police force and prison population since 2006, in 2014 a new law on State Intelligence Services and the National Intelligence Organisation (*Milli İstihbarat Teşkilatı*, MİT) expanded the surveillance and data collection power of the latter. According to the EU, this law "extended the scope of the service's duties, increased the already broad immunity of its staff and increased access to information from all public institutions and banks, without restrictions and without adequate judicial or parliamentary oversight" (European Commission, 2014: 11). The law also granted Turkish intelligence services immunity from judicial control in their conduct concerning wiretapping and surveillance (European Commission, 2014: 13). The law also prevents a direct judicial investigation of MİT members concerning their conduct. It states that public prosecutors should first inform the undersecretary of MİT when they receive any tips or complaints concerning the conduct of MİT members. Public prosecutors cannot take any further procedural act and protection measures if the conduct is in relation with the duties and activities of MİT (Devlet İstihbarat Hizmetleri ve Milli İstihbarat Hizmetleri Kanunu, n.d., Article 26). Human Rights Watch warned that this law can immunise intelligence personnel who commit serious human rights violations such as torture (Human Rights Watch, April 29, 2014). It added that "[t]he law also effectively places the intelligence agency above the law since the agency decides if its own activity should be prosecuted" (Human Rights Watch, April 29, 2014).

The hypertrophy of the state's repressive apparatus corresponded to a period in which global records in the protection of civil and political rights, not least the freedom of press, have painted a disturbing picture since 2007. For 13th consecutive years after 2006, the number of countries around the world experiencing declines in freedom outnumbered those registering gains (Freedom House, 2019: 1). According to the 2019 World Press Freedom Index by Reporters without Borders (2016a), Turkey ranked 157th out of 180 countries, falling behind Russia (149th), Mexico (144th), and Iraq (156th) (Reporters Without Borders, 2016). The Reporters without Borders' report stated that Turkey is "the world's biggest jailer of professional journalists" (Reporters Without Borders, 2016b). According to Larry Diamond (2015: 150), Turkey has been one of the states that "had worse average freedom scores at the end of 2013 than they did at the end of 2005".

Similarly, according to the findings of Freedom House, Turkey was positioned in "Not Free status" in 2019 (Freedom House, 2019). An earlier report titled "Freedom of the Press 2013: A Global Survey of Media Independence" had also stated that constitutional guarantees of freedom of the press and expression are not fully put into practice due to restrictive provisions in the criminal code and anti-terrorist act. The report reiterated what Reporters without

Borders' report continuously stated. According to Freedom House, "Turkey remains among the nations with the most journalists behind bars in the world" (Freedom House, 2013: 35).

In addition to the formal limitations on civil liberties, the particular capitalist structure of Turkish media severely limits democracy. The capitalists who own holding companies, active in the construction, energy, and mining sectors, have interests in running a pro-government media outlet in order to access government contracts and benefit from privatisation (Corke, et al., 2014: 12–13). According to Ayşe Buğra and Osman Savaşkan (2014: 79), the public procurement law was changed 29 times between 2003 and 2013 and over 100 amendments were made to the law in respect of its scope, applications, and exceptions. In 2013 alone, the government issued approximately NTL 90 billion ($40 billion) worth of public procurements (Kamu İhale Kurumu [Public Procurement Authority], 2014: 1). Through close links with the government and Erdoğan, the capitalists in the pro-government media sector benefited from public tenders and media handovers (Buğra and Savaşkan, 2014: 95–101). Some examples include Doğuş Holding's (NTV, Star TV) acquisition of a $702 million tender in 2013 to operate Galataport in İstanbul and İhlas Holding's (Türkiye, İhlas New Agency, TGRT TV) $1.86 billion deal in 2013 to gentrify the Gaziosmanpaşa area in Istanbul (Corke et al., 2014). Not surprisingly, after the Demirören Holding purchased the *Milliyet* newspaper in 2011, the company owner asked Erdoğan who to appoint as the editor-in-chief of the newspaper (Corke et al., 2014: 12). Moreover, following the purchase of Doğan Media Group in March 2018—one of the biggest media conglomerates in Turkey, whose chairman was an open critic of Erdoğan—by Demirören Holding, the AKP will control 73% of all newspapers circulated in Turkey (*Birgün*, 21 March 2018).

Meanwhile, political opponents of the party faced serious tax charges. As a form of selective and discretionary use of legal instruments, the Doğan media group was levied a $2.5 billion fine in September 2009 due to tax charges (Arsu and Tavernise, 2009). In the 2009 EU Progress Report of Turkey, this fine was declared to "potentially undermine the economic viability of the Group and therefore affect freedom of press in practice" (European Commission, 2009: 18). In 2013, two Koç Holding subsidiaries, TÜPRAŞ and Aygaz, were targeted by finance inspectors to conduct a "routine" inspection after Erdoğan charged Divan Hotel, owned by Koç, of harbouring Gezi protesters (*Hürriyet Daily News*, 25 July 2013). A detailed review of global competitive reports by the World Economic Forum (2006: 407; 2019: 563) reveals that there has been a steady deterioration of Turkey's judicial independence since 2006; Turkey fell 54 places from 2006 (50th) to 2019 (104th). A minimum level of judicial independence and a predictable, rational, and systematic legal system are necessary for the operations of capitalists to invest in productive sectors, if not in speculative areas, and to calculate and assess risks (Weber, 1978: 883). As Berk Esen and Sebnem Gumuscu (2017) suggest, the politicisation of state institutions—such as debt collection and tax inspection—and the erosion of the rule of law has led to a situation where the AKP can punish its dissidents and reward its loyalists through rents and tranfering capital.

All these backlashes in civil liberties are in contradiction with the Schumpeterian understanding of democracy, in which "a considerable amount of freedom of press" is a principle in competing for political leadership (Schumpeter, 2003: 272). However, competition for leadership is geared towards the AKP advantage. According to the OSCE's Office for Democratic Institutions and Human Rights' (ODIHR) report on Turkey's presidential election in August 2014, unfair competition among candidates marked the election with regard to the "misuse of administrative resources and the lack of a clear distinction between key institutional events and campaign activities", as well as significantly biased media coverage, including state television, in favour of Erdoğan (Office for Democratic Institutions and Human Rights, 2014: 1–3).[6]

4 Sub-imperialism and Neo-Ottomanism in Foreign Policy: Strategic Depth or Strategic Failure?

Although the reversal of the previous wave of democratisation was not inevitable, the structure of the Turkish model—as Cihan Tuğal (2016a: 15, 36) argues, "the marriage of formal democracy, free market capitalism, and (a toned down) conservative Islam"—made the sustainability, if not the possibility, of democratisation under a neoliberal doctrine impossible. However, the AKP's authoritarian turn since 2011 is the product of both the "fall of the Turkish model" and the repercussions of Turkey's sub-imperialist foreign policy on domestic policy, where neo-Ottoman fantasies played a key role. It is important to highlight that the realignment of Turkish foreign policy under the doctrine of neo-Ottomanism is a product of decades-long capitalist development in

---

[6] According to the Organisation for Security and Cooperation in Europe (OSCE), state television, "TRT 1 devoted 51 per cent of coverage to Mr. Erdoğan, with Mr. İhsanoğlu and Mr. Demirtaş received 32 per cent and 18 per cent, respectively. In addition, 25 per cent of Mr. İhsanoğlu's coverage was negative in tone, while Mr. Erdoğan's coverage was almost all positive" (Office for Democratic Institutions and Human Rights, 2014: 18). The report also stated that Erdoğan combined his presidential campaigning with the inauguration of big state projects such as high-speed train between İstanbul and Ankara and Başakşehir football stadium in İstanbul (Office for Democratic Institutions and Human Rights, 2014: 14, fn. 39).

which Turkey's regional economic power complemented its political-military power after the transition to an export-led economic model in the 1980s. In other words, sub-imperialism and its form in the Turkish context—neo-Ottomanism—is in accordance with the political and economic needs of Turkish capitalism as a whole. But how to account for Turkey's mutation into a sub-imperialist state that can implement a regional and neo-Ottomanist foreign policy? The following sub-section firstly examines the concept of sub-imperialism and then discusses it within Turkey's political-military and economic power.

4.1 Sub-imperialism in Question

The term "sub-imperialism" was originally coined by sociologist Ruy Mauro Marini (1965, 1972) to describe Brazil's regional economic and political power after the 1964 military coup that overthrew President João Goulart. The process of converting a dependent country to sub-imperialism was not, however, confined to Brazil. Indeed, the crisis of world capitalist accumulation of the late 1970s created opportunities for a limited number of dependent countries—such as Brazil, Mexico, Argentina, Israel, Saudi Arabia, Iran under the Shah, India, and South Africa—to become global intermediary powers on the back of the development of their own productive forces (Gunder Frank, 1979).

Asymmetric power relations within the global order consist of a trichotomy of categories of actors that maintain dependence: "*imperialist center, subimperialist agents and dominated periphery countries*" (Väyrynen and Herrera, 1975: 168). The sub-imperial agents are "intermediaries in the relations between center and periphery when they are simultaneously both dominant and dominated units; more dominated than dominant, however" (Väyrynen and Herrera, 1975: 165). Sub-imperialist agents' dependence on the core can take technological, financial and commercial forms, with sub-imperialist powers tied to the core through the imperialist centre's know-how, big transnational corporations, foreign debts and trade (Väyrynen and Herrera, 1975: 171). The USA dominates dependency structures "as a center nation of first rank over the West European industrial states (and similarly over Japan) as centers of second rank", owing to its penetration of European markets and the financial sector, the status of the dollar as the leading international currency, technological supremacy and its protective military role for Europe (Gantzel, 1973: 205–206).

On the one hand, a sub-imperial agent is located at the centre of the periphery and exerts regional hegemony by playing the role of an imperial power while simultaneously having a peripheral relationship to the core (Shaw, 1979: 348). The sub-imperial agent, therefore, encapsulates a combination of "*dependence* on one or more central nations, the economic and military *capacity*, as well as the regional political military and economic *expansion*" (Väyrynen, 1979: 353). Regional political, military and economic expansion provides the sub-imperialist agent with the autonomy and manoeuvrability to assert its power in foreign policy without a necessary break from the imperialist core (Väyrynen, 1979: 367; Väyrynen and Herrera, 1975: 171). On the other hand, the core maintains global dependency through sub-imperial powers that provide regional channels for raw materials and finished products in a three-layered exchange system (Grundy, 1976: 561). This in turn reduces the core's military and political costs for capitalist accumulation (Gunder Frank, 1979: 283). For the core, the importance of a sub-imperialist state lies in the fact that it provides a "bridgehead for the transnational corporations" of the imperialist centre (Väyrynen and Herrera, 1975: 173). As Raimo Väyrynen and Luis Herrera (1975: 170–171) suggest, "[s]ubimperialism is ... military control by dominant actors through go-between armies, economic exploitation thorough go-between corporations and banks as well as political domination through go-between political elites".

As an example, Marini highlights how Brazil in the 1960s and 1970s shared the core characteristics of a sub-imperialist country: regional domination coupled with dependence on an imperialist core through various mechanisms (Marini, 1965, 1972). During the sub-imperialist stage of Brazilian capitalism, which extended until 1985 under a military government, Brazilian foreign policy was based on the conscious acceptance of US quasi-monopoly rule in the South Atlantic. Brazil enabled this domination though its policy of continental interdependence (Marini, 1965: 19–20). This does not, however, lead to the conclusion that Brazil pursued a policy of submission to US interests. Rather, it stood for the active, collaborative imperialist interdependence of Brazilian capitalist interests with American interests by "assuming in this [imperialist] expansion the position of a key nation" (Marini, 1965: 22).

As an example of this imperialist alignment with the US, Marini points to Brazil's Castelo Branco regime (1964–1967), which joined the US in its invasion of the Dominican Republic in 1965, applauded the US decision to send military aid to Latin America through the Organisation of American States (OAS), and insisted on the continent's military integration under the aegis of the US army (Marini, 1965: 21). The "communist threat" that hovered over Brazil and the Dominican Republic was the main reason for this collaboration. As one Brazilian colonel claimed:

> The Armed Forces brilliantly stopped communism from taking over Brazil. Another brilliant example is their participation in the Dominican Republic in the operation initiated by the American marines where they

also stopped communism from taking over that country (as quoted in Burns, 1967: 208).

While this imperialist integration provided the Brazilian bourgeoisie with the opportunity to intensify its industrial and technological modernisation through the influx of foreign capital, this influx was also advantageous to the US, as it needed to export its obsolete equipment (Marini, 1965: 22). As a result, Brazilian capital and foreign monopolies cooperated in exploiting Brazilian workers and in their shared claims over Brazil's export earnings (Marini, 1972: 16–17).

The exploitation of trade revenues was a product of Brazil's rapid GDP growth under the military regime. As Gunder Frank (1979: 293) explains:

> From 1968 to 1974, Brazilian GDP grew at sustained annual rates of 10% and industrial production at 11% a year… Exports sextupled between 1964 and 1975, rising from $1,430 million to $8,200 million… The most spectacular increase, however, was registered by the export of manufactures or industrial products that increased their share from 7–10% to 15–20% (depending on definition) of total exports that themselves sextupled.

Nevertheless, while playing the role of an imperialist centre, Brazil under the military regime was highly dependent on US and Western technology. The German Mercedes, for instance, provided the Brazilian army and marines with engines for their combat vehicles, while the French Thomson-CSF supplied the Brazilian air defence systems (Väyrynen, 1979: 361–362).

Turning to the Turkish case, it can be argued that Turkey's dependent relationship with the US, economic expansion to its less developed neighbours, and attempts to play the role of an imperialist core in the region all point to it as an example of sub-imperialism. Indeed, Turkey's sub-imperialist expansion into the Middle East is the product of a decades-long process; a process of establishing an economic infrastructure through ISI and strengthening its military power during the Cold War under the auspices of the US. It can be argued that Turkey's economic expansion since the 1980s' transition to export-led growth complemented its military capacity, thus rendering the country sub-imperialist.

4.2   *The Military Dimension of Turkey's Sub-imperialist Role*

Turkey has been trying to play the role of regional police under the auspices of the US. During the Cold War, Turkish foreign policy was largely driven by its tenacious attachment to the Western alliance and against the Soviet Union

(Hale, 2013: 80). In line with the containment policy regarding the "communist threat" in Europe, Turkey was added to the Truman Doctrine in 1947; one year later, Turkey received Marshall Aid funding under the European Recovery Programme. Moreover, Turkey has been a member of NATO since 1952 (Hale, 2013: 83–87). US military assistance ($2.271 billion between 1948 and 1964 along with the deliveries of surplus equipment equivalent to $328 million) and economic aid (totalling $1,380 billion between 1950 and 1962) were indeed instrumental in Turkey's economic growth under the Menderes governments of the 1950s and in fortifying Turkey's defences (Hale, 2013: 89–90). "U.S. economic aid to Turkey between 1950 and 1964 was equivalent to 17 percent of total gross investment and 35 percent of total public investment in Turkey". (Leo Tansky in Uslu, 2003: 99). Between 1964 and 1969, this economic assistance, an average of $284 million per year, exceeded half of Turkey's foreign exchange earnings (Hale, 2013: 109).

In return, Turkey played its role as regional surrogate—a role that echoed US imperialism in the Middle East—by becoming one of "the local cops on the beat" in the periphery, a phrase later used by Nixon's Defence Secretary Melvin Laird (Noam Chomsky in Chomsky and Achcar, 2007: 55 Chomsky, 1999: 535). Turkey's status as the only Muslim country in NATO was "crucial for preserving stability in the Middle East and, in a broader sense, neutralizing the region as an arena in the East-West conflict" (Rustow, 1987: 110). This imperialist collaboration revealed itself, for instance, at the Bandung Conference in 1955, where Turkey allied with Western powers to "prevent the conference from being a spring-board for the communists or even the neutrals" (Kimche as cited in Ahmad, 1977: 396). However, Turkey's attachment to the Western alliance in the 1950s strained its relations with the Arab World. The US-sponsored Baghdad Pact (later known as CENTO) between Iran, Iraq, Pakistan, and the UK in 1955 was protested across the Arab world, especially in Egypt (Hale, 2013: 92). Arab nationalist governments denounced Turkey as "an agent of American policy in the Middle East" (International Crisis Group, 2010: 2). Turkey and Iraq, under US guidance, were even accused of plotting to overthrow the Syrian regime in August 1957 (Bishku, 2012: 40). This, however, did not prevent Nasser from establishing a political union with Syria in 1958 known as the United Arab Republic (Bishku, 2012: 40). In the same year, Turkey made the İncirlik Air Base available to the US for its intervention in Lebanon (Hale, 2013: 95).

Turkey also backed French imperialism against Algerian independence movements between 1954 and 1962. In addition, it was also one of the first countries to recognise Israel in 1949 (International Crisis Group, 2010: 2). Less than a decade later, in 1958, Turkey under Menderes and Israel under Ben-Gurion formed a secret alliance known as "the peripheral alliance" or "Phantom

Pact", which also involved Iran and Ethiopia. The aim of this alliance was to ward off Nasser's Pan-Arabism and Soviet influence in the region, and guard against the upheavals in Iraq. The bilateral alliance between Israel and Turkey "included cooperation on diplomatic, military, and economic levels" (Bengio, 2010: 44). The alliance included cooperation in industrial development in Turkey and increasing trade between the two countries. Economic cooperation included developments in agriculture, irrigation pipes, and the planning of the Keban Dam. Militarily, the alliance included exchanges of intelligence and military industrial know-how, the training of Turkish armed forces, and permission for the Israeli air force to use Turkish territory. In return, Turkey agreed to side with Israel, calling on NATO and the Pentagon to increase Israel's military capacity (Bengio, 2010: 44).

The intensive courtship between Turkey and Israel yielded a trilateral cooperation between MOSSAD, SAVAK and MAH (later to be called MİT—National Intelligence Organisation) in forming an organisation called "Trident", which functioned as an intelligence sharing mechanism (Bengio, 2010: 45). The Turkish army was the guardian of this relationship (Bengio, 2010: 52). This alliance continued until the annulment of the intelligence connection in 1966, when the issue of Cyprus emerged as a key determinant of Turkish foreign policy (Bengio, 2010: 54–64).

Turkey, seeking to maintain imperialism in the region, stood at odds with the independence movement in Cyprus and sided with other NATO members who opposed Cypriot self-determination (Fırat, 2010: 357–358). Instead, the Turkish state advocated partitioning the island after 1955 (Hasgüler, 2002). Although four years of Greek revolt against British colonialism ended with the proclamation of the Republic of Cyprus in August 1960 (Hasgüler, 2002: 237), this resolution did not stabilise the island. Post-1960 Cyprus was a battleground for outside powers trying to subvert its independence, while an internal nationalist tug of war developed between the EOKA under General George Grivas and the TMT (*Türk Mukavemet Teşkilatı*—The Turkish Resistance Organisation) in liaison with the Turkish Colonel Alparslan Türkeş. (Hitchens, 1997: 47). Turkey's deep state was also active in Cyprus and inflamed intercommunal tension in order to legitimise partition (Yalçın Okut, 2015, personal communication). Sabri Yirmibeşoğlu, a retired Turkish General and Secretary-General of the National Security Council (1988–1990), confessed to carrying out a false flag operation in Cyprus during an interview. He admitted that Turkey's deep state "burnt down a mosque in order to [blame it] on the enemy [Greek Cypriots] to increase public resistance" (*Today's Zaman*, 24 September 2010).

When an Athens-junta-sponsored coup, aided by EOKA-B units, was staged against Archbishop Makarios in Cyprus on 15 July 1974, Turkey started a military incursion on the northern part of the island with two military operations on 20 July and 14 August. Before the incursion, the Commander of the Turkish Naval Forces Kemal Kayacan threatened Prime Minister Bülent Ecevit, saying: "...if, as in the past, we draw back at the last minute, neither we as commanders, nor you as the Prime Minister, can survive..." (as quoted in Birand, 1985: 15). Furthermore, the partition policy was wholeheartedly pushed by the fundamentalist National Salvation Party under Erbakan, who was in coalition with Ecevit at that time. Hasan Aksay, a parliamentarian from the National Salvation Party, even suggested in the *Milli Gazete* that the military occupy the whole of the island (İslamoğlu, 1974: 64–65). The US's attitude toward the Cyprus crisis— i.e. imposing an arms embargo on Turkey—caused Greece's withdrawl from NATO's military wing (Couloumbis, 1983: 97; Hitchens, 1997: 131). Greece only returned six years later, in 1980.

Nevertheless, the embargo set the stage for the development of the local defence industry and thus the establishment of the Turkish Land Forces in 1974 (Undersecretariat for Defence Industries, 2010). The Turkish Armed Forces (TAF) unified the land, air, and naval forces under the Turkish Armed Forces Foundation (*Türk Silahlı Kuvvetlerini Güçlendirme Vakfı,* TAFF), which formed in 1987 and expanded capitalist economic activity. TAFF has since functioned as a military corporation. Law number 3388 sets out the Foundation's objective as developing the national war industry, forming new war industry branches, purchasing war industry equipment and supplies, and importantly, contributing to enhancing the warfare capacity of the Turkish Armed Forces (Resmi Gazete [Official Gazette]. June 25, 1987: 16). Concomitantly, the Foundation enjoys economic benefits such as exemptions from inheritance and succession taxes, stamp tax, and corporation tax even though its separate economic enterprises are subject to corporation tax (Resmi Gazete [Official Gazette]. June 25, 1987: 17). TAFF is particularly significant in its direct involvement in the warfare industry. It owns the biggest shares in Aselsan (Military Economic Industries), Havelsan (Military Aerospace Industries), Roketsan (Military Rocket Industries) and TAI (Turkish Aerospace Industries), which are the largest military-industrial enterprises in Turkey. For instance, Aselsan, which maintains the leading position in the Turkish military economy, ranked as the 15th largest industrial enterprise in net production-based sales in Turkey in 2018 (İSO, 2017). It also ranked as the 85th largest arms producing and military services company in the world in 2012 (excluding Chinese companies), with $870 million in arms sales and $163 million in total profit. According to the Stockholm International Peace Research Institute (SIPRI), Aselsan employed 5,205 people in 2011 (Perlo-Freeman and Wezeman, 2014: 216).

The Defence Industry Support Fund (DISF), which has functioned under the control of the Undersecretariat for Defence Industries since 1985, is another organisation significant to linking the TAF with the capitalist economic rationale. DISF forms the main extra-budgetary resource for Turkey's defence expenditure (Akça, 2010b: 16), and aims to modernise the armed forces and develop the national defence industry in accordance with Law number 3238. Unsurprisingly, DISF is endowed with economic privileges for its income generation. Law number 3238 provides a wide range of resources for DISF, although it has been subject to major amendments since 2002. DISF's income is based on various resources, such as the grant in aid submitted to the annual budget, a share of income and revenues from corporate taxes, funds from the Ministry of Defence's budget, a share of private consumption tax, National Lottery revenue, national racetrack betting revenue, and national numbers games, as well as transfers from the foundations established to support the TAF, grants, revenue generated for paid military services, donations, aid, and revenue generated by the Fund's assets (Akça, 2010b: 16). Between 1985 and 2000, $11.6 billion was collected in the Fund, of which 70.1% was spent on military projects (Akça, 2009: 256). According to the 2012 Activity Report of the Directorate of Defence Industry, between 2000 and 2012 the Fund had an income of over $14 billion (Savunma Sanayii Müsteşarlığı [Undersecretariat for Defence Industries], (2012: 31).

4.3   Continuity in Turkish Foreign Policy in the 1990s

In the geopolitical order of post-Cold War era, NATO swiftly mutated into a "security" organisation—a broader designation than the bounded concept of "defence" that characterised the Cold War era—and expanded into countries in Soviet Russia's zone of influence. NATO extended its military jurisdiction under the "new strategic concept" of security set out in the Rome Atlantic Summit of November 1991, and took on a political role while charging itself with managing possible risks and preventing political, economic, and social instabilities that arise even beyond its territories (Achcar, 2000: 61–62). The importance of the Turkish military in the new geopolitical order did not diminish, but rather increased. According to the 2014 report of the Stockholm International Peace Research Institute (SIPRI), Turkey became the world's 14th largest military spender, with $19.1 billion spent in 2013 (Perlo-Freeman, Solmirano and Wilandh, 2014: 182).[7] Although there was a decrease in Turkish military expenditure as a percentage of GDP, from 2.8% in 2004 to 2.3% in 2013, military expenditure in constant US$ (2011) prices increased from 16.6 billion

---

7   Calculated using market exchange rates in current US$ for 2013.

in 2004 to 18.7 billion in 2013 (Perlo-Freeman, et al., 2014). The Turkish armed forces, consisting of 359,273 active military personnel out of a total 398,513 as of January 2017 (*Hürriyet*, 2 January 2017) is also one of the largest armies in NATO.

In the aftermath of the Cold War, the Turkish state continued its regional surrogacy role. In the first Gulf War in 1990/1991, Turkey under Turgut Özal backed US imperialism in countering Iraq's invasion of oil-rich Kuwait. During the first Gulf War, Turkey opened its İncirlik air bases, among others, for coalition forces' use (Hale, 2013: 160). Özal attempted to turn this crisis into an opportunity by siding with the US, as he firmly believed that the US would remove Saddam Hussein and neautralise Iraqi military power (Robins, 1991: 71). However, Saddam Hussein stayed in power for over a decade and crushed, with US consent, Kurdish and Shiite popular uprisings in both northern and southern Iraq in 1991 (Achcar, 2004: 234–239). It was only *after* these popular uprisings were crushed that the UN passed Resolution 688 on 5 April 1991, which enforced a no-fly zone in northern Iraq (Hale, 2013: 161). This was followed by the deployment of an international force—known as "Operation Provide Comfort" and later "Provide Comfort"—to the İncirlik Air Base in Turkey for a non-NATO operation. Despite opposition from the general public, this operation was routinely renewed by the Turkish parliament upon the "recommendations of the National Security Council". "Operation Northern Watch" replaced "Provide Comfort" in 1997 (Hale, 2013: 161–163; Jenkins, 2001: 75).

The role of the Turkish military in foreign policy administration included playing its part within US imperialism in the post-Cold War "unipolar moment", even beyond its own neighbourhood. The Turkish military joined "Operation Restore Hope" in Somalia between 1992 and 1994 and Turkish Lieutenant General Çevik Bir was appointed commander of the coalition forces in 1993. The Turkish military participated in IFOR (Implementation Force) in Bosnia and SFOR (Stabilization Force) in Kosovo; it also deployed a peacekeeping force in Palestine in the 1990s (Uzgel, 2003: 196). In the Kosovo War of 1998/1999, Turkey only served "the Machiavellian desire of the Clinton-Albright administration to marginalize the role of Russia and the institutions of which it is a pillar, like the UN and the Organization for Security and Cooperation in Europe (OSCE)" (Achcar, 1999: 17). Turkey was also involved in NATO's International Security Assistance Force (ISAF) in Afghanistan and took over its command in 2002 (Uzgel, 2003: 196) and 2005.

Turkey's military expansion beyond the region suggests that Turkey consolidated its position as a "military sub-imperialist country" in the 1990s (Erkiner, 2000: 149). Armament, military modernisation, and a "Military Training and Cooperation Agreement" with Israel signed in 1996 were key to advancing

Turkey's sub-imperialism (Erkiner, 2000: 34–40). In 1985, a long-term military modernisation programme was initiated to establish a domestic arms industry (Günlük-Şenesen, 2002; 1993). The programme initially allocated $10–12 billion over a 10-year period, and was extended for 30 years in 1996 with a budget of $150 billion. Due to economic problems, the programme was revised in 2000 and its budget decreased (Günlük-Şenesen, 2002: 107). Between 1994 and 1998, Turkey became the third largest recipient of weapons globally, mainly from the US and Germany (Hen-Tov, 2004).

With respect to the "Military Training and Cooperation Agreement" signed with Israel in 1996, the military high command took the lead in forming and executing the agreement by bypassing the jurisdiction of the foreign ministry (Bengio, 2010: 108). This agreement enabled Turkey to acquire military know-how, participate in joint air and naval exercises with Israel, cooperate in advanced weapons systems production, share intelligence, and modernise its fighter planes (Bengio, 2010: 110–115; Hale, 2013: 227). The relationship between Israel and Turkey in the second half of the 1990s produced "the biggest-ever foreign contract for Israel's aircraft industry", which was about $700 million (Bengio, 2010: 114).

Domestically, the military was the prime actor in relations with Syria. In 1998, Turkey amassed troops along the Syrian border to force the country to expel the PKK leader Öcalan (Hale, 2013: 232–234). The Turkish General Staff initiated a plan—called "controlled crisis management"—to pressure Syria to expel Öcalan (Jenkins, 2001: 73). On 16 September 1998, First Army Commander General Atilla Ateş said near the Syrian border: "Our patience is exhausted. If the necessary measures are not taken, we as the Turkish nation will be forced to take every kind of measure" (as quoted in Jenkins, 2001: 73).

4.4 The Economic Foundation of Neo-Ottomanism: Turkish Exports and Capital in the Region

With the shift of Turkey's economic structure from an inward-looking capital accumulation model based on national-developmentalism to an export-oriented industrialisation model based on competition after the 1980s, Turkey's economic power was subsumed into its military power. In the process of transforming into a sub-imperialist power, Turkish exports increased from nearly $3 billion in 1980 to nearly $172 billion in 2019 (Figure 18). This export expansion has necessitated that Turkish goods must be sold not only inside domestic borders but also beyond its borders.

This shift in the economic model under neoliberalism moved Turkey to export manufactured goods while the structural adjustment programmes imposed on the Arab countries under the *infitah* (opening) from the 1970s brought

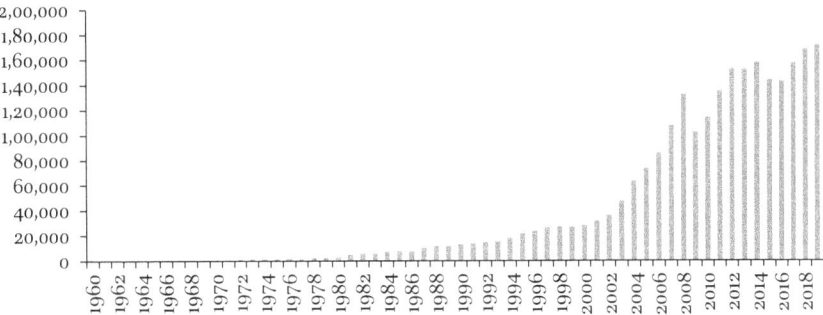

FIGURE 18   Turkish exports by years (million $), 1960–2019
SOURCE: *FOREIGN TRADE BY YEARS*, BY TÜİK (N.D.).

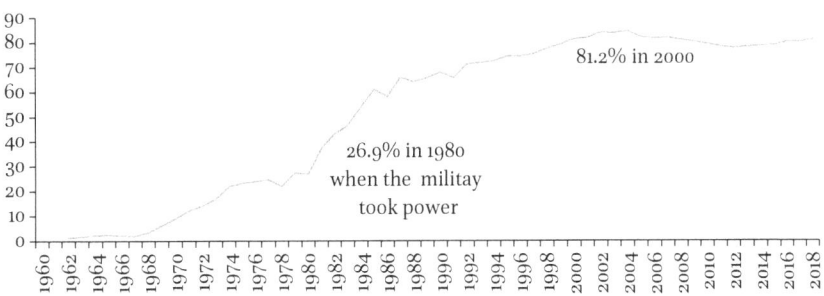

FIGURE 19   Export of manufactured goods (% of exports), 1960–2018
SOURCE: THE WORLD BANK (2020).

forth crony capitalism under patrimonial and neopatrimonial states (Achcar, 2013, Chapters 1 and 2). Figure 19 illustrates that the percentage of the manufactured goods in Turkey's total exports tripled from 26.9% in 1980—the year neoliberalism was inaugurated under military dictatorship, a trajectory similar to that of Chile under General Pinochet between 1973 and 1990—to 81% in 2000. Even though there was a slight decrease in the percentage of manufactured goods in total exports in 2009, the ratio has still been above 75%, hitting 80.9% in 2018 (Figure 19).

In this new economic setting, the increasing need of the Turkish economy to export its goods led to the intensification of its relations with the Middle East (Tür, 2011). The restructuring of Turkish finance capital on the basis of competition after the 2001 crisis and the increasing influence of peripheral capital since the 1980s conditioned the new activism of foreign policy (Kutlay, 2011). This transformation of state-society relations resulted in what Kemal Kirişci (2009) has called a "trading state". According to Kirişci (2009: 33–34), in

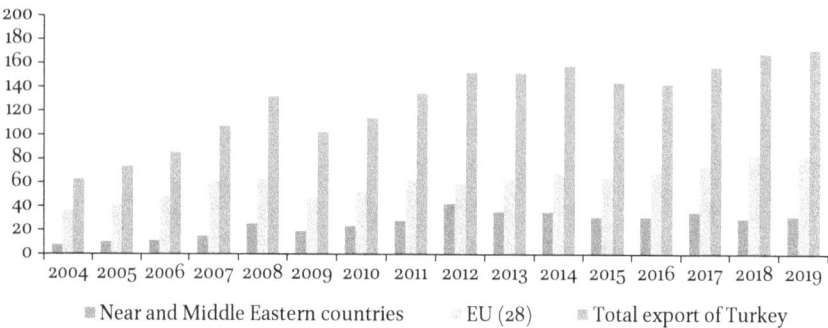

FIGURE 20   Turkish exports by two country groups (billion $), 2004–2019
SOURCE: *EXPORTS BY COUNTRY GROUP AND YEAR, BY TÜİK (N.D.).*

a trading state, new economic actors participate in decision-making processes in foreign policy matters and exert greatest power to steer foreign policy to be in line with economic priorities. In foreign policy administration, the priorities of new agents feature the geographical division of economic interests. As Davutoğlu has stressed, while TUSKON expands to Africa, TÜSİAD has an interest lobbying the EU for Turkey's membership. MÜSİAD, on the other hand, is active in Arab Gulf countries (Davutoğlu, 2008: 83–84).

To show this trajectory, under AKP rule Turkish exports to Near and Middle Eastern Countries increased more rapidly between 2004 and 2013 than exports to EU countries. The former increased from $7.9 billion in 2004 to $35.4 billion in 2014, a quadruple rise in a decade, whilst the latter increased from $36.7 billion in 2004 to $68.4 billion in 2014 (Figure 20). It should be stressed that Near and Middle Eastern countries together with North African countries are the only two regions where Turkey extracts a trade surplus. According to the Turkish Statistical Institute, while Near and Middle Eastern countries and North African countries absorbed $35.4 billion and $9.8 billion worth of Turkish products, respectively, in 2014 they only exported $3.4 billion and $20.5 billion worth of products to Turkey, thus yielding a trade surplus of more than $21 billion (TÜİK, n.d.). This also explains the subimperialist expansion of Turkey into the Middle East.

In the face of the Eurozone crisis since late 2009, the Middle Eastern market subsequently provided a new arena for Turkish peripheral capitalism (Kaya, 2011: 86). During the 2007/2008 global financial crisis, which evolved into the Euro crisis in the European Union, the Near and Middle Eastern market became even more important than the European market for Turkish goods. Another major reason for the increase in trade volume with the Middle East is that the increase of oil prices since 2002, after hitting bottom in 1998, increased demand for imports to oil-rich Middle Eastern countries (Tezcür and Grigorescu, 2014). While in 2002 crude oil prices were as low as $29.92 per barrel, they were slightly over $100 in 2008 and had decreased to $89.08 per barrel by November 2014 (McMahon, 2014).[8]

It is worth recognising that Turkey engages with exporting capital notwithstanding its small scale. In 2010, FDI stocks of Turkish companies exceeded $20 billion, with developed countries absorbing more than half with $11.6 billion (United Nations Conference on Trade and Development, 2012: 16–17). However, Turkey's FDI stocks amounted to only 2.9% of its GDP in 2010, while inward FDI stocks were equivalent to 25% of Turkey's GDP in 2010 (United Nations Conference on Trade and Development, 2012: 4). On the other hand, the increase of Turkish investments in North Africa is also noteworthy. Turkish corporations in 2001 only had investment values of $1 million in Libya; $5 million in Tunisia; and $5 million in Egypt. By 2010 it increased to $168 million, $142 million and $103 million in each of these three countries respectively (United Nations Conference on Trade and Development, 2012: 16). Figures 21 and 22 demonstrate the increase in Turkey's enormous inward and outward investments in the 2000s.

Similar to the findings of UNCTAD above, in 2011 the Ankara Chamber of Commerce showed that close to 3,500 Turkish companies have operated in 103 countries, mainly doing business in the energy and banking sectors. Whereas the total value of direct investment of Turkish companies was only $3.7 billion

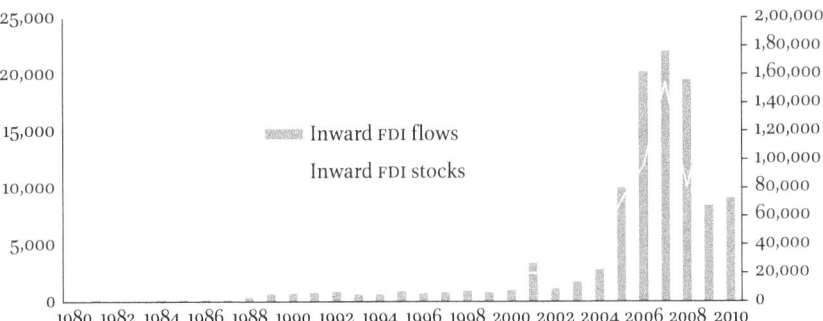

FIGURE 21   Inward FDI flows and FDI stocks in Turkey (million $), 1980–2010
SOURCE: UNITED NATIONS CONFERENCE ON TRADE AND DEVELOPMENT, UNCTAD (2012: 5–6).
Note: The vertical axis on the right shows the inward FDI stocks; the vertical axis on the left shows the inwards FDI flows.

---

8   By August 2016, inflation adjusted oil prices were as low as $34.13 per barrel.

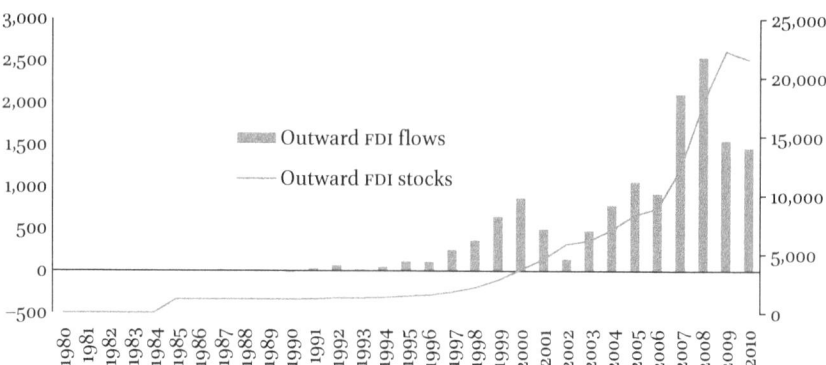

FIGURE 22   Outward FDI flows and FDI stocks of Turkey (million $), 1980–2010
SOURCE: UNITED NATIONS CONFERENCE ON TRADE AND DEVELOPMENT,
UNCTAD (2012: 5–6).
Note: The vertical axis on the right shows the outward FDI stocks; the vertical axis on the left shows the outward FDI flows.

in 2001, it rose to $23.6 billion by October 2010. The value of FDI of Turkish companies in the energy sector was recorded at $4 billion. In 2010, Turkish companies abroad invested $4 billion in energy; $3 billion on banking; $1.6 billion in financial institutions; $2 billion in manufacturing; $1.6 billion in commerce; $1.5 billion in information and communication; and $444 million in construction. The need to diversify across investment markets reflects the different geographical location of export of capital by Turkish capitalism. With respect to the amount of FDI abroad of Turkish companies, the Netherlands, Azerbaijan, Malta, Germany, the USA, Luxembourg, Kazakhstan, and the UK constitute the main geography of Turkish FDI (Ankara Chamber of Commerce, 2011).

However, sub-imperialist Turkey is heavily dependent on the technology and know-how of foreign capital. Turkish capitalism integrated into dependence chains and increased its exports on the basis of providing cheap labour for transnational corporations (TNCs) in return for access to technology. This has resulted in Turkey's positioning as a springboard for TNCs. For instance, while the automotive industry accounted for 25% of total exports in 2013 (Automotive Manufacturers Association, 2014), it is technologically dependent mainly on French (Renault), German (Mercedes-Benz), Japanese (Toyota), and South Korean (Hyundai) capitalism (United Nations Conference on Trade and Development, 2012: 22). Turkey's other important export sectors (electrical and electronic equipment and household appliances) are subordinated to Dutch (Vestel Electronics),[9] German (BSH Group and Siemens), French (Areva T&D)

---

9   The Vestel Electronics Company was indeed opened in Manisa in 1985 as a FDI of British Polly Peck International under Asil Nadir (*Milliyet*, 4 May 1985: 9) an advertisement in the

and Italian (Indesit) technology (United Nations Conference on Trade and Development, 2012: 22). Having said that, some of the largest home-based TNCs enlist the help of foreign capital in a number of sectors, including: retail and whole trade (OMV Petrol Ofisi and Opet Petroleum); transport, storage and communications (Turkish Airlines and Turkcell); metals and metal products (Ereğli Iron and Steel Factories); electrical and electronic equipment (Arçelik); construction (ENKA); and finance (Koç, Sabancı and İş Bankası) (United Nations Conference on Trade and Development, 2012: 20).

4.5 Turkish Companies as Agents of Regional Economic Power

According to a survey conducted in 2013 by Kadir Has University, the Foreign Economic Relations Board (*Dış Ekonomik İlişkiler Kurulu*, DEİK), and the Vale Columbia Center on Sustainable International Investment, the top 29 non-financial Turkish multinationals on the basis of their foreign assets had $36.7 billion in 2012, with TPAO and Anadolu Group accounting for more than $4 billion each (Table 13). These 29 non-financial multinational companies had $23.4 billion in foreign sales in 2012, with 115,539 workers abroad employed in 426 foreign affiliates on five continents. The survey shows that 326 out of 426 foreign affiliates of these multinational corporations were concentrated in Europe and Central Asia in 2012, while 53 were concentrated in the Middle East and Africa (DEİK, 2014: 1). The survey also shows the accelerated process of monopolisation; the five largest Turkish multinationals controlled 58% of total assets or $21.4 billion (Table 13).

With regard to the geographical diversification of Turkish companies, while they have reached technology and high-skilled labour in the EU, they have also sought a cheap labour force in Africa and Asia. The supply of natural resources in Central Asian countries appeals to Turkish capitalism, as well. In particular, Turkish Petroleum Corporation (*Türkiye Petrolleri Anonim Ortaklığı*, TPAO), a state-owned enterprise, is active in this "spatio-temporal fix". TPAO has been operating in Kazakhstan for crude oil exploration and production activities through the joint venture company KazakhTurkMunai Ltd (KTM), of which TPAO has 49% of shares. In Azerbaijan, TPAO is a shareholder in three exploration, development, and production projects. The projects are Azeri, Chirag, Guneshli Project; Shah Deniz Project; and Alov Project in which TPAO has shares of 6.75%, 9% and 10%, respectively. The company holds 6.53% shares of Baku-Tbilisi-Ceyhan Main Export Oil Pipeline Project and 9% of shares in the South Caucasus Pipeline Project, which transports Shah Deniz natural gas to

newspaper before its shares were transferred to the Dutch Collar Holding in 1991. The company has been a part of the Zorlu Holding in Turkey since 1994.

TABLE 13   29 Largest Turkish multinationals* (million $), 2012

Name	Industry	Assets		Sales		Number of employment		Number of foreign affiliates
		Foreign	Total	Foreign	Total	Foreign	Total	
TPAO	Oil and gas	4,872	8,423	1,535	3,453	49	5,000	4
Anadolu Group	Conglomerate	4,443	11,109	2,597	6,110	13,750	27,500	20
Enka Construction	Infrastructure and Real Estate	3,779	8,156	1,365	5,720	10,331	21,290	42
Koç Holding	Conglomerate	3,333	60,579	1,857	47,119	8,289	82,158	41
Doğuş Group	Conglomerate	3,104	31.151	149	6,110	6,213	30.250	50
Yıldırım Holding	Conglomerate	1,867	2,619	300	1.050	4,200	7,100	9
Sisecam A.S.	Glass manufacturing	1,368	4,845	705	2,967	6,090	17,838	15
Yıldız Holding	Food and Beverage	1,277	3,629	444	6,887	7,500	36,000	7
Tekfen Holding	Conglomerate	1,250	2,296	1,563	2,264	11,752	17,532	11
Zorlu Energy Group	Energy	1,120	2,768	234	292	0	864	3
TAV Holding	Conglomerate	1,081	2.937	226	1,425	3,837	22,704	8
Turkcell	Communications	1,057	10,360	595	5,836	1,418	13,901	14
BoruSAn Holding	Conglomerate	973	3,394	325	3,949	1,455	5,072	10
Sabancı Holding	Conglomerate	828	97,421	245	6,546	2,827	57,556	34
Çalık Holding	Conglomerate	816	7,613	523	2,745	8,103	19,940	15
Hayat Holding	Conglomerate	780	3,085	243	1,828	3,463	7,914	7
Gübretaş	Fertiliser	686	1,197	528	1,237	415	1,103	1
Alarko Group	Conglomerate	651	1,200	488	899	1,323	4,879	8

TABLE 13   29 Largest Turkish multinationals* (million $), 2012 (cont.)

Name	Industry	Assets		Sales		Number of employment		Number of foreign affiliates
		Foreign	Total	Foreign	Total	Foreign	Total	
Orhan Holding	Conglomerate	534	778	300	1,050	2,044	7,300	11
Doğan Holding	Conglomerate	486	4,815	275	1,753	4,073	13,750	64
Türk Telekom	Communications	444	9,558	-	7,057	1,200	37,524	2
Turkish Airlines	Airlines	400	10,431	5,962	8,281	2,228	15,857	0
Ekol Logistics	Logistics	375	750	125	350	1,200	6,791	7
Eczacıbaşı Holding	Conglomerate	371	2,686	569	3,307	1,994	11,730	18
Kürüm Holding	Iron and Steel	281	522	318	849	400	1,031	2
Teklas	Automotive	175	400	28	139	522	1,283	2
Çelebi Holding	Conglomerate	167	297	119	307	6,491	10,619	6
Eroğlu Holding	Textiles	148	269	850	1,133	5,214	12,117	13
Evyap	Consumer Products	98	772	53	630	536	2,205	2
Total		36,766	294,062	23,415	131,290	115,539	501,740	426

SOURCE: DEİK (2014).

* Note: The benchmark for these multinational companies is to invest more than $100 million in foreign assets. Information is based on the responses of the MNCs to the survey.

the border of Georgia and Turkey (TPAO, *Türkiye Petrolleri Anonim Ortaklığı*, Turkish Petroluem Corporation. 2013). In Libya, TPAO has been operating exploration activities since 2000 and its drilling activities have been active since 2010; in Iraq, it was awarded a contract to develop the Badra Oil Field, Missan Oil Field, Siba Gas Field, and Mansuriya Gas Development Projects. Besides this, TPAO has business development activities in hydrocarbon rich regions such as the Russian Federation, Indonesia, Sudan, Yemen, North Africa, and

South America (TPAO, *Türkiye Petrolleri Anonim Ortaklığı*, Turkish Petroleum Corporation. 2013).

Noteworthy mergers and acquisitions by Turkish companies between 2007 and 2013 included the following purchases:[10] Russian SABMiller by Anadolu Efes for $1.9 billion in 2011; Belgium Godiva by Yıldız Holding for $850 million in 2007; Greek Astir Palace Resort by Doğuş Holding for $598 million in 2013; Razi Petrochemical Company, the largest fertiliser facility of Iran, by Gübretaş for $532 million in 2008; the world's third largest container carrier, French CMA CGM, by Yıldırım Holding for $500 million in 2010; Belarusian Telecommunications Network (BeST) by Turkcell for $500 million in 2008; Miran exploration block in Iraqi Kurdistan by Genel Energy for $450 million in 2012; Russian coking coal and steel producer Mechel Chrome by Yıldırım Holding for $425 million in 2013; TradeMedia East, a leading advertising publishing company in Eastern Europe and Russia, by Doğan Holding for $336.5 million in 2007; South African's Defy by a Koç Holding company, Arçelik, for $323.7 million in 2011; Malta Freeport Terminals by Yıldırım Holding for $285.5 million in 2011; Hungarian data services provider Invitel by Türk Telekom for $269.7 million in 2010; Bina Bawi Exploration Block in Iraqi Kurdistan by Genel Energy for $240 million in 2012; and U.S. DeMet's Candy Co. by Yıldız Holding for $221 million in 2013 (Deloitte, 2012: 7–8; 2013: 6–8).

Recently, Yıldız Holding acquired the 184-old British United Biscuits in 2014, thus becoming the world's third largest biscuits maker (*Hürriyet Daily News*, 3 November 2014). Turkish Holdings also continue to facilitate resource extraction from the MENA region. Tosyalı Holding invested in the largest iron and steel plant in Algeria, a country that supplied the largest quantities of natural gas to Turkey in 2013 after Russia and Iran (Daragahi, 2014). In Iraqi Kurdistan, Turkish companies accounted for 55% of foreign companies in 2010, mainly concentrating on building projects including roads, airports, and a police academy (Fielding-Smith, 2010). Not surprisingly, the revolutionary process in MENA not only frightened the despotic regimes in the region but also foreign companies doing business there. Turkish Eroğlu Holding, which invested $150 million in denim garment manufacturing in Ismailia in Egypt, complained about the workers' demand during the revolutionary process, which included the reduction of work week from 48 hours to 42 hours and the increase of wages from $110–120 to $200. Ümmet Eroğlu, member of the Board of Directors of Eroğlu Holding, did not hesitate to label Egyptian workers as "capricious"

---

10   For the sake of clarity, this book included the biggest ten mergers and acquisitions between 2007 and 2013 by Turkish companies for those which had a transaction value more than $200 million.

and said that there is not an unemployment problem in Egypt but a worker problem (Yüzbaşıoğlu, 2011).

Turkish construction firms underwrote 433 foreign projects amounting to $26.1 billion in 2012, mainly in Turkmenistan, Iraq, the Russian Federation, Saudi Arabia, Iran, Ethiopia, United Arab Emirates, Qatar, and Morocco (Türkiye Müteahhitler Birliği [Turkish Contractors Association], 2013: 20). ENKA Holding, one of the largest contractor firms in the world, participated in a large number of power plant constructions in Sulaymaniyah, Dohuk, and Erbil in Iraqi Kurdistan, including motorways, bridges and tunnels in Balkans; a new "city" in Oman under the Blue City Project; and business centres, public buildings, shopping malls and industrial plants, mainly in Russia (ENKA, 2014). In December 2010, a Turkish consortium won a construction bid to rebuild Sadr City in Baghdad with residences for more than a half million people in 75,000 units, valued at $11.3 billion (Karataş, 2010). According to UNCTAD, two Turkish multinational companies, Turkcell (73rd) in telecommunications and ENKA (99th) in construction and real estate sectors, belong to the top 100 list of non-financial companies from developing and transition economies, with foreign assets in 2012 exceeding $6 billion and $3 billion, respectively (United Nations Conference on Trade and Development, 2013).

The influence of Turkish entrepreneurs, especially in Central Asia, is not limited to doing business in profitable areas. They also benefit from crony capitalism under the dictatorial regimes of Central Asia. Ahmet Çalık, founder of Çalık Holding, became energy advisor and was appointed Minister of Textiles under President Niyazov in Turkmenistan for fifteen years (Hendrick, 2013: 171). Muammer Türkyılmaz, founding member of Başkent Education Firms—the Gülen community's financial and administrative umbrella organisation in Turkmenistan—was promoted to Deputy Minister of Education by the current President Berhimuhamedov in 2007 (*Zaman*, 17 March 2007). Ali Bayram, an influential figure in the educational field of the Gülen Movement, had no difficulty in being appointed honorary member of the Committee for Education of the Parliament of Kazakhstan after President Turgut Özal (1989–1993) supported him by writing a reference letter to Nazarbayev in 1992 (Yüksel, 2005).

Turkish companies and the state have not only rushed to snap up investment in manufacturing and services but also investment in agriculture by grabbing large tracts of land especially in Africa. For instance, in 2014 Turkey signed a big land deal setting up a joint venture between the Turkish General Directorate of Agricultural Enterprises and an institution from Sudan to lease 780,000 hectares of farmland for cultivation. Mehdi Eker, Turkey's Food, Agriculture, and Livestock Minister since 2005, expressed Turkey's plan in Sudan, which is situated within the basin of the River Nile: "Turkey will help its technology, mechanization and animal breeding. The company will export its production to the world" (*World Bulletin*, April 29, 2014). On the other hand, it is darkly ironic that Darfur, a region in Western Sudan, faces a food crisis while Sudan opens its borders for agro-business. According to a 2012 United Nations World Food Programme Report (2012: 24), "out of total of 9.36 million people in Darfur, 960,000 people are estimated to be food insecure and 2.51 million are vulnerable to food insecurity".

4.6 Political Tools for Turkish Sub-imperialism

As an umbrella organisation of Turkish capitalists, excluding TUSKON, the Foreign Economic Relations Board (*Dış Ekonomik İlişkiler Kurulu*, DEİK) sets the economic priorities of Turkish capitalism. DEİK was established as a Turkish government initiative by Özal in 1986 under the auspices of the Union of Chambers and Commodity Exchanges of Turkey (*Türkiye Odalar ve Borsalar Birliği*, TOBB). This business association conducts the foreign relations of the Turkish private sector, explores inward and outward investment opportunities, helps businesses increase their exports, and coordinates business activities (DEİK, 2011). With a new structure tying the organisation to the Ministry of Economy by a law enacted in September 2014, DEİK (2011) is charged with "managing the foreign economic relations of the Turkish private sector". Through 120 Business Councils, DEİK has established counterpart organisations and by 2014 had 900 member companies; Turkish capitalists benefit from direct contact with state leaders, build corporate cooperation worldwide, and take part in foreign policy formulation. DEİK's Board of Directors, which includes 35 members, comprises representatives of Turkey's small and big capitalists. Former head of MÜSİAD Ömer Cihad Vardan (2008–2012) was assigned in 2014 by the Ministry of Economy to the new presidency of the organisation (DEİK, 2011).[11]

At the heart of this proactive foreign policy, Turkey has strenuously mobilised a range of economic and political tools available to it for the purposes of

---

11   The role of DEİK in foreign economic policy is shaped by a corporatist relationship with the state (Atlı, 2011). While DEİK is privileged by taking part in policy-making process with respect to foreign policy, bargaining is conditioned upon acquiescent approval of some particular state policies. Atlı highlights two specific examples in which DEİK yielded to state policies. One was the cancellation of a conference in 2007 by the Turkish-American Business Council after the US House of Representatives' Foreign Relations Committee decided to recognise the Armenian Genocide. The other one was the suspension of the Turkish-Greek Business Council's operations in 1999 after Greece was supportive of the PKK (Atlı, 2011: 123). With the new regulation of DEİK enacted in September 2014, the Minister of Economy is endowed with the selection of the chairperson of DEİK.

regional integration. This has been blessed by the US, since Turkey has constituted a major sub-imperialist player for US interests in MENA in the context of diminished American legitimacy in the region following the Iraqi invasion in 2003. Under the "zero problems with neighbours" policy, which was rigorously implemented until the revolutionary process erupted in the Arab region in 2011, the AKP sought to comply with the features of a "trading state". By playing the role of an imperialist core, Turkey actively facilitated trade and lubricated the neoliberal transformation of its vicinity. A 2010 Report by the International Crisis Group (ICG) states that "[p]romoting free trade, facilitating transfers of technology and expertise and carrying out infrastructure integration projects all evoke a win-win attitude which has become a catchphrase of Turkish diplomacy, by contrast with the zero-sum equation that traditionally has dominated the region" (International Crisis Group, 2010: 13). Under AKP rule since 2002, Turkey signed successive free trade agreements with MENA countries: Morocco, Tunisia, Syria, and Palestine in 2004; Egypt in 2005; Jordan in 2009; and Lebanon in 2010.[12] In addition, the Balkans have appeared as economic geography to Turkey's conclusion of successive free trade agreements. Turkey currently has free trade agreements with Albania signed in 2006; Montenegro in 2008; Serbia 2009; and Kosovo together with earlier ones signed with Macedonia in 1999 and Bosnia-Herzegovina in 2002 (Republic of Turkey Ministry of Economy, 2014).[13] Turkey also lifted visa requirements for some Middle Eastern countries such as Syria, Lebanon, Jordan, and Saudi Arabia in 2009 and Libya in 2010 (Aygül, 2014: 409).

Just before the revolutionary process ignited in MENA in December 2010, the private sectors of Turkey, Jordan, Syria, and Lebanon formed a "Levant Quartet" for further economic and cultural integration and increased economic stability (Tür, 2011: 597). This project was hailed as an "EU of the Middle East" (Kurtaran, 2010). Turkey had also provided mediation in Syria-Israel peace talks in 2008. Syrian President Bashar al-Assad was even hosted in southern Turkey by "his friend" Prime Minister Recep Tayyip Erdoğan in August 2008 (*Today's Zaman*, 6 August 2008). The love affair between Erdoğan and al-Assad peaked when joint cabinet meetings were held on 13 October 2009, before it

---

12   The free trade agreement with Syria was suspended on 6 December 2011. Lebanon has not ratified the Association Agreement establishing Free Trade.
13   The free trade agreement signed with Kosovo is still under ratification process. Turkey also has free trade agreements with EFTA countries (Iceland, Liechtenstein, Norway, and Switzerland) signed in 1991; Israel in 1996; Georgia in 2007; Chile in 2009, Mauritius in 2011 and South Korea in 2012. Free Trade Agreements with Malaysia and Moldova are under ratification process (Republic of Turkey Ministry of Economy, 2014).

turned sour in 2011 during the revolutionary process in MENA (Demirtaş, 2013: 111).

Another political linchpin of Turkey's pro-active foreign policy with respect to its sub-imperialist expansion is its foreign aid policy, which entails the "good governance" component of the Post-Washington Consensus. This policy is motivated by Turkey's strategic calculations and aims of enhancing Turkey's presence in its sphere of influence (Altunisik, 2014). Founded in 1992 after the dissolution of the Soviet Union in 1991, the Turkish Cooperation and Coordination Agency (*Türk İşbirliği ve Koordinasyon Ajansı Başkanlığı*, TİKA) has been one of the institutional tools of Turkish foreign policy ever since. It initially aimed to provide assistance to the "Turkic" republics, and its first Programme Coordination Office was inaugurated in Turkmenistan. TİKA expanded its sphere of influence and increased the number of its Programme Coordination Offices from 12 in 2002 to 33 in 2012 (TİKA, n.d.). Through this state organisation, there has been a tremendous increase in Turkish foreign aid. While official Turkish development assistance amounted to only $85 million in 2002, it reached $2.5 billion in 2012 (TİKA, 2012: 13).[14] Not surprisingly, Middle East countries were the largest recipients of Turkish bilateral official development assistance in 2012 with approximately $1.1 billion, followed by Africa with $750 million (TİKA, 2012: 93).[15]

This foreign aid also went hand in hand with the restructuring of coercive apparatuses of foreign countries, an illustration of Turkey's attempt to legitimise the "good governance" concept through building "effective institutions". Turkey was involved in training Tunisian police and gendarmerie forces in 2013, supported Mohamed Morsi for his election in Egypt and gave social infrastructure and services assistance to Egypt in 2012. In Libya, Turkey participated

---

14   According to OECD, "[o]fficial development assistance is defined as those flows to countries and territories on the DAC [Development Assistance Committee] List of ODA [Official Development Assistance] Recipients ... and to multilateral development institutions which are provided by official agencies, including state and local governments, or by their executive agencies; and each transaction of which is administered with the promotion of the economic development and welfare of developing countries as its main objective; and is concessional in character and conveys a grant element of at least 25 per cent..." (OECD, Organisation for Economic Co-operation and Development. 2008, November. Is it ODA?. Retrieved from http://www.oecd.org/investment/stats/34086975.pdf).

15   Bilateral official development assistance includes direct assistance by the public sector, assistance through national or international NGOs, and assistance made by public-private partnership (OECD, Organisation for Economic Co-operation and Development. 2008, November. Is it ODA?. Retrieved from http://www.oecd.org/investment/stats/34086975.pdf).

in a state building process and trained 800 Libyan Police Academy cadets in İstanbul, while the bulk of foreign aid to Yemen mainly comprised of health assistance in 2012 (Altunisik, 2014: 342–343). With the election in 2004 of Ekmeleddin İhsanoğlu as Secretary-General of the Organisation of Islamic Cooperation (OIC)—the first Turkish citizen to serve in this post since its foundation in 1969—Turkey acquired the opportunity to reform the OIC to adopt "good governance" and "expansion of political participation" in its Ten-Year Programme of Action in 2005 and its Charter in 2008 (Kirişçi, 2013: 208).

5 Neo-Ottomanism in Practice

The sub-imperialist stage of Turkish capitalism is articulated into a political project called Neo-Ottomanism. Neo-Ottomanism is the "ideal expression of the dominant material relations". It is the ideological cement of Turkish capitalism in alignment with the expansionary needs of the export-oriented Turkish economy after the 1980s. It is worth noting that Turkey's expansionary foreign policy was initially crystallised after the dissolution of the Soviet Union in 1991 in the context of new geopolitical order. Turkey's expansionary foreign policy in the 1990s was rested upon reaching a zone of influence; "a Turkish World stretching from the Adriatic to the Great Wall of China". The phase was first used by Henry Kissinger in World Economic Forum in Davos on 1 February 1992 in a session called "Turkey Having Vast Opportunities for Regional and Global Collaboration" and the same vision was promoted by Prime Minister Süleyman Demirel in the same year (Erkiner, 2000: 26). This expansionary policy espoused a nationalist and Islamic discourse in order to reach the "Turkic states" of former Soviet Russia countries. However, Turkey's plan to unite these Central Asian countries by integrating them under a Turkish Bank and Turkish Common Market—promoted at the 1992 Ankara Summit—was a failure since Russia had a more profound sphere of control in those countries (Erkiner, 2000: 28–29). Additionally, in the 1990s, Turkey lacked economic power commensurate with its military power to make large energy investments in Azerbaijan, Kazakhstan and Turkmenistan (Erkiner, 2000: 144).

It is in the post-Bonapartist/Kemalist era of the 2000s that Turkey has adopted an active stance in foreign policy in terms of embracing an Ottoman past to affect "the dynamic flow of history, rather than an ordinary and passive component of it". (Davutoğlu, 2013: 865). Ahmet Davutoğlu who was chief foreign policy advisor to Erdoğan and then Minister of Foreign Affairs (2009–2014) before becoming Prime Minister in 2014, said in a speech in Sarajevo in October 2009:

"As in the 16th century, when the Ottoman Balkans were rising, we will once again make the Balkans, the Caucasus and the Middle East, together with Turkey, the centre of world politics in the future. That is the goal of the Turkish foreign policy, and we will achieve it" (Bekdil, 2013).

The need for a proactive diplomacy and foreign policy was detailed in Davutoğlu's book *Stratejik Derinlik: Türkiye'nin Uluslararası Konumu* (Strategic Depth: Turkey's International Position) written in 2001. According to him, Turkey needs to fervently seize on its geography and history as "two constant variables" since it is positioned at the intersections of multiple regions and centred on the legacy of the Ottoman Empire (Davutoğlu, 2014c).

> Turkey enjoys multiple regional identities and thus has the capability as well as the responsibility to follow an integrated and multidimensional foreign policy. The unique combination of our history and geography brings with it a sense of responsibility. To contribute actively towards conflict resolution and international peace and security in all these areas is a call of duty arising from the depths of a multidimensional history for Turkey (Davutoğlu, 2009: 12).

This is why, according to Davutoğlu, "historical depth, geographical positioning and rich legacy in international affairs" compels the country to pursue a proactive foreign policy. According to him, "those who fail to understand the flow of history and do not position themselves in the world accordingly will be overtaken by the rapid pace of events and will end up paying a heavy price for it" (Davutoğlu, 2012: 3). Turkey as a pivotal-country is located at the intersection of three geopolitical and concentric geographical areas, and therefore should take advantage of this "cognizance of geography": (1) "the near land basin" including the Balkans, the Middle East and the Caucasus; (2) "the near maritime basin" including the Black Sea, Adriatic, the East Mediterranean Sea, the Red Sea, the Persian Gulf, and Caspian Sea; and (3) "the near continental basin", including Europe, North Africa, Southern Asia, and Central and Eastern Asia (Davutoğlu, 2014c: 118).

Davutoğlu capitalises on different geostrategic theories and concepts by Haushofer (*Lebensraum*), Mackinder (*pivot area/Heartland*), Spykman (*Rimland*), Mahan (*sea power/geostrategy*), and Seversky (*strategic air power* and *area of decision*) (Davutoğlu, 2014c: 102–109).[16] The expansionist foreign policy

---

16   Halford Mackinder (1861–1947) published "The Geographical Pivot of History" in 1904 in which he attached a particular geostrategic importance to the control of Eastern Europe.

espoused by Davutoğlu calls for enlarging Turkey's *Hinterland* far beyond its natural borders. As he states, "the defence of Eastern Thrace and Istanbul now begins in the Adriatic Sea and Sarajevo, and the defence of Eastern Anatolia and Erzurum begins in the Northern Caucasus and Grozny" (Davutoğlu as quoted in Ozkan, 2014a: 124).

Harking back to Ottoman history plays an instrumental role in challenging the Kemalist narrative of the official ideology, which aimed to break away from the Ottoman legacy. According to Davutoğlu, "dehistoricisation" and disconnect with this past resulted in alienation of society from its "inner self". The product of this alienation is a "divided self" and consequently a frail embracement of a "false self" (Davutoğlu, 2014c: 59). According to him, the "exclusionary and reductionist ideology of history" embraced during the nation-state formation process led to perceiving the Ottoman era "as an archaic construct that represented the pre-modern era" (Davutoğlu, 2014a: 22–23). The new political elites, referring to Mustafa Kemal and his entourage, radically broke away from Ottoman civilisation; they associated with a particular identity, culture and institutions in order to join Western civilisation (Davutoğlu, 2014c: 81–82). Therefore, Turkey's fundamental conflict, it is suggested, lies in the disparity between the society that inherited the political and cultural Ottoman legacy and the political system imposed by a political elite who aimed at joining another civilisation (Davutoğlu, 2014c: 83).

Neo-Ottomanism challenges Kemalist foreign policy and "republican strategic culture" (Evans, 2014, Parts 3 and 4). Under the Bonapartist regime espoused by Mustafa Kemal, foreign policy was based on two objectives: the preservation of the nation-state and the borders of National Pact (*Misak-ı Milli*) and adherence to the Western bloc. In the Cold War period, Turkey continued to conduct this foreign policy, which aimed to preserve its borders against the

---

According to him, for world domination, the control of Euro-Asia is needed; for the control of Euro-Asia, the control of heartland [The heartland, today, refers to the area covering Russia, Central Asia and the Caspian Basin] is needed; and for the control of the heartland, the control of Eastern Europe is needed. Karl Haushofer (1869–1946), on the other hand, relied on Ratzel's theory called *Lebensraum* (habitat or living space) in which a perceived anthropomorphised state, like a living organism, needs new spaces and colonies to live. This was used to legitimise the Nazi expansion. Another geostrategist is Nicholas Spykman (1893–1943) who gave importance to the control of an area called *Rimland*, covering an area of Western Europe, Turkey, Iraq, Pakistan, Afghanistan, India, China, Korea and East Siberia. He is known as the founding father of the containment policy of the U.S. after the Second World War. While Alfred Thayer Mahan (1840–1914) suggested controlling the peripheral sea in order to contain the expansionary potential of a dominant power, Alexander P.de Seversky (1894–1974) prioritised air power in global strategy in a bipolar world (Davutoğlu, 2014c: 102–109).

Soviet Union by aligning itself with NATO, rather than "achieving a distinctive position in the international system" (Davutoğlu, 2014c: 69–71). Therefore, "republican strategic culture" was a reaction to the long decay of the Ottoman Empire from the early 19th century. It evolved into an obsession with homogeneity and national unity under the Kemalist regime and set aside the role of Islam in politics. On the other hand, the "neo-Ottoman strategic culture" developing after the 1980s espoused sub-national identities and active, sometimes interventionist foreign policy with an ambition to be a regional power (Evans, 2014, Parts 3 and 4). In this new setting of a "neo-Ottoman strategic culture", Turkishness denotes being a member of the Ottoman legacy. In a 2014 interview with Richard Falk, Davutoğlu (2014b) stressed:

> Even when we make reference to "the Turkish people", it has been correctly observed that, "It's a culmination of all the ethnic and religious groups of the Ottoman state: Balkan nations, Caucasian nations, Middle Eastern nations, all mixed into Turkey". This past has a continuity with the present. What we need is to restore these values, especially the strong political sense of order and cultural belonging that we owe to each other.

This challenge to Kemalist "republican strategic culture" and foreign policy, however, departs from Erbakan's direct assault on Westernisation and his attempt to form an alternative path to European integration, through development of economic cooperation between major Muslim countries of Bangladesh, Egypt, Indonesia, Iran, Malaysia, Nigeria, Pakistan and Turkey (in the Developing Eight—D8). Under the AKP, the overarching relationship with the East supplements Turkey's alliance with the West, rather than being a substitute for it (Taspinar, 2008: 14).[17]

---

17 According to some authors, Turkish foreign policy has pursued a Pan-Islamist line under Davutoğlu (Kıvanç, 2015; Ozkan, 2014). For Kıvanç (2015), Davutoğlu's book titled *Stratejik Derinlik* (Strategic Depth) is based on a Pan-Islamic and unscientific approach. Ozkan, on the other hand, outlines in his article the reflections of Pan-Islamism by delving extensively into Davutoğlu's early writings *in the second half of the 1980s and the 1990s* when he referred to atrocities and war crimes by Serbian armed forces in Bosnian War as "Christian terrorism and fundamentalism", the wars in Afghanistan and Chechnya as "jihad", Chechnyan warriors as "mujahedeen", and Israel as "geopolitical tumour" (Ahmet Davutoğlu in Ozkan, 2014: 127–130). He, however, overlooks the mutations of Islamic fundamentalists in Turkey in the late 1990s. Rather he sees continuity in their ideology.

Needless to say, this proactive foreign policy alongside Turkey's "multiple regional identities" attributes the EU membership to "Turkey's strategic choice" and "one of the most important projects of the Republican era" (Davutoğlu, 2010: 13). However, as a foreign policy strategy, Turkey should refrain from attaching *only* to EU membership (Davutoğlu, 2014c). The strategy should involve "rearrangement of relations with power centres in a substitute mode and the establishment of a hinterland in which long-term cultural, economic and political links are fortified" (Davutoğlu, 2014c: 118). This, indeed, stems from Turkey's multiple identities. "In terms of its area of influence, Turkey is a Middle Eastern, Balkan, Caucasian, Central Asian, Caspian, Mediterranean, Gulf, and Black Sea country" (Davutoğlu, 2008: 78). Therefore, Davutoğlu advocates a renewal of self-reliance by mobilising a "strategic mindset" which draws its strength from summoning up a legacy of the Ottoman Empire; it should rely on its "strategic depth" (Davutoğlu, 2014c).

6   The State Crisis Ahead of Turkey's Failed Coup

A fundamental question facing contemporary Turkish politics is how an army faction could stage a coup attempt against a democratically elected government, considering that Turkey had already undergone a democratisation process and implemented democratic reforms of civil-military relations. This chapter asks: under what political conditions may disruption of bourgeois rule lead to violent capture of state power by a coup? The chapter suggests that when bourgeois hegemony is severely threatened by a particular socio-political turmoil while the bourgeoisie as a whole is unable to exert operative control over society, the core state apparatus tends to substitute itself for direct rule of the bourgeoisie while presenting itself as the "savior of the nation". In particular, the chapter argues that the resurgence of war in the Kurdish region of Turkey and the divergence of the AKP's foreign policy from imperialist order have decisively tipped the balance of forces in favor of the military. A reversal of the previous wave of democratisation and the inability of the AKP to maintain a new bourgeois hegemony have destroyed effective control over society. Notably, the Turkish army's position *vis-à-vis* the civilian authority has been strengthened by the combination of the unresolved Kurdish question domestically and Turkey's regional role as a sub-imperialist country that intervened in the Arab revolutionary process so as to steer and control the latter.

Turkey has been at the zenith of a process of general crisis of the State since around 2013 when the Gezi protests unfolded as a political response to the neoliberal, authoritarian, and conservative policies of the AKP (Yörük and Yüksel,

2014: 122). The sectarian turn in Turkish foreign policy was boosted following the Gezi Park protests of summer 2013. When a neoliberal urban renewal project aimed to demolish Gezi Park, the only green public space in Taksim, to construct an Ottoman-style barracks and a shopping mall, nation-wide protests erupted in May 2013. The Gezi protesters mostly raised political demands against the authoritarian and conservative moves of the AKP and challenged the commercialisation of a public space (Yörük and Yüksel, 2014: 122–123). However, the government and its supporters attempted to link the Gezi protests with the Alevi community (Karakaya-Stump, 2014). It was stated that 78% of those who were taken into custody during the protests were Alevis, according a police report (Şardan, 2013). On the other hand, Prime Minister Erdoğan demonised the CHP with allegations of provocation and attempts to mobilise the Alevis for the protests (*Hürriyet*, 26 June 2013). Pro-government newspapers speculated about a possible Alevi revolt in August 2013 (Kütahyalı, 2013). Even the corruption scandal on 17 December 2013, which resulted in the arrest of sons of three AKP ministers with key figures in the party circle, was depicted by the pro-AKP media as an extension of the Gezi protests (Karagül, 2015).

However, the AKP regime, as the bearer of the common interests of capitalists, had substantially accomplished its task in Turkey before 2013, namely, to enable the bourgeoisie to control the hard core of the state power, the military. Before 2013, the AKP had undertaken an integral hegemonic project through the EU harmonisation process so as to push the military power to retreat to its barracks. In order to enable this historical function, the conservative AKP was able to absorb civil society and Islamic radicalism within a neoliberal Islam, gaining liberals' support as well (Tuğal, 2009). However, viewed through the lens of Italian Marxist Antonio Gramsci, Turkey's bourgeois class had already been saturated following its political accomplishment to civilianise the political sphere. Since then, the AKP has been unable to absorb the whole society by gaining a new constitutive hegemony and has thus resorted to an aggressive propagation of a right-wing populist rhetoric that formulates society as being divided between "us" and "them".

Tenacious blaming of Fethullah Gülen, self-exiled preacher in the US, for organising a "parallel state structure" within the state and of staging a coup conceals a reality of political turmoil and subsequent organic crisis which prepared the ground for the coup attempt. The organic crisis of the AKP to a large extent commenced, rather paradoxically, after its complete victory in the 2011 general elections. The party won nearly 50 per cent of the votes and since then, the AKP's bid for power ruled out any compromise in political decision-making processes. In addition to this domestic situation, the way in which Turkey's political leadership handled the Arab Uprisings and the effects of Europe's economic turmoil on Turkey intensified the organic crisis. Therefore, the appearance of minimal hegemony has been a consequence of contradictions within the power bloc, which came to the surface after 2011. Aziz Babuşçu, the AKP chairman of İstanbul province between 2007 and 2015 and since 2015 an MP, confessed, before the eruption of Gezi protests in May 2013, to the partition of alliance with their former stakeholders:

> Those who were our stakeholders one way or the other in our 10 years of rule will not be stakeholders in the next 10 years. In the past 10 years there were those who shared our efforts to cleanse the ranks and to define freedom, law and justice. Let's say, although they did not fully agree with us, some of those liberal segments were stakeholders in that process. But the future is the era of building. This era will not be as they want. Therefore those stakeholders will not be with us. Those who were with us this or that way yesterday, tomorrow will join ranks with forces that will oppose us because the Turkey that will be built and developed will not be the future they will accept. That is why our task is a lot harder (Aziz Babuşçu as cited in Cengiz, 2013).

In his bid for power, Erdoğan continued to hold control over the AKP even after he was elected as a President in 2014, a trajectory similar to that of Putin and Medvedev between 2008 and 2012 in Russia where the former embodied real political power even though the Russian constitution assigned more power to the latter. In the June 7 general election in 2015 the pro-Kurdish HDP passed the threshold by gaining 13 per cent of the votes and ended the one-party majoritarian rule of the AKP. The leadership under Erdoğan did not welcome the election results and Turkey in turn passed through a second general election in six months. The outcome of this second election, which was held in November 2015, was that the AKP vote rose from 41 per cent to nearly 50 per cent. However, the reshuffling of elections in a six-month period created a political climate in which the democratic defeat of Erdoğan through peaceful elections was unlikely (Sezgin, 2016).

Last but not least, Prime Minister Erdoğan latched on to an abrasive populist trope not only to win upcoming elections but also to criticise and muzzle his political opponents as "elitists", resulting in a further polarisation of society along cultural fault lines. Populism, here, refers to *"an ideology that considers society to be ultimately separated into two homogenous and antagonistic groups, 'the pure people' versus 'the corrupt elite', and which argues that politics should be an expression of the volonté générale (general will) of the people"* (Mudde, 2004: 543). This political ideology exalts of a unified homogenous "people" through the mediation of a charismatic leader, who claims to embody "the interests of the nation" (Canovan, 1999: 5). This charismatic leader addresses a particular logic of articulation to construct a popular subject for a mode of representation (Laclau, 2005). By portraying the CHP as the party of "crème de la crème" and "White Turks", the AKP was to be the party of "Negroes" (*Yeni Şafak*, 17 March 2014). While denouncing the CHP as an elitist party, which demanded to monopolise "all privileges and opportunities" into its hands, Erdoğan called himself a "Negro Turk" (Küçük, 2013). In a protest against construction of a road in METU, a leading university in Ankara, Turkey, protesters were portrayed as "leftists", "atheists" and "terrorists" that the CHP embraced while the AK Party youth was said to have only "computers and pens" rather than "Molotov cocktails in their hands" (*Today's Zaman*, 6 March 2014). It then became possible for the AKP leadership to increasingly "interpellate" political subjects through an Islamic mode of articulation or identification. Insofar as the AKP has been successful in portraying itself as the embodiment of the will of "the people" while depicting the CHP as the party of the "elitists", it has served in reducing the social cleavages to cultural splits, obfuscating power struggles within both constructed "people" and the "elite", and thereby glossing over the destructiveness of neoliberalism creating and exacerbating social and economic insecurities. Meanwhile, democracy is reduced to the ballot box and any anti-government demonstration is depicted as an attempt to impose the will of the minority over the majority (Özbudun, 2014: 157).

In addition, the populist rhetoric employed by Erdoğan facilitated institutional fragmentation. While populist political strategy is built on direct and quasi-personal appeal of the leader to the disparaged masses by circumventing intermediary institutions (Weyland, 1999), populism emboldened by Erdoğan also mobilised a "politics of ressentiment" that pits Turkey's secular middle classes against real possessors of the nation, the Sunni-Muslim majority (Kandiyoti, 2014). The consequence was that "this repeated othering behavior by a leading figure cultivates an atmosphere in which animosity is the norm and violence is not only tolerated, but actually rewarded" (Hintz, 2016b). Therefore, a highly polarised society, divided along cultural lines such as conservative/secular, Kemalist/Islamist, modern/traditional, hindered the forming of an effective hegemony that would absorb social resentment.

On top of this, the failure of the peace process to resolve the decades-long Kurdish conflict tipped the country into a spiral of violence. According to Human Rights Foundation of Turkey (2016), the resumption of war in the Kurdish region of Turkey's southeast after 2015 and daylong curfews in those parts left at least 338 civilians dead. More than 1.6 million residents were affected between August 16, 2015 and April 20, 2016. Remarkably, the reversal of the previous wave of democratic reforms implemented by the AKP between 2002 and 2007 emboldened the military to become involved in political decision-making processes such as the Kurdish issue and foreign policy. It can be suggested that Turkey achieved the first phase of political democratisation, while failing to achieve its successive phase of democratic consolidation. With regards to the Kurdish issue, the military compromised with the AKP and regained one of its reserved domains and prerogatives: immunity from prosecution in counter-terrorism operations in southeast Turkey (*Reuters*, 24 June 2016). However, the military was bestowed impunity while the impunity of MPs, especially those of pro-Kurdish HDP, was stripped.

The AKP's reconciliation with the old regime resembles, albeit with important political differences, that of Ennahda, sometimes described as the Tunisian Muslim Brotherhood founded by Rached Ghannouchi and Abdelfattah Mourou in 1981 under the name of "The Movement of Islamic Tendency". Ennahda conceded to share power with the old regime in the context of revolutionary and counter-revolutionary waves in the Arab world. This was because the party was not able to neutralise the revolutionary wave in Tunisia and because of the difficulty of imposing Sharia rule in a situation where the state apparatus, media and economy were under the control of the old regime (Achcar, 2016: 158). However, in the Turkish case the AKP strategically allied with the old regime to counter Gülen-linked state personnel in the police force and the judiciary. Ennahda's accommodation of the old regime went so far that Ghannouchi (2016a) announced in an interview with *Le Monde*, just before Ennahda's 10th conference, that he would declare the party's separation from political Islam and rebrand it as a civic democratic movement (*Le Monde*, 19 May 2016). He also reiterated his aim to separate mosques from politics; to implement "benign capitalism" that would balance the freedom of entrepreneurship with social justice; to create an entrepreneurial culture; and to expand exports and negotiations with the EU for free trade agreements, all signalling a transformation in Tunisian Islamic politics that echoes the AKP experience (Ghannouchi, 2016). On the other hand, the AKP's adoption of an accommodating stance towards Kemalist forces—that the party had neutralised through democratizing reforms up until 2011—has been a result of a political process unleashed when the Gülen movement asked the AKP for more political power and spoils. Another factor that brought together the interests of the AKP and the old regime was a regional context that enabled the Kurds in Syria to form autonomous zones in north of the country.

Relatedly, the AKP's foreign policy since 2011 facilitated the decay of stable bourgeois rule in the country and caused disgruntlement within the military. The United States' ambivalence towards the AKP is closely related to the divergence of policies between an imperialist and a sub-imperialist force with respect to the Syrian civil war. In the early phase of the uprising, Turkey took the lead in organizing the Syrian National Council in İstanbul in October 2011 in which the Syrian Muslim Brotherhood was a dominant force for decision-making and policymaking (Achcar, 2016: 44; Carnegie Endowment for International Peace, 2016). Moreover, the Free Syrian Army, composed of dissenters from the Syrian army, was sheltered in Turkey (Ilgıt and Davis, 2013). However, when the uprising mutated into a civil war due to the suppression of uprising without compunction by *shabbihas*, Assad's special forces (Achcar, 2013: 224–227, 2016), the support of Turkey and Qatar for Islamic fundamentalist forces went beyond Muslim Brotherhood networks. Al-Nusra Front, which was formed in 2013 as a Syrian branch of Islamic State of Iraq (ISI) and then left ISIS and al-Qaeda, could spread its message though the broadcasting of its leader, Abu Muhammad al-Julani, in Qatar-funded Al Jazeera (Achcar, 2016: 39–40). Besides, there have been allegations that Turkey backed jihadist organisations such as al-Nusra Front for overthrowing Assad and counterbalancing Kurdish cantons in northern Syria (Stein, 2015) along with Jaish al-Fatah or the Army of Conquest, and Ahrar al-Sham (Sengupta, 2015). That three trucks under the control of National Intelligence Organisation (*MİT*, in its Turkish acronym) were searched in January 2014 and were found to be loaded with weapons on their way to Syria seemed to support allegations of Turkey's support for Islamic fundamentalist groups (Taştekin, 2015).

The New York Times reported that Qatar purchased anti-aircraft missiles and small-arms cartridges from Sudan that were delivered to the Syrian opposition through the Turkish border (Chivers and Schmitt 2013 in Achcar, 2016: 18). US Vice President Joe Biden confirmed reports of such support to the Syrian rebels during a speech at Harvard Kennedy School in October 2014. He stated that tripartite allies of the US in the region (Turkey, Qatar and Saudi Arabia) "poured hundreds of millions of dollars, and tens of thousands of tons of weapons into anyone who would fight against al-Assad, accepted the people who would be in supply for al-Nusra and al-Qaeda and extremist elements of jihadists coming from other parts of the world" (as cited in Tanış, 2014). Biden's "Freudian slip" was later corrected by himself with a clarification that he had not meant that US allies in the region *intentionally* promoted the expansion of the Islamic State or other groups (Usher, 2014). On this point, it should be added that Turkey branded al-Nusra as a terrorist organization only in June 2014—however, without a legally binding sanction, according to law professor Ersan Şen (as cited in Daloglu, 2014). Turkey also started airstrikes against ISIS as late as summer 2015 under international pressure to do so (Tuysuz and

Bilginsoy, 2016) and allowed the US to use its İncirlik air base to attack IS only in July 2015 (Sly and DeYoung, July 23, 1015).

Needless to say, while the US has prioritised the war against ISIS and has consequently given military support to Syrian Kurds that have been fighting against them, during the siege of the Kurdish enclave of Kobani in September 2014 in particular, Turkey initially refused to open up a corridor to the border town for Kurdish fighters and weapons to pass through. This instigated a Kurdish insurrection in Turkey in October 2014 that left dozens of people dead (Letsch, 2014a, 2014b), an event which became another element that facilitated political instability in country. It was only after US pressure that Turkey opened up reinforcement to the city with the help of Turkey's allies, the Free Syrian Army, and Iraqi peshmerga fighters (Achcar, 2016: 43). In other words, those labelled a terrorist organisation by Turkey are seen by the US as *de facto* ally in its war against the Islamic State (IS). The Democratic Union Party (PYD, in its Kurdish acronym), which operates in northern Syria and has links with the outlawed PKK, and the Women's Protection Units (YPJ, in its Kurdish acronym), have been pioneers in the fight against IS. These units have been supported by arms airdropped by the US. The strategic failure of the AKP only confirms that Turkey's "zero-problems foreign policy" implemented by former Prime Minister Ahmet Davutoğlu was eviscerated in the context of the Arab uprisings. Worse still, miscalculations in foreign policy brought the repercussions of Syrian civil war inside Turkey, with large cities such as İstanbul and Ankara affected either by PKK attacks or hit by ISIS suicide bombers.

The coup attempt of 15 July in Turkey unfolded in a severely polarized society, one that the political leadership had consciously facilitated. Nevertheless, the coup attempt should be depicted neither as a botched coup nor a hoax concocted by Erdoğan himself. Parallels have been drawn offhand between the coup attempt and the Reichstag fire in Germany in 1933, an event which the Nazis capitalised upon in order to declare emergency constitutional powers to mobilise its supporters and to curb democratic rights. It is true that Erdoğan himself called the coup attempt "a gift from God" and turned it into an opportunity to purge not only Gülen-linked civil servants but also all kinds of opposition by means of state of emergency and decree laws. However, the scale of killings that followed the coup attempt, which left 265 dead and 1,440 wounded, gives an indication of what the consequences could have been had the coup succeeded.

It is undeniable that the Gülen movement, as propagated through the concept of *Hizmet* (Service) by his sympathisers, has a stake in civil society and the state. According to Carol Migdalovitz's report to US Congress, the Gülen movement "controls a network of schools around the world, including some in the United States; universities; banks with more than $5billion in assets; non-governmental organizations; and newspapers, magazines, and networks in Turkey and other countries" (Migdalovitz, 2010: 21). As it was argued in the beginning of this chapter, the neoliberal transformation of the Turkish education system aided the expansion of the Gülen movement; poor but promising students relied upon Gülenist schools to achieve social mobility, thus bringing many into contact with movement. Lieutenant Colonel Levent Türkkan, who was the aide of Chief of General Staff General Hulusi Akar and participated in the coup attempt, testified that he came from a poor farmer family that did not have any fields to cultivate. He added that he was a bright student who wanted to be a soldier and attended Gülen-linked schools in his middle-school years. He denounced the movement for exploiting his ambition to be a soldier and for leaking exam questions for the Işıklar Military Academy before the exam (Benli, July 20, 2016).

The Gülen movement sympathisers have also been infiltrating state institutions, especially the military, since the 1970s. In 1986, Ruşen Çakır, a well-known journalist and expert on Islamic movements in Turkey, reported the dismissal of Gülen-linked military high school students who had infiltrated the prestigious İstanbul Kuleli, Bursa Işıklar, and İzmir Maltepe military high schools by way of practising *taqiya* (religiously-sanctioned dissimulation) and concealing their religious beliefs (Çakır and San, 1986). Former Police Chief Hanefi Avcı also reiterated that the movement was also active in national police and national intelligence service where they conspired against the leading figures in the military (Avcı, 2010).

In addition to the use of the Islamic notion of *taqiya* to infiltrate to the state institutions, members of the movement employed a tactical avoidance of direct confrontation with the state establishment and obedience to the state where it was necessary. Indeed, colonisation of the state by various Islamic sects was not restricted to the Gülen movement. According to Deniz Kandiyoti (2016: 38–39), colonisation of the state is associated with the decay of a Weberian meritocratic appointment system of civil servants in the state bureaucracy in favor of followers of various Islamic orders in Turkey. Nevertheless, the Gülen community was more systematic than other Islamic sect in its attempt to infiltrate state institutions. For instance, in a sermon delivered by Gülen and shown on Turkish television in 1999, he advocated a Machiavellian strategy of *taqiya* to attain political goals:

> You must move in the arteries of the system without anyone noticing your existence until you reach all the power centers ... until the conditions

are ripe, they [the followers] must continue like this. If they do something prematurely, the world will crush our heads, and Muslims will suffer everywhere, like in the tragedies in Algeria, like in 1982 [in] Syria ... like in the yearly disasters and tragedies in Egypt. The time is not yet right. You must wait for the time when you are complete and conditions are ripe, until we can shoulder the entire world and carry it ... You must wait until such time as you have gotten all the state power, until you have brought to your side all the power of the constitutional institutions in Turkey ... Until that time, any step taken would be too early—like breaking an egg without waiting the full forty days for it to hatch. It would be like killing the chick inside. The work to be done is [in] confronting the world. ... I know that when you leave here—[just] as you discard your empty juice boxes, you must discard the thoughts and the feelings that I expressed here (as cited in Sharon-Krespin, 2009).

At the apex of his obedience to the state, Gülen supported the 1980 military coup in Turkey. He even criticised those who took streets in 1989 to protest the headscarf ban in Turkish universities, urging them not to partake in "anarchy". He ridiculed them by saying that that most of protesters were either men in loose, black garment covering the body from head to toe or women in indecent dress (Fethullah Gülen,1989 in Çakır, 2012: 118).

Taking into account the unprecedented growth of the Gülen movement and the alliance and then detachment of the AKP from this movement, the coup attempt seems to be the last violent outburst of a four-year war that has been unfolding between Recep Tayyip Erdoğan and Fethullah Gülen since 2012. In other words, borrowing Carl von Clausewitz's aphorism from his 1832 book *On War*, this war is merely "the continuation of policy by other means" (Von Clausewitz, 2007: 28).

Retrospectively, the political war between Erdoğan and Gülen appears to have crystallised in February 2012 with the attempt by Sadrettin Sarıkaya, a specially authorised prosecutor, to detain Hakan Fidan, the head of Turkish Intelligence. Indeed, according to Ruşen Çakır, the war was the result of a conflict on how to fill the vacuum in political power that was created between 2007 and 2012 when military tutelage was downgraded by judicial means through the Ergenekon and Sledgehammer cases, in which Gülen-linked prosecutors and judges played an important role (Çakır and Sakallı, 2014: 40). However, this political war escalated in November 2013 when the AKP moved to close down college prep schools, which were largely under the control of Gülen followers. The move was counteracted by Gülen-linked police in December 2013 in what became known as the 17/25 December operations, which involved the leaking of information that led to a corruption scandal centred on the companions of Erdoğan and sons of four AKP ministers (Çakır and Sakallı, 2014). As a response, judicial operations set in motion the de-Gülenisation of the state and approximately 6,000 security personnel were shuffled by December 2014 (Hamsici, December 16, 2014).

In its final phase, a couple of days before the coup attempt, on July 9 İzmir Deputy Chief Prosecutor Okan Bato demanded arrests for several active military personnel accused of producing fake evidences in military espionage trials and of being members of the "Fethullahist Terror Organisation". Bato also claimed that new arrest warrants would be issued (Shaw and Şık, July 21, 2016). In addition, it transpired that there would be a massive purge of Gülen-linked military personnel after the Supreme Military Council's meeting (Yüksek Askeri Şura, YAŞ) that would be convened on July 28. This prompted a final attempt by Gülen-linked military personnel, who mounted a pre-emptive attack in order to obliterate a possible purge.

De-Gülenisation of the state accelerated following the 15 July coup attempt. Deputy Prime Minister Bekir Bozdağ asserted that 110,778 civil servants were dismissed, of whom only 3,604 were reinstated by January 2018 (*Hürriyet Daily News*, 31 January 2018). Arrest warrants were issued for 140 out of 387 judges from the Court of Appeals and for 48 out of 156 judges from the Council of State (*Hürriyet Daily News*, 16 July 2016). The Head of the Court of Cassations also declared that 4,500 judges and prosecutors were under investigation for alleged links with Gülen by March 2018 (*Hürriyet Daily News*, 5 March 2018). He, therefore, complained of the inexperience of nearly 9,000 newly appointed judges and prosecutors, who constitute half of the Turkish judiciary (*Hürriyet Daily News*, 5 March 2018). 196 out of 326 generals and admirals were retired, resigned or dismissed while the number of commissioned officers decreased from 32,189 in July 2016 to 24,705 in July 2017 (*Hürriyet Daily News*, 23 July 2017), consequently weakening the core state apparatus. The dismissal tsunami also engulfed 11,500 left-wing teachers who were accused of having links with the PKK. By the end of 2017, 5,822 academics had been dismissed from 118 public universities in Turkey (Akdeniz and Altıparmak, 2018: 39).

The US adopted a tepid approach to the coup attempt in its early phase, which can be attributed to the ambivalent relationship between Turkey's sub-imperialist foreign policy and the US's imperialist order in the Middle East. In response to unfolding events in Turkey on the coup day, US Secretary of State John Kerry only stated that he "hoped for peace, stability and continuity in Turkey" (*Reuters*, 15 July 2014) without castigating the coup attempt, instead taking an ambivalent wait-and-see policy regarding which side would triumph. General Joseph Votel, US Central Command Commander, expressed his concern over the purges of Gülen-linked military personnel, who were also considered to be US military interlocutors, since this would possibly undermine US military operations against IS (Paletta, 2016). In an article written for *Huffington Post* one week after the coup by Graham Fuller, former vice chairman of CIA's National Intelligence Service, the Gülen movement was whitewashed as "one of the most encouraging faces of contemporary Islam in the world" and one of the "rational, moderate, socially constructive and open-minded organisations" amongst the Islamic movements (Fuller, 2016). Not surprisingly, Gülen (August 27, 2015) himself has been courted by the USA in its fight against "Islamic extremism" since he continuously denounced violence and put some responsibility upon Muslims for the "smeared image of ... faith". This opened doors to Gülen; Fuller (2016) reiterated his willingness to be a referee for Gülen's eligibility for a US green card in 2006. All these ambivalent approaches to the coup attempt aggravated a political climate of anti-Americanism in Turkey, characterised by the suggestion that the USA abetted the coup attempt masterminded by Gülen himself.

Without doubt, had the coup succeeded, Turkey would have been going through a civil war that would have resembled that of the late 1970s and the fate of Erdoğan would have resembled that of Mohamed Morsi in Egypt, who was toppled on 3 July 2013. Turkey's fate would have been similar to the Algerian case, in which the Islamic Salvation Front was about to win the 1992 general elections but was pushed aside by the military coup which opened the way for a bloody ten-year civil war. In light of these comparisons, the failure of the coup attempt is promising. However, it should be added that its failure does not necessarily mean the triumph of democracy. Erdoğan successfully accommodated the mainstream opposition parties, with the exception of the HDP, in the Yenikapı anti-coup rally where a new language of "national unity" was introduced. Shrouded by this "national unity" discourse, it became ordinary to close down news agencies, radio stations, newspapers, and magazines that were charged of having link with "Gülenist terrorism" as well as Alevi radio stations, Kurdish newspapers and television programmes, including one channel for children. In this context, trustees were appointed to major Kurdish-run municipalities in the southeastern and eastern part of Turkey and the HDP parliamentarians and co-chairs were arrested (*Hürriyet Daily News*, 17 November 2016).

On the other hand, the coup attempt also sheds light on a paradox particular to Turkey: that the most regressive and fundamentalist segments of society, Islamic fundamentalists and hard-line nationalists, were bearers—if not implementers—of a democratic function in thwarting the coup within the context of the absence or weakness of progressive forces in society. The factions of the state bureaucracy under AKP control, mainly the police force, Special Force Command, and importantly the Presidency of Religious Affairs, swiftly acted to thwart the coup by mobilising masses through *salah* (prayers) being read by 110,000 imams at 85,000 mosques (Tremblay, 2016). Calls for the restoration of the death penalty and slogans in favor of Sharia law articulated by the masses demonstrated a desire for "vigilante vengeance" against those who attempted the coup (Hintz, 2016a). This was not surprising; the euphoria for building a democratic bloc that progressive forces spearheaded after 2015 June elections had been swiftly suffocated by the "politics of fear" being propagated by the AKP.

All in all, the Turkish case only works to revoke the mainstream democratisation theory of Adam Przeworski that claims that affluent democracies do not turn into authoritarian regimes (Browlee, 2016). Creeping authoritarianism and populism that divides society only feeds the destabilisation of the country and increases the rise of political risks, consequently setting the country back to another cycle of Bonapartist coups. This confirms the suggestion made Gramsci in the *Prison Notebooks* that the ruling classes cannot retain efficient hegemony over society when "either … the ruling class has failed in some major political undertaking for which it has requested, or forcibly extracted, the consent of the broad masses (war, for example), or … huge masses (especially of peasants and petit-bourgeois intellectuals) have passed suddenly from a state of political passivity to a certain activity, and put forward demands which taken together, albeit not organically formulated, add up to a revolution" (Gramsci, 1971: 210). Whether the political leadership under President Erdoğan has understood the political context of the coup has so far remained an open question.

CHAPTER 6

Concluding Observations

Throughout this book, Bonapartism has been used as an analytical tool to conceptualise the Kemalist state. As a product of precarious circumstances and a political crisis, Bonapartism is an exceptional form of the capitalist state whereby the state secures the reproduction of capitalist social relations. Distinctively, in Bonapartist political regimes, real power does not rest with the political representatives of the dominant classes, but with the executive apparatus of the state. It has been shown that Bonapartism recapitulated and institutionalised itself after the passing of a "national hero" in relation to circumstances and existing class relations. In this context, the Kemalist regime safeguarded the conditions of capital accumulation and created the conditions for the growth of Turkish bourgeoisie, which was too weak to consolidate its political hegemony. Nevertheless, as this thesis has shown, the Kemalist state's economic pillar started to slowly crumble after the transition to export-led capitalism eroded national developmentalism. In this transition, the military dictatorship of 1980–1983 played an instrumental role.

This book has suggested that the AKP has represented a departure from its predecessors by successfully uniting the general interests of the "devout bourgeoisie" with those of the big bourgeoisie for civilianisation of the political power apparatus. The political trajectory of Necmettin Erbakan's successive Islamic fundamentalist parties, on the other hand, had been successful only in representing the interests of the peripheral capitalists. Therefore, the central argument of this book is that the mutation of Islamic politics in Turkey was instrumental in achieving the severance of military control from parliamentary power. In other words, the AKP used the mutation of Islamic politics as a means to neutralise the military by co-opting the liberals and entering into an alliance with the Islamic community of Fethullah Gülen, which had a strong presence in the judiciary and the police force. By doing this, the AKP waged a democratic struggle to vest power in the elected parliament and carry the democratic transition until 2010/2011. However, once the AKP to a large extent presided over the military in 2010/2011, it did not refrain from centralising political power in its hands, thereby drifting to authoritarianism and losing its integral hegemony over society.

With respect to foreign policy, it has been shown that in relation to the transformation of the Turkish economy after the 1980s and the demise of the Kemalist state, the AKP has found a fertile ground to realign Turkish foreign policy under the doctrine of neo-Ottomanism. Neo-Ottomanism has been an ideological anchor of Turkish capitalism since the 1980s when Turkey's regional economic power complemented its political-military capacity and power. The expansion of Turkish capitalism into Middle Eastern countries mobilised a mild form of pan-Islamic ideology and a policy of "zero-problem with neighbours" by recognising the Ottoman legacy. However, neo-Ottomanist expansionary policy has encountered a sectarian rift in Turkish foreign policy owing to two political developments: the mutation of the Syrian uprising into a civil war and Turkey's domestic political instability, which peaked with the Gezi protests in the summer of 2013.

The revolutionary process in the Arab world in 2011 presented Erdoğan with a ripe opportunity to further implement his neo-Ottomanist expansionary foreign policy. At the initial stage of the Arab revolutionary process, he was praised in the Arab world when on 2 February 2011 he called for Mubarak's resignation—the first leader to do so (Edelman et al., 2013: 71–72). This was an important step, along with two events that popularised Erdoğan in the Arab world: his condemnation of Israeli President Shimon Peres in the Davos Summit for conducting a war in Gaza in 2008–2009; and the raiding of the *Mavi Marmara* flotilla by Israeli naval forces in the Mediterranean Sea in May 2010 after it tried to break the Israeli blockage of Gaza, which created a major crisis between Turkey and Israel (Samaan, 2013). Erdoğan's Cairo visit in September 2011 was also welcomed in the Arab world, during which he promoted the Turkish model of secularism to the Egyptian Muslim Brotherhood (Edelman et al., 2013: 72). His pro-Muslim Brotherhood policy continued after the election of the Brotherhood candidate, Mohamed Morsi, as Egyptian president in June 2012. Turkey pledged in September 2012 to provide Egypt with a $2 billion financial package to assist the Egyptian economy (Edelman et al., 2013: 72). Qatar also pledged $2 billion to finance the Egyptian budget deficit and invested an $18 billion in tourism and industrial projects (Werr, 2012). In this context, Turkey's interests converged with those of Qatar, which financed the Muslim Brotherhood and Islamic fundamentalist forces in the wake of the Arab uprising (Achcar, 2013a; Ulrichsen 2014; Steinberg, 2012)[1] based on a neo-Ottoman, pan-Islamic view that the Muslim Brotherhood would prevail in the post-revolutionary process.

---

1   Qatar under Hamad bin Khalifa Al Thani, who came to power with a palace coup in 1995, had capitalised on the break-up of the relationship between the Muslim Brotherhood and the Saudi Kingdom, which permitted US troops to station on its soil in the first Gulf War in 1991 (Achcar, 2013: 125–128).

Turkey's pro-Muslim Brotherhood policy was not limited to Egypt. In 2012 Turkey accommodated and then gave a residence permit to former Iraqi Vice President Tariq Al-Hashimi from the Iraqi Islamic Party, the Iraqi branch of the Muslim Brotherhood when the Shiite-dominated Nouri Maliki government issued an arrest warrant for him in December 2011 (Yezdani, 2012). In addition, Tawakkul Karman, who represents the Yemeni Congregation for Reform (*Al-Islah*, the reformist wing of the Yemeni Muslim Brotherhood) (Jacob, 2011), was granted Turkish citizenship in October 2012 (*Hürriyet Daily News*, 12 October 2012). With respect to Syria, Turkey initially pursued a dual role. On the one hand it used diplomacy to push Assad to make some political reforms at the initial stage of the uprising. On the other hand, it helped Syrian opposition organise in Turkey (Ayata, 2015: 102–103). When Assad refused to make political reforms, Turkey suspended its diplomatic relations with Syria that September and staunchly pursued a policy of "regime change" (Ayata, 2015: 103). For this aim, Turkey hosted the establishment of the Syrian National Council (SNC) in İstanbul in August 2011 (*Al Arabiya News*, 23 August 2011) an umbrella organisation that brings together various opposition forces but is dominated by the Muslim Brotherhood (Carnegie Middle East Center, 2013). When in November 2012 the US dismissed the SNC for not adequately representing the Syrian opposition and urged the inclusion of more Syrian opposition forces, a new body called the "National Coalition of Syrian Revolutionary and Opposition Forces" replaced the SNC, crystallising the divergent views between Turkey and the US (Edelman et al., 2013: 42). Turkey responded in December 2012 by facilitating a meeting that unified the command structure within the Free Syrian Army known as the "Supreme Military Council Command of Syria" under General Salim Idriss (MacFarquhar and Saad, 2012).

However, when the Syrian uprising turned into "a full-scale civil war" in 2012 (Achcar, 2013a: 224) this impacted on Turkish foreign policy, which became increasingly shaped by sectarian calculations (Edelman et al., 2013: 46). When Lebanon's Shiite Hezbollah joined the war in Syria in support of Assad in 2013, Deputy Prime Minister Bekir Bozdağ ridiculed Hezbollah (meaning the Party of God) by saying that it should change its name to the Party of Satan (Taştekin, 2013). Interestingly enough, when Israel attacked Hezbollah in Syrian Golan Heights in January 2015, Turkey remained silent and did not criticise Israel, showing that Turkey prioritises an anti-Assad stance over anti-Israel rhetoric (Tremblay, 2015). This anti-Assad stance and sectarian rift in Turkish foreign policy was followed by allegations that Turkey supported the fundamentalist *Ahfad al-Rasoul* (Grandsons of the Prophet) Brigade against Kurdish militias in northern Syria in November 2012 (Al-Shistani, 2013). In interviews with the representatives of Islamic fundamentalist forces in Syria, such as *Ahrar ash-Sham*

(Free Men of the Levant) and *Jabbat al-Islamiyya* (the Islamic Front), these forces all warmly praised the Turkish "humanitarian aid" and "hospitality" (Çiçek, 2013, 2014). It has also been alleged that the Islamic coalition under *Jaish al-Fatah* (Army of Conquest), which includes the al-Nusra Front, was supported by Turkey, Qatar, and Saudi Arabia in the capture from regime forces of the northern Syrian city of Idlib in March 2015 (Hassan, 2015). The fall of the city to Islamic forces was praised by the pro-AKP media as the "big victory of the Syrian opposition" (*Sabah*, 28 March 2015). Furthermore, in a sign of sectarian calculation, Turkey allied with the Sunni bloc, which included most of the Gulf countries along with Egypt, Sudan, Morocco, and Jordan, in order to undermine the Iranian influence in the Gulf region and in Yemen particularly. President Erdoğan reassured Saudi Arabia of Turkey's political and possible logistical support to the Saudi-led airstrikes against the Shiite-oriented Houthi movement in Yemen and denounced Iran for pursuing a sectarian role in the region (*France 24*, 27 March 2015).

Nevertheless, the sectarian rift in Turkish foreign policy did not lead to a break in Turkish-Iranian relations, since Turkey's attitude towards its neighbour has many layers. On one hand, it is clear that Turkey and Iran have prioritised contradictory interests with regards the preservation of Bashar al-Assad in Syria (Ayman, 2014: 18). On the other hand, the establishment of self-rule in Syrian Kurdistan, known as Rojava, led to a rapprochement between Turkey and Iran in terms of security cooperation, since both countries perceive the possibility of a Kurdish conflict in their territories as a national security threat (Lawson, 2014: 1354–1358). In addition, both countries have an interest in energy cooperation. While Turkish capitalism very much depends on secure access to the oil and the natural gas deposits of Iran, Iran needs a transit country like Turkey in order to reach the European market (Bahgat, 2014: 121).

On that point, it should be added that the sectarian shift and increasing deterioration of relations with Syria also has a domestic dimension. When two car bombs exploded in the town of Reyhanlı, in Hatay province on the border with Syria in May 2013, Erdoğan did not refrain from emphasising the sectarian affiliations of those who died. He expressed his condolences for 53 "Sunni" citizens and charged the CHP with having links with Assad (*Radikal*, 14 June 2013). This only exacerbated the sectarian tension in Turkey. Three months earlier in February 2013 Erdoğan had remarked that *cemevleri*, places of worship for the Alevis, who make up an estimated 10% to 20% of the population in Turkey (Çarkoğlu and Bilgili, 2011: 353), are nothing but cultural centres, since Islam dictates that the mosque is the only place of worship (*Radikal*, 22 February 2013). When a complex that would combine side-by-side a mosque and a *cemevi* was inaugurated in an Alevi neighbourhood of Tuzluçayır, in Ankara in

September 2013 (Bayram and Tercanlı, 2013), some Alevi organisations raised concerns that this project was aimed at making the *cemevi* an auxiliary establishment of a mosque (Tremblay, 2013). Worryingly, sectarian tension focused on residency. A 2012 law (Law No 6360) concerning the establishment of new municipalities split the Antakya municipality in Hatay province in two, along religious and ethnic lines (Letsch, 2013). The Alawite neighbourhoods brought together under a new local municipality, "Defne", and cut off from the more developed municipality "Antakya", a demarcation referred to by residents as "the Berlin Wall" (Letsch, 2013).

1 Basic Structural Economic Limitations of Turkey's Sub-imperialist Expansion: the Sustainability and Capacity Problem of the Turkish Economy

The sub-imperialist economic and ideological expansion of Turkey reveals the basic contradiction in achieving economic growth: *the increasing gap between Turkey's exports and imports*. In other words, the fundamental deep paradox of sustaining economic growth in Turkey is possible only by incurring a trade deficit. According to the Turkish Statistical Institute, Turkey's exports in 2019 amounted to slightly more than $172 billion, while its imports were slightly more than $203 billion, thus constituting a trade deficit of around $30 billion (Figure 23).

A 2010 Turkish Central Bank working paper, which surveyed 145 big manufacturing Turkish firms, concluded that the manufacturing sector predominantly

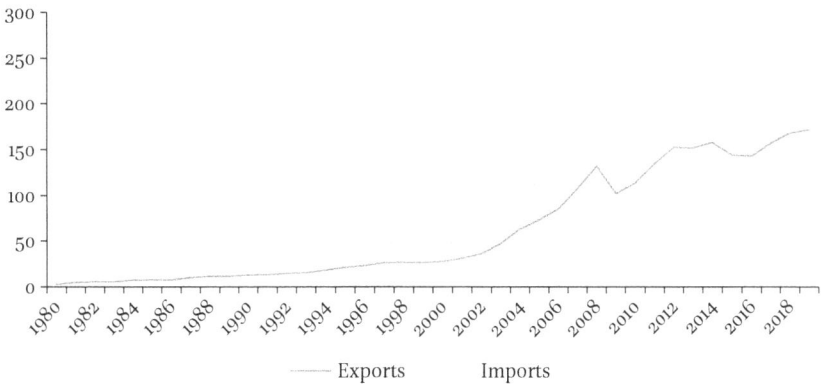

FIGURE 23 Turkish exports and imports (billion $), 1980–2019
SOURCE: *FOREIGN TRADE BY YEARS*, BY TÜİK (N.D.).

used foreign intermediate and investment goods as inputs in its production. The paper showed that the more Turkey went beyond its traditional labour-intensive manufacturing (such as textiles, leather, garments, and agriculture) and the more it specialised and transformed its manufacturing into sectors such as motor vehicles and electrical machines, the more the economy necessitated raw materials, equipment and engines, which are insufficiently produced domestically (Saygılı et al., 2010). For instance, although Turkey has a 50% market share in colour television production in the EU, this product has low value-added since the picture tube, chip set, and other electronic components must be imported (in Saygılı sh., 2010: 115). The binary characteristics of the Turkish economy suggest that while specialisation in the economy necessitates controlling outlets and markets for raw materials and intermediate goods in its production, it also creates a deficit problem due to the fact that these inputs cannot be provided from domestic supply.

The second striking problem which is linked to Turkey's trade deficit is the combination of the low level of high-technology exports and a decline in competiveness. With respect to competitiveness, Turkey dropped to 61th out of 141 countries in 2019 according to *The Global Competitiveness Report 2019* by the World Economic Forum (2019). An earlier report in 2014 had highlighted the worst indicator of Turkey with regard to the global competitiveness index: female participation in the labour force (World Economic Forum, 2014). According to official statistics, the women's labour force participation rate in Turkey was 29.9% as of January 2015 (TÜİK, 2015).

On the other hand, the ratio of high-technology exports to manufactured exports is still nominal while the rate of manufactured products in Turkish exports has been showing a rapid increase since the 1980s—nearly a threefold jump from 27% in 1980 to 80% in 2016. Apparently, according to World Bank, World Development Indicators, there has been a clear stagnation in the ratio of high-technology exports to manufactured exports in the last two decades, representing a ratio of 2% in 1989 and 2016 (The World Bank, 2020). Yet, other emerging countries have much higher ratios of high technology exports to total exports of manufactured goods. In this respect, South Korea and China seem to have rapidly ramped up their high-technology exports, which cover more than a quarter of their total exports, amounting to 26% in 2016. On the other hand, Malaysian high-technology exports constituted nearly a half of their total exports in 2016 at 43% (Figure 24).

In order to tackle these two structural problems, the AKP announced in 2012 a "Decree on Government Subsidies for Investments" so as to strengthen the international competitiveness of firms by encouraging high-tech, large-scale and strategic investment incentive schemes (Resmi Gazete [Official Gazette],

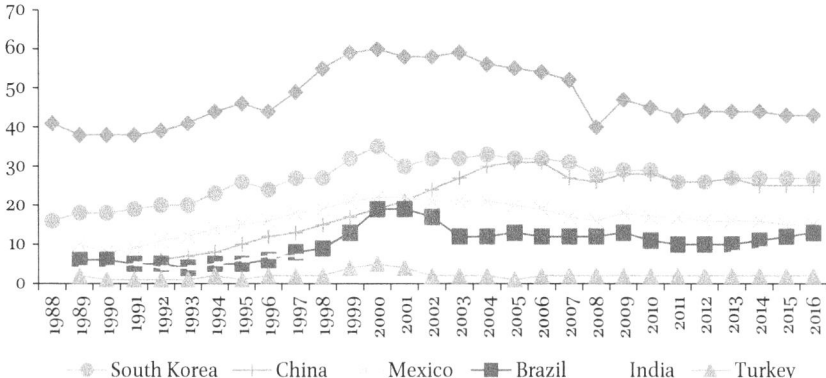

FIGURE 24 High-technology exports in some selected emerging countries and Turkey (% of manufactured exports)
SOURCE: THE WORLD BANK (2020).

June 19, 2012). Incentive tools, depending on the characteristics of the investment and schemes—general, regional, large-scale and strategic investment incentive schemes—include VAT exemption, customs duty exemption, tax reduction, social security premium support both for employer's and employee's shares, income tax deductions, interest support, land allocation, and VAT refunds (Resmi Gazete [Official Gazette], June 19, 2012, Article 4). This new investment system divides Turkey into six regions according to the socio-economic development index. Private investment for the least developed provinces, especially those of the Sixth Region, which mostly cover Kurdish region of Turkey's southeast, is encouraged. The decree also introduced "specific priority investments" in which investors are encouraged without the state stipulating which specific region they will invest in. The priority investment sectors include high value added sectors such as automotive, pharmaceuticals, space, and defence industries, as well as transportation, mining, tourism, and education. In order to reduce the dependency of Turkish industry on imports and increase international competitiveness, strategic investment and large-scale incentive schemes promote high tech and high value added products (Republic of Turkey Ministry of Economy, n.d.).

2   Is Erdoğan an Islamic Bonaparte?

The AKP's obvious authoritarian track since 2013, the concentration of power by President Erdoğan, and Islamisation from above have led some progressive and liberal scholars in Turkey to argue that Erdoğan himself is a Bonaparte of the 21st century. They put forward strong *prima facie* observations about the similarities between 19th century France under Bonaparte and Turkey under Erdoğan. Fethi Açıkel, for instance, suggested that the transition from a parliamentary system to a presidential one marks the rise of Bonapartism in Turkey, as the term refers to one-man rule with nostalgia for the past and disregard for the separation of power. According to Açıkel, Turkish Bonapartism under Erdoğan is strictly attached to Islam not only as a religion but as an ideology, as the AKP's foreign policy aims at being the leader of the Sunni world. Secondly, according to Açıkel, the AKP seeks to re-write Turkish history, erase Kemalist symbols, trivialise the Republic and attach more importance to Ottoman symbols and rituals (Yazıcıoğlu, 2015). Erkin Özalp, on the other hand, highlights the political conditions that gave rise to Bonapartist regimes. He states that in both France in Turkey, Bonapartism was not the result of the leaders' personal traits or charisma, but rather the objective conditions and wrong policies of republicans and Democrats (Duran, 2016). Cihan Tuğal (2016b) argues that Erdoğan's Turkish state has slid between right-wing Bonapartism and neo-fascism over the last few years. Liberal columnist Cengiz Çandar also attributes a similarity between Bonaparte's 18th Brumaire and Erdoğan's 17 December (2013), when the government initiated a war against the Gülenists by changing the structure of the High Council of Judges and Prosecutors and increasing the power of the National Intelligence Organisation. According to Çandar (2014), this was not a purge of Gülenists, but a "civilian coup" initiated by Erdoğan. Baran Serhad (2016) highlights that the botched coup of 2016 became a springboard for Erdoğan's Bonapatism. However, Erdoğan's Bonapartism is fragile due to the fact that he cannot rise above the classes and is supported only by the conservative bourgeoisie. Barış Yıldırım and Foti Benlisoy (2017), on the other hand, make a Marxist analysis, suggesting that Erdoğan's Bonapartism is the result of the parliamentary inability to prevent state fragmentation and the disunity of the bourgeoisie.

Moreover, Turkey is not unique in being labelled as Bonapartist, as French left and right-wing scholars also labelled French President Charles de Gaulle (1959–1969) as a Bonaparte due to his one-man rule. René Rémond drew an analogy between Gaullism and Bonapartism due to the former's features of "control of the media of mass communications; reassuring property owners and business accompanied by 'social concerns'; Saint-Simonian technocratic reformism; an assertive foreign and military policy and an authoritarian, monocratic political regime, supported by a centralized administrative elite, notably through the partisan activities of the prefects" (Hayward, 2004: 222). On this point, it is undeniable that de Gaulle came to power in a context that expected a resolution to the political crisis caused by the Algiers putsch of 13 May 1958 and initiated a plebiscite to ratify the new constitution that set up France's Fifth Republic. This is why Mitterrand easily equated 13 May 1958 with "de Gaulle's December 2, 1851": "between de Gaulle and the republicans there is first and always the *coup d'état*" (Hayward, 2004: 224). However, this analysis overlooked the fact that de Gaulle subordinated his personal rule to national sovereignty, as he resigned after the rejection of the French constitutional referendum in 1959; a very un-Napoleon move (Hayward, 2004: 227).

A similar line of reasoning relates to Erdoğan. He, himself, rests on the legitimacy of popular sovereignty even though the parliament lost its functioning power. As argued, he mobilises an illiberal populism in which republican elites are portrayed as people against the natonal will. However, even though the physiognomy of Erdoğan's Turkey and Bonaparte's France seem to resemble each other in terms of the dictatorial power granted to leaders, it should first be stressed that Bonapartist rule rests on the autonomisation of the *executive* power, specifically the military. In this sense, "executive" does not refer to the executive branch of a representative parliamentary government, as would be argued by liberal thinkers such as de Tocqueville or Montesquieu; rather, for Marx, it refers to "enormous bureaucratic and military organisation, with its vast and ingenious state machinery, with a host of officials numbering half a million, besides an army of another half million" (Marx, 1972: 104). Having said this, it is important to highlight that these writers tend to replace the characteristics of a militaristic regime with a civilian authoritarian regime. Erdoğan's dictatorial rule does not rest on the military but rather on national legitimacy and parliamentary majority, which arises from the ballot box. Even more, it is hard to argue that Erdoğan holds full control over the military, taking into account the botched coup in 2016.

3   Any Hope: Waiting for Godot?

The sectarian calculations in foreign policy and the authoritarian drift of Erdoğan suffered a setback in the 2015 parliamentary elections with the success achieved by the Peoples' Democratic Party (*Halkların Demokratik Partisi*, HDP). The HDP crossed the 10% electoral barrier and acquired more than six million votes. As an umbrella party of the Kurdish people, environmentalists, feminists, Alevis, and the LGBT community, the HDP has implemented an electoral strategy against the concentration of power in the hands of Erdoğan while it has embraced a radical democratic programme that transcends formal democratisation and calls for a substantial democratisation. It also challenges the commercialisation of education, health, and more broadly daily life. This challenge was crucial in two aspects. First, the victory of the HDP *initially* ended the thirteen-year single-party dominance of the AKP, thereby temporarily killing the presidential project of Erdoğan. Second, the rise of the HDP, along with the party programme, still carries the potential to reinvigorate left-wing politics in Turkey and challenge neoliberalism. However, the failure of the coalition talks between the AKP and the CHP, and then, between the AKP and the MHP, led Turkey to hold an early general election on 1 November 2015. The AKP won a landslide victory, receiving almost 50% of all votes against the backdrop of renewed war with the Kurds. Erdoğan employs Machiavellian politics—*accusata/scusata*—in which every vile political action is excused in the name of protecting the integrity of the nation and preserving security. Within this context, Erdoğan allied with the ultra-nationalist right—the Nationalist Movement Party (MHP)—to retain power. In the 2017 constitutional referendum, initiated under the state of emergency, Erdoğan was also backed by the MHP in changing the system from a parliamentary to a presidential one, but only won by a slim, contested margin. They have also allied for the 2019 presidential elections under the term the "People's Alliance" (*Cumhur İttifakı*). These abrupt shifts from a relatively liberal stance to a staunchly nationalist one demonstrate that Erdoğan has established a new illiberal social contract with nationalists, the remnants of the Ancien Régime and the military by destroying his own efforts at procedural democratisation (Eliçin, 2016). This shift was epitomised by the military incursion in Afrin, which blocked the formation of an autonomous Kurdistan in northern Syria; an incursion that was also supported by the "social democratic" Republican People's Party. However, it can be argued that this new social contract is fragile and disruptive due to the spiral of violence in Turkey since 2015, after the failure of the peace process. Thus, the immediate future of the AKP will be contingent upon its handling of the Kurdish issue, which has already been shown to be its Achilles' heel, and simultaneously upon the AKP's ability to remain united despite the contradictions that have been developing within the party such as the foundation of Future Party in December 2019 by former Prime Minister Ahmet Davutoğlu. Under these circumstances, any hope that Turkey will find itself back on the rails of procedural democratisation under AKP rule seems to be in vain, reminiscent of Samuel Beckett's *Waiting for Godot*, where Godot will never arrive. Therefore, it is reasonable to conclude that the history of the Republic of Turkey swings like a pendulum between military rule and civilian authoritarianism.

References

Acar, F. (2002) Turgut Özal: Pious Agent of Liberal Transformation. In: Heper M. and Sayarı S. (eds) *Political Leaders and Democracy in Turkey*. Maryland: Lexington Books, 163–180.

Achcar, G. (1997) The Arab World: Absence of democracy. *Le Monde diplomatique*. Available at: http://mondediplo.com/1997/06/arabdem.

Achcar, G. (1999) Is NATO's Onslaught a "Just War"?. *Monthly Review: An Independent Socialist Magazine* 51(2): 15–19.

Achcar, G. (2000) Rasputin Plays at Chess: How the West Blundered into a New Cold War. In: Ali T. (ed.) *Masters of the Universe? : Nato's Balkan Crusade*. London and New York: Verso, 57–98.

Achcar, G. (2004) *Eastern Cauldron: Islam, Afghanistan, Palestine and Iraq in a Marxist Mirror*. London: Pluto Press.

Achcar, G. (2011) *The Arabs and the Holocaust: The Arab-Israeli War of Narratives* (trans. by Goshgarian, G. M.). New York: Picador.

Achcar, G. (2013) *The People Want: A Radical Exploration of the Arab Uprising*. London: Saqi Books.

Achcar, G. (2016) *Morbid Symptoms: Relapse in the Arab Uprising*. London: Saqi Books.

Afetinan, A. (1982) *İzmir İktisat Kongresi: 17 Şubat–4 Mart 1923*. Ankara: Türk Tarih Kurumu Basımevi.

Ağaoğulları, M.A. (2003) Aşırı Milliyetçi Sağ. In: Schick, I.C. and Tonak E.A. (eds) *Geçiş Sürecinde Türkiye*. İstanbul: Belge Yayınları, 189–236.

Ahmad, F. (1977) *The Turkish Experiment in Democracy 1950–1975*. London: C. Hurst for the Royal Institute of International Affairs.

Ahmad, F. (1991) Politics and Islam in Modern Turkey. *Middle Eastern Studies* 27(1): 3–21.

Ahmad, F. (1993) *The Making of Modern Turkey*. London: Routledge.

Akça, İ. (2009) Kolektif Bir Sermayedar Olarak Türk Silahlı Kuvvetleri. In: İnsel, A. and Bayramoğlu, A. (eds) *Bir Zümre, Bir Parti, Türkiye'de Ordu*. İstanbul: Birikim Yayınları, 225–269.

Akça, İ. (2010a) Ordu, Devlet ve Sınıflar: 27 Mayıs 1960 Darbesi Örneği Üzerinden Alternatif Bir Okuma Denemesi. In: Paker E.B. and Akça İ. (eds) *Türkiye'de Ordu, Devlet ve Güvenlik Siyaseti*. İstanbul: İstanbul Bilgi Üniversitesi Yayınları, 351–406.

Akça, İ. (2010b) *Military-Economic Structure in Turkey: Present Situation, Problems, and Solutions*. İstanbul: TESEV.

Akçalı, E. and Perinçek, M. (2009) Kemalist Eurasianism: An Emerging Geopolitical Discourse in Turkey. *Geopolitics* 14(3): 550–569.

Akçam, T. (2012) *The Young Turks' Crime Against Humanity: The Armenian Genocide and Ethnic Cleansing in the Ottoman Empire*. Princeton and Oxford: Princeton University Press.

Akdeniz, Y. and Altıparmak, K. (2018) *Turkey: Freedom of Expression in Jeopardy*. Available at: https://www.englishpen.org/wp-content/uploads/2018/03/Turkey_Freedom_of_Expression_in_Jeopardy_ENG.pdf.

Akin, E. and Karasapan, Ö. (1988) The Rabita Affair. *Middle East Report* (153): 15.

Akkaya, Y. and Çetik, M. (1999) *Türkiye'de Endüstri İlişkileri*. İstanbul: Tarih Vakfı Yayınları.

AK Party (2010) *Anayasa Değişiklik Paketi ile İlgili Sorular ve Cevaplar*. Available at: http://www.akparti.org.tr/upload/documents/ak_parti_ref_kitab_180710.pdf.

AK Party (n.d.) *Conservative Democrat Political Identity*. Available at: http://www.akparti.org.tr/english/akparti/2023-political-vision#bolum_.

AK Party (n.d.) *Party Programme*. Available at: http://www.akparti.org.tr/english/akparti/parti-programme#bolum_.

Aktay, Y. and Özensel, E. (2005) İsmet Özel: Dostların Eşiğindeki Diaspora. In: Bora, T. and Gültekingil M. (eds) *Modern Türkiye'de Siyasi Düşünce: İslamcılık*. İstanbul: İletişim, 782–798.

Samim, A. (1981) The Tragedy of the Turkish Left. *New Left Review* 126(I): 60-85.

Samim A. (1987) The Left. In: Schick İ.C. & Tonak E. A. (eds) *Turkey in Transition*. New York: Oxford University Press.

Akyol, M. (2013) Behind the war over prep schools. *Hürriyet Daily News*, 16, November. Available at: http://www.hurriyetdailynews.com/behind-the-war-over-prep-schools.aspx?pageID=449&nID=57991&NewsCatID=411.

Aladağ, A. (2013) *Hegemonya Yeniden Kurulurken Sol Liberalizm ve Taraf*. İstanbul: Patika Kitap.

Al Arabiya News (14 September 2011) Egypt's Muslim Brotherhood criticizes Erdogan's call for a secular state. Available at: http://www.alarabiya.net/articles/2011/09/14/166814.html.

Al Arabiya News (23 August 2011) After Istanbul meeting, Syrian dissidents form "national council" to oust Assad. Available at: http://www.alarabiya.net/articles/2011/08/23/163729.html.

Al-Azm, S. (1993) Islamic Fundamentalism Reconsidered: A Critical Outline of Problems, Ideas, and Approaches, Part I. *Comparative Studies of South Asia, Africa And The Middle East* 13(1 and 2): 93–121.

Alkan, T. (1984) The National Salvation Party in Turkey. In: Heper, M. and Israeli, R. (eds) *Islam and Politics in the Modern Middle East*. London: Croom Helm, 79–102.

Al-Shistani, M.B. (2013) Turkey and Syria's Jihadis: More than Free Passage?. *The Turkey Analyst* 6(10), 22, May. Available at: http://www.turkeyanalyst.org/publications/turkey-analyst-articles/item/13-turkey-and-syria%E2%80%99s-jihadis-more-than-free-passage?.html.

Altan, M. (1993) Türkiye'nin bütün sorunu politik devletten liberal devlete geçememesidir. In: Özal, T., Menderes, A., Altan, M., Özdemir, H., Çandar, C., Akat, A.S., Erdoğan, R.T. *Yeni arayışlar, yeni yönelimler: 2. Cumhuriyet tartışmaları*. Ankara: Başak Yayınları.

Altunisik, M.B. (2014) Turkey as an "Emerging Donor" and the Arab Uprisings. *Mediterranean Politics* 19(3): 333–350.

Anayasa Mahkemesi Kararlar Dergisi (1972) No: 9. 2nd edition. Ankara: Ankara Üniversitesi Basımevi: Available at: www.anayasa.gov.tr/files/pdf/kararlar_dergisi/kd_09.pdf.

Ankara Chamber of Commerce (14 January 2011) *Ekonominin Gurbet Kuşları*. Available at: http://www.atonet.org.tr/yeni/index.php?p=1736&l=1.

Arat, Y. (1998) Feminists, Islamists, and Political Change in Turkey. *Political Psychology* 19(1): 117–131.

Arıcanlı, T. and Rodrik D. (1990) An Overview of Turkey's Experience with Economic Liberalization and Structural Adjustment. *World Development* 18(10): 1343–1350.

Arsu, S. and Tavernise S. (2009) Turkish media group is fined $2.5 billion. *The New York Times*, 9, September. Available at: http://www.nytimes.com.

ASKON (Anadolu Aslanları İşadamları Derneği) (2010) *Kurum Kültürü*. Available at: http://www.askon.org.tr/kurum-kulturu.

ASKON (Anadolu Aslanları İşadamları Derneği) (n.d.) *Tanıtım Kataloğu Türkçe-English*. Available at: http://www.askon.org.tr/dosyalar/askon_tr_eng.pdf.

ASKON (Anadolu Aslanları İşadamları Derneği) (n.d.) *Türkiye'nin en büyük ihracatçıları içerisinde 9 ASKON üyesi*. Available at: http://www.askon.org.tr/turkiyenin-en-buyuk-ihracatcilari-icerisinde-9-askon-uyesi.

Atlı, A. (2011) Businessmen as Diplomats: The Role of Business Associations in Turkey's Foreign Economic Policy. *Insight Turkey* 13(1): 109–128.

Atasoy, Y. (2005) *Turkey, Islamists and Democracy: Transition and Globalization in a Muslim State*. New York: I.B. Tauris.

Automotive Manufacturers Association (2014) Türkiye'nin 500 Büyük Sanayi Kuruluşu İçinde Otomotiv Sanayii. Available at: http://www.osd.org.tr/yeni/wp-content/uploads/2014/07/iso500-2013.pdf.

Avcı, H. (2010) *Haliç'te Yaşayan Simonlar: Dün Devlet Bugün Cemaat*, 17th edition. Ankara: Angora.

Avşar, G., Özdil, K. and Kırmızıdağ, N. (2014) *The Other Side of the Ergenekon: Extrajudicial Killings and Forced Disappearances*. TESEV Publications. Available at: http://www.tesev.org.tr/assets/publications/file/13022014105122.pdf.

Axiarlis, E. (2014) *Political Islam and the Secular State in Turkey: Democracy, Reform and the Justice and Development Party*. New York: I.B. Tauris and Co. Ltd.

Ayata, B. (2015) Turkish Foreign Policy in a Changing Arab World: Rise and Fall of a Regional Actor?. *Journal of European Integration* 37(1): 95–112.

Ayata, S. (1996) Patronage, Party, and State: The Politicization of Islam in Turkey. *Middle East Journal* 50(1): 40–56.

Aydın, Z. (2005) *The Political Economy of Turkey*. London: Pluto Press.
Aydinli, E. (2009) A Paradigmatic Shift for the Turkish Generals and an End to the Coup Era in Turkey. *Middle East Journal* 63(4): 581–596.
Aydinli, E. (2011) Ergenekon, New Pacts, and the Decline of the Turkish "Inner State". *Turkish Studies* 12(2): 227–239.
Aygül, C. (2014) Locating Change in Turkish Foreign Policy: Visa Policies of the Justice and Development Party in the 2000s. *Turkish Studies* 15(3): 402–418.
Ayman, S.G. (2014) Turkey and Iran: Between Friendly Competition and Fierce Rivalry. *Arab Studies Quarterly* 36(1): 6–26.
Baehr, P. and Richter M. (2004) (eds) *Dictatorship in History and Theory: Bonapartism, Caesarism, and Totalitarianism*. Washington & New York: German Historical Institute and Cambridge University Press.
Bahgat, G. (2014) Iran-Turkey Energy Cooperation: Strategic Implications. *Middle East Policy* 21(4): 121–132.
Balci, B. (2003) Fethullah Gülen's [sic] Missionary Schools in Central Asia and their Role in the Spreading of Turkism and Islam. *Religion, State and Society* 31(2): 151–177.
Balci, B. (2014) *The Gülen Movement and Turkish Soft Power*. Available at Carnegie Endowment for International Peace: http://carnegieendowment.org/2014/02/04/g%C3%BClen-movement-and-turkish-soft-power.
Bali, R.N. (2013) *Antisemitism and Conspiracy Theories in Turkey*. İstanbul: Libra.
Bardakçi, M. (2013) Coup Plots and the Transformation of Civil-Military Relations in Turkey under AKP rule. *Turkish Studies* 13(3): 411–428.
Barkey, H.J. (1990) *The State and the Industrialization Crisis in Turkey*. Boulder, Colo.: Westview Press.
Başkaya, F. (2008) *Paradigmanın İflası: Resmi İdeolojinin Eleştirisine Giriş*. Ankara: Özgür Üniversite Kitaplığı.
Başkaya, F. (2009) *Devletçilikten 24 Ocak Kararlarına: Türkiye Ekonomisinde İki Bunalım Dönemi*, 4th edition. Ankara: Özgür Üniversite.
Başkaya, F (2010) *Yediyüz: Osmanlı Beyliğinden 28 Şubat'a: Bir Devlet Geleneğinin Anatomisi*, 4th edition. Ankara: Özgür Üniversite.
Bayar, A.H. (1996) The Developmental State and economic policy in Turkey. *Third World Quarterly* 17(4): 773–785.
Bayat, A. (2007) *Islam and Democracy: What is the Real Question?*. Paper 8. Leiden, ISIM (The International Institute for the Study of Islam in the Modern World): Amsterdam University Press.
Bayram, M. and Tercanlı K. (2013) Cami ve Cemevinin temel atma töreni öncesi olay. *Hürriyet*, 9, September. Available at: http://www.hurriyet.com.tr/gundem.
Bayramoğlu, A. (2009) Asker ve Siyaset. In: İnsel, A. and Bayramoğlu, A. (eds) *Bir Zümre, Bir Parti, Türkiye'de Ordu*, 4th edition. İstanbul: Birikim Yayınları, 59–118.

Bekdil, B. (2013) The historic march of our holy nation..., *Hürriyet Daily News*, 16, August. Available at: http://www.hurriyetdailynews.com.

Bengio, O. (2010) *The Turkish-Israeli Relationship: Changing Ties of Middle Eastern Outsiders*. New York: Palgrave Macmillan.

Benli, M.H. (2016) Top Turkish commander's aide admits allegiance to Gülenists. *Hürriyet Daily News*, 20, July. Available at: http://www.hurriyetdailynews.com/top-turkish-commanders-aide-admits-allegiance-to-gulenists-.aspx?PageID=238&NID=101851&NewsCatID=341.

Beşikçi, İ. (2010) Türk Siyasal Hayatı: Resmi İdeoloji, Kemalizm ve Kürtler. In: Beşikçi, İ., Kutlay, N., Üstel, F., Özarslan, O., ... Çelik, E. *Resmi İdeoloji ve Kemalizm*. İstanbul: Akademi Yayın, 13–26.

Bianet (3 November 2014) At least 14,555 workers die on the job under AKP rule. Available at: http://www.bianet.org/english/labor/159654-at-least-14-555-workers-die-on-the-job-under-akp-rule.

Bianet (14 January 2020) Ninety-five Percent of Workers Killed in Occupational Homicides Precarious, Non-Union. Available at: http://bianet.org/english/print/218573-ninety-five-percent-of-workers-killed-in-occupational-homicides-precarious-non-union.

Bila, Fikret. (4 March 1997) Güreş: Uymazlarsa Bozulur. *Milliyet*. Retrieved from http://gazetearsivi.milliyet.com.tr.

Bila, F. (2007) Eski genelkurmay başkanı orgeneral Doğan Güreş: ABD-AB, Türkiye'nin bölünmesini istiyor. *Milliyet*, 4, November. Available at: http://www.milliyet.com.tr.

Birand, M.A. (1987) *The Generals' Coup in Turkey: An Inside Story of 12 September 1980*. London: Brassey's Defence Publishers.

Birand, M.A. (1985) *30 Hot Days*. London: K. Rustem and Brother.

Birgün (21 March 2018) Doğan Medya grubu Demirören's satıldı. Available at: https://www.birgun.net/haber-detay/dogan-medya-grubu-demiroren-e-satildi-208892.html.

Bishku, M.B. (2012) Turkish-Syrian Relations: A Checkered History. *Middle East Policy* 19(3): 36–53.

Boratav, K. (2006) *Türkiye'de Devletçilik*, 2nd edition. Ankara: İmge Kitabevi.

Boratav, K. (2011) *Türkiye İktisat Tarihi: 1908–2009*, 15th edition. Ankara: İmge Kitabevi.

Bourdieu, P. (1986) The Forms of Capital. In: Richardson, J. (ed.). *Handbook of Theory and Research for the Sociology of Education*. New York: Greenwood Press.

Brockett, G. D. (2009) Provincial Newspapers as a Historical Source: *Büyük Cihad* and the Great Struggle for the Muslim Turkish Nation (1951-53). *International Journal of Middle East Studies* 41(3): 437–455.

Browlee, J. (2016) Why Turkey's authoritarian descent shakes up democratic theory. *The Washington Post*, 23, March. Available at: https://www.washingtonpost.com/

news/monkey-cage/wp/2016/03/23/why-turkeys-authoritarian-descent-shakes-up-democratic-theory/.
Bulut, F. (1997) *Ordu ve Din*. Ankara: Doruk Yayımcılık.
Buğra, A. (1991) Political Sources of Uncertainty in Business Life. In: Heper, M. (ed.). *Strong state and economic interest groups: the post 1980 Turkish experience*. New York: Walter de Gruyter.
Buğra, A. (1994) *State and Business in Modern Turkey: A Comparative Study*. Albany: State University of New York Press.
Buğra, A. (1998) Class, Culture, and State: An Analysis of Interest Representation by Two Turkish Business Associations. *International Journal of Middle East Studies* 30(4): 521–539.
Buğra, A. and Savaşkan, O. (2014) *New Capitalism in Turkey: The relationship between Politics, Religion and Business*. Cheltenham: Edward Elgar Publishing.
Burns, E.B. (1967) Tradition and Variation in Brazilian Foreign Policy. *Journal of Inter-American Studies* 9(2): 195–212.
Cagaptay, S. (2004) Race, Assimilation and Kemalism: Turkish Nationalism and the Minorities in the 1930s. *Middle Eastern Studies* 40(3): 86–101.
Cagaptay, S. (2010) What's Really Behind Turkey's Coup Arrests?. *Foreign Policy*, 25, February. Available at: http://www.foreignpolicy.com/articles/2010/02/25/whats_really_behind_turkeys_coup_arrests.
Cammack, P. (1990) Statism, New Institutionalism and Marxism. *Socialist Register 26*: 147–170.
Canovan, M. (1999) Trust the People! Populism and the Two Faces of Democracy. *Political Studies* 47(1): 2–16.
Carnegie Endowment for International Peace (2016) *The Syrian National Council*. Available at: http://carnegieendowment.org/syriaincrisis/48334.
Carnegie Middle East Center (25 September 2013) The Syrian National Council. Available at: http://carnegie-mec.org/publications/?fa=48334.
Carver, T. (2004) Marx's Eighteenth Brumaire of Louis Bonaparte: Democracy, Dictatorship, and the Politics of Class Struggle. In: Baehr, P. and Richter M. (eds) *Dictatorship in History and Theory: Bonapartism, Caesarism, and Totalitarianism*. Washington and New York: German Historical Institute & Cambridge University Press, 103–128.
Cengiz, O.K. (2013) The Return of "Mujahid" in Turkey. *Al Monitor*, 19, June. Available at: http://www.al-monitor.com/pulse/originals/2013/06/erdogan-mujahid-turkey-religious-akp.html.
Chang, D. (2008) *Capitalist Development in Korea: labour, capital and the myth of the developmental state*. London: Routledge.
Chomsky, N. (1999) *Fateful Triangle: The United States, Israel & The Palestinians*. London: Pluto Press.

Chomsky, N. and Achcar, G. (2007) *Perilous Power The Middle East and US Foreign Policy*. UK: Hamish Hamilton.

Cizre, U. and Walker, Jo. (2010) Conceiving the New Turkey After Ergenekon. *The International Spectator* 45(1): 89–98.

Cizre, U. (2011) Disentangling the Threads of Civil-Military Relations in Turkey: Promises and Perils. *Mediterranean Quarterly* 22(2): 57–75.

Cizre, Ü. and Yeldan, E. (2005) The Turkish Encounter with Neo-Liberalism: Economics and Politics in the 2000/2001 Crises. *Review of International Political Economy* 12(3): 387–408.

Cizre-Sakallioglu, U. and Cınar, M. (2003) Turkey 2002: Kemalism, Islamism and Politics in the Light of the February 28 Process. *The Southern Atlantic Quarterly* 102 (2–3): 309–332.

Cokgezen, M. (2000) New fragmentations and new cooperations in the Turkish bourgeoisie. *Environment and Planning C: Government and Policy* 18(5): 525–544.

Constitutional Court of the Republic of Turkey (2020a) *Statistics*. Available at: http://www.anayasa.gov.tr/en/Statistics/.

Constitutional Court of the Republic of Turkey (2020b) *Kararlar Bilgi Bankası*. Available at: http://www.anayasa.gov.tr/Kararlar/KararlarBilgiBankasi/.

Council of the European Union (2001) Council Decision of 8 March 2001 on the principles, priorities, intermediate objective and conditions contained in the Accession Partnership with the Republic of Turkey. *Official Journal of the European Communities*. L/85/13. Available at: http://eur-lex.europa.eu/legal-content/EN/TXT/PDF/?uri=CELEX:32001D0235&from=EN.

Council of the European Union (23 January 2006) Council Decision of 23 January 2006 on the principles, priorities and conditions contained in the Accession Partnership with the Republic of Turkey. *Official Journal of the European Union*, L 22/34. Available at: http://eur-lex.europa.eu/legal-content/EN/TXT/PDF/?uri=CELEX:32006D0035&from=EN.

Council of the European Union (26 February 2008) Council Decision of 18 February 2008 on the principles, priorities and conditions contained in the Accession Partnership with the Republic of Turkey and repealing Decision 2006/35/EC. *Official Journal of the European Union*, L 51/4. Available at: http://eur-lex.europa.eu/legal-content/EN/TXT/PDF/?uri=CELEX:32008D0157&from=EN.

Cook, S. (2007) *Ruling but not governing: the military and political development in Egypt, Algeria, and Turkey*. Baltimore: The John Hopkins University Press.

Corke, S., Finkel, A., Kramer, D.J., Robbins C.A. and Schenkkan, N. (2014) Democracy in Crisis: Corruption, Media and Power in Turkey. *A Freedom House Special Report*. Available at: https://freedomhouse.org/sites/default/files/Turkey%20Report%20-%20Feb%203,%202014.pdf.

Couloumbis, T.A. (1983) *The United States, Greece, and Turkey: The troubled triangle.* New York: Praeger.

Court of Cassation (n.d.) Sami Selçuk'un 1999–2000 Adli Yıl Açılış Konuşması. Available at: http://www.yargitay.gov.tr/belgeler/site/acilisKonusma/1999-2000.pdf.

Credit Suisse (2014) *Global Wealth Databook 2014.* Available at: https://publications.credit-suisse.com/tasks/render/file/?fileID=5521F296-D460-2B88-081889DB12817E02.

Çakır, R. (1994) *Ne Şeriat Ne Demokrasi: Refah Partisini Anlamak*, 2nd edition. İstanbul: Metis Yayınları.

Çakır, R. (2005) Milli Görüş Hareketi. In: Bora, T. and Gültekingil, M. (eds) *Modern Türkiye'de Siyasi Düşünce: İslamcılık*, 2nd edition. İstanbul: İletişim, 544–575.

Çakır, R. (2012) *Ayet ve Slogan: Türkiye'de İslami Oluşumlar*, 10th edition. İstanbul: Metis Yayınları.

Çakır, R. and Sakallı, S. (2014) *100 Soruda Erdoğan X Gülen Savaşı.* İstanbul: İletişim.

Çakır, R. and San C. (1986) Orduya sızan dinci grup: Fethullahçılar. *Nokta* 51: 22–25.

Çalmuk, F. (2005) Erbakan. In Bora, T. and Gültekingil, M. (eds) *Modern Türkiye'de Siyasi Düşünce: İslamcılık*, 2nd edition. İstanbul: İletişim, 550–567.

Çandar, C. (2014) Napoléon'un 18 Brumaire'i, Erdoğan'ın 17 Aralık'ı. *Radikal*, 23, February. Available at: http://www.radikal.com.tr/yazarlar/cengiz-candar/napolonun-18-brumairei-erdoganin-17-araliki-1178080/.

Çarkoğlu, A., and Bilgili, N.Ç. (2011) A Precarious Relationship: The Alevi Minority, the Turkish State and the EU. *South European Society and Politics* 16(2): 351–364.

Çarkoğlu, A. and Toprak, B. (2007) *Religion, Society and Politics in a Changing Turkey.* İstanbul: TESEV.

Çetin, M. (2010) *The Gülen Movement: Civic Service Without Borders.* New York: Blue Dome Press.

Çiçek, N. (2013) Ahrar'uş Şam Hareketinin liderleri Timeturk'e konuştu. *Timeturk*, 22, February. Available at: http://www.timeturk.com/tr.

Çiçek, N. (2014) İslam Cephesi'nden Hamavi Nevzat Çiçek'e konuştu. *Timeturk*, 25, January. Available at: http://www.timeturk.com/tr.

Çongar, Y. (1997) Washington'dan, orduya uyarı. *Milliyet*, 14, June, p. 14. Available at: http://gazetearsivi.milliyet.com.tr.

Dahl, R. (2000) *On Democracy.* New Haven, Conn. and London: Yale University Press.

Daloglu, T. (2014) Turkey finally designates Jabhat al-Nusra a terrorist group. *Al-Monitor*, 6, June. Available at: http://www.al-monitor.com/pulse/originals/2014/06/turkey-al-nusra-terrorist-organization-syria-al-qaeda.html.

Daragahi, B. (2014) Turkish businesses embrace opportunities in north Africa in spite of Libya risk. *Financial Times*, 21, September. Available at: http://www.ft.com.

Davutoğlu, A. (2008) Turkish Foreign Policy Vision: An Assessment of 2007. *Insight Turkey* 10(1): 77–96.

Davutoğlu, A. (2009) Turkish Foreign Policy and the EU in 2010. *Turkish Policy Quarterly* 8(3): 11–17.

Davutoğlu, A. (2012) Principles of Turkish Foreign Policy and Regional Political Structuring. *Center for Strategic Research (SAM) Vision Papers* (3): 3–12.

Davutoğlu, A. (2013) Turkey's humanitarian diplomacy: objectives, challenges and prospects. *Nationalities Papers: The Journal of Nationalism and Ethnicity* 46(6): 865–870.

Davutoğlu, A. (2014a) Turkish-Armenian Relations in the Process of de-Ottomanization or "Dehistoricization": Is a "Just Memory" Possible?. *Turkish Policy Quarterly*: 21–30.

Davutoğlu, A. (2014b) Turkish PM in conversation, Part 2: Old Turkey, New Turkey. *openDemocracy*, 17, December. Available at: https://www.opendemocracy.net/ahmet-davutoglu-richard-falk/turkish-pm-in-conversation-part-2-old-turkey-new-turkey.

Davutoğlu, A. (2014c) *Stratejik Derinlik: Türkiye'nin Uluslararası Konumu*, 95th edition. İstanbul: Küre Yayınları.

DEİK (*Dış Ekonomik İlişkiler Kurulu*) (2011) DEİK Info. Available at: http://en.deik.org.tr/287/DeikHakkinda.html.

DEİK (*Dış Ekonomik İlişkiler Kurulu*) (2014) Despite Stronger US Dollar Turkish OFDI Continues to Grow. Available at: www.deik.org.tr/Contents/FileAction/5187.

Delibas, K. (2015) *The Rise of Political Islam in Turkey: Urban Poverty, Grassroots Activism and Islamic Fundamentalism*. London and New York: I.B. Tauris.

Deloitte (2012) *Turkey Outbound M&A*. Available at: http://www.deloitte.com/assets/dcom-turkey/local%20assets/documents/turkey_en_outbound%20m&a_250112.pdf.

Deloitte (2013) *Turkish Outbound M&A 2012–2013*. Available at: https://www2.deloitte.com/content/dam/Deloitte/tr/Documents/mergers-acqisitions/Turkish%20Outbound%20MA_2014%20%283%29.pdf.

Demir, F. (2009) Financial liberalization, private investment and portfolio choice: Financialization of real sectors in emerging markets. *Journal of Development Economics* 88(2): 314–324.

Demirel, A. (2011) *Birinci Meclis'te Muhalefet: İkinci Grup*, 6th edition. İstanbul: İletişim Yayınları.

Demirel, T. (2004) Soldiers and civilians: the dilemma of Turkish democracy. *Middle Eastern Studies* 40(1): 127–150.

Demirel, T. (2010) 2000'li Yıllarda Asker ve Siyaset: Kontrollü Değişim ile Statüko Arasında Türk Ordusu. *SETA Analiz* (18). Ankara: Siyaset, Ekonomi ve Toplum Araştırmaları Vakfı.

Demirtaş, B. (2013) Turkish-Syrian Relations: From Friend "Esad" to Enemy "Esed". *Middle East Policy* 20(1): 111–120.

Devlet İstihbarat Hizmetleri ve Milli İstihbarat Hizmetleri Kanunu (n.d.) Available at: https://www.mit.gov.tr/2937.pdf.

Diamond, L. (2015) Facing Up to the Democratic Recession. *Journal of Democracy* 26(1): 141–155.

Diyanet İşleri Başkanlığı (2020) *İstatistikler*. Available at: http://stratejigelistirme.diyanet.gov.tr/sayfa/57/istatistikler.

Dogan, M.G. (2010) When Neoliberalism Confronts the Moral Economy of Workers: The Final Spring of Turkish Labor Unions. *European Journal of Turkish Studies* [Online], 11.

Dogru, H.E. (2016) *The "Benevolent Hand" of the Turkish State: Mass Housing Administration, State Restructuring and Capital Accumulation in Turkey*. Unpublished doctoral thesis, York University: Canada.

Doğan, P. & Rodrik, D. (2010) *Balyoz: Bir Darbe Kurgusunun Belgeleri ve Gerçekler*, 3rd edition. İstanbul: Destek Yayınevi.

Draper, H. (1974) Marx on Democratic Forms of Government. *Socialist Register* 11: 101–124.

Draper, H. (1977) *Karl Marx's Theory of Revolution I: State and Bureaucracy. 1*. New York and London: Monthly Review Press.

Dreyfuss, R. (2005) *Devil's Game: How the United States Helped Unleash Fundamentalist Islam*. New York: Metropolitan Books.

Dufour, M. and Orhangazi, Ö. (2009) The 2000–2001 Financial Crisis in Turkey: A Crisis for Whom?. *Review of Political Economy* 21(1): 101–122.

Duggan, L. (2003) *The Twilight of Equality?: Neoliberalism, Cultural Politics, and the Attack on Democracy*. Boston: Beacon Press.

Duran, Z. (2016) Erkin Özalp'le "Fransız Üçlemesi" üzerine: Erdoğan ile Bonaparte arasındaki benzerlikler şaşırtıcı ... an Interview with Erkin Özalp. *İleriHaber*, 12, November. Available at: http://ilerihaber.org/icerik/erkin-ozalple-fransiz-uclemesi-uzerine-erdogan-ile-bonaparte-arasindaki-benzerlikler-sasirtici-62921.html.

Dzyubenko, O. (2014) U.S. vacates base in Central Asia as Russia's clout rises. *Reuters*, 3, June. Available at: http://www.reuters.com.

Edelman E.S., Cornell, S.E., Lobel, A. and Makovsky, M. (2013) *The Roots of Turkish Conduct: Understanding the Evolution of Turkish Policy in the Middle East*. Washington: Bipartisan Policy Center. Available at: http://bipartisanpolicy.org/wp-content/uploads/sites/default/files/The%20Roots%20of%20Turkish%20Conduct.pdf.

Eğilmez, M. (5 December 2013) Dış Borçlarımız. Available at: http://www.mahfiegilmez.com/2013/12/ds-borclarmz.html.

Eliçin, I. (16 November 2016) An Interview with Gilbert Achcar. Available at: https://www.youtube.com/watch?v=EesgQBdkt6.

Eligür, B. (2010) *The Mobilization of Political Islam in Turkey*. New York: Cambridge University Press.

REFERENCES 235

Emre, A. (2008) Boşluklu şehirler. *Yeni Şafak*, 7, August. Available at: http://www.yenisafak.com.tr.

E-MÜSİAD (*Müstakil Sanayici ve İş Adamları Derneği*) (2014) *Üye Firmalar*. Available at: http://www.e-musiad.com/Firma/KatalogSektor.aspx.

Engels, F. (1866) Engels to Marx 13 April. *Karl Marx Frederick Engels Collected Works*. Vol. 42, 266. London: Lawrence & Wishart.

Engels, F. (1991) The Origin of the Family, Private Property, and the State. In: *Marx and Engels Selected Works*. London: Lawrence and Wishart, 442–560.

ENKA, (ENKA *İnşaat ve Sanayi A.Ş.*) (2014) Projects. Available at: http://www.enka.com/Enka.aspx?MainID=67&ContentID=67.

Erbakan, N. (1971) *Türkiye ve Ortak Pazar*. İzmir: Furkan Yayınları.

Erbakan, N. (1975) *Milli Görüş*. İstanbul: Dergah Yayınları.

Erbakan, N. (1991a) *Türkiye'nin Temel Meseleleri*. Ankara: Rehber Yayıncılık.

Erbakan, N. (1991b) *Adil Ekonomik Düzen*. Ankara: Semih Ofset.

Erbakan, N. (2013a) Giriş. In: *Davam*. Ankara: MGV Yayınları.

Erbakan, N. (2013b) Medeniyet Davamız. In: *Davam*. Ankara: MGV Yayınları.

Erbakan, N. (2013c) Türkiye'nin Meseleleri ve Çözümleri. In: *Prof. Dr. Necmettin Erbakan Külliyatı*. Vol. 2. Ankara: MGV Yayınları, 369–389.

Erbakan, N. (2013d) Türkiye'nin Temel Meseleleri. In: *Prof. Dr. Necmettin Erbakan Külliyatı*. Vol. 3. Ankara: MGV Yayınları, 7–107.

Erbakan, N. (2013e) Milli Görüş ve Anayasa Değişikliği. In: *Prof. Dr. Necmettin Erbakan Külliyatı*. Vol: 3. Ankara: MGV Yayınları, 341–359.

Erbakan, N. (2013f) Milli Görüş ve 3. Beş Yıllık Plan. In: *Prof. Dr. Necmettin Erbakan Külliyatı*. Vol: 5. Ankara: MGV Yayınları, 39–74.

Ercan, F. (2002) The Contradictory Continuity of the Turkish Capital Accumulation Process: A Critical Perspective on the Internationalization of the Turkish Economy. In: Balkan, N. and Savran S. (eds) *The Ravages of Neo-liberalism: Economy, Society and Gender in Turkey*. New York: Nova Science Publishers, 21–37.

Ergan, U. (2015) Turkish army: find those behind Balyoz "plot". *Hürriyet Daily News*, 2, April. Available at: http://www.hurriyetdailynews.com.

Erkiner, E. (2000) *Alt Emperyalizm ve Türkiye*. İstanbul: Pencere Yayınları.

Esen, B. (2014) National-Building, Party-Strength, and Regime Consolidation: Kemalism in Comparative Perspective. *Turkish Studies* 15(4): 600–620.

Esen, B. and Gumuscu, S. (2017) Building a Competitive Authoritarian Regime: State-Business Relations in the AKP's Turkey. *Journal of Balkan and Near Eastern Studies* 20(4): 349–372.

European Commission (1998) *Regular Report from the Commission on Turkey's progress towards Accession*. Available at: http://ec.europa.eu/enlargement/archives/pdf/key_documents/1998/turkey_en.pdf.

European Commission (2000) *2000 Regular Report from the Commission on Turkey's Progress Towards Accession*. Available at: http://ec.europa.eu/enlargement/archives/pdf/key_documents/2000/tu_en.pdf.

European Commission (2001) *2001 Regular Report on Turkey's progress towards accession*. Available at: http://ec.europa.eu/enlargement/archives/pdf/key_documents/2001/tu_en.pdf.

European Commission (2002) *2002 Regular Report on Turkey's progress towards accession*. Available at: http://ec.europa.eu/enlargement/archives/pdf/key_documents/2002/tu_en.pdf.

European Commission, EC. (2003) *2003 Regular Report on Turkey's progress towards accession*. Available at: http://ec.europa.eu/enlargement/archives/pdf/key_documents/2003/rr_tk_final_en.pdf.

European Commission (2004) *2004 Regular Report on Turkey's progress towards accession*. Available at: http://ec.europa.eu/enlargement/archives/pdf/key_documents/2004/rr_tr_2004_en.pdf.

European Commission (2005) *Turkey 2005 Progress Report*. Available at: http://ec.europa.eu/enlargement/archives/pdf/key_documents/2005/package/sec_1426_final_progress_report_tr_en.pdf.

European Commission (2006) *Turkey 2006 Progress Report*. Available at: http://ec.europa.eu/enlargement/pdf/key_documents/2006/nov/tr_sec_1390_en.pdf.

European Commission (2007) *Turkey 2007 Progress Report*. Available at: http://ec.europa.eu/enlargement/pdf/key_documents/2007/nov/turkey_progress_reports_en.pdf.

European Commission (2009) *Turkey 2009 Progress Report*. Available at: http://ec.europa.eu/enlargement/pdf/key_documents/2009/tr_rapport_2009_en.pdf.

European Commission (2012) *Turkey 2012 Progress Report*. Available at: http://ec.europa.eu/enlargement/pdf/key_documents/2012/package/tr_rapport_2012_en.pdf.

European Commission (2014) *Turkey 2014 Progress Report*. Available at: http://ec.europa.eu/enlargement/pdf/key_documents/2014/20141008-turkey-progress-report_en.pdf.

European Council (21–22 June 1993) *European Council in Copenhagen 21–22 June 1993 Conclusions of the Presidency*. Available at: http://www.consilium.europa.eu/ueDocs/cms_Data/docs/pressData/en/ec/72921.pdf.

European Court of Human Rights (13 February 2003) Case of Refah Partisi (The Welfare Party) and Others v. Turkey. *Reports of Judgements and Decisions 2003-II*, Applications nos. 41340/98, 41342/98, 41343/98 and 41344/98. Available at: http://hudoc.echr.coe.int/sites/eng/pages/search.aspx?i=001-60936#{"itemid":["001-60936"]}.

Evans, R. (22 October 2014) Turkey's Shifting Strategic Culture: Part 3—From Republican to Neo-Ottoman. *Geopoliticus*. Available at: http://www.fpri.org/geopoliticus/2014/10/turkeys-shifting-strategic-culture-part-3-republican-neo-ottoman.

Evans, R. (29 October 2014) Turkey's Competing Strategic Cultures: Part 4—Now and Into the Future. *Geopoliticus*. Available at: http://www.fpri.org/geopoliticus/2014/10/turkeys-competing-strategic-cultures-part-4-now-and-future-0.

Evin, A. (1994) Demilitarization and Civilianization of the Regime. In: Heper, M. and Evin, A. (eds) *Politics in the Third Turkish Republic*. Oxford: Westview Press, 23–40.

Evren, K. (1983) Inaugural Speech. In: *Second Economic Congress of Turkey (2–7 Nov. 1981): Opening-Closing Sessions and Committee Reports*. Ankara: State Planning Organisation, 9–19.

Evren, K. (1991) *Kenan Evren'in Anıları. 3*. İstanbul: Milliyet Yayınları.

Eygi, M.Ş. (2012a) Müslümanlar ve demokrasi. *Milli Gazete*, 28, March. Available at: http://www.milligazete.com.tr.

Eygi, M.Ş. (2012b) Laiklik hakkında konvansiyonel yalanlar. *Milli Gazete*, 26, November. Available at: http://www.milligazete.com.tr.

Eygi, M.Ş. (2013) Bu gazete ve TV'lerle Türkiye selamete ve huzura kavuşmaz. *Milli Gazete*, 2, July. Available at: http://www.milligazete.com.tr.

Fırat, M. (2010) Relations with Greece. In: Oran, B. (ed.) *Turkish Foreign Policy, 1919–2006: Facts and analyses with documents*. Salt Lake City: University of Utah Press, 344–367.

Fielding-Smith, A. (2010) Turkey finds a gateway to Iraq. *Financial Times*, 14, April. Available at: http://www.ft.com.

Finefrock, M.M. (1981) Laissez-Faire, the 1923 Izmir Economic Congress and Early Turkish Developmental Policy in Political Perspective. *Middle Eastern Studies* 17(3): 375–392.

Förster, M. and Pearson, M. (2002) Income Distribution and Poverty in the OECD Area: Trends and Driving Forces. *OECD Economic Studies* (34): 7–39.

France 24 (27 March 2015) Turkey supports Saudi mission in Yemen, says Iran must withdraw. Available at: http://www.france24.com/en/20150326-turkey-support-saudi-yemen-erdogan-interview-france-24/.

Freedom House (2013) Freedom of the Press 2013. Available at: https://freedomhouse.org/sites/default/files/FOTP%202013%20Full%20Report.pdf.

Freedom House (2019) *Freedom in the World 2019*. Available at: https://freedomhouse.org/sites/default/files/Feb2019_FH_FITW_2019_Report_ForWeb-compressed.pdf.

Fukuyama, F. (1989) The End of History?. *The National Interest*. Available at: http://www.wesjones.com/eoh.htm.

Fukuyama, F. (1991) Liberal Democracy as a Global Phenomenon. *PS: Political Science and Politics* 24(4): 659–664.

Fukuyama, F. (1992) *The End of the History and the Last Man*. New York: The Free Press.

Fuller, G. (July 22, 2016). The Gulen Movement Is Not a Cult—It's One of the Most Encouraging Faces of Islam Today. *Huffington Post*. Retrieved from http://www.huffingtonpost.com/graham-e-fuller/gulen-movement-not-cult_b_11116858.html.

Ganser, D. (2005) *NATO's Secret Armies: Operation Gladio and Terrorism in Western Europe*. London and New York: Frank Cass.

Gantzel, K.J. (1973) Dependency Structures as the Dominant Pattern in World Society. *Journal of Peace Research* 10(3): 203–215.

Gellner, E. (1981) *Muslim Society.* Cambridge: Cambridge University Press.

Genel Kurmay Başkanlığı Birinci Ordu ve Sıkıyönetim Komutanlığı (1973) *Komünistler İşçilerimizi Nasıl Aldatıyorlar?*. Selimiye: İstanbul.

General Secretariat of the National Security Council (1982) *12 September in Turkey: Before and After*. Ankara: Ongun Kardeşler.

Gevgilili, A. (1981) *Yükseliş ve Düşüş*. İstanbul: Altın Kitaplar Yayınevi.

Geyikdağı, M. (1984) *Political Parties in Turkey: The Role of Islam*. New York: Praeger Publishers.

Ghannouchi, R. (2016) From Political Islam to Muslim Democracy: The Ennahda Party and the Future of Tunisia. *Foreign Affairs* (September/October Issue). Available at: https://www.foreignaffairs.com/articles/tunisia/political-islam-muslim-democracy.

Göçek, F. (2011) *The Transformation of Turkey: Redefining State and Society from the Ottoman Empire to the Modern Era*. London and New York: I.B. Tauris.

Göle, N. (1997) Secularism and Islamism in Turkey: The Making of Elites and Counter-Elites. *Middle East Journal* 51(1): 46–58.

Gramsci, A. (1971) *Selections from the Prison Notebooks* (ed. and trans. by Hoare, Q. and Smith, G.N.). New York: International Publishers.

Grugel, J. (2002) *Democratization: A Critical Introduction*. Hampshire and New York: Palgrave.

Grundy, K.W. (1976) Intermediary Power and Global Dependency: The Case of South Africa. *International Studies Quarterly* 20(4): 553–580.

Gumuscu, S. and Sert, D. (2009) The Power of the Devout Bourgeoisie: The Case of the Justice and Development Party. *Middle Eastern Studies* 45(6): 953–968.

Gunder Frank, A. (1979) Unequal Accumulation: Intermediate, Semi-Peripheral, and Sub-Imperialist Economies. *Review (Fernand Braudel Center)* 2(3): 281–350.

Gunter, M. (2008) *The Kurds Ascending: The Evolving Solution to the Kurdish Problem in Iraq and Turkey*. New York and Hampshire: Palgrave Macmillan.

Gunter, M. (2014) Turkey, Kemalism, and the "Deep State". In: Romano, D. and Gurses, M. (eds) *Conflict, Democratization, And the Kurds in the Middle East*. New York: Palgrave Macmillan, 17–39.

Gülalp, H. (2001) Globalization and Political Islam: The Social Bases of Turkey's Welfare Party. *Middle East Studies* 33: 433–488.

Gülalp, H. (2003) *Kimlikler Siyaseti: Türkiye'de Siyasal İslamın Temelleri*. İstanbul: Metis Yayınları.

Gülen, F. (2004) *Key Concepts in the Practice of Sufism: Emerald Hills of the Heart Vol 1* (rev. ed. and trans. by Ünal, A.). Rutherford, USA: The Light, Inc. and Işık Yayınları.

Gülen, F. (18 October 2005) "Bazı Yerlere Henüz Ulaşılamadı". Available at: http://fgulen.com/tr/turk-basininda-fethullah-gulen/fethullah-gulen-hakkinda-haberler/

fethullah-gulen-hakkinda-2005-haberleri/9214-Aktuel-Bazi-Yerlere-Henuz-Ulasilamadi.

Gülen, F. (2015) Fethullah Gulen: Turkey's Eroding Democracy. *The New York Times*, 3, February. Available at: http://www.nytimes.com/2015/02/04/opinion/fethullah-gulen-turkeys-eroding-democracy.html?ref=topics.

Gülen, F. (2015) Muslims Must Combat the Extremist Cancer. *The Wall Street Journal*, 27, August. Available at: http://www.wsj.com/articles/muslims-must-combat-the-extremist-cancer-1440718377.

Güney, M.K. (19 May 2015) Ekonomi Kimin İçin Büyüyor? Türkiye'de Servet Bölüşümü Adaletsizliği. *Research Institute on Turkey*. Available at http://riturkey.org/2015/05/ekonomi-kimin-icin-buyuyor-turkiyede-servet-bolusumu-adaletsizligi-k-murat-guney/.

Günlük-Şenesen, G. (1993) An overview of the arms industry modernization programme in Turkey. In: *SIPRI Yearbook 1993: World Armaments and Disarmament*. Oxford: Oxford University Press, 521–532.

Günlük-Şenesen, G. (2002) Turkey's Globalization in Arms: The Economic Impact. In: Balkan, N. and Savran, S. (eds) *The Ravages of Neo-liberalism: Economy, Society and Gender in Turkey*. New York: Nova Science Publishers, 105–116.

Güngen, A.R. and Erten, Ş. (2005) Approaches to Serif Mardin and Metin Heper on State and Civil Society in Turkey. *Journal of Historical Studies* 3: 1–14.

Gürgen, D. (2011) Occupational accidents kill 10,000 in ten years. *Hürriyet Daily News*, 22, December. Available at: http://www.hurriyetdailynews.com.

Gürsoy, Y. (2012) The changing role of the military in Turkish politics: democratization through coup plots?. *Democratization* 19(4): 735–760.

Hale, S. (1997) The Women of Sudan's National Islamic Front. In: Beinin, J. and Stork, J. (eds) *Political Islam: Essays from Middle East Report*. California: University of California Press.

Hale, W. (1994) *Turkish Politics and the Military*. London and New York: Routledge.

Hale, W. (2011) The Turkish Republic and its Army, 1923–1960. *Turkish Studies* 12(2): 191–201.

Hale, W. (2013) *Turkish Foreign Policy since 1774*, 3rd edition. Oxon: Routledge.

Hale, W. and Özbudun, E. (2010) *Islamism, Democracy and Liberalism in Turkey: The Case of the AKP*. London and New York: Routledge.

Hamsici, M. (2014) 10 Soruda: 17–25 Aralık operasyonları. *BBC Türkçe*, 16, December. Available at: http://www.bbc.com/turkce/haberler/2014/12/141212_17_25_aralik_operasyonu_neler_oldu_10_soruda.

Harris, G.S. (1965) The Role of the Military in Turkish Politics. *Middle East Journal* 19(2): 169–176.

Harris, G.S. (1970) The Causes of the 1960 Revolution in Turkey. *Middle East Journal* 24(4): 438–454.

Harvey, D. (2005) *A Brief History of Neoliberalism*. New York: Oxford University Press.

Hasgüler, M. (2002) The Cyprus Issue from the Cold War to the Present. In: Balkan, N. and Savran, S. (eds) *The Politics of Permanent Crisis: Class, Ideology and State in Turkey*. New York: Nova Science Publishers, 231–247.

Hassan, H. (2015) Syria's revitalized rebels make big gains in Assad's heartland. *Foreign Policy*, 28, April. Available at: http://foreignpolicy.com.

Hayward, J. (2004) Bonapartism and Gaullist Heroic Leadership: Comparing Crisis Appeals to an Impersonated People. In: Baehr, P. and Richter, M. (eds) *Dictatorship in History and Theory: Bonapartism, Caesarism, and Totalitarianism*. Washington and New York: German Historical Institute and Cambridge University Press.

Hazareesingh, S. (2004) Bonapartism as the Progenitor of Democracy: The Paradoxical Case of the French Second Empire. In: Baehr, P. and Richter, M. (eds) *Dictatorship in History and Theory: Bonapartism, Caesarism, and Totalitarianism*. Washington and New York: German Historical Institute and Cambridge University Press, 129–152.

Held, D. (2006) *Models of Democracy*, 3rd edition. Cambridge: Polity Press.

Hendrick, J.D. (2009) Globalization, Islamic activism, and passive revolution in Turkey: the case of Fethullah Gülen. *Journal of Power* 2(3): 343–368.

Hendrick, J.D. (2013) *Gülen: The Ambiguous Politics of Market Islam in Turkey and the World*. New York and London: New York University Press.

Hen-Tov, E. (2004) The Political Economy of Turkish Military Modernization. *Middle East Review of International Affairs* 8(4).

Heper, M. (1976) The Recalcitrance of the Turkish Public Bureaucracy to "Bourgeois Politics": A Multi-Factor Political Stratification Analysis. *Middle East Journal* 30(4): 485–500.

Heper, M. (1981) Islam, Polity and Society: A Middle Eastern Perspective. *Middle East Journal* 35(3): 345–363.

Heper, M. (1985) *The State Tradition in Turkey*. Walkington: The Eothen Press.

Heper, M. (ed.) (1991) *Strong state and economic interest groups: the post 1980 Turkish experience*. New York: Walter de Gruyter.

Heper, M. and Ahmet E. (eds) (1988) *State, Democracy and the Military, Turkey in the 1980s*. Berlin and New York: Walter de Gruyter.

Hintz, L. (2 August 2016a) The dark side of the popular mobilization that stopped Turkey's coup (Project on Middle East Political Science Briefing No: 30. Available at: http://pomeps.org/2016/08/03/briefing-30-turkeys-coup-attempt/.

Hintz, L. (2 August 2016b) The heinous consequences of Turkey's polarization. (Project on Middle East Political Science Briefing No: 30. Available at: http://pomeps.org/2016/08/03/briefing-30-turkeys-coup-attempt/.

Hitchens, C. (1997) *Hostage to History: Cyprus from the Ottomans to Kissinger*. London and New 3York: Verso.

Huber, E. and Stephens, D.J. (1999) The Bourgeoisie and Democracy: Historical and Contemporary Perspetives. *Social Research* 66(3): 759–788.

Human Rights Foundation of Turkey (2016) *Fact Sheet on Declared Curfews Between August 16, 2015 and April 20, 2016 and Civilians who Lost Their Lives.* Available at: http://en.tihv.org.tr/fact-sheet-on-declared-curfews-between-august-16-2015-and-april-20-2016-and-civilians-who-lost-their-lives/.

Human Rights Watch (1999) *Violations of Free Expression in Turkey.* Available at: http://www.hrw.org/legacy/reports/1999/turkey/.

Human Rights Watch (2007) *Human Rights Concerns in the Lead up to July Parliamentary Elections.* Available at: http://www.hrw.org/legacy/backgrounder/eca/turkey0707/turkey0707web.pdf.

Human Rights Watch (29 April 2014) Turkey: spy agency law opens door to abuse. Available at: http://www.hrw.org/news/2014/04/29/turkey-spy-agency-law-opens-door-abuse.

Human Rights Watch (11 December 2014) Security bill undermines rights. Available at: http://www.hrw.org/news/2014/12/11/turkey-security-bill-undermines-rights.

Huntington, S. (1991) *The Third Wave: Democratization in the Late Twentieth Century.* Noman and London: University of Oklahoma Press.

Huntington, S. (1993) The Clash of Civilizations?. *Foreign Affairs* 72(3): 22–49.

Huntington, S. (1996) *The Clash of Civilizations and the Remaking of World Order.* New York: Simon and Schuster.

Hür, A. (2013) İttihatçı ve kemalistlerin alevi-bektaşi politikaları. *Radikal*, 30, June. Available at: http://www.radikal.com.tr.

Hürriyet (3 November 2002) İş dünyası: ampul yandı: icraatı görelim. Available at: http://arama.hurriyet.com.tr/arsivnews.aspx?id=107455.

Hürriyet (14 July 2003) TSK 35. madde değiştirildi. Available at: http://www.hurriyet.com.tr/gundem/23718265.asp.

Hürriyet (29 April 2007) Genelkurmay'dan çok sert açıklama. Available at: http://www.hurriyet.com.tr/gundem/6420961.asp?gid=180.

Hürriyet (26 July 2008) Ergenekon'un 1 numarası ve liderler kadrosu. Available at: http://arama.hurriyet.com.tr/arsivnews.aspx?id=9520170.

Hürriyet (13 April 2009) Ergenekon'da 12'nci dalga. Available at: http://www.hurriyet.com.tr/gundem/11419713.asp.

Hürriyet (5 July 2012) Özel yetkili mahkemeler kaldırıldı. Available at: http://www.hurriyet.com.tr/gundem/20919163.asp.

Hürriyet (26 June 2013) Başbakan'dan eylemcilerin sığındığı otele şok suçlama. Available at: http://www.hurriyet.com.tr/gundem/23580769.asp.

Hürriyet (2 January 2017) TSK personel sayısını açıkladı. Available at: http://www.hurriyet.com.tr/gundem/tsk-personel-sayisini-acikladi-40324227.

Hürriyet Daily News (23 May 1999). Human rights diary. Available at: http://www.hurriyetdailynews.com/human-rights-diary.aspx?pageID=438&n=human-rights-diary-1999-05-23.

Hürriyet Daily News (29 August 2000) Istanbul DGM lifts Gulen arrest warrant. Available at: http://www.hurriyetdailynews.com/default.aspx?pageid=438&n=istanbul-dgm-lifts-gulen-arrest-warrant-2000-08-29.

Hürriyet Daily News (3 August 2002) Kilinc: EU will never accept Turkey. Available at: http://www.hurriyetdailynews.com/default.aspx?pageid=438&n=kilinc--eu-will-never-accept-turkey-2002-03-08.

Hürriyet Daily News (21 December 2002) Sezer vetoes changes to pave for Erdogan's premiership. Available at: http://www.hurriyetdailynews.com/default.aspx?pageid=438&n=sezer-vetoes-changes-to-pave-for-erdogans-premiership-2002-12-21.

Hürriyet Daily News (21 May 2006) Government cautious those with responsibility. Available at: http://www.hurriyetdailynews.com/government-cautions-those-with-responsibility.aspx?pageID=438&n=government-cautions-those-with-responsibility-2006-05-21.

Hürriyet Daily News (6 February 2008) Baykal makes harsh criticism of headscarf move. Available at: http://www.hurriyetdailynews.com/default.aspx?pageid=438&n=baykal-makes-harsh-criticism-of-headscarf-move-2008-02-06.

Hürriyet Daily News (9 February 2012) Ankara in shock over probe on intel chiefs. Available at: http://www.hurriyetdailynews.com/ankara-in-shock-over-probe-on-intel-chiefs.aspx?pageID=238&nID=13359&NewsCatID=338.

Hürriyet Daily News (21 September 2012) Court hits ex-top soldiers hard. Available at: http://www.hurriyetdailynews.com/court-hits-ex-top-soldiers-hard.aspx?pageID=238&nID=30704&NewsCatID=338.

Hürriyet Daily News (11 October 2012) Şemdinli incident not "organized". Available at: http://www.hurriyetdailynews.com/semdinli-incident-not-organized.aspx?pageID=238&nID=32164&NewsCatID=338.

Hürriyet Daily News (12 October 2012) Turkish ID more important than Nobel, Karman says. Available at: http://www.hurriyetdailynews.com/turkish-id-more-impotant-than-nobel-karman-says.aspx?pageID=238&nid=32246.

Hürriyet Daily News (25 July 2013) Tax probe at Koç-owned firms drives shares down. Available at: http://www.hurriyetdailynews.com/tax-probe-at-koc-owned-firms-drives-shares-down-.aspx?PageID=238&NID=51378&NewsCatID=345.

Hürriyet Daily News (5 August 2013) 19 sentenced to life in Turkey's Ergenekon coup trial, including ex-military chief. Available at: http://www.hurriyetdailynews.com/court-announces-verdicts-in-turkeys-ergenekon-coup-plot-trial-ex-army-chief-sentenced-to-life.aspx?pageID=238&nID=52034&NewsCatID=339.

Hürriyet Daily News (3 November 2014) Turkish company acquires British biscuit giant, becoming global number 3. Available at: http://www.hurriyetdailynews.com/turkish-company-acquires-british-biscuit-giant-becoming-global-number-3.aspx?pageID=238&nID=73836&NewsCatID=345.

Hürriyet Daily News (16 July 2016) Coup attempt shakes up Turkish judiciary with big shift, detention reported. Available at: http://www.hurriyetdailynews.com/half-of-new-turkish-judges-and-prosecutors-are-inexperienced-court-of-cassations-head-128287.

Hürriyet Daily News (17 November 2016) Turkey appoints trustees to four municipalities. Available at: www.hurriyetdailynews.com/police-detain-van-major-in-turkeys-southeast-appoints-administrators.aspx?pageID=238&nID=106224&NewsCatID=341.

Hürriyet Daily News (23 July 2017) Number of Turkish generals decreases 40 percent with post-coup attempt dismissals. Available at: http://www.hurriyetdailynews.com/number-of-turkish-generals-decreases-40-percent-with-post-coup-attempt-dismissals--115852.

Hürriyet Daily News (31 January 2018) 107,174 state workers dismissed since failed 2016 coup: Turkish Deputy PM Bozdağ. Available at: http://www.hurriyetdailynews.com/107-174-state-workers-dismissed-since-failed-2016-coup-turkish-deputy-pm-bozdag-126595.

Hürriyet Daily News (5 March 2018) Half of new Turkish judges and prosecutors are inexperienced: Court of Cassations head. Available at: http://bianet.org/english/politics/180625-minister-of-justice-bozdag-36-000-people-arrested-in-feto-investigation?bia_source=rss.

Hürriyet Daily News (19 July 2019) Capacity of prisons yo exceed 300,00. Available at: https://www.hurriyetdailynews.com/capacity-of-prisons-to-exceed-300-000-145097.

IBRD (International Bank for Reconstruction and Development) (1951) *The Economy of Turkey: An Analysis and Recommendations for A Development Program*. Report of a Mission sponsored by the International Bank for Reconstruction and Development in collaboration with the Government of Turkey. Baltimore: The John Hopkins Press.

Ilgıt, A. and Rochelle, D. (2013) Many Roles of Turkey in the Syrian Crisis. Middle East Research and International Project (MERİP). Available at: http://www.merip.org/mero/mero012813.

IMF, The International Monetary Fund (15 May 2001) IMF Approves Augmentation of Turkey's Stand-by Credit to US$19 Billion. Press Release, No: 01/23. Available at: https://www.imf.org/external/np/sec/pr/2001/pr0123.htm.

International Crisis Group (7 April 2010) *Turkey and the Middle East: Ambitions and Constraints*, Europe Report No: 203. Available at: http://www.crisisgroup.org/~/media/files/europe/turkey-cyprus/turkey/203%20turkey%20and%20the%20middle%20east%20-%20ambitions%20and%20constraints.ashx.

International Telecommunication Union (2020) *Statistics*. Available at: https://www.itu.int/en/ITU-D/Statistics/Pages/stat/default.aspx.

Investment Support and Promotion Agency (2010) *Labor Force and Employment in Turkey*. Available at: https://www.joi.or.jp/modules/investment/custom/documents/TUR_1007_R-Labor_Force_in_Turkey-EU.pdf.

Islamische Gemeinschaft Milli Görüş (n.d.) *What does "Milli Görüş" mean?*. Available at: http://www.igmg.org/gemeinschaft/islamic-community-milli-goerues/what-does-milli-goerues-mean.html.

Islamische Gemeinschaft Milli Görüş (n.d.) *Wer sind wir?, Biz kimiz?, Who are we?*. Available at: http://www.igmg.org/fileadmin/pdf/teskilat/IGMG_tanitim_burosu-ru_3_Sprache.pdf.

İlyasoğlu, A. (1996) *İslâmcı Kadın Hareketinin Bugünü Üzerine*. Birikim 91: 60–65.

İnan, E. (1997) Ekonomide mektup restleşmesi. *Sabah*, 7, March. Available at: http://arsiv.sabah.com.tr.

İnce, Ö. (2011) Bu nasıl darbeci ordu?. *Hürriyet*, 9, March. Available at: http://www.hurriyet.com.tr.

İnsel, A. (2003) "The AKP and Normalizing Democraracy in Turkey". *South Atlantic Quarterly* 102(2–3): 293–308.

İslamoğlu, M. (1974) *Erbakan Ecevit'e Karşı*, 2nd edition. İstanbul: Tüba Yayınları.

ISO (İstanbul Sanayi Odası) (2017) *Turkey's Top 500 Industrial Enterprises-2012*. Available at: http://www.iso500.org.tr/500-buyuk-sanayi-kurulusu/2018/.

Jacob, C. (2011) Nobel Peace Prize Laureate Tawakkul Karman—A Profile. *The Middle East Media Research Institute* (MEMRI). Available at: http://www.memri.org.

Jacoby, T. (2014) The Ergenekon Inquiry in Turkey: Democratisation or Witch-Hunt. *Orient* 56(1): 14–19.

Jenkins, G. (2001) *Context and Circumstance: The Turkish Military and Politics*. New York: Oxford University Press.

Jenkins, G. (2009) *Between Fact and Fantasy: Turkey's Ergenekon Investigation*. Silk Road Paper, Central Asia-Caucasus Institute and the Silk Road Studies Program. Available at: http://www.silkroadstudies.org/new/docs/silkroadpapers/0908Ergenekon.pdf.

Jessop, B. (2008) *State Power: A Strategic-Relational Approach*. Cambridge: Polity Press.

Kaldor, M. and Vejvoda, I. (1997) Democratization in Central and East European Countries. *International Affairs* 73(1): 59–82.

Kamu İhale Kurumu (2014) *Kamu Alımları İzleme Raporu 2013: Dönem 01.01.2013–31.12.2013*. Available at: http://www1.ihale.gov.tr/Duyurular2012/2013_y%C4%B1lsonu_kamu_alimlari_istatistik_raporu.pdf.

Kandiyoti, D. (2014) No laughing matter: Women and the new populism in Turkey. *OpenDemocracy*, 1, September. Available at: https://www.opendemocracy.net/5050/deniz-kandiyoti/no-laughing-matter-women-and-new-populism-in-turkey.

Kandiyoti, D. (2016) The mutation of the Turkish state: the long view. *The Middle East at SOAS*, 12(5): 38–39.

Karabelias, G. (1999) The Evolution of Civil-Military Relations in Post-War Turkey, 1980–95. *Middle Eastern Studies* 35(4): 130–151.

Karabelias, G. (2009) The Military Institution, Atatürk's Principles, and Turkey's Sisyphean Quest for Democracy. *Middle East Studies* 45(1): 57–69.

Karagül, İ. (2015) Terör dalgası, o belgeler ve Gezi-Paralel ittifakı. *Yenişafak*, 3, April. Available at: http://www.yenisafak.com.

Karakaya-Stump, A. (2014) Alevizing Gezi. *Jadaliyya*, 26, March. Available at: http://www.jadaliyya.com/pages/index/17087/alevizing-gezi.

Karataş, N. (2010) Turkish contractors to rebuild Sadr City in Baghdad. *Hürriyet Daily News*, 12, October. Available at: http://www.hurriyetdailynews.com.

Karaveli, H.M. (2009) The Power of the Gülen Movement Causes Concern After the New Arrests in the Ergenekon Investigation. *The Turkey Analyst* 2(8). Available at: http://www.turkeyanalyst.org/.

Kardaş, Ü. (2009) Askeri Gücün Anayasal Bir Yargı Alanı Yaratması Yürütme Erkini Etkin Bir Şekilde Kullanması. In: İnsel, A. and Bayramoğlu, A. (eds) *Bir Zümre, Bir Parti, Türkiye'de Ordu*, 4th edition. İstanbul: Birikim Yayınları, 295–310.

Karpat, K.H. (1970) The Military and Politics in Turkey, 1960–64: A Socio-Cultural Analysis of a Revolution. *The American Historical Review* 75(6): 1654–1683.

Kaya, Y. (2011) "Turkey's Turn to the East" and the Intra-Class Contradictions in Turkey. *Global Discourse: An Interdisciplinary Journal of Current Affairs and Applied Contemporary Thought* 2(2): 81–95.

Kayalı, K. (2012) *Ordu ve Siyaset: 27 Mayıs–12 Mart*, 5th edition. İstanbul: İletişim Yayınları.

Kayaoglu, A. (2014) Socioeconomic impact of conflict: state of emergency ruling in Turkey. *Defence and Peace Economics*: 1–20.

Kazan, Ş. (2003) *Refah Gerçeği. 2*. Ankara: Keşif Yayınları.

Kazan, Ş. (2003) *Refah Gerçeği. 3*. Ankara: Keşif Yayınları.

Kazgan, G. (2008) *Türkiye Ekonomisinde Krizler (1929–2001): "Ekonomi Politik" Açışından Bir İrdeleme*, 2nd edition. İstanbul: İstanbul Bilgi Üniversitesi Yayınları.

Kendal, N. (1993) Kurdistan in Turkey. In: Chaliand, G. (ed.) *A people without a country: the Kurds and Kurdistan*. London: Zed Books, 38–94.

Kepenek, Y. and Yentürk, N. (2003) *Türkiye Ekonomisi* 13th edition. İstanbul: Remzi Kitapevi.

Keyder, Ç. (1979) The Political Economy of Turkish Democracy. *New Left Review* I(115): 3–44.

Keyder, Ç. (1987a) *State and Class in Turkey: A Study in Capitalist Development*. London: Verso.

Keyder, Ç. (1987b) The Political Economy of Turkish Democracy. In: Schick, I. and Tonak, E. (eds) *Turkey in Transition: New Perspectives*. New York: Oxford University Press.

Kıvanç, Ü. (2015) *Pan-İslâmcının Macera Kılavuzu: Davutoğlu Ne Diyor, Bir Şey Diyor Mu?* İstanbul: Birikim Yayınları.

Kirişci, K. (2009) The transformation of Turkish foreign policy: The rise of the trading state. *New Perspectives on Turkey* 40: 29–57.

Kirişçi, K. (2013) The EU, Turkey, and the Arab Spring: Challenges and Opportunities for Regional Integration. In: Düzgit, S.A., Duncker, A., Huber, D., Keyman, E. and Tocci, N. (eds) *Global Turkey in Europe: Political, Economic, and Foreign Policy Dimensions of Turkey's Evolving Relationship with the EU*. Roma: Edizioni Nuova Cultura, 195–220.

Köni, H. (2012) Saudi Influence on Islamic Institutions in Turkey Beginning in the 1970s. *Middle East Journal* 66(1): 97–110.

Kösebalaban, H. (2002). Turkey's EU Membership: A Clash of Security Cultures. *Middle East Policy* 9(2): 130–146.

Krygier, M. (1985) Marxism and bureaucracy: A paradox resolved. *Politics* 20(2): 58–69.

Kurkcu, E. (1996) The Crisis of the Turkish State. *Middle East Report, Turkey: Insolvent Ideologies, Fractured State* (199): 2–7.

Kurtaran, G. (2010) Mediterranean quartet taking step toward union, says Syrian minister. *Hürriyet Daily News*, 12, March. Available at: http://www.hurriyetdailynews.com.

Kutlay, M. (2011) Economy as the "Practical Hand" of "New Turkish Foreign Policy": A Political Economy Explanation. *Insight Turkey* 13(1): 67–88.

Küçük, M. (2009) Çarpıcı açıklamalar. *Hürriyet*, 22, January. Available at: http://www.hurriyet.com.tr.

Küçük, M. (2013) Ben zenci Türk'üm. *Hürriyet*, 24, February. Available at: http://www.hurriyet.com.tr.

Kütahyalı, R.O. (2013) Aleviler kışkırtılıyor. *Sabah*, 16, July. Available at: http://www.sabah.com.tr.

Lacey, M. (2003) Turks reject U.S. criticism of opposition to Iraq war. *The New York Times*, 7, May. Available at: http://www.nytimes.com.

Laclau, E. (2005) Populism: What's in a Name?. In: Panizza F. (ed.) *Populism and the Mirror of Democracy*. London and New York: Verso, 32–49.

Laçiner, Ö. (2007) Şimdi Alternatif Zamanı. *Birikim*, 220–221: 43–49.

Lake, A. (1993/94) From Containment to Enlargement. *The DISAM Journal of International Security Assistance Management* 16(2): 68–78.

Law 3713 on Fight Against Terrorism (1991) Available at: http://www.mevzuat.gov.tr/MevzuatMetin/1.5.3713.pdf (in Turkish).

Lawson, F.H. (2014). Syria's mutating ciwil war and its impact on Turkey, Iraq and Iran. *International Affairs* 90(6): 1351–1365.

Le Monde (19 May 2016a) Rached Ghannouchi: "Il n'y a plus de justification à l'islam politique en Tunisie". Available at: http://www.lemonde.fr/international/article/2016/05/19/rached-ghannouchi-il-n-y-a-plus-de-justification-a-l-islam-politique-en-tunisie_4921904_3210.html.

Lerner, D. and Robinson, R.D. (1960) Swords and Ploughshares: The Turkish Army as a Modernizing Force. *Word Politics* 13(1): 19–44.

Letsch, C. (2013) Syrian conflict brings sectarian tensions to Turkey's tolerant Hatay province. *The Guardian*, 3, September. Available at: http://www.theguardian.com.

Letsch, C. (2014a) Kobani: anger grows as Turkey stops Kurds from aiding militias in Syria. The *Guardian*, 8, October. Available at: https://www.theguardian.com/world/2014/oct/08/kobani-isis-turkey-kurds-ypg-syria-erdogan.

Letsch, C. (2014b) Kurdish peshmerga forces arrive in Kobani to bolster fight against ISIS. *The Guardian*, 1, November. Available at: https://www.theguardian.com/world/2014/nov/01/kurdish-peshmerga-kobani-isis-syria.

Levitsky, S. and Way, L.A. (2002) Elections Without Democracy: The Rise of Competitive Authoritarianism. *Journal of Democracy* 13(2): 51–65.

Levitsky, S. and Way, L.A. (2010) *Competitive Authoritarianism: Hybrid Regimes After the Cold War*. New York: Cambridge University Press.

Lewis, B. (1961) *The Emergence of Modern Turkey*. Oxford: Oxford University Press.

Lyons, M.N. (2008) Two Ways of Looking at Fascism. *Socialism and Democracy* 22(2): 121–156.

MacFarquhar, N. and Hwaida, S. (2012). Rebel groups in Syria make framework for military. *The New York Times*, 7, December. Available at: http://www.nytimes.com.

Madi, Ö. (2014) From Islamic Radicalism to Islamic Capitalism: The Promises and Predicaments of Turkish-Islamic Entrepreneurship in a Capitalist System (The Case of İGİAD). *Middle Eastern Studies* 50(1): 144–161.

Mandel, E. (1969) *The Marxist Theory of the State*. New York: Pathfinder Press.

Mardin, Ş. (1973) Center-Periphery Relations: A Key to Turkish Politics?. *Daedalus* 102(1): 169–190.

Mardin, Ş. (1995) Civil Society and Islam. In: Hall, J. (ed.) *Civil Society: Theory, History, Comparison*. Cambridge: Polity.

Marini, R.M. (1965) Brazilian "Interdependence" and Imperialist Integration, *Monthly Review* 17(7): 10–29.

Marini, R. (1972) Brazilian Subimperialism. *Monthly Review* 23(9): 14–24.

Marois, T. (2012) *States, Banks and Crisis: Emerging Finance Capitalism in Mexico and Turkey*. Cheltenham: Edward Elgar.

Marsden, G. (1980) *Fundamentalism and American Culture: The Shaping of Twentieth-Century Evangelicalism 1870–1925*. New York: Oxford University Press.

Marx, K. (1970 [1843]) *Critique of Hegel's "Philosophy of Right"*. In: Cowling, M., Elton, G.R., Kedourie, E., Pocock, J.G.A., Pole, J.R. and Ullman, W. (eds) New York: Cambridge University Press.

Marx, K. (1972 [1852]) *The Eighteenth Brumaire of Louis Bonaparte*, 6th edition. Moscow: Progress Publishers.

Marx, K. (2000 [1871]) *The Civil War in France*. In: D. McLellan (ed.) *Karl Marx selected writings*, 2nd edition. New York: Oxford University Press, 584–603.

Maudūdi, S.A.A. (1967) *The Islamic Law and Constitution*, 3rd edition. Lahore: Islamic Publications.

McMahon, T. (17 December 2014) Historical Crude Oil Prices (Table). Available at: http://inflationdata.com/Inflation/Inflation_Rate/Historical_Oil_Prices_Table.asp.

Mendoza, M. (2011) Terrorist convictions reach 35,000. *The Independent*, 4, September. Available at: http://www.independent.co.uk.

McGhee, G.C. (1954) Turkey Joins the West. *Foreign Affairs* 32(4): 617–630.

Migdalovitz, C. (2010) *Turkey: Politics of Identity and Power*. (Congressional Research Service Report for Congress). Available at: http://fpc.state.gov/documents/organization/147289.pdf.

Miliband, R. (1965) Marx and the State. *The Socialist Register* 2: 278–296.

Milli Selamet Partisi 1973 Seçim Beyannamesi (1973) İstanbul: Fatih Yayınevi. Available at: https://acikerisim.tbmm.gov.tr/xmlui/bitstream/handle/11543/815/197600578_1973.pdf?sequence=1&isAllowed=y.

Milliyet (27 December 1995) Çağrı. p.11. Available at: http://gazetearsivi.milliyet.com.tr.

Milliyet (27 November 1996) Çiller: Abdullah Çatlı şerefli. p.15. Available at: http://gazetearsivi.milliyet.com.tr.

Milliyet (7 March 1997) Sivil dayanışmadan milletvekillerine mektup. p.17. Available at: http://gazetearsivi.milliyet.com.tr.

Milliyet (12 August 1997) Erbakan'ın MGK'daki zor anları. Available at: http://www.milliyet.com.tr/1997/08/12/siyaset/erbakan.html.

Milliyet (4 September 1999) 28 Şubat sureci bin yıl da sürer. p.14. Available at: http://gazetearsivi.milliyet.com.tr.

Milliyet (5 November 2002a) TÜSİAD'dan Avrupa'ya: AKP İslamcı değil. Available at: http://www.milliyet.com.tr/2002/11/05/ekonomi/eko02.html.

Milliyet (5 November 2002b) AB için AK Parti-CHP işbirliği... . Available at: http://www.milliyet.com.tr/2002/11/05/son/sontur23.html.

Milliyet (30 July 2008) "AKP kapatılmasın" kararı çıktı. Available at: http://www.milliyet.com.tr/default.aspx?aType=SonDakika&ArticleID=972729.

Milliyet (27 November 2014) Türkiye'de, siyasi parti kuruluşunda rekor. Available at: http://www.milliyet.com.tr/turkiye-de-siyasi-parti/siyaset/detay/1976048/default.htm.

Momayezi, N. (1998) Civil-Military Relations in Turkey. *International Journal on World Peace* 15(3): 3–28.

Mooers, C. (1991) *The Making of Bourgeois Europe: Absolutism, Revolution, and the Rise of Capitalism in England, France and Germany*. London: Verso.

Moore, B. (1966) *Social Origins of Dictatorship and Democracy: Lord and Peasant in the Making of the Modern World*. Middlesex: Penguin University Books.

Moore, C. (1990). Islamic Banks and Competitive Politics in the Arab World and Turkey. *Middle East Journal* 44(2): 234–255.

Mudde, C. (2004) The Populist Zeitgeist. *Government and Opposition* 39(4): 542–563.

Mumcu, U. (1993) *Rabıta*, 5th edition. İstanbul: Tekin Yayınevi.

Munck, R. (2005) Neoliberalism and Politics, and the Politics of Neoliberalism. In: Saad-Filho, A. and & Johnston, D. (eds) *Neoliberalism: A Critical Reader.* London; Ann Arbor, MI: Pluto Press, 60–69.

Mutlu, S. (2011) The Economic Cost of Civil Conflict in Turkey. *Middle Eastern Studies* 47(1): 63–80.

MÜSİAD (*Müstakil Sanayici ve İş Adamları Derneği*) (1993a) *Orta Ölçekli İşletmeler ve Bürokrasi.* İstanbul: Müsiad Yayınları.

MÜSİAD (*Müstakil Sanayici ve İş Adamları Derneği*) (1993b) *Kit'lenme! ve Özelleştirme.* İstanbul: Müsiad Yayınları.

MÜSİAD (*Müstakil Sanayici ve İş Adamları Derneği*) (1994a) *Economic Cooperation Among Islamic Countries.* No: 8. İstanbul: Müsiad Yayınları.

MÜSİAD (*Müstakil Sanayici ve İş Adamları Derneği*) (1994b) *İş Hayatında İslam İnsanı (Homo Islamicus).* No: 9. İstanbul: Müsiad Yayınları.

MÜSİAD (*Müstakil Sanayici ve İş Adamları Derneği*) (1996) *A New Perspective of the World at the Threshold of the 21st Century.* İstanbul: Müsiad Yayınları.

MÜSİAD (*Müstakil Sanayici ve İş Adamları Derneği*) (2000) *Anayasa Reformu ve Yönetimin Demokratikleşmesi.* Available at: http://www.musiad.org.tr/F/Root/burcu2014/Ara%C5%9Ft%C4%B1rmalar%20Yay%C4%B1n/Pdf/Ara%C5%9Ft%C4%B1rma%20Raporlar%C4%B1/Anayasa_Reformu_ve_Yonetimin_Demokratiklesmesi.pdf.

MÜSİAD (*Müstakil Sanayici ve İş Adamları Derneği*) (2011) Türkiye Cumhuriyeti Anayasa Önerisi. No: 75. İstanbul: Müsiad Yayınları.

MÜSİAD (*Müstakil Sanayici ve İş Adamları Derneği*) (2012) MÜSİAD *Tüzük.* Available at: http://www.musiad.org.tr/Tuzuk.aspx.

MÜSİAD (*Müstakil Sanayici ve İş Adamları Derneği*) (2014) MÜSİAD *Fair.* Available at: http://www.musiadfair.com/eng/.

MÜSİAD (*Müstakil Sanayici ve İş Adamları Derneği*) (2020) MÜSİAD*'la Tanışın.* Available at: http://www.musiad.org.tr/tr-tr/musiadla-tanisin.

Nalbantoğlu, H.Ü. (1993) Modernity, State and Religion: Theoretical Notes towards a Comparative Study. *Sojourn: Journal of Social of Issues in Southeast Asia* 8(2): 345–360.

Nalçacı, E. (2012) İkinci Cumhuriyetin kuruluşuna eşlik eden ideolojik salgı: Vesayet rejimi, In: Nalçacı, E. and Özeren, S. (eds) *İkinci Cumhuriyet'in Düzeni.* İstanbul: Yazılama.

Narli, N. (2000) Civil-military relations in Turkey. *Turkish Studies* 1(1): 107–127.

Nas, T.F. (2008) *Tracing the Economic Transformation of Turkey from the 1920s to EU Accession*. Leiden: Martinus Nijhoff.

Nas, T.F. and Odekon, M. (1992) (eds) *Economics and Politics of Turkish Liberalization*. London and Toronto: Associated University Press.

National Programme of Turkey for the Adoption of the EU Acquis (2008) Available at: http://www.abgs.gov.tr/index.php?p=42260&l=2.

Ntvmsnbc (17 July 2000) Erbakan given prison term. Available at: http://arsiv.ntvmsnbc.com/news/15748.asp.

Nye, R.P. (1977) Civil-Military Confrontation in Turkey: The 1973 Presidential Election. *International Journal of Middle East Studies* 8(2): 209–228.

Ozgur, I. (2012) *Islamic Schools in Modern Turkey: Faith, Politics, and Education*. New York: Cambridge University Press.

OECD, Organisation for Economic Co-operation and Development (1999) *OECD Economic Surveys: Turkey 1999*. Available at: http://www.keepeek.com/Digital-Asset-Management/oecd/economics/oecd-economic-surveys-turkey-1999_eco_surveys-tur-1999-en#page1.

OECD, Organisation for Economic Co-operation and Development (2002) *Small and Medium Size Enterprise Outlook 2002*. OECD Publishing, Available at: http://www.oecd-ilibrary.org/industry-and-services/oecd-small-and-medium-enterprise-outlook-2002_sme_outlook-2002-en.

OECD, Organisation for Economic Co-operation and Development (2013) Average annual hours actually worked per worker. *OECD.StatExtracts*. Available at: http://stats.oecd.org/Index.aspx?DatasetCode=ANHRS.

OECD, Organisation for Economic Co-operation and Development (2014) *Society at Glance 2014: OECD Social Indicators, The crisis and its aftermath*. OECD Publishing. Retrieved from http://www.oecd-ilibrary.org/docserver/download/8113171e.pdf?expires=1415903615&id=id&accname=guest&checksum=9F86E55D62B0C66EE6DC6B1F97553B2C.

OECD, Organisation for Economic Co-operation and Development (2014b) *OECD Economic Surveys: Turkey 2014*. OECD Publishing. Available at: http://www.keepeek.com/Digital-Asset-Management/oecd/economics/oecd-economic-surveys-turkey-2014_eco_surveys-tur-2014-en#page1.

OECD, Organisation for Economic Co-operation and Development (2014c) Society at a Glance 2014 Highlights: TURKEY, OECD Social Indicators. Excerpted from *Society at Glance 2014: OECD Social Indicators, The crisis and its aftermath*. Available at: http://www.oecd.org/turkey/OECD-SocietyAtaGlance20142014-Highlights-Turkey.pdf.

OECD, Organisation for Economic Co-operation and Development (2020a) Trade Union Density. *OECD.StatExtracts*. Available at: https://stats.oecd.org/Index.aspx?DataSetCode=TUD.

OECD, Organisation for Economic Co-operation and Development (2020b) Collective Bargaining Coverage. *OECD.StatExtracts*. Available at: https://stats.oecd.org/Index.aspx?DataSetCode=TUD.

OECD, Organisation for Economic Co-operation and Development (2020c) Minimum relative to average wages of full-time workers. *OECD.StatExtracts*. Available at: https://stats.oecd.org/Index.aspx?DataSetCode=TUD.

Office for Democratic Institutions and Human Rights (2014) *Republic of Turkey Presidential Election 10 August 2014 OSCE/ODIHR Limited Election Observation Mission Final Report*. Available at: http://www.osce.org/odihr/elections/turkey/126851?download=true.

Olson, E. (1985) Muslim Identity and Secularism in Contemporary Turkey: "The Headscarf Dispute". *Anthropological Quarterly* 58(4): 161–171.

Onaran, Ö. and Oyvat, C. (2015) *The political economy of inequality, redistribution and boom-bust cycles in Turkey*. Working Papers GPERC16. Greenwich Political Economy Research Centre: University of Greenwich. Available at: http://gala.gre.ac.uk/14067/.

Onaran, Ö. (2009) Crises and post-crisis adjustment in Turkey, Implications for labor. In: Öniş, Z. and Şenses F. (eds) *Turkey and the Global Economy: Neo-liberal restructuring and integration in the post-crisis era*. London; New York: Routledge, 243–261.

OPEC, Organisation of the Petroleum Exporting Countries (2020) *OPEC share of world crude oil reserves, 2018*. Available at: https://www.opec.org/opec_web/en/data_graphs/330.htm.

Ozcan, G. and Çokgezen, M. (2003) Limits to Alternative Forms of Capitalization: The Case of Anatolian Holding Companies. *World Development* 31(12): 2061–2084.

Ozkan, B. (2014) Turkey, Davutoglu and the Idea of Pan-Islamism. *Survival: Global Politics and Strategy* 56(4): 119–140.

Öniş, Z. (1997) The Political Economy of Islamic Resurgence in Turkey: The Rise of Welfare Party in Perspective. *Third World Quarterly* 18(4): 743–766.

Öniş, Z. (1998) Stabilisation and Growth in a Semi-Industrial Economy: An Evaluation of the Recent Turkish Experiment, 1977–1984. *State and Market: The Political Economy of Turkey in Comparative Perspective*. İstanbul: Boğaziçi University Press.

Öniş, Z. (2003) Domestic Politics versus Global Dynamics: Towards a Political Economy of 2000 and 2001 Financial Crises in Turkey. In: Öniş, Z. and Rubin, B. (eds) *The Turkish Economy in Crisis*. London: Frank Cass, 1–30.

Öniş, Z. (2004) Turgut Özal and His Economic Legacy: Turkish Neo-Liberalism in Critical Perspective. *Middle Eastern Studies* 40(4): 113–134.

Özal, T. (1991) *Turkey in Europe and Europe in Turkey*. Nicosia: K. Rustem and Brother.

Özbudun, E. (2000) *Contemporary Turkish Politics: Challenges to Turkish Politics*. Colorado and London: Lynne Rienner Publishers.

Özbudun, E. (2007) Democratization Reforms in Turkey, 1993–2004. *Turkish Studies* 8(2): 176–196.

Özbudun, E. (2014) AKP at the Crossroads: Erdoğan's Majoritarian Drift. *South European Society and Politics* 19(12): 155–167.

Özbudun, E. and Gençkaya, Ö.F. (2009) *Democratization and the Politics of Constitution-making in Turkey*. Budapest: Central European University Press.

Özdağ, Ü. (1997) *Menderes Döneminde Ordu-Siyaset İlişkileri ve 27 Mayıs İhtilalı*. İstanbul: Boyut Kitapları.

Özdalga, E. (2002) Necmettin Erbakan: Democracy for the Sake of Power. In: Heper, M. and Sayarı, S. (eds) *Political Leaders and Democracy in Turkey*. Lanham, Md.: Lexington Books.

Özkan F. (2009) Türkiye'nin gerçek burjuva sınıfı biziz!. *Star*, 20, July Available at: https://m.star.com.tr/yazar/Turkiyenin_gercek_burjuva_sinifi_biziz-yazi-520953/.

Öztürk, Ö. (2014) Türkiye'de İslamcı Büyük Burjuvazi. In Balkan, N., Balkan, E. and Öncü, A. *Neoliberalizm, İslamcı Sermayenin Yükselişi ve AKP*. İstanbul: Yordam Kitap, 181–213.

Özyürek, E. (2006) *Nostalgia for the Modern: State Secularism and Everyday Politics in Turkey*. Durham and London: Duke University Press.

Paletta, D. (2016) Pentagon Allies Jailed in Turkey Amid Coup Backlash, General Says. *The Wall Street Journal*, 28, July. Available at: http://blogs.wsj.com/washwire/2016/07/28/pentagon-allies-jailed-in-turkey-amid-coup-backlash-general-says/.

Pamuk, Ş. (1984) İthal İkamesi, Döviz Darboğazları ve Türkiye, 1947–1979. In: Boratav, K., Keyder, Ç. and & Pamuk, Ş. *Krizin Gelişimi ve Türkiye'nin Alternatif Sorunu*. İstanbul & Ankara: Kaynak Yayınları, 37–68.

Parla, T. (2009) Türkiye'de Merkantilist Militarizm 1960–1998. In İnsel, A and Bayramoğlu, A. (eds) *Bir Zümre, Bir Parti, Türkiye'de Ordu*, 4th edition. İstanbul: Birikim Yayınları, 201–223.

Park, B. (2008) Turkey's Deep State: Ergenekon and the Threat to Democratisation in the Republic. *The RUSI Journal* 153(5): 54–59.

Park, B. (2009) Ergenekon: power and democracy in Turkey. *OpenDemocracy*, 17, September. Available at: https://www.opendemocracy.net/article/ergenekon-power-and-democracy-in-turkey-0.

Participation Banks Association of Turkey (n.d.) *Participation Banks 2013 Sector Report*. Available at: http://www.tkbb.org.tr/Documents/YillikSektorRaporlari/TKBB_ing_low.pdf.

Perlo-Freeman, S., Ferguson, N., Kelly, N., Solmirano, C. and Wilandh, H. (2014) Military expenditure data, 2004–2013. *SIPRI Yearbook 2014*. Oxford: Oxford University Press, 221–250.

Perlo-Freeman, S., Solmirano, C. and Wilandh, H. (2014) Global developments in militaryr expenditure. *SIPRI Yearbook 2014*. Oxford: Oxford University Press, 175–182.

Perlo-Freeman, S. and Wezeman, P.D. (2014) Top 100 arms-producing and military services companies in the world excluding China, 2012. *SIPRI Yearbook 2014: Armaments, Disarmament and International Security*. Oxford: Oxford University Press, 206–220.

Polat, N. (2011) The Anti-Coup Trials in Turkey: What Exactly is Going On?, *Mediterranean Politics* 16(1): 213–219.

Pope, N. and Pope, H. (1997) *Turkey Unveiled: Atatürk and After*. London: John Murray.

Poulantzas, N. (1973) *Political Power and Social Classes*. London: NLB, Sheed and Ward.

Poulantzas, N. (1974) *Fascism and Dictatorship: The Third International and the Problem of Fascism*. London: NLB.

Poulantzas, N. (1975) *Classes in Contemporary Capitalism*. London: NLB.

Presidency of Turkey, Presidency of Strategy and Balance (2018) *Some Indicators Related to the Consolidated Budget*. Available at: http://www.sbb.gov.tr/ekonomik-ve-sosyal-gostergeler/#1540022258789-43a5759e-f454.

Privatisation Administration, Republic of Turkey Prime Ministry (2018) *2018 Yılı Faaliyet Raporu*. Available at: https://ms.hmb.gov.tr/uploads/sites/6/2019/04/2018-Faaliyet-Raporu-11-04-2019.pdf.

Przeworski, A. (1991) *Democracy and the market: Political and economic reforms in Eastern Europe and Latin America*. Cambridge: Cambridge University Press.

Radikal (21 April 2007) Nokta dergisi kapanıyor. Available at: http://www.radikal.com.tr/haber.php?haberno=219024.

Radikal (5 July 2008) Başbakan Ergenekon'un savcısıysa ben avukatıyım. Available at: http://www.radikal.com.tr/politika/basbakan_ergenekonun_savcisiysa_ben_avukatiyim-886827.

Radikal (11 November 2008) Vecdi Gönül ırkçı gibi konuştu. Available at: http://www.radikal.com.tr/politika/vecdi_gonul_irkci_gibi_konustu-907860.

Radikal (25 March 2009) Ergenekon'un İkinci İddianamesinin Tam Metni. Available at: http://www.radikal.com.tr/turkiye/ergenekonun_ikinci_iddianamenin_tam_metni-927957.

Radikal (5 August 2009) 3. Ergenekon iddianamesine onay. Available at: http://www.radikal.com.tr/turkiye/3_ergenekon_iddianamesine_onay-948339.

Radikal (22 February 2013). Erdoğan: Alevilik din değil; Ali ile alakaları yok. Available at: http://www.radikal.com.tr/politika/erdogan_alevilik_din_degil_ali_ile_alakalari_yok-1122494.

Radikal (14 June 2013) Erdoğan: Reyhanlı'da 53 sünni vatandaşımız şehit edildi. Available at: http://www.radikal.com.tr/politika/erdogan_reyhanlida_53_sunni_vatandasimiz_sehit_edildi-1137612.

Republic of Turkey Ministry of Economy (2014) *Free Trade Agreements*. Available at: http://www.economy.gov.tr/portal/faces/home/free-trade/turkey-free?_afrLoop=43754780108203&_afrWindowMode=0&_afrWindowId=itpxulp0g_385#!%40%40%3F_afrWindowId%3Ditpxulp0g_385%26_afrLoop%3D43754780108203%26_afrWindowMode%3D0%26_adf.ctrl-state%3Ditpxulp0g_439.

Republic of Turkey Ministry of Family and Social Policy (2012) *Haziran 2012 Sosyal Yardım İstatistikleri Bülteni*. Available at: http://www.aile.gov.tr.

Republic of Turkey Ministry of Economy (n.d.) *Investment Incentives Turkey*. Available at: http://www.incentives.gov.tr/index.cfm?sayfa=9B6A6BDE-F1AB-4A70-CBE5770FF56F50BE.

Republic of Turkey Ministry of Family and Social Policy (2015) 2014 Faaliyet Raporu. Available at: http://sgb.aile.gov.tr/data/54f1fc41369dc5920c515f67/aspb-faaliyetraporu2014.pdf.

Republic of Turkey Ministry of Foreign Affairs, Directorate for EU Affairs (2019) *Chronology of Turkey-European Union Relations (1959–2015)*. Available at: https://www.ab.gov.tr/turkey-eu-relations_4_en.html.

Republic of Turkey Ministry of Justice, General Directorate of Prisons and Detention Houses. (2016) *Ceza İnfaz Kurumlarının Yıllara Göre Mevcutları*. Available at: http://www.cte.adalet.gov.tr/index.html.

Republic of Turkey Ministry of Labour and Social Security (n.d.) *İşçi ve Sendika Üye Sayıları*. Available at: http://www.csgb.gov.tr/csgbPortal/csgb.portal?page=uye.

Republic of Turkey, Ministry of Treasury and Finance (2018) *Gross External Debt Stock of Turkey (Archive)*. Available at: https://www.hmb.gov.tr/kamu-finansmani-istatistikleri.

Republic of Turkey, Ministry of Treasury and Finance (2019) *Ekonomik Göstergeler, Ocak 2019*. Available at: https://ms.hmb.gov.tr/uploads/2019/02/Ekonomik-G%C3%B6stergeler-Ocak-2019-e.pdf.

Resmi Gazete (25 June 1987) *Türk Silahlı Kuvvetlerini Güçlendirme Vakfı Kanunu*. Law Number: 3388. Available at: http://www.resmigazete.gov.tr/main.aspx?home=http://www.resmigazete.gov.tr/arsiv/19498.pdf&main=http://www.resmigazete.gov.tr/arsiv/19498.pdf.

Resmi Gazete (18 July 2006) *Terörle Mücadele Kanununda Değişiklik Yapılmasına Dair Kanun*. Law Number: 5532. Available at: http://www.resmigazete.gov.tr/main.aspx?home=http://www.resmigazete.gov.tr/eskiler/2006/07/20060718.htm&main=http://www.resmigazete.gov.tr/eskiler/2006/07/20060718.htm.

Resmi Gazete (19 June 2012) *Yatırımlarda Devlet Yardımları Hakkında Karar*. Law/Decree Number: 2012/3305, Available at: http://www.resmigazete.gov.tr/eskiler/2012/06/20120619-1.htm.

Robins, P. (1991) *Turkey and the Middle East*. Institute of International Relations. New York: Foreign Relations Press.

REFERENCES

Rodinson, M. (2004) Maxime Rodinson on "Islamic Fundamentalism": An Unpublished Interview with Gilbert Achcar. *Middle East Report* (233): 2–4.

Roper, B.S. (2013) *The History of Democracy: A Marxist Interpretation*. London: Pluto Press.

Reporters Without Borders (2016a) *2019 World Press Freedom Index*. Available at: https://rsf.org/en/ranking.

Reporters Without Borders (2016b) *Turkey*. Available at: https://rsf.org/en/turkey.

Reuters (15 July 2014). "Kerry says hopes for peace and stability in Turkey". Available at: http://www.reuters.com/article/us-turkey-security-usa-russia-idUSKCN0ZV2NQ.

Reuters (24 June 2016) "Turkey grants immunity to security forces fighting militants". Available at: http://www.reuters.com/article/us-turkey-security-kurds-idUSKCN0ZA1IV.

Rubin, M. (2008) Erdogan, Ergenekon, and the Struggle for Turkey. *Mideast Monitor*, 8, August Available at: http://www.meforum.org/1968/erdogan-ergenekon-and-the-struggle-for-turkey.

Rueschemeyer, D., Stephens, E.H., and Stephens, J.D. (1992) *Capitalist Development and Democracy*. Cambridge: Polity Press.

Rustow, D. (1987) *Turkey: American's Forgotten Ally*. New York: Council on Foreign Relations.

Saadet Partisi (2010a) Erbakan. Available at: http://www.saadet.org.tr/kisi/necmettin-erbakan.

Saadet Partisi (2010b) Program. Available at: http://www.saadet.org.tr/kurumsal/i-giris/689.

Sabah (22 May 1997) Tarihi uyarı. Available at: http://arsiv.sabah.com.tr/1997/05/22/f07.html.

Sabah (28 March 2015) Fetih Ordusu İdlib'i aldı. Available at: http://www.sabah.com.tr/dunya/2015/03/28/fetih-ordusu-idlibi-aldi.

Said, E. (2003) *Orientalism*. London: Penguin Books.

Sakallioglu, U.C. (1996) Parameters and Strategies of Islam-State Interaction in Republican Turkey. *International Journal of Middle East Studies* 28(2): 231–251.

Sakallıoğlu, Ü.C. (1997) The Anatomy of the Turkish Military's Political Autonomy. *Comparative Politics* 29(2): 151–166.

Samaan, J. (2013) "The Rise and Fall of the 'Turkish Model' in the Arab World". *Turkish Policy Quarterly* 12(3): 61–69.

Samim, A. (1981) The Tragedy of the Turkish Left. *New Left Review* 126(I): 60–85.

Samim A. (1987) The Left. In: Schick İ.C. & Tonak E. A. (eds) *Turkey in Transition*. New York: Oxford University Press.

Sarıbay, Y.A. (2005) Milli Nizam Partisi'nin Kuruluşu ve Programının İçeriği. In: Bora, T. and Gültekingil, M. (eds) *Modern Türkiye'de Siyasi Düşünce: İslamcılık*, 2nd edition. İstanbul: İletişim, 576–590.

Satterthwaite, J.C. (1972) The Truman Doctrine: Turkey. *Annals of the American Academy of Political and Social Science* 401: 74–84.

Savran, G. (1987) Marx'ın Düşüncesinde Demokrasi: Siyasetin Eleştiri. *11. Tez*. 6: 52–66.

Savran, S. (2002) The Legacy of the Twentieth Century. In: Balkan, N. and Savran, S. (eds) *The Politics of Permanent Crisis: Class, Ideology and State in Turkey*. New York: Nova Science Publishers, 1–20.

Savran, S. (2010) *Türkiye'de Sınıf Mücadeleri: Cilt 1: 1908–1980*. İstanbul: Yordam Kitap.

Savunma Sanayii Müsteşarlığı (2012) *Savunma Sanayii Müsteşarlığı Faaliyet Raporu 2012*. Available at: http://www.ssm.gov.tr/anasayfa/kurumsal/Faaliyet%20Raporlar/2012%20Y%C4%B1l%C4%B1%20Faaliyet%20Raporu.pdf.

Sayarı, S. (1992) Politics and Economic Policy-Making in Turkey, 1980–1988. In: Nas, T.F. and Odekon, M. (eds) *Economics and Politics of Turkish Liberalization*. London and Toronto: Associated University Presses, 26–43.

Saygılı, Ş., Cengiz C., Cihan Y., and Hamsici, T. (2010) *Türk İmalat Sanayiin İthalat Yapısı*. The Central Bank of the Republic of Turkey. Working Paper, 10/02. Available at: http://www.tcmb.gov.tr/wps/wcm/connect/8b16265d-2fcb-4ce3-944b-dd2cfb967750/WP1002.pdf?MOD=AJPERES&CACHEID=8b16265d-2fcb-4ce3-944b-dd2cfb967750.

Schick, İ. and Tonak, E. (eds) (1987) *Turkey in Transition: New Perspectives*. New York: Oxford University Press.

Schmitter, P.C. and Karl, T.L. (1991) What Democracy is … and Is Not. Journal of Democracy 2(3): 75–88.

Schumpeter, J.A. (2003) *Capitalism, Socialism & Democracy*, 5th edition. London and New York: Routledge.

Schwarzmantel, J. (1995) Capitalist Democracy Revisited. *Socialist Register* 31: 207–224.

SeçimHaberler (2019) 31 Mart 2019 Yerel Seçim Sonuçları. Available at: https://secim.haberler.com/2019/yerel-secimler/.

Selian, A. (2002) *ICTs in Support of Human Rights, Democracy and Good Governance*. Available at: https://www.itu.int/osg/spu/wsis-themes/humanrights/ICTs%20and%20HR.pdf.

Sengupta, K. (2015) Turkey and Saudi Arabia alarm the West by backing Islamist extremists the Americans had bombed in Syria. *The Independent*, 12, May. Available at: http://www.independent.co.uk/news/world/middle-east/syria-crisis-turkey-and-saudi-arabia-shock-western-countries-by-supporting-anti-assad-jihadists-10242747.html.

Serhad, B. (2016). Failed Coup: A Springboard to Bonapartism. *Left Voice*, 9, August. Available at: http://www.leftvoice.org/Failed-Coup-A-Springboard-to-Bonapartism.

Server Holding (2019) Available at: http://www.serverholding.com/.

Sezgin, Y. (2016) How Erdogan's anti-democratic government made Turkey ripe for unrest. *Turkey's coup attempt*. (Project on Middle East Political Science Briefing No.30). Available at: http://pomeps.org/2016/08/03/briefing-30-turkeys-coup-attempt/.

Sharon-Krespin, R. (2009) Fethullah Gülen's Great Ambition: Turkey's Islamist Danger. *The Middle East Quarterly* 16(1): 55–66.

Shaw, C. and Şık, A. (2016) How Turkey invited and then quashed an attempted coup: the inside scoop. *De Correspondent*, 21, July. Available at: https://decorrespondent.nl/4972/how-turkey-invited-and-then-quashed-an-attempted-coup-the-inside-scoop/1300816787644-095a0b2f.

Shaw, T.M. (1979) The Semiperiphery in Africa and Latin America: Subimperialism and Semiindustrialism. *The Review of Black Political Economy* 9(4): 341–358.

SHP (*Sosyal Demokrat Halkçı Parti*, Social Democratic Populist Party) (1989) Sosyal Demokrat Halkçı Parti'nin Doğu ve Güneydoğu Sorununa Bakışı ve Çözüm Önerileri. In: *Cumhuriyet Halk Partisi Raporları*. Available at: http://www.chp.org.tr/wp-content/uploads/rapor_1989.pdf.

Singer, M. (1977) *The Economic Advance of Turkey 1938–1960*. Ankara: Turkish Economic Society Publications.

Sly, L. and Karen D. (2015) Turkey agrees to allow U.S. military to use its base to attack Islamic State. *The Washington Post*, 23, July. Available at: https://www.washingtonpost.com/world/middle_east/turkey-agrees-to-allow-us-military-to-use-its-base-to-attack-islamic-state/2015/07/23/317f23aa-3164-11e5-a879-213078d03dd3_story.html.

Sørensen, G. (2008) *Democracy and Democratization: Processes and Prospects in a Changing World*, 3rd edition. Boulder, Colorado: Westview Press.

Sönmez, A. (1967) The reemergence of the idea of planning and the scope of targets of the 1963–1967 plan. In: İnanç, İ.S. (ed.) *Planning in Turkey: selected papers*. Ankara: METU Publications, 28–43.

Sönmez, M. (1992) *Türkiye'de Holdingler: Kırk Haramiler*, 5th edition. Ankara: Arkadaş Yayınevi.

Söyler, M. (2013) Informal institutions, forms of state and democracy: the Turkish deep state. *Democratization*: 20(2): 310–334.

Söyler, M. (2014) The Deep State: Forms of Domination, Informal Institutions and Democracy. In *Heinrich Böll Stiftung Türkei*. Available at: http://tr.boell.org/de/2014/06/16/deep-state-forms-domination-informal-instutions-and-democracy.

Söyler, M. (2015) *The Turkish Deep State: State Consolidation, Civil-Military Relations and Democracy*. Abingdon, Oxon & New York: Routledge.

Stein, A. (2015) Turkey's Evolving Syria Strategy: Why Ankara Backs Al-Nusra but Shuns ISIS. *Foreign Affairs*, 9, February. Available at: https://www.foreignaffairs.com/articles/turkey/2015-02-09/turkeys-evolving-syria-strategy.

Steinberg, G. (2010) The Muslim Brotherhood in Germany. In: Rubin, B. (ed.) *The Muslim Brotherhood: The Organization and Policies of a Global Islamist Movement*. Hampshire: Palgrave Macmillan.

Steinberg, G. (2012) *Qatar and the Arab Spring: Support for Islamists and New Anti-Syrian Policy*. Stiftung Wissenschaft und Politik (SWP) Comment 7. Berlin: German Institute for International and Security Affairs.

Steinherr, A., Tukel, A. and Ucer, M. (2004) The Turkish Banking Sector, Challenges and Outlook in Transiton to EU Membership. *Bruges European Economic Policy Briefings*. No. 9.

Sunier, T. and Landman, N. (2015) *Transnational Turkish Islam: Shifting Geographies of Religious Activism and Community Building in Turkey and Europe*. Hampshire: Palgrave Macmillan.

Şardan, T. (2013) Gezi'den kalanlar ve farklı bir analiz. *Milliyet*, 25, November. Available at: http://www.milliyet.com.tr.

Şaylan, G. (1988) Ordu ve Siyaset; Bonapartizmin Siyasal Kültürü. In: *Bahri Savcı'ya Armağan*. Ankara: Mülkiyeliler Birliği Vakfı Yayınları, 449–459.

Şen, M. (2010) Transformation of Turkish Islamism and the Rise of the Justice and Development Party. *Turkish Studies* 11(1): 59–84.

Şen, S. (1996) *Cumhuriyet Kültürünün Oluşum Sürecinde Bir İdeolojik Aygıt Olarak Silahlı Kuvvetler ve Modernizm*. İstanbul: Sarmal Yayınevi.

Şenses, F. (2003) Economic Crisis as an Instigator of Distributional Conflict: The Turkish Case in 2001. *Turkish Studies* 4(ii): 92–119.

Şenses, F. (1994) The Stabilization and Structural Adjustment Program and the Process of Turkish Industrialization: Main Policies and Their Impact. In: Şenses, F. (ed.) *Recent Industrialization Experience of Turkey in a Global Context*. Westport: Greenwood Press, 50–73.

Tachau, F. and Heper, M. (1983) The State, Politics, and the Military in Turkey. *Comparative Politics* 16(1): 17–33.

Tanış, T. (2014) Biden says Erdoğan admitted ISIL mistake. *Hürriyet Daily News*, 3, October. Available at: http://www.hurriyetdailynews.com/biden-says-erdogan-admitted-isil-mistake.aspx?pageID=238&nID=72530&NewsCatID=359.

Taraf (20 January 2010) Darbenin adı Balyoz. Available at: http://www.taraf.com.tr/haber-darbenin-adi-balyoz-46614.

Taspinar, Ö. (2008) Turkey's Middle East Policies: Between Neo-Ottomanism and Kemalism. *Carnegie Papers*. Available at: http://carnegieendowment.org/files/cmec10_taspinar_final.pdf.

Taş, H. (2014) Turkey's Ergenekon Imbroglio and Academia's Apathy. *Insight Turkey* 16(1): 163–179.

Taştekin, F. (2013) Turkey's Sunni Identity Test. *Al Monitor*, 21, June. Available at: http://www.al-monitor.com.

Taştekin, F. (2015) Turkish military says MIT shipped weapons to al-Qaeda. *Al-Monitor*, 15, January. Available at: http://www.al-monitor.com/pulse/originals/2015/01/turkey-syria-intelligence-service-shipping-weapons.html.

TBMMa (*Türkiye Büyük Millet Meclisi*, The Grand National Assembly of Turkey) (2012) *Ülkemizde Demokrasiye Müdahale Eden Tüm Darbe ve Muhtıralar ile Demokrasiyi İşlevsiz Kılan Diğer Bütün Girişim ve Süreçlerin Tüm Boyutları ile Araştırılarak Alınması Gereken Önlemlerin Belirlenmesi Amacıyla Kurulan Meclis Araştırma Komisyonu Raporu*. Vol: 1, Term: 24, Legislative Session: 3, No: 376.

TBMMb (*Türkiye Büyük Millet Meclisi*, The Grand National Assembly of Turkey) (2012) *Ülkemizde Demokrasiye Müdahale Eden Tüm Darbe ve Muhtıralar ile Demokrasiyi İşlevsiz Kılan Diğer Bütün Girişim ve Süreçlerin Tüm Boyutları ile Araştırılarak Alınması Gereken Önlemlerin Belirlenmesi Amacıyla Kurulan Meclis Araştırma Komisyonu Raporu*. Vol: 2, Term: 24, Legislative Session: 3, No: 376.

TBMMc (*Türkiye Büyük Millet Meclisi*, The Grand National Assembly of Turkey) (n.d.) Milli Nizam Partisi: Program ve Tüzük. Available at: https://acikerisim.tbmm.gov.tr/xmlui/bitstream/handle/11543/799/197600503.pdf?sequence=1&isAllowed=y.

TESEV (2009) *Security Sector in Turkey: Questions, Problems, and Solutions*. İstanbul: TESEV.

TESEV (2013) *Military, Police and Intelligence in Turkey: Recent Transformations and Needs for Reforms*. Policy. İstanbul: TESEV.

Tezcür, G.M. and Grigorescu, A. (2014) Activism in Turkish Foreign Policy: Balancing European and Regional Interests. *International Studies Perspectives* 15(3): 257–276.

Therborn, G. (1977) The rule of capital and the rise of democracy. *New Left Review* 103: 3–41.

The Constitution of the Turkish Republic (1961) Law number 334 of July 9, 1961. In the Official Gazette number 10859 of July 20, 1961.

The World Bank (1980) *Turkey: Policies and Prospects for Growth*. Report No: PUB2657. Available at: http://www-wds.worldbank.org/external/default/WDSContentServer/IW3P/IB/2001/01/20/000178830_98101903335718/Rendered/PDF/multi_page.pdf.

The World Bank (1981) *Turkey-Second Structural Adjustment Loan Project*. Report No: P3034. Available at: http://documents.worldbank.org/curated/en/1981/04/723438/turkey-second-structural-adjustment-loan-project.

The World Bank (2020) *World Development Indicators*. Created on various times. Available at: http://databank.worldbank.org/data/views/reports/chart.aspx#.

Thornburg, M.W., Spry, G. and Soule, G.H. (1949) *Turkey: An Economic Appraisal*. New York: The Twentieth Century Fund.

TİKA (*Türk İşbirliği ve Koordinasyon Ajansı Başkanlığı*, Turkish Cooperation and Coordination Agency) (2012) *Turkish Development Assistance 2012*. Available at: http://store.tika.gov.tr/yayinlar/kalkinma-yardimi/TurkishDevelopmentAssistance2012.pdf.

TİKA (*Türk İşbirliği ve Koordinasyon Ajansı Başkanlığı, Turkish Cooperation and Coordination Agency*) (n.d.) *About* TİKA. Available at: http://www.tika.gov.tr/en/about-us/1#.

Today's Zaman (8 March 2008) Appeals court unanimously upholds Fethullah Gülen acquittal. Available at: http://www.todayszaman.com/national_appeals-court-unanimously-upholds-fethullah-gulen-acquittal_135894.html.

Today's Zaman (6 August 2008) Erdoğan meets Assad in Bodrum for peace talks. Available at: http://www.todayszaman.com/diplomacy_erdogan-meets-assad-in-bodrum-for-peace-talks_149488.html.

Today's Zaman (22 January 2010) Constitutional Court rules out civilian trials for military. Available at: http://www.todayszaman.com/tz-web/news-199331-constitutional-court-rules-out-civilian-trials-for-military.html.

Today's Zaman (24 September 2010) Retired general confesses to burning mosque to fire up public. Available at: http://www.todayszaman.com/national_retired-general-confesses-to-burning-mosque-to-fire-up-public_222544.html.

Today's Zaman (6 August 6, 2012) Başbuğ thanks Erdoğan for his support. Available at: http://www.todayszaman.com/news-288775-basbug-thanks-erdogan-for-his-support.html.

Today's Zaman (6 March 2014) CHP files complaint against Erdoğan for labelling ODTÜ students "terrorists". Available at: http://www.todayszaman.com/national_chp-files-complaint-against-erdogan-for-labeling-odtu-students-terrorists_341306.html.

Today's Zaman (4 September 2014) Highlights of major corruption, bribery operations of Dec. 17, 25. Available at: http://www.todayszaman.com/anasayfa_highlights-of-major-corruption-bribery-operations-of-dec-17-25_357703.html.

Toker, C. (2008) *Abdüllatif Şener "Adım da benimle beraber büyüdü"*. İstanbul: Doğan Kitap.

Toprak, B. (2006) Islam and Democracy in Turkey. In: Çarkoğlu, A. and Rubin, B. (eds) *Religion and Politics in Turkey*. London and New York: Routledge.

Toprak, B. (1993) Islamist Intellectuals: Revolt against Industry and Technology. In: Heper, M. Öncü, A. and Kramer, H. (eds) *Turkey and the West: Changing Political and Cultural Identities*. London: I. B Tauris, 237–257.

Toprak, Z. (1982) Türkiye'de "Milli İktisat" (1908–1918). Ankara: Yurt Yayınları.

TPAO (*Türkiye Petrolleri Anonim Ortaklığı*, Turkish Petroluem Corporation) (2013) *International Projects*. Retrieved from http://www.tpao.gov.tr/eng/?tp=m&id=29.

Tremblay, P. (2013) Turkish Alevis Refuse "Sunnification". *Al Monitor*, 11, September. Available at: http://www.al-monitor.com.

Tremblay, P. (2015) Why Israel's Hezbollah strike didn't bother Turkey's Islamists. *Al Monitor*, 22, January. Available at: http://www.al-monitor.com.

Tremblay, P. (2016) How Erdogan used the power of the mosques against coup attempt. *Al-Monitor*, 25, June. Available at: http://www.al-monitor.com/pulse/originals/2016/07/turkey-coup-attempt-erdogan-mosques.html.

Tuğal, C. (2007) NATO's Islamists: Hegemony and Americanization in Turkey. *New Left Review* 44: 5–34.

Tuğal, C. (2009) *Passive Revolution: Absorbing the Islamic Challenge to Capitalism*. California: Stanford University Press.

Tuğal, C. (2016a) *The Fall of the Turkish Model: How the Arab Uprisings Brought Down Islamic Liberalism*. London and New York: Verso.

Tuğal, C. (2016b) Turkey coup aftermath: between neo-fascism and Bonapartism. *Opendemocracy*, 18, July. Available at: https://www.opendemocracy.net/cihan-tugal/turkey-coup-aftermath-between-neo-fascism-and-bonapartism.

Tunçkanat, H. (1996) *27 Mayıs 1960 Devrimi (diktadan demokrasiye)*. İstanbul: Çağdaş Yayınları.

Tura, A.R. (1998) *Kemalist Devlet*. İstanbul: Kardelen Yayınları.

Turan, İ. (1988) Political Parties and Party System in Post-1983 Turkey. In: Heper, M. and Evin, A. (eds) *State, Democracy, and the Military Turkey in the 1980s*. Berlin and New York: Walter de Gruyter, 63–80.

Turkish Court of Account (2011) *Law No. 6085 on Turkish Court of Accounts* (Unofficial Copy). Official Journal No: 27790. Available at: http://www.sayistay.gov.tr/mevzuat/6085/6085English.pdf.

TUSKON, *Türkiye İşadamları ve Sanayiciler Konfederasyonu*, Turkish Confederation of Businessmen and Industrialists (n.d.) *About Us*. Available at: http://www.tuskon.org/?p=content&cl=kurumsal&i=3.

Tuysuz, G. and Bilginsoy, Z. (2016) Ministry: Turkey joins coalition airstrikes against ISIS in Syria. *CNN*, 29, August. Available at: http://edition.cnn.com/2015/08/29/europe/turkey-airstrikes/.

TÜİK (2005) *Mahalli İdareler Seçimi The Election of Local Administrations, 28.03.2004*. No: 2935. Available at: http://www.turkstat.gov.tr/IcerikGetir.do?istab_id=225.

TÜİK (2009) *Mahalli İdareler Seçimi 29.03.2009*. No: 3584. Available at: http://www.tuik.gov.tr/Kitap.do?metod=KitapDetay&KT_ID=12&KITAP_ID=237.

TÜİK (2012) *Milletvekilleri Genel Seçimleri 1923–2011*. No: 3685, Ankara: TÜİK.

TÜİK (2015) *Labour Force Statistics, January 2015*, 15, April. Available at: http://www.turkstat.gov.tr/PreHaberBultenleri.do?id=18636.

TÜİK (n.d.) *Number of fixed telephone, mobile telephone and internet subscribers. Transportation and Communication*. Available at: http://www.turkstat.gov.tr/PreIstatistikTablo.do?istab_id=1580.

TÜİK (n.d.) *Seasonally Adjusted Main Labour Force Indicators*. Available at: http://www.turkstat.gov.tr/UstMenu.do?metod=temelist.

TÜİK (n.d.) *The Poverty Rates According to Poverty Line Methods. Income, Consumption and Poverty.* Retrieved from http://www.turkstat.gov.tr/UstMenu.do?metod=temelist.

TÜİK (n.d.) *Prison Population.* Available at: http://www.turkstat.gov.tr/UstMenu.do?metod=temelist.

TÜİK (n.d.) *Foreign Trade by Years.* Available at: http://www.turkstat.gov.tr/UstMenu.do?metod=temelist.

TÜİK (n.d.) *Exports by Country Group and Year.* Available at: http://www.turkstat.gov.tr/UstMenu.do?metod=temelist.

Tür, Ö. (2011) Economic Relations with the Middle East Under the AKP-Trade, Business Community and Reintegration with Neighboring Zones. *Turkish Studies* 12(4): 589–602.

Türkiye Müteahhitler Birliği (Turkish Contractors Association) (2013) *İnşaat Sektörü Analizi.* Available at: http://www.tmb.org.tr/arastirma_yayinlar/tmb_bulten_ocak2013.pdf.

TÜSİAD (*Türk Sanayicileri ve İşadamları Derneği*, Turkish Industry & Business Association) (1992) *The Turkish Economy'92.* İstanbul: TÜSİAD.

TÜSİAD (*Türk Sanayicileri ve İşadamları Derneği*, Turkish Industry and Business Association) (1997) *Türkiye'de Demokratikleşme Perspektifleri.* Available at: http://www.tusiad.org/__rsc/shared/file/demoktur.pdf.

TÜSİAD (*Türk Sanayicileri ve İşadamları Derneği*, Turkish Industry and Business Association) (1999) Türkiye'de Demokratik Standartların Yükseltilmesi: Tartışmalar ve Son Gelişmeler. Available at: http://www.tusiad.org/__rsc/shared/file/demokrat.pdf.

TÜSİAD (*Türk Sanayicileri ve İşadamları Derneği*, Turkish Industry and Business Association) (2002) *Türkiye'de Girişimcilik.* Available at: http://www.tusiad.org/tr/yayinlar/raporlar/item/1880-turkiyede-girisimcilik.

TÜSİAD (*Türk Sanayicileri ve İşadamları Derneği*, Turkish Industry and Business Association) (2011) *2011 Çalışma Raporu.* Available at: http://www.tusiad.org/bilgi-merkezi/tusiad-faaliyet-raporlari/tusiad-faaliyet-raporu-2011/.

TÜSİAD (*Türk Sanayicileri ve İşadamları Derneği*, Turkish Industry and Business Association) (2013) *TÜSİAD by Numbers.* Available at: http://www.tusiad.org/tusiad/tusiad-by-numbers/.

Ulrichsen, K.C. (2014) *Qatar and the Arab Spring: Policy Drivers and Regional Implications.* Washington: Carnegie Endowment for International Peace. Available at: http://carnegieendowment.org/files/qatar_arab_spring.pdf.

Umit, C. (2011) Disentagling the Threads of Civil-Military Relations in Turkey: Promises and Perils. *Meditterrenan Quarterly* 22(2): 57–75.

Undersecretariat for Defence Industries (2010) Historical Development. Available at: http://www.ssm.gov.tr/home/tdi/Sayfalar/historical.aspx.

United Nations Conference on Trade and Development, UNCTAD (2012) *Investment Country Profiles Turkey*. Available at: http://unctad.org/en/PublicationsLibrary/webdiaeia2012d6_en.pdf.

United Nations Conference on Trade and Development, UNCTAD (2013) The Top 100 non-financial TNC's from developing and transition economies, ranked by foreign assets, 2012. Available at: unctad.org/Sections/dite_dir/docs/WIR2014/WIR14_tab29.xls.

Usher, B.P. (2014) Joe Biden apologised over IS remarks, but was he right?. *BBC*, 7, October. Available at: http://www.bbc.com/news/world-us-canada-29528482.

Uslu, N. (2003) *The Turkish-American Relationship Between 1947–2003: The History of a Distinctive Alliance*. New York: Nova Science Publishers.

Uzgel, İ. (2003) Between Praetorianism and Democracy: The Role of the Military in Turkish Foreign Policy. *The Turkish Yearbook of International Relations* 34: 177–211.

Uzgel, İ. (2009) Ordu Dış Politikanın Neresinde?. In: İnsel, A. and Bayramoğlu, A. (eds) *Bir Zümre, Bir Parti, Türkiye'de Ordu*, 4th edition. İstanbul: Birikim Yayınları, 311–334

Ünal, A. & Williams, A. (2000) *Advocate of Dialogue: Fethullah Gülen*. Virginia: The Foundation.

Ünver, H.A. (2009). Turkey's "Deep-State" and the Ergenekon Conundrum. *The Middle East Institute Policy Brief* (23): 1–25.

Üskül, Z. (1997) *Siyaset ve Asker*. İstanbul: İmge Kitabevi.

Vardan, Ö.C. (2012) *Cihad ve MÜSİAD*. İstanbul: Timaş.

Väyrynen, R. and Herrera, L. (1975) Subimperialism: From Dependence to Subordination. *Instant Research on Peace and Violence* 5(3): 165–177.

Väyrynen, R. (1979) Economic and Military Position of the Regional Power Centers. *Journal of Peace Research* 16(4): 349–369.

Volpi, F. (2003) *Islam and Democracy: The Failure of Dialogue in Algeria*. London: Pluto Press.

Von Clausewitz, C. (2007) *On War*. Oxford: Oxford University Press.

Weber, M. (1978) *Economy and Society: An Outline of Interpretive Sociology*. G. Roth, & C. Wittich. (eds) Berkeley, Los Angeles & London: University of California Press.

Weber, M. (2005) *The Protestant Ethic and the Spirit of Capitalism*. London & New York: Routledge.

Weiker, W.F. (1963) *The Turkish Revolution, 1960–1961: aspects of military politics*. Washington: Brookings Institute.

Weiker, W.F. (1973) *Political Tutelage and Democracy in Turkey: The Free Party and its Aftermaths*. Leiden: Brill.

Weyland, K. (1999) Neoliberal Populism in Latin America and Eastern Europe. *Comparative Politics* 31(4): 379–401.

Werr, P. (2012) Turkey to provide Egypt with $2 billion in finance. *Reuters*, 15, September. Available at: http://www.reuters.com.

Wolff, P. (1987). *Stabilization Policy and Structural Adjustment in Turkey, 1980–1985: The Role of the IMF and World Bank in an Externally Supported Adjustment Process*. Berlin: German Development Institute (GDI).

Wood, E.M. (1995) *Democracy against Capitalism: renewing historical materialism*. Cambridge: Cambridge University Press.

World Bulletin (29 April 2014) Turkey, Sudan sign agriculture cooperation protocol. Available at: http://www.worldbulletin.net/haber/134979/turkey-sudan-sign-agriculture-cooperation-protocol.

World Economic Forum (2006) *The Global Competitiveness Report 2006–2007*. Available at: http://www3.weforum.org/docs/WEF_GlobalCompetitivenessReport_2006-07.pdf.

World Economic Forum (2014) *The Global Competitiveness Report 2014–2015*. Available at: http://www3.weforum.org/docs/WEF_GlobalCompetitivenessReport_2014-15.pdf.

World Economic Forum (2019) *The Global Competitiveness Report 2019*. Available at: http://www3.weforum.org/docs/WEF_TheGlobalCompetitivenessReport2019.pdf.

World Food Programme (2012) *Darfur: Comprehensive Food Security Assessment: Sudan 2012–2013*. Available at: http://documents.wfp.org/stellent/groups/public/documents/ena/wfp263983.pdf.

Wright R. and Tyson, A.S. (2005) U.S. evicted from air base in Uzbekistan. *The Washington Post*, 30, July. Available at: http://www.washingtonpost.com.

Yalçın, N. (1992) PKK'nın amacı tahrik. *Milliyet*, 6, September. p.17. Available at: http://gazetearsivi.milliyet.com.tr.

Yalman, G. (2009) *Transition to Neoliberalism: The case of Turkey in the 1980s*. İstanbul: İstanbul Bilgi University Press.

Yanardağ, M. (2009) *Ergenekon ve Sosyalistler*, 2nd edition. İstanbul: Siyah Beyaz.

Yanardağ, M. (2015) *Liberal İhanet*, 5th edition. İstanbul. Kırmızı Kedi Yayınları.

Yarar, E. (n.d.) *21. Yüzyıla Girerken Dünyaya Yeni Bir Bakış*. Available at: http://emusiad.net/img/arastirmalaryayin/pdf/arastirma_raporlari_18_2.pdf.

Yaşar, E.M. (2005) Dergah'tan Parti'ye, Vakıftan Şirkete Bir Kimliğin Oluşumu ve Dönüşümü İskerderpaşa Cemaati. In Bora, T. and Gültekingil, M. (eds) *Modern Türkiye'de Siyasi Düşünce: İslamcılık*, 2nd edition. İstanbul: İletişim, 323–340.

Yavuz, M. H. (1997) Political Islam and Welfare (Refah) Party in Turkey. *Comparative Politics* 30(1): 63–82.

Yavuz, M.H. (2009) *Secularism and Muslim Democracy in Turkey*. Cambridge: Cambridge University Press.

Yavuz, M.H. (2003a) *Islamic Political Identity in Turkey*. New York: Oxford University Press.

Yavuz, M.H. (2003b) The Gülen Movement. In: Yavuz, M.H. and Esposito, J.L. (eds) *Turkish Islam and the Secular State: The Gülen Movement.* New York: Syracuse University Press, 19–47.

Yazıcıoğlu, Y. (31 October 2015) Erdoğan'a "İslami Bonapart" Benzetmesi. An Interview with Fethi Açıkel. Available at: https://www.amerikaninsesi.com/a/erdogan-a-islami-bonapart-benzetmesi/3031141.html.

Yeni Şafak (16 July 2008) Evet milletin savcısıyım. Available at: http://www.yenisafak.com.tr/politika/evet-milletin-savcisiyim-129065.

Yeni Şafak (17 March 2014) Erdoğan: Onlar beyaz Türk'müş biz zenci…. Available at: http://www.yenisafak.com.tr/politika/erdogan-onlar-beyaz-turkmus-biz-zenci-626643.

Yerel Yönetimler Portalı (2014) Seçim Sonuçları. Available at: http://www.yerelnet.org.tr/basvuru_kaynaklari/secim_sonuclari/index.php?yil=1963.

Yeşilada, B. (2002) The Virtue Party. *Turkish Studies* 3(1): 62–81.

Yezdani, İ. (2012) Turkey gives al-Hashemi, his team residence permit. *Hürriyet Daily News*, 31, July. Available at: http://www.hurriyetdailynews.com.

Yıldırım, B. and Benlisoy, F. (2017) Turkey's Fragile Bonapartism. *Left Voice*, 6, January. Available at: http://www.leftvoice.org/Turkey-s-Fragile-Bonapartism.

Yörük, E. and Yüksel, M. (2014) Class and Politics in Turkey's Gezi Protests. *New Left Review* 89: 103–123.

YSK (*Yüksek Seçim Kurulu*) (2014) 30 Mart 2014 Mahalli İdareler Genel Seçimi. Available at: http://www.ysk.gov.tr/ysk/content/conn/YSKUCM/path/Contribution%20Folders/HaberDosya/BelediyeBaskanligi2014.pdf.

Yükleyen, A. (2012) *Localizing Islam in Europe: Turkish Islamic Communities in Germany and the Netherlands.* New York: Syracuse University Press.

Yüksel, H. (2005) Gülen'in Eğitim İmparatorluğu. *Yeni Aktüel* (13): 22–32.

Yüzbaşıoğlu, S. (2011) Mısırlı işçi patron dövüyor. *Sabah*, 17, February. Available at: http://www.sabah.com.tr.

Zakaria, F. (2003) *The Future of Freedom: Illiberal Democracy at Home and Abroad.* New York: W.W. Norton & Company.

Zaman (17 March 2007) Türkmen milli eğitimi, Türk okullarının kurucusuna emanet. Available at: http://www.zaman.com.tr/gundem_turkmen-milli-egitimi-turk-okullarinin-kurucusuna-emanet_514689.html.

Zaman (18 June 2014) AYM: Balyoz davasında, hak ihlali yapıldı. Available at: http://www.zaman.com.tr/gundem_aym-balyoz-davasinda-hak-ihlali-yapildi_2225327.html.

Zürcher, E. (2004) *Turkey: A Modern History*, 3rd edition. London: I.B. Tauris.

Index

AKP vi, xi, 6–7, 15–17, 21–22, 85–86, 88, 95, 107, 128–130, 134–135, 137–139, 142–144, 146–149, 151, 154, 157–159, 161–163, 167–168, 170–173, 176–177, 188, 197, 202–209, 211–212, 214–215, 218, 220–221, 224
army 2–3, 13, 15, 37, 40, 42–43, 46, 48, 50–51, 58, 63–65, 77, 83, 103, 124, 130, 140, 151, 153–155, 157–159, 167–168, 179–180, 182, 203, 223
ASKON v, 85, 93–94
authoritarianism 7, 22–23, 42, 130, 172–173, 214–215, 224

Bonapartism v, 1, 9–15, 17, 20–21, 25, 49, 52, 56, 62, 78, 134, 153, 215, 222
bourgeois democratic transition 6–7, 17
bourgeoisie xi, 1–3, 7, 9–14, 17, 19–21, 25–27, 29, 33–34, 37–43, 53, 58, 60, 62, 64, 67, 81, 84–86, 92–95, 100, 130, 135, 180, 203–204, 215, 222
bureaucracy 2–3, 6, 11, 13, 26, 40, 43, 50–51, 62, 70, 91, 104, 161, 210, 214

capital accumulation 3, 10, 12, 31, 33–34, 60, 62, 95, 186, 215
centre-periphery 4–6
civil society 1–2, 7, 19–20, 82, 104, 126–127, 159, 171, 204, 210
Cold War v, vi, 41, 44, 50, 64, 80, 98, 121, 130–133, 180, 184–185, 201
coup v, xi, 6, 9, 13–14, 16, 20, 22, 36, 41, 43, 46, 48–50, 56, 58, 60, 64–68, 72, 74, 82, 94–95, 103, 106, 125, 127, 133, 143, 160, 163, 165–166, 169–170, 172, 178, 182, 203–204, 209–214, 222–223

Davutoğlu 188, 199–203, 209, 224
Demirel 3, 13, 30, 47, 49–50, 63–64, 68, 73, 83, 100, 104, 158, 199
democracy 1, 6–8, 17–22, 37, 83, 119–121, 124, 128, 130, 132–134, 149–150, 157, 159, 172–173, 176–177, 206, 213
democratic transition v, xi, 6–7, 15, 17, 21–22, 36, 95, 129–130, 149, 157, 173, 215

democratisation vi, xi, 7, 17–18, 21–22, 79–80, 130, 133–134, 138, 149, 167–168, 177, 203, 207, 214, 223
developmentalism 15, 24–25, 31, 60, 62, 86, 95, 186, 215
dictatorship 20, 53, 60, 64, 67, 69–70, 135, 174, 187, 215

Erbakan vi, 64, 93, 98, 100–101, 103–106, 112–119, 121–123, 125, 128–129, 142, 144, 159, 183, 202, 215
Erdoğan vii, 23, 85, 121, 128–129, 138, 159, 161–162, 167, 170, 176–177, 197, 199, 204–206, 209, 211–214, 216, 218, 221, 223

Gülen vi, 22, 94–95, 130, 163, 165–168, 170–171, 195, 204, 207, 209–213, 215

Heper 1–4

Islamic fundamentalism 71, 85, 97, 108, 124, 133, 138, 143, 159
Islamisation 69

Just Order 113, 115

Kemalism v, 1, 8, 14–15, 24–25, 29, 32, 48–49, 60, 64, 106
Kemalist regime 5, 12–13, 202, 215

liberalisation v, 15, 22, 31, 38, 54, 60, 68, 79, 81, 83–84, 121, 133–135, 142, 152

Marx 9–11, 19–21, 67, 93, 132, 223
MGK 49–51
military tutelage 8, 15, 17, 22, 95, 134, 157, 168, 170, 173, 211
MÜSIAD ix, 84–85, 87–93, 110–112, 128, 138, 150, 188, 196

national view vi, 116
NATO 39–40, 43, 64, 131, 158, 165, 181–185, 202
Neoliberal 108, 149
Neoliberalism v, 64, 148
Neo-Ottomanism vi, 177, 186, 199, 201, 216

INDEX

OYAK   56–58, 156
Özal   73–78, 84, 95, 105, 126, 138, 185, 196

PKK   16, 83

Refah   55, 106, 108–109, 118, 120–121, 124–125, 128, 157

Schumpeter   18, 177
state   v–vi, xi, 1–22, 24–26, 28–29, 31–34, 38, 40–44, 46, 49, 51–52, 54, 56–58, 60, 63, 65, 67–76, 78–81, 83–89, 92, 95, 99–101, 103–106, 108, 111–113, 115, 118–119, 121–122, 124–127, 129–132, 135–137, 142, 146, 149, 151–152, 154–156, 159, 160–163, 165–168, 171, 173, 175, 177–179, 182, 185, 187, 191, 195–199, 201–204, 207, 209–212, 214–215, 221–224
state-society relations   3, 6, 71, 187
Sub-imperialism   vi, 178

Turgut Özal   v, 15, 21, 63, 73, 75, 105, 126, 135, 138, 165–166, 185, 195
TÜSIAD   ix, 1, 33, 47, 61, 63, 76–77, 84–91, 124, 126, 138, 149–151, 188
TUSKON   v, 94, 167, 188, 196

Welfare Party   vi, 55, 100, 106, 111, 128, 159
   see also Refah

www.ingramcontent.com/pod-product-compliance
Lightning Source LLC
Chambersburg PA
CBHW071336080526
44587CB00017B/2852